D0934638

DATE			

BAKER & TAYLOR

The State and the Poor

The State
and the Poor

*Public Policy
and Political Development
in India and the United States*

John Echeverri-Gent

UNIVERSITY OF CALIFORNIA PRESS
Berkeley · Los Angeles · Oxford

University of California Press
Berkeley and Los Angeles, California

University of California Press, Ltd.
Oxford, England

Library of Congress Cataloging-in-Publication Data

Echeverri-Gent, John.
    The state and the poor : public policy and political development in India and the
United States / John Echeverri-Gent.

        p.   cm.
    Includes bibliographical references and index.
    ISBN 0-520-08082-3 (alk. paper)
        1. Rural poor—Government policy—India.   2. Rural poor—Government policy—
United States.   3. Rural development—Government policy—India.   4. New Deal,
1933–1939.   5. India—Social conditions—1947–   6. United States—Social conditions—1933–1945.
    I. Title.
    HC440.P6E243   1993
    362.5'8'0954—dc20   92–28991
                                                                                                         CIP

Printed in the United States of America

9 8 7 6 5 4 3 2 1

The paper used in this publication meets the minimum requirements of American National Standard for Information Sciences—Permanence of Paper for Printed Library Materials, ANSI Z39.48-1984.♾

Contents

Figures, Maps, and Tables

Acknowledgments

One of the most rewarding aspects of working on this book is that it has brought me into contact with many extraordinarily capable and generous people. I have accumulated many debts while completing the project, and I take great pleasure in expressing my gratitude for the help and friendship I have received along the way.

Lloyd and Susanne Rudolph initiated me into serious exploration of state and society in South Asia. Ira Katznelson introduced me to the study of American political development. He also taught me the fruits of viewing Marx and Weber as complementary rather than competing. Theda Skocpol has profoundly influenced my understanding of state institutions, and John Padgett encouraged me to explore the insights of organization theory. All these friends and colleagues have given valuable suggestions after reading various incarnations of this book since its first appearance as a Ph.D. dissertation at the University of Chicago. I continue to be grateful for their support.

Many of the ideas in this book were initially developed in the Rudolphs' seminar on South Asian political economy and John Padgett's seminar on organization theory. I am grateful for my fellow participants' criticism and camaraderie. My discussions with other graduate students at the University of Chicago have shaped the problems I have addressed and the approaches I have taken in this book. I am especially indebted to John Bowman, Margaret Weir, and Jim Johnson.

I also thank the men and women of Maharashtra and West Bengal, where I performed my fieldwork; I sincerely appreciate their generosity and gracious hospitality. Officials in the Government of India and the state governments of Maharashtra and West Bengal were extremely helpful to me as I conducted my research in India. I am grateful to Dr. S. P. Aiyar of Bombay University for serving as my adviser during my dissertation research in India. Samuel S. Lieberman was especially helpful when I began spinning my wheels in the Maharashtra dust. Since our first days in Pune, Sandy has been a repeated source of assistance and encouragement. M. D. Bhandare of the American Institute of Indian Studies graciously helped my wife and me settle into Pune. M. B. Desai and Bhagwan G. Kunte assisted with the translations from Marathi. My research in West Bengal greatly benefited from the help of Suraj Bandyopadhyay, Rakhari Chatterji, P. K. Sen, Ashok Maiti and N. C. Adak. Mohini Mohan Hembran, N. C. Adak, and S. N. Rajen helped with interviews and translation work from Bengali. During difficult times, Uma Das Gupta not only facilitated my work but went beyond her call of duty as India's regional officer at the U.S. Educational Foundation. I also wish to thank Richard Crawford for his assistance at the National Archives in Washington, D.C.

My colleagues in the Department of Government and Foreign Affairs at the University of Virginia have provided a stimulating working environment. I am especially grateful to Herman Schwartz, Steve Finkel, and Jim Savage for their comments on different aspects of the work. Walter Hauser of the Department of History and the Center of South Asian Studies has also provided me with comments on parts of the manuscript and has greatly enhanced my understanding of politics and history in South Asia. Ronald Herring, Atul Kohli, Mel Leffler, Nelson Lichtenstein, Brian Balogh, Richard Kirkendall, and Don Hadwiger have also generously provided me with useful criticism of various parts of the book. I also am indebted to the comments of the three anonymous readers who reviewed my manuscript for the University of California Press. Manu Goswami, Aida Hozic, John Blakeman, and Shallini Charles provided valuable assistance at various points in my research.

Funding for my initial research in India was made possible by a Fulbright-Hays Fellowship provided through the United States Department of Education. I made two later trips with the help of a grant from the University of Virginia and then as a senior fellow with the American Institution of Indian Studies. Funding for writing up my research was provided by grants from the University of Chicago's Committee on South Asian Studies and the Center for Advanced Studies at the University of Virginia. Parts of the book were also written while I was a

McArthur Fellow at the Overseas Development Council. I am grateful to Naomi Schneider and Erika Büky for their skillful supervision of the book's publication, and Dorothy Conway for her conscientious copyediting.

Earlier versions of parts of this text appeared in *Asian Survey, The Policy Studies Journal, World Development,* and *Contemporary South Asia.* I thank the publishers of these journals for permitting me to include revised materials from those articles in this book.

Finally, I wish to express my gratitude to my parents, Barbara and John Gent, for their unwavering support. They instilled in me many of the values that are reflected in this book, and their ethic of hard work helped me to finish it. The zest for life of my daughters, Simone Gabriela and Andrea Alexis, has been a repeated source of inspiration during the book's research and writing. I dedicate this book to my wife and colleague-in-life, Elisavinda Echeverri-Gent. She has been of help in virtually every way possible. By providing intellectual stimulation in matters having little to do with this book, she has been crucial to keeping it in proper perspective.

Introduction:
Institutions, Rationality,
and Poverty Alleviation

How can poverty alleviation programs alter the constraints presented by rigid social structures and promote more equitable development? Would state agencies rationally implement policies if they were insulated from political pressures? Is political conflict inevitably detrimental to effective public policy? This book examines these issues by elaborating a new conceptual framework for analyzing public policy implementation and applying it to three different poverty alleviation programs. It advances our understanding of the politics of rural poverty alleviation and offers a new strategy for ameliorating the plight of the poor. In the process, it assesses the contributions of the "new institutionalism" to political analysis.

Three disciplinary traditions have served as important channels for developing versions of the new institutionalism: economic approaches to institutions, particularly transaction cost analysis and agency theory,[1] macrocomparative analysis in sociology and political science,[2] and the study of institutions in organizational theory.[3] Each approach links institutional analysis to rationality in a different way. The economic approach to institutions begins with the assumption of rational decision making by self-interested individuals. It modifies the microeconomic assumption of global rationality by stressing the importance of bounded rationality, information costs, and information asymmetry. At the macro level, it contends that economic institutions efficiently obtain their objectives despite the conflicts between self-interested individuals and their strategic use of information.

While drawing on transaction cost analysis and agency theory, the analysis presented in this book critiques the microfoundations of the economic approach as well as its linkage between individual and institutional rationality. Even though the economists' approach enhances the realism of the microeconomic tradition's depiction of individual rationality by accounting for the importance of incomplete information and information costs, it retains the assumption that preferences are exogenous to strategic interaction. The economists make no allowance for the role of culture in shaping understandings and objectives and, ultimately, producing different forms of rationality.[4] In short, the economists' approach does not provide adequate conceptual tools to explain preference formation and change.

The economists' assumption that institutional arrangements represent efficient equilibrium solutions or at least provisional points on the way to such an equilibrium fails to account adequately for the resilience of the sources of institutional irrationality. Most transaction cost analysis and agency theory fail to account for the protean nature of individual resistance to organizational control. Individuals are too ingenious in the pursuit of self-interest and organizational change too cumbersome for organizational structures to prevent individuals from pursuing their own interests in ways that subvert institutional objectives. The analysis also suffers from its conflation of rationality with power. Economic approaches to institutions often neglect the possibility that authorities have the power to impose institutional structures that advance their interests even when they are inefficient from a societal perspective.[5] Finally, the economists' methodological individualism and their concentration on how institutions are generated from the strategic interaction of self-interested individuals do not provide adequate analytical tools to explain how institutions constrain individuals.[6] Institutions are not merely the aggregation of the preferences and power of their constituents; they also shape the preferences and power of those subject to them.

The macrocomparative tradition provides a better understanding of institutional constraints. It improves upon the microfoundations offered by the economic approach with its contention that preferences are not exogenously given but historically constituted. Central to its analysis is its stress on how institutional structures shape the rationality of individuals and social groups.

The critique of the macrocomparativists developed in this book is not the common lament that analysts in the macrocomparative tradition have called for a "state-centered" analysis that precludes proper analysis of state-society relations.[7] While early institutionalists may have been guilty of overexuberance in calling for "a paradigmatic shift" in analysis, a close reading of their work points toward the need to better conceptualize state-society relations rather than denying their importance.[8] The criticism here is that much of macrocomparative institutionalism concentrates on the politics of policy formation, stressing the role played by social and political elites. As a consequence, it adopts a top-down perspective, which obfuscates the conflicting rationalities at different levels of state institutions.[9] The importance of these conflicts becomes especially apparent in studies of policy implementation. These studies demonstrate how the directives of policy elites are often transformed as a result of the conflicting interests of officials at the grass roots. This book takes to heart Michael Lipsky's exhortation to study "street-level" bureaucrats because "the decisions of street-level bureaucrats, the routines they establish, and the devices they invent to cope with uncertainties and work pressures, effectively *become* the public policies they carry out." [10] It attempts to redress the macrocomparativists' top-down bias by focusing on the activities of grass-roots officials. Balancing the macrocomparativist top-down perspective with a bottom-up approach sheds new light on central concepts such as state autonomy and state capacity.

At the micro level, approaches to institutions developed by organization theorists have until recently tended to view individual rationality less as the strategic pursuit of self-interest and more as reference to cultural norms that legitimize particular alternatives. At the macro level, they view the process of institutionalization as shaped primarily from cultural "logics of appropriateness," even when this results in divergence from rationality in terms of economic efficiency.

This book attempts to advance the organization theorists' perspective by exploring the creative tension between the cultural sources of rationality and the view of rationality as the strategic pursuit of self-interest. The stress on cultural sources of rationality raises the important issue of the origins and evolution of the cultural norms; yet the explanations advanced by the organization theorists remain at a preliminary stage. This book attempts to advance our understanding by locating the development of cultural norms in the context of the strategic interaction of actors in the pursuit of self-interest. It shows how culture is simultaneously an object that actors attempt to manipulate to support their interests and a constraint that impedes some strategies and enables others.

Each of the three approaches to institutions offers insight to the relationship between state institutions and society. Although their insights are incomplete, they are complementary. At the risk of oversimplifying, we might say that the economic approach to institutions concentrates on mechanisms that promote institutional efficiency. The macrocomparativists present relations between social groups and state institutions primarily in terms of the political dynamics of history, and the organization theorists stress the cultural norms as the nexus between state institutions and society. This book develops a conceptual framework that synthesizes the insights from these approaches in a way that advances our understanding of state-society relations.

THE CONCEPTUAL FRAMEWORK

The book is based on the premise that policy implementation, as the site of tangible exchanges between state and society, provides a strategic point for developing our analysis.[11] It presents a conceptual framework for the analysis of policy implementation. The framework is informed by three perspectives. The first is the *Rational Process Perspective*. Beginning with the assumption that policymakers are characterized by bounded rationality, this perspective stresses that planning and the monitoring of implementation are the most important features of policy implementation. Together, they create a process of "dynamic rationality," which shapes the course of implementation by improving the correspondence between its means and ends. The second analytical viewpoint, the *Conflictual Process Perspective,* asserts that conflict is endemic in implementing agencies and largely determines the course of implementation. These two perspectives help us to understand the complexity of the internal dynamics of implementing organizations. Their analysis of relations between government agencies and their social environment, however, has serious shortcomings.

Finally, the *Organizational Environment Perspective* examines state-society relations by conceptualizing the ways in which the activity of policy-implementing agencies is embedded in its societal context. It applies insights developed from organization theory to argue that relations of resource dependence are important factors in shaping the process of implementation. It adds that the institutional environment of state agencies conditions their policy implementation by creating "institutionalized rules" or cultural norms, which shape the perceptions and actions of decision makers. This perspective also explores the characteristics that distinguish state agencies from other organizations. In particular, it stresses how the "constitutive impact" of public policy shapes the opportunities and constraints for collective political action in the social environment of implementing agencies.[12]

The methodology used in applying the analytical framework is neo-Weberian. Each perspective captures a particular logic of implementation and is used as an ideal type. One advantage of this approach lies in the heuristic benefits accumulated from applying relatively parsimonious models to analyze complex circumstances. At the same time, the framework's multiple perspectives create a "Rashomon" effect, adding new insights and speculative dimensions to our understanding. The inclusion of alternative perspectives exploits the theoretical parsimony of the models while limiting the reductionism that frequently accompanies it. In addition, each perspective can be used to explain deviations from the predictions of the others.

THE COMPARATIVE STRATEGY

Each of the three case studies examined in this book involves the implementation of rural antipoverty programs. One case demonstrates how the Resettlement Administration and the Farm Security Administration implemented these programs during the American New Deal. The other two demonstrate the implementation of povery alleviation programs in India: the Employment Guarantee Scheme in the Indian state of Maharashtra and the National Rural Employment Programme in the Indian state of West Bengal.

Can the New Deal programs insightfully be compared with the programs in India? The comparison is unorthodox yet informative. It illuminates important structural parallels as well as interesting differences. In each case, rigid social hierarchies privileged the position of local elites and provided them with the capacity to distort implementation or generate powerful opposition to the programs. As this study shows, the elites are not necessarily opposed to poverty alleviation programs, but they can be expected to deploy their formidable economic, social, and political resources to protect their positions of dominance. In many cases, the elites' position atop the social hierarchy and their ties to local government officials enabled them to exploit public resources for private benefit. The New Deal and Indian rural poverty alleviation programs faced the common challenge of finding a means to deliver program benefits to the poor while circumventing the capacity of social elites to distort implementation. This same challenge confronts the implementation of poverty alleviation programs throughout the world.

An important premise of the comparison is that the New Deal rural antipoverty programs were oriented predominantly to the South, even though they were national in scope. For example, the rural rehabilitation program, accounting for 59 percent of all Resettlement Administration and Farm Security Administration expenditures from 1936 to 1946, channeled 53 percent of its funds into the eleven Confederate states plus Oklahoma. The next-largest program was the tenant-purchase program. Its loans to help tenants purchase their farms comprised 13 percent of all expenditures. Seventy percent of these loans were made in fifteen Southern states. Perhaps most important, reaction to the programs was most vociferous in the South. Southern politicians dominated the politics that shaped and ultimately terminated the programs.

A "Colonial Economy" and the Developing World

The economy of the American South bore remarkable structural similarities to that of India and other developing countries. There is a long scholarly tradition, adhered to by some of the most eminent historians of the South, that analyzes the Southern economy as a "colonial economy." The main thrust of the argument is that the South was an agrarian periphery that was linked to more industrialized areas of the world, especially the northeastern United States, through its export of primary commodities and its import of industrial goods and capital. Despite the region's abundant natural resources, the development of Southern industry was limited by unequal exchange, the underdevelopment of its financial system, and the domination of "foreign" capital.[13]

In the comparison presented here, the dominance of outside capital in shaping the South's industrial development is less important than the rough parallels between the South's agrarian economy in the 1930s and that of developing countries such as India. The Southern economy was predominantly rural and agricultural. Despite its commercial orientation, Southern agricultural production remained on a small-scale, labor-intensive basis. While the size of the holdings were not as small as in India, the American South shared with India the problem of extensive underemployment resulting from the imbalance between rural population and employment opportunities. Tenancy and sharecropping were widespread. The rural poor, in the American South, as in India, took frequent resort to consumption loans at usurious interest rates in order to see them through difficult times. The extensive tenancy, sharecropping, and usury led to extensive debt and widespread poverty. Agricultural economist D. Gale Johnson estimated that 46 percent of American farm families lived below the poverty line in 1929.[14]

Rigid agrarian structures with widespread poverty characterize both India and the American South through the first four decades of the twentieth century. True, overpopulation is even a more serious problem in India than it was in the rural South, and India's agrarian structure may have a larger share of agricultural laborers and fewer tenants. Nevertheless, in each case, the rural poor had very limited opportunities to improve their livelihood. Systems of patronage limited the independence of the poor, and the more affluent landowners were able to translate their control over land into various forms of social power. In the American South as well as in India, relations of economic dependence and patronage have been an important factor shaping the implementation of rural poverty alleviation programs.

Caste, Race, and Social Hierarchy

The South's agrarian system encompassed social as well as economic relations. Here, once again, we find intriguing parallels and differences between the American South and India. There is a long tradition within American history of referring to Southern race relations in terms of "caste,"[15] and many prominent scholars have drawn insightful comparisons between the position of African-Americans and scheduled castes in the two societies.[16] The parallels are useful to the extent that they highlight the rigid social hierarchies of each society, with African-Americans and scheduled castes at the bottom. Endogamy, sexual taboos, social segregation, exploitation, and violence supported the caste and racial division. Extending the parallels much further, however, obscures central differences between the two cases.

Although rigid social hierarchy was prevalent in both cases, the nature of the hierarchies differed, and they were embedded in very different societies. The intended beneficiaries of the antipoverty programs studied here were not only African-Americans and scheduled castes but also poor whites and other caste groups. In India, the rural poor compose a relatively larger share of the population than in the United States. The disparate political demographics make them a more attractive constituency, especially after the transformation of Southern agriculture in the decades following the end of the Great Depression.

Louis Dumont has argued that India's caste system is based on the society's inegalitarian values, whereas racism in the United States contradicts America's egalitarian values.[17] The cases studied in this book contradict Dumont's observation. Racism and social hierarchy in America's South were underpinned by aristocratic values, at least until the emergence of the civil rights movement, whereas caste in India is contradicted by the egalitarian values that undergird the political system in contemporary India. True, the South gave birth to Jeffersonian and Jacksonian democracy. It also was the seat of the populist movement in the 1890s. Although these traditions lived on, by the beginning of the twentieth century they were subordinated to political institutions reflecting elitist as well as racist values. Measures such as the literacy test and the poll tax excluded poor whites as well as African-Americans. Whereas these measures were central features of Southern politics during the first half of the twentieth century, they are an anathema to India's democratic practice. In contemporary India, policies such as the reservation of parliamentary constituencies and public sector employment for members of the scheduled castes and tribes encourage the participation of the deprived, even though the dependence and coercion that reinforce the country's social hierarchy sometimes prevent them from pursuing their interests.

Politics of Populism, Factionalism, and Elite Domination

One of the most interesting parallels between the American South and India is that in both we find a politics of populism accompanied by weak party organization and political factionalism. During its heyday in the 1890s, populism proved a serious threat to elite domination in the American South. It was this threat that, in part, led to the disfranchisement of African-Americans and poor whites. The colorful rhetoric of populists persisted after disfranchisement. The American South had its Pitchfork Ben Tillman; Eugene Talmadge, "the Wild Man from Sugar Creek"; Huey ("the Kingfish") Long—just as India has its Devi (the *Tau*) Lal, Sharad Joshi, and Mahendra Singh Tikait. In both instances, populists have attempted to rally rural interests against the cities, big business, and outside interests.

While the Democratic Party and the Congress Party[18] dominated politics in the American South and India for extended periods, rural politicians in each country relied on the support of personalistic factions that rarely outlasted the career of their leaders. In the American South, "friends and neighbors" politics created local bases of support. To extend their support, Southern politicians were obliged to reach an accommodation with county "rings" or cliques of planters, merchants, and judges who controlled local "vote banks." During the first two decades of India's independence, its political leaders also mobilized support through local elites. Ever since Indira Gandhi's *garibi hatao* (remove poverty) campaign of 1971, they have come to rely increasingly on the appeals of populist rhetoric. The result has been a tendency toward plebiscite politics that has weakened party organization and incited rampant factionalism within the Congress as well as in its political opposition.[19]

Though populism was accommodated within the parameters of elite domination in each country, the politics of the rural South proved more conservative than that of rural India. The disfranchisement of African-Americans and poor whites was fundamental to this conservatism. The planter elites of the black belt provided the impetus behind it. Their success in eliminating the votes of African-Americans and poor whites undercut the Republican opposition and curtailed the possibilities for programmatic partisan competition. Groups in the bottom echelons of India's social structure, in contrast, remain an active and potentially strategic constituency. Most Indian politicians profess a commitment to ameliorating the plight of the rural poor. There remains a gaping hiatus between their rhetoric and the realities of Indian poverty alleviation programs.

The political ascendance of farmers' organizations in national politics provides a final parallel. Although the South's representatives in Congress were divided on an array of issues, they stood united in their support for the commercial interests of Southern agriculture and in their opposition to federal intervention in Southern race relations. The incorporation of the South into the farm bloc in the 1930s consolidated what quickly became one of the most powerful lobbies in Congress.[20] During the 1940s, the farm bloc allied with congressional conservatives to end most of the New Deal poverty alleviation programs. To this day, it remains largely successful in promoting the interests of affluent farmers. In India also, farmers' organizations play an increasingly important role in shaping India's rural development policies.[21] Still, they have yet to establish an institutionalized link to India's rural development policymakers comparable to the farm organizations' links with the congressional agricultural committees. It remains to be seen whether they will follow the American organizations and succeed in shaping India's rural development programs to promote the interests of its large farmers.

ADMINISTRATIVE STRUCTURES AND POVERTY ALLEVIATION

Comparison of the case studies in this book enables one to examine the advantages and disadvantages of different administrative structures for the implementation of poverty alleviation programs. Administrative structure is an important variable affecting the impact of antipoverty programs because it shapes the capabilities of administrators and their responsiveness to the poor. In addition, it is a variable that is most easily manipulated by policymakers. Each of the cases in this book is implemented by a different administrative structure. From 1935, rural poverty programs during the New Deal were implemented by a single agency—first the Resettlement Administration and then the Farm Security Administration. The Employment Guarantee Scheme in Maharashtra is implemented through a complex administrative network that incorporates the specialized expertise of seven different agencies. Elected local councils have been placed in charge of implementing the National Rural Employment Programme in West Bengal.

PUBLIC POLICY AND POLITICAL DEVELOPMENT

This book combines methodological approaches to develop a better understanding of the relationship between public policy and political development. In the two Indian cases, data were collected largely through extensive interviews with government officials and relevant members of the public. Contemporary government records were also a rich source of information. While these sources afforded an excellent view of state-society relations and the impact of government programs on political mobilization, they lack the historical perspective to shed much light on the relationship between public policy and political development.

The American case was researched largely through archival records, historical records, and secondary literature. The historical perspective that it affords is vital in developing a better understanding of the relation between public policy and political development. Despite their professions of faith in economic liberalism, American policymakers have historically promoted agricultural development through extensive state intervention. Studying the history of American rural development is especially useful because it offers the opportunity to examine the sequences of policy that shaped the trajectory of the country's development. An important objective of this study is to explain the dynamics underpinning these policy sequences—in particular, the ways in which the political and economic impact of policy interventions creates conditions that structure the possibilities for later interventions.

During the New Deal, policies to promote agrarian capitalism enhanced the political power of commercial farmers by increasing the resources under their control and providing them with incentives for political mobilization. The mobilization of the affluent farmers in turn shaped the government agencies concerned with rural development in a fashion that reflected the farmers' interests. This dynamic inevitably constrained the ways in which the state could intervene to alleviate rural poverty. While the New Deal programs encouraged the mobilization of a substantial but highly dispersed constituency, they threatened the interests and the ideology of commercial farmers. The Farm Security Administration attempted to enhance its political support by cultivating a constituency relationship with the National Farmers Union, a rival of the American Farm Bureau Federation that was more sympathetic to the rural poor. Ultimately, the American Farm Bureau Federation and other organizations of commercial farmers were able to align with the anti–New Deal congressional coalition to bring about the Farm Security Administration's demise.

Comparison of the Indian cases highlights the advantages and disadvantages of the different ways in which public policy encourages the mobilization of the poor. While these programs promoted the political organization of the poor, they created incentives that encouraged distinctive modes of collective action. The Employment Guarantee Scheme in Maharashtra empowered the poor through its guarantee of employment. The guarantee creates incentives for their political mobilization.

It encourages an array of groups—political parties as well as nongovernmental organizations—to organize the poor or at least be more sensitive to their interests. The pluralistic pattern of mobilization helped to make government officials implementing the program more responsive by promoting alternative channels through which the poor could press their claims. Indeed, the mobilization of the poor placed administrators in a political market, compelling them to supply more employment in areas of high demand and less work in districts with low demand. Implementation of the National Rural Employment Programme in West Bengal enabled the ruling Communist Party of India (Marxist) to use patronage to extend its organization among the rural poor. The patronage, however, tended to weaken the capacity of the poor for independent political mobilization and for pressuring government officials and the ruling party to be responsive.

THEORETICAL CONCLUSIONS
AND POLICY IMPLICATIONS

By applying the rational, conflictual, and organizational environmental perspectives to the examination of policy implementation, we can begin to explore the relationships among the perspectives. A "politics of rationality" exists because planning and the monitoring of implementation are usually conditioned in important ways by political considerations. Although most analysts stress the detrimental consequences of politics for implementation, the study contends that policy objectives can be better achieved when the "rationality of politics" is enhanced.

Some analysts advocate insulating state agencies from politics and enhancing their autonomy. In urging that state autonomy be increased, they frequently discount the predatory interests of the state. They also fail to recognize that networks of exchange between states and society may enable states to direct the use of resources controlled by non-state actors in ways that advance policy objectives.

To protect against the predatory tendencies of the state, and to secure the cooperative use of resources by nonstate actors, one needs mechanisms that make state agencies responsive to social needs. For poverty alleviation programs, these mechanisms are usually political. But using politics to ensure the state's responsiveness to the needs of the poor raises the "paradox of participation." Making poverty alleviation programs responsive to the poor calls for a political process that represents their interests. But as long as the poor remain poor, they are disadvantaged in securing equitable representation. Public policy can help to resolve this paradox if it creates incentives for the political mobilization of the poor. This mobilization often can be structured to pressure administrators to promote policy objectives. The political impact of public policy is likely to have repercussions for the long term as well. Its cumulative consequences shape the patterns of political mobilization that ultimately condition the trajectory of a society's political and economic development.

What types of policies are likely to produce more equitable development if one considers the political as well as the economic impact of public policy? The concluding chapter of this book argues for a strategy that combines Amartya Sen's advocacy that the objective of development should be to expand people's capabilities with Theodore W. Schultz's stress on investment in human capital.[22] A well-educated, healthy, and productive work force will improve a country's productivity, promote growth, and ensure a political process that is responsive to the people's needs.

Designing policies according to the principle of *targeted universalism* is essential to the success of such a strategy.[23] Policy analysts frequently contend that targeting beneficiaries is the most effective way to implement policies funded with limited resources. While this approach makes economic sense, it can lead to political suicide. Reducing the beneficiaries of a policy limits its constituency. Narrowing a program's target group can undercut its political viability. Is there a way to gain the efficiency of targeting while avoiding its political liabilities?

Targeting *policy tasks* rather than constituencies offers an answer. Efficiency can be enhanced when policy tasks are limited to those that are feasible in the context of the available resources and expertise. The principle of universalism also enhances efficiency. By reducing the discretion of local officials to determine the beneficiaries of a program, it limits their opportunities for corruption. At the same time, universal eligibility for benefits makes programs more politically viable by creating broad coalitions of support. In addition to enhancing the political viability of current programs, these coalitions can be instrumental in providing the impetus for even more equitable future programs and, ultimately, for laying the basis for more equitable trajectories of economic and political development.

CHAPTER I

Organizational Processes of Policy Implementation

Votes count in the choice of governing personnel but other
resources decide the actual policies pursued by the
authorities.

—*Stein Rokkan*

To study public policy implementation is to study a relationship between state and society. When we learn how state agencies implement
policy, we can begin to understand the advantages and disadvantages
of state autonomy. We also learn how social structure constrains public
policy and how public policy conditions the agency of social groups.
Before we can grapple with these issues, we need a framework to conceptualize the dynamics of implementation. This chapter presents an
analytical framework that combines the insights of implementation
studies with organization theory and political economy.

Existing studies of policy implementation tend to maintain either of
two basic assumptions about organizational behavior. For some, the
most important characteristic is the bounded rationality of decision
makers as they confront complex problems with limited cognitive
means. Their cognitive shortcomings often result in counterproductive
actions. Decision makers, however, learn from their mistakes, thereby
improving their understanding and modifying organizational activity
to correspond more closely to policy objectives. Others view organizations as collectivities encompassing self-interested individuals. For these
scholars, organizational behavior is largely a product of the pursuit of
individual self-interest. Since organizations include heterogeneous interests, they usually suffer from conflicts. In this view, the politics of resolving these conflicts is the central dynamic of policy implementation.

Both of these perspectives have produced studies making important
contributions to our understanding of policy implementation, but each

also has its limitations. The conceptual framework presented in this chapter synthesizes the insights gained from these different analytical traditions: the Rational Process Perspective and the Conflictual Process Perspective. In my view, neither of these perspectives adequately conceptualizes relationships between implementing agencies and their societal environment. A new approach, the Organizational Environment Perspective, uses organization theory to develop a better conceptualization of the relations between implementing agencies and their environment. It draws on the resource dependence model of interorganizational relations to argue that the behavior of agencies is shaped by their need to acquire resources from their environment. Resource dependence involves asymmetric exchanges of economic, political, and information resources. A dependent agency, however, is rarely powerless, since it employs the resources under its control in strategies to overcome its dependence. The Organizational Environment Perspective employs the concept of "institutionalized rules" to show that culture shapes these exchanges by encouraging some patterns of action and institution building and constraining others. Though there is much to be gained by applying organization theory to policy implementation, the perspective includes an assessment of its limitations. In particular, it contends that organization theory's conceptualization of organizations as a generic phenomenon fails to account for the distinctiveness of government agencies and their unique capabilities. The unique capabilities of government agencies have important consequences for policy implementation and can be employed to mitigate resource dependence that is detrimental to effective policy implementation.

TRADITIONAL PERSPECTIVES ON POLICY IMPLEMENTATION

The Rational Process Perspective

Planning and monitoring create the primary dynamic of implementation, according to the Rational Process Perspective. Planners design organization structures to maximize efficiency after taking into account implementation technologies, information-processing needs, and environmental uncertainty.[1] Many analysts now contend that transaction costs largely determine how organizations demarcate their boundaries and their internal structure.[2]

Advocates of the Rational Process Perspective stress the bounded rationality of decision makers. Their rationality is "bounded" because the complexity of the problems they confront exceeds their cognitive capabilities.[3] They develop channels for administrative feedback to monitor the impact of their decisions. As a result, policy implementation is characterized by dynamic rationality, since decision makers periodically examine feedback and adjust their decisions to improve the correspondence between implementation performance and policy objectives.

An efficient organization manipulates the causes of inefficiency well.[4] Collecting information about inefficiency is crucial to effective performance, since it enables decision makers to improve methods of implementation in order to better achieve their policy objectives. In this sense, organizational learning is history-dependent, since an organization's routines are based primarily on past experience as interpreted through organizational feedback.[5] Not only are routines and other aspects of organizational structure designed (and redesigned) to achieve policy goals, but the proponents of the Rational Process Perspective have also become increasingly aware that authorities often alter the indicators of success, and even policy objectives, after learning the consequences of implementation.[6] The dynamic rationality of policy implementation relates means and ends in both directions.

Early advocates of the Rational Process Perspective were often charged with neglecting the effect of conflict among members of an organization. Economists have attempted to redress this deficiency with the development of agency theory.[7] Agency theory investigates how authorities can utilize monitoring systems and incentives to control the opportunistic behavior of their subordinates. Policy analysts have applied this theory to policy implementation in a number of studies, but they have usually found serious limitations. In contrast to the economists' general optimism that information can be gathered and incentives structured so as to minimize inefficiencies, political scientists have shown us that variables not often accounted for in economists' models limit the ability of superiors to control their subordinates. These variables include the high costs of designing incentive structures and the implausibility of acquiring perfect information about agent motivations, the bureaucrats' understanding of and commitment to their organizational mission, legal constraints, and the support of an agency's political allies.[8]

In sum, even though the attribution of rationality to government bureaucracy has been an object of growing skepticism since Max Weber asserted that bureaucracy was the most technically efficient form of organization yet contrived, the Rational Process Perspective continues to illuminate important aspects of policy implementation. It highlights two strategic points for examining implementation: planning (that is, designing an administrative network that will provide the most effective implementation) and monitoring (collecting and analyzing administrative feedback, with the objective of making the implementation process more efficient). According to this perspective, then, implementation is rational, not in the sense that it reaches any absolute level of rationality but because it is characterized by a process of dynamic rationality in which authorities progressively fashion implementation so that it corresponds more closely to policy objectives.

This perspective's emphasis on planning and monitoring excludes other important considerations. It fails to consider, for example, that information gathering and analysis may be intended more to bolster the legitimacy of decision-making processes than to inform their outcome.[9] It also underestimates the complexities that arise when organizational constituents provide information according to their strategic advantage.[10] What is rational for one level of organization may be irrational from the perspective of another. Although authorities attempt to enhance the responsiveness of implementing agencies by creating rules and incentives to constrain conflicting interests, these measures often fail to subdue self-interested behavior. Indeed, some contend that conflicts of interest are the central dynamic shaping the course of policy implementation.

The Conflictual Process Perspective

The Conflictual Process Perspective stresses that the agencies involved in policy implementation are more than just means to obtain program objectives. They are collectivities whose members have a diverse range of interests. These interests conflict, and disputes are resolved through bargaining and struggles. Conflict is the central feature of policy implementation. This emphasis leads proponents of the perspective to be pessimistic about the prospects for effective policy implementation.

The very conditions that promote effective implementation in the Rational Process Perspective spawn conflict, according to this perspective. A division of labor may enhance organizational capacity by providing for specialization within a coordinated network; however, specialization encourages recruitment of members with different backgrounds and skills. Personnel occupying different units within an organization accumulate different experiences, which engender different outlooks. In situations of interdependence, these disparate viewpoints constitute an important source of conflict.[11]

Vertical differentiation within organizational hierarchies is another basis for conflict. Conflict arises even when personnel perform their jobs conscientiously. While managers take measures to promote efficient use of organizational resources, subordinates strive to ensure the availability of ample resources in order to perform their responsibilities. Managers are socialized to take long-term, strategic perspectives. Subordinates tend to have a more parochial outlook and identify with the immediate interests of their clients. Managers take measures to maximize their control, but subordinates attempt to protect their discretion.[12]

Though conflict may be endemic in organizations, struggles to resolve conflicts are more visible in some organizations than others. Organizations with ambiguous goals sustain higher levels of conflict, as do those with scarce resources and those facing technological uncertainty or controversy over the appropriate means to achieve organizational objectives. Struggles increase with the importance of issues. However, the salience of conflict can be reduced if power is sufficiently centralized to allow those who dominate the organization to preempt struggles by imposing their preferences.[13]

Even where organizational actors share a commitment to rational decision making, advocates of this perspective focus on the politics of rationality. While rationality entails decision-making procedures involving means-end calculations, decisions determining organizational objectives and measures taken to achieve them are embedded in a conflictual process driven by the efforts of various groups to advance their positions. At times, the decision-making procedures themselves can become an issue of dispute. What is rational for one organizational member may not be rational for others.[14]

In contrast to the Rational Process Perspective, in which organizational structure is an instrument used by authorities to promote rational implementation, advocates of the Conflictual Process Perspective stress its conflictual determinants. Many theorists view organizational structure as a reflection of the distribution of power. Organizational structure inevitably becomes an object of conflict, since it bestows power and authority among an organization's members.[15] The institutionalization of power within organizational structures, in turn, conditions new struggles.

Implementation frequently involves the creation of an administrative network requiring the coordination of different agencies. Interorganizational conflict is usually even more problematic than intraorganizational conflict, since the very measures taken to curb intraorganizational conflict—e.g., the socialization of personnel and the articulation of an organizational mission—tend to exacerbate interorganizational ones. Conflict also arises because the policy mandates coordinating activities in different agencies are often vague, and because they create programs tacked onto the ongoing activities of agencies without providing additional resources.[16] Relations among agencies in an administrative network are characterized by a series of games, in which each actor tries to gain access to program resources not under its control while at the same time extracting better terms from other actors seeking access to resources that it does control.[17] The problems highlighted by the Conflictual Process Perspective point toward the conclusion that impediments to effective implementation proliferate with increases in the multiplicity of decision points and the complexity of joint action.[18]

The Conflictual Process Perspective extends its analysis to relations between administrative networks and actors in their societal environment—interest groups, political parties, and other agencies—who are interested in implementation. The perspective's conceptualization of relations between agencies and groups in their environment is often limited by the case study approach adopted by many of its proponents. This approach often leads to underspecified variables and circular logic.

James Q. Wilson provides an important departure.[19] In his view, the relations between interest groups and bureaucracies depend on the structure of interests in their policy domain. Wilson offers a typology of four political environments that generate distinctive outcomes. First, where programs provide goods and services to a limited number of beneficiaries and the costs of the programs are dispersed over a large number of people, relations between agencies and their social environment will be characterized by "client politics" in which highly mobilized program beneficiaries will predominate. Second, where the costs of a program are concentrated and the benefits are dispersed, Wilson contends that relations between an agency and its environment will be characterized by "entrepreneurial politics." Such programs and agencies are likely to be created through the efforts of political entrepreneurs who succeed in mobilizing widespread public support, but those who bear the costs will mobilize to minimize the negative impact of implementation on their interests while the entrepreneur will struggle to maintain popular pressure to ensure that implementation continues to pursue its original objectives. The third type of environment character- izing implementation is where a policy produces high per capita costs and high per capita benefits but no group predominates. This environ- ment produces an "interest-group politics" where beneficiaries and cost-bearers alike are highly mobilized and agencies are most likely to respond to those who succeed in tipping the scales in their favor. Fi- nally, some agencies implement programs that have widely dispersed costs and benefits. Few interest groups are mobilized in this environ- ment, and the subsequent "majoritarian politics" results in substantial autonomy for the agency whose actions do not arouse hostile opposi- tion.

Wilson's typology is formed according to the impact of public policy on the incentives for collective action within a policy domain; however, it has little to say about the sources of power of different actors. If we wish to explain policy outcomes, then we must account for the relative power of the various actors involved as well as their incentives for col- lective action. Furthermore, we must do a better job of explaining how discourse within policy communities shapes the interests and objectives of government agencies and the social groups in their domain.

In sum, the Conflictual Process Perspective captures important as- pects of the policy implementation process. Implementing agencies are made up of heterogeneous interests, whose conflicts shape the course of implementation. The perspective points to three strategic locations for analyzing these conflicts: conflicts between self-interested organiza- tional members and policy objectives, between organizational units, and between the implementing agencies and social groups forming part of a policy network.

Though adherents to the Conflictual Process Perspective have made many important contributions to our understanding of policy imple- mentation, their work is also marred by various shortcomings. They overlook the role that rational processes of implementation play in shaping organizational behavior. While they consider conflict between implementing agencies and their environment an important factor shaping implementation, their theoretical observations are underdevel- oped. Power is the currency of the Conflictual Process Perspective, but the determinants of power are usually underspecified. Finally, in their assumption that implementation is shaped by the politics of self-interest, they neglect the ways in which self-interest emerges and the fashion in which culture encourages some courses of action while constraining others. Recent developments in organization theory have focused on these issues.

THE ORGANIZATIONAL
ENVIRONMENT PERSPECTIVE

The Organizational Environment Perspective draws on two currents in organization theory to develop a more sophisticated understanding of the relationship between implementing agencies and their societal environment. First, it employs the resource dependence model to illuminate how implementation is shaped by the exchange of economic, political, and information resources. Then it explains how these exchanges are conditioned by the institutional environment. "Institutionalized rules" are especially important, since they constitute a cultural terrain that facilitates some courses of action and constrains others. Though there is much to be gained by applying these concepts to policy implementation, the perspective demonstrates that a full understanding must also include an assessment of organizational theory's limitations. In particular, organization theory's generic conceptualization of organizations fails to account for the distinctiveness of government agencies and their unique capabilities. The Organizational Environment Perspective demonstrates that these features have important implications for policy implementation.

The Resource Dependence Model
of Interorganizational Relations

Pfeffer and Salancik have developed the most comprehensive statement of the resource dependence model of interorganizational relations. Their model is based on the premise that survival is the paramount objective for organizations and that, in order to survive, organizations must acquire resources from their environment.[20] Such transactions constitute relations of dependence. Environmental actors that control needed resources exert power over a dependent organization's structure and activity.

What determines the relative dependence of organizations? First, dependence is a function of the importance of an externally controlled resource. Importance is determined by the extent to which a resource is critical to organizational performance and the quantity of the resource that is necessary. Second, external dependence is positively associated with the concentration of control over the resource. Third, dependence also varies with the uncertainty of supply. The supply of resources from some actors is more certain when they make commitments or when they lack alternative courses of action. Those actors who retain discretion to dispose of their resources in a variety of attractive ways will wield more power than those who lack such discretion. The concurrence of importance, concentration, and uncertainty multiplies the effect.[21]

These factors, in themselves, do not cause dependence; rather, dependence is a consequence of asymmetric exchange.[22] Organizations usually possess countervailing power. They can counteract resource dependence if they control other resources that are important to environmental actors. They generally employ these resources in strategies to overcome their dependence.

Pfeffer and Salancik's conceptualization of the way resource dependence shapes organizational activity improves upon the more mechanical understanding of correlations between organizations and environments offered by earlier organization theorists.[23] They provide a sophisticated understanding of how resource dependence conditions the internal dynamics of organizations. Dependence on environmental resources affects the distribution of power within an organization. Those subunits responsible for coping with more important dependencies acquire greater power in intraorganizational decision making. Resource dependence also shapes the criteria for selecting decision makers. It encourages the selection of a decision maker whose qualifications and views are congenial to powerful environmental actors. This selection process, in turn, shapes the organization's responses to its environment.[24]

Pfeffer and Salancik stress the contingent nature of these processes. They view intraorganizational dynamics as driven by members who use their power to shape outcomes in their favor. Resource dependence mediates their prospects for success. Simultaneously, the struggles that occur within organizations affect the impact of resource dependence.[25]

Dependence is in large part a function of two environmental dimensions: the concentration or dispersion of control over important resources and the relative abundance of resources. Agencies operating in an environment where control over important resources is concentrated in a few actors will tend to become dependent on them. These actors are also likely to develop a larger absolute stake in the agency's action and a greater incentive to respond to changes in its behavior.[26] In addition, their prospects for collective action improve as their number declines. Organizational autonomy will increase to the extent that dispersion of resources engenders competition among actors in the environment.[27] Thus, implementing agencies will tend to be more autonomous in environments where crucial resources are widely dispersed among competing actors.

Resources can be dispersed among a large number of actors, however, and still be concentrated through organizational networks. In some countries, political parties play an important role in mobilizing resources and influencing policy implementation.[28] In the United States, their role has declined while that of various peak associations, public interest groups, and trade associations has increased.[29] As the system has become more fragmented, coalitions have assumed greater importance.[30] In each case, resources are concentrated to the extent that managers, political entrepreneurs, and others have established centralized control. The mere existence of a centralized leadership does not mean centralized control over resources, since conflicts between organizational leaders and the general membership can impede resource mobilization. Concentration of control over resources is contingent on the skills and strategies of various organizational leaders.

Resource abundance in the environment is negatively associated with resource dependence. The more abundant the resources, the less likely it is that control over a particular resource will be concentrated, and the more likely that substitutes will be available. Government agencies will be less dependent in an environment where resources are abundant.

Changes in the relative concentration and abundance of environmental resources go a long way toward explaining Robert Salisbury's "paradox of interest groups in Washington."[31] At a time when the number and variety of organized interests represented in Washington are at an all-time high, their influence is on the decline despite their increasingly sophisticated strategies to exert influence. The influence of particular groups tends to decline as the number of groups represented in a policy domain increases. Moreover, as the plurality of interests grows, political support is more readily available for alternative policy positions. According to Salisbury, the proliferation of interests has transformed many a traditional "iron triangle," making government authorities less dependent on the support of particular interests.

The resource dependence model also suggests that the vulnerability of a government agency to resource dependence increases as its control over resources becomes more dispersed, since environmental actors will have more opportunities to exert their influence. Implementing agencies with decentralized structures of authority and administrative networks that are comprised of multiple agencies will be more vulnerable to resource dependence. An agency's vulnerability also depends on the abundance of its resources. Resource abundance not only enhances an agency's power in its relations with environmental actors; it also reduces the likelihood that subunits will enter into alliances with environmental actors in order to enhance their own power.

Government Agencies and the Exchange of Economic, Political, and Information Resources

One of the biggest attractions of the resource dependence perspective is its conception of dependence as a relation of asymmetric exchange. In this conceptualization, dependent organizations may still possess important resources, which they employ to reduce their dependence. Three types of resources are important to an explanation of policy implementation: economic, political, and information resources.

Elites in the private sector control economic resources through their discretion over investment and the organization of the economy. Their decisions affect the availability of "jobs, prices, growth, the standard of living and [the] economic security of everyone."[32] Business decisions have substantial impact on policy implementation. Securing the cooperation of economic elites is often essential to successful implementation.

No matter how powerful the economic elites, government officials are not imprisoned by interests imposed on them from society. The state controls an array of goods and services that are in great demand: credit, subsidies, licenses, tariffs, various forms of regulation, infrastructure, commodities produced in the public sector, public sector employment, and technological innovations.[33] The state's economic resources can determine the fate of entire industries. A good example is the aerospace industry, where the government has exercised its control over patents, cross-licensing arrangements, sales contracts, research and development funds, finance for capital improvements, and bailouts to encourage the establishment of firms and to maintain their health. The history of the aerospace industry is replete with instances where changes in government objectives have been followed by changes in the objectives of firms within the industry.[34]

Political resources are also exchanged between government agencies and society. These range from the authority to exercise legal sanctions to the capacity to mobilize political support. Analysts have long observed the impact of powerful political actors on policy implementation. Philip Selznick's classic study of the Tennessee Valley Authority remains one of the most insightful works of this genre. He concludes that an implementing agency, if it is to endure, cannot rely on "the diffuse support of elements not directly involved in its work." Instead, it must "find support among local institutions and develop smooth working relations with them." [35]

These observations overstate the dependence of a government agency on local institutions. They neglect the fact that strong support from superior authorities may enable an agency to overcome local resistance. Selznick's own work identifies the Soil Conservation Service as an agency that bucked the oppposition of the American Farm Bureau Federation and other adversaries because the SCS had strong backing within the Department of Agriculture and diffuse popular support.[36]

Government agencies also use their own political resources to counteract political opposition in their environment. Agencies can distribute resources in ways that weaken opposition and strengthen supportive groups. The resources of agencies are often used to facilitate the organization of supportive constituencies. For instance, the U.S. Extension Service worked to create state farm bureaus, and federal air pollution officials built support for environmental policy initiatives during the 1960s by mobilizing potential supporters.[37] James D. Thompson has remarked that prestige is the "cheapest" way to acquire power.[38] Implementing agencies can use their authority to strengthen supportive groups by vesting them with more prestige than their opponents. Finally, the employees of an agency often develop into a powerful constituency in their own right.

The third type of resource, control over information, has long been recognized as a source of power in inter- and intraorganizational relations.[39] The information resources possessed by private organizations are especially important, since implementation often takes place in an environment where there is no market feedback. Because their survival is often more tightly coupled with societal conditions, private sector organizations are often better attuned to social circumstances. For instance, business firms can credibly claim to be in close touch with conditions of supply and demand in their markets or with the technologies in their possession. Trade associations often develop specialized expertise about the industry they represent. Public interest organizations can plausibly assert that they possess greater familiarity with the needs of their constituencies on particular issues.[40] Implementing authorities appear particularly vulnerable to dependence on external sources of information when they initiate new policies. At this time, they frequently lack the experience necessary to anticipate the consequences of their actions, and they rely on outside expertise to avoid appearing misguided or incompetent.[41] As implementation proceeds, government agencies continue to depend on information provided by other groups to evaluate a policy's impact.

State agencies also possess important information resources. They control the dissemination of information concerning important, and often arcane, regulations and procedures; and they can use this resource to reward allies and penalize enemies. An extreme example is the Brazilian government's failure to disseminate information concerning flooding schedules, thereby causing widespread social disruption.[42] Agency officials can also use their control over information to select that which reflects positively on their agency while withholding disadvantageous data. Government agencies also largely determine the standards by which policies are evaluated; and these standards may be adjusted to suit official interests. Government policies usually set the agenda for political analysis.[43] Furthermore, by funding research, government agencies exert control over implementation analysis.

To the extent that organizational networks develop around policy implementation, implementing agencies are likely to have more power. Centrality of position within information networks is a source of power.[44] It enhances the efficacy of strategies to pit competing demands against one another and manipulate responses through differential disclosure. The growing interdependence of government programs makes their impact difficult to predict, and it obscures the interests of different social groups. These trends have increased the importance of information resources and enhanced the dependence of interest groups on the informational resources of the government.[45]

Explaining the consequences of resource dependence requires complex analysis. Organizations often develop sophisticated "resource management" strategies.[46] They can attempt to minimize their dependence by diversifying their resource mix.[47] They can try to increase their autonomy by ensuring predictable supplies of resources. Organizations may also deploy resources to create allies that enhance their power. In spite of the complex considerations involved, recent methodological advances have been made in measuring resource dependence. Using an input-output model, Salancik has developed an index of influence in dependency networks; and Laumann and Knoke have synthesized network theory with Coleman's exchange models to develop measures of the power of actors within the energy and health policy domains. Their model consistently predicts outcomes in these policy areas.[48]

In conclusion, the resource dependence model asserts that policy implementation will be shaped by the relative power of government agencies and actors in their environment as determined by the resources under their control. Three points of exchange appear to be strategically important to an understanding of policy implementation: (1) exchanges between policy-formulating authorities and implementing agencies, (2) exchanges between implementing agencies and actors in their environment, and (3) exchanges between environmental actors and policymakers (see figure 1).

Public Policy and Institutionalized Rules

Proponents of the resource dependence model have been criticized for their preoccupation with the environment as a source of material inputs.[49] The inclusion of political and information resources in our broader conceptualization of resource dependence responds to this criticism to some extent. Still, the resource dependence model remains inadequate because it fails to consider that actors make sense of their information through cognitive maps that shape their understanding of what is possible and appropriate.[50] To understand the evolution of policy implementation, we must account for the ways that institutionalized rules shape the cognition and values of decision makers.[51]

Institutionalized rules are cultural theories about how society works and consequent prescriptions for attaining social objectives.[52] Institutionalized rules are created after innovative responses to organizational problems become so widely diffused that they gain general acceptance as legitimate solutions to such problems.[53] Some social practices become institutionalized because they resonate with cultural values that

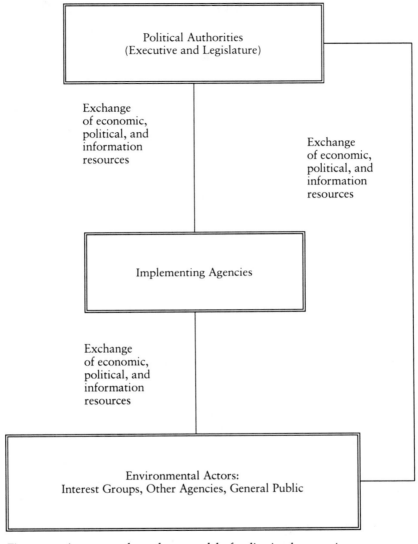

Figure 1.   A resource dependence model of policy implementation.

accord them legitimacy whether or not they are efficacious.[54] Authoritative institutions—including professional associations, governmental agencies, and educational institutions—articulate and legitimate institutionalized rules.[55]

Institutionalized rules have cognitive as well as normative consequences. They condition decision makers' intuitive understanding by defining implementation problems in particular ways. In the process, they prescribe some practices and proscribe others.[56] Organizations often alter their procedures to accommodate institutionalized rules even when these modifications do not benefit performance. For example, the diffusion of municipal civil service reforms from 1900 to 1930 initially resulted from the increased efficiency that they engendered. The reforms continued to spread—regardless of whether they enhanced efficiency— because of the legitimacy that they provided.[57]

Government agencies are generally more susceptible to the constraints imposed by institutionalized rules than other organizations. Ambiguous policy goals and difficulties in evaluating the technologies of government agencies lead to uncertainty among government officials.[58] The status of government agencies as public sector organizations makes them more vulnerable to popular evaluation. As Lynn notes, "the difficulty of government work is that it not only has to be well done, but the public has to be convinced that it is being well done.[59] In this context, "institutionalized rules" become very attractive. They provide external legitimation and promote internal consensus among organizational members. Because institutionalized rules are likely to be stable, the legitimacy that they bring helps to buffer government agencies from changes in their environment.[60] Finally, institutionalized rules are likely to predominate more in public sector agencies than in the private sector, because in the public sector there is generally no mechanism like the market to weed out inefficient practices. As a consequence, political legitimacy often becomes a more important criterion for survival than economic efficiency.[61]

Resource dependence and institutionalized rules stand in an interactive relationship. While resource dependence conditions the development of institutionalized rules, institutionalized rules shape the nature of resource exchanges. Resource dependence influences both the creation and the dissemination of institutionalized rules.

All other things being equal, the more powerful the social actor, the more likely it will succeed in institutionalizing rules favoring its interests.[62] The disparate distribution of resources in a society results in a selection process favoring better-endowed actors.[63] This selection process operates at three sites.[64] The first is the discourse that occurs among policy experts. While this discourse generally includes alternative perspectives advocated by different coalitions, each perspective is based on core values and an internal logic that promotes the development of some ideas and filters out others.[65] State institutions are the second site of selection. The knowledge, skills, and learning that people acquire reflect the incentives embedded in their institutional context.[66] The learning process that guides the innovation of policy-relevant ideas is in large measure derived from experience with previous policies.[67] Innovations with greater feasibility in a particular institutional context are also more likely to be adopted. Competition for popular support among political leaders is the third site where cultural selection occurs. Political leaders and political parties promote ideas that increase their support, and they discourage ideas that diminish their popularity.[68]

Although resource dependence shapes the development of institutionalized rules, institutionalized rules are not merely a reflection of resource dependence. Institutional rules, in an important sense, must be shared, not simply imposed. Widespread acceptance is essential to obtain legitimacy. Gaining acceptance requires that the rules be intuitively plausible and consistent with the sense of appropriateness derived from cultural values. In addition, as the spread of Western norms of rationality to other societies illustrates, the source of institutionalized rules may be exogenous to networks of resource dependence.[69] Externally generated institutional rules can shape the perceptions of powerful and dependent organizations alike, although the more powerful are likely to exert greater influence over the assimilation of such rules. Finally, institutionalized rules can alter relations of resource dependence. In a fascinating study, Ritti and Silver show how institutionalized rules have transformed antagonistic relations between a regulatory agency and its regulatees into mutually beneficial ones by creating rituals that enhance the legitimacy of each.[70]

Institutionalized rules constitute a cultural terrain whose contours shape the nature of exchanges by facilitating some strategies while impeding others.[71] This terrain is created by the historical sedimentation of different rules whose ambiguity or inconsistency may suggest different courses of action.[72] In fact, different social groups frequently employ different institutionalized rules to advocate alternative courses of action. Even then, institutionalized rules condition action by limiting the perceived alternatives. At times, they can create a "cultural lag," which causes people to miss new opportunities to advance their interests because they are reluctant to abandon culturally legitimated patterns of action. As March and Olsen's study of institutional reform demonstrates, measures designed to make bureaucracies more efficient are often jettisoned when they contradict culturally given "logics of appropriateness."[73]

In sum, the Organizational Environment Perspective offers a novel way to examine how the environment of implementing agencies shapes the rational and conflictual processes depicted by the conventional wisdom. The need to gain access to environmental resources shapes the design of organizational structure as well as the adjustments that occur in the course of implementation. Institutionalized rules limit the set of alternatives under consideration and influence their evaluation. They simultaneously enhance the efficacy of some alternatives by endowing them with legitimacy. The Organizational Environment Perspective also advances our understanding of the conflictual dynamics of implementation. It helps to explain how the structure of environmental resources conditions intraorganizational conflict by strengthening the position of those who control access to important resources. It likewise enhances our understanding of the conflicts that arise between agencies and actors in their environment by providing a more rigorous specification of the sources of power that shape these processes. Institutionalized rules shape political processes by enhancing the efficacy of some strategies of action. By endowing actors with legitimacy, institutionalized rules also strengthen their bargaining positions.

Limitations of Organization Theory: Unique State Capacities

Organization theory is deficient in explaining the activity of implementing agencies because it fails to take into account the distinctiveness of state organizations. The singular position of the state in society provides government officials with access to unique capabilities. Legitimate coercion is one example of a unique state capacity whose impact on interorganizational relations has rarely been explored by organizational theorists. Another capacity unique to the state organizations is the constitutive impact of public policy—that is, the ability of policies to shape the identities of various social groups and regulate the ways in which they interact. All organizations possess policies that have a constitutive impact on their members. The impact of public policy is distinctive because of its scope. While the constitutive impact of a private organization is confined to its members, the constitutive impact of public policy affects all social actors within its jurisdiction, whether locality or nation.

The constitutive impact of public policy occurs at three levels. The broadest is the political constitution or legal regime. This level affects policy implementation because legal regimes shape the identities of those participating in implementation and limit the ways in which they interact. They are important factors in determining the identity of citizens, since they define their legal rights and obligations.[74] They also delimit the identities of such important political actors as private corporations and nonprofit organizations. Finally, legal regimes usually proscribe certain forms of interaction between various actors.

Policy mandates are the second level at which public policy has a constitutive impact. Mandates delimit the domain of societal actors affected by implementation. They are largely responsible for distributing the relative costs and benefits among various social groups. These costs and benefits condition the groups' incentives for collective action. They also shape the formation of political coalitions.

Consider the contrast resulting from the different domains delimited by the mandates for "old" and "new" regulatory agencies. The jurisdiction of the old agencies usually coincided with industry boundaries. Since agencies such as the Interstate Commerce Commission, the Securities and Exchange Commission, the Food and Drug Administration, and the Civil Aeronautics Board regulated the important activity of a particular industry, the industry's interest in the agency was intense. In contrast, the impact of these agencies on citizens' lives was compartmentalized, and public interest was less intense. As a result, the actions of these agencies were less likely to spur collective action among the public than from the industries. In the new regulatory agencies, policy mandates delimited different domains. Because agencies such as the Environmental Protection Agency (EPA) have only a compartmentalized impact on a diverse array of industries, collective action by these industries is limited. At the same time, the EPA's responsibilities coincide with an issue that is of great concern to public interest groups. Throughout the 1970s, business groups were unable to exert much influence over the EPA while the agency remained responsive to environmental groups. Business was able to rein it in only after the election of a president intent on weakening the agency.[75]

Finally, public policy shapes the organization and behavior of social actors through implementation procedures. These procedures are formed as a consequence of the overall structure of the political system, the policy mandate, and the organizational routines of implementing agencies.[76] For instance, private corporations, universities, and other social actors that are dependent on government funding are profoundly affected by governmental accounting and budgeting procedures. In the United States, the constitutional separation of powers frequently makes these actors accountable to an array of agencies (such as the General Accounting Office, the General Services Administration, and the Office of Management and Budget), in addition to the agency that implements the program in which they are participating. The dispersion of government authority may lead to diffusion of authority within the social actor. Budget cycles and appropriations processes, in addition to allocating resources, establish the timing, constraints, and opportunities for social actors who wish to bring their influence to bear on the allocation process.

Implementation procedures can determine who gains access to authorities. For example, the procedures followed by the U.S. Atomic Energy Commission and later the Nuclear Regulatory Commission, in regulating the construction of nuclear power plants, favor producer interests at the expense of public interest organizations. Licenses for construction were granted on the basis of case-by-case hearings. These procedures promoted a close working relationship between agency personnel and the staff of producer interests. At the same time, they discouraged the participation of other groups by raising their costs and limiting their influence. Had the agencies adopted procedures to regulate through the elaboration of general rules, the participation of other groups would have received more encouragement, since their costs would be lower and their impact wider.[77]

Economists and corporate managers have long understood the importance of the constitutive impact of public policy. George Stigler, for instance, has observed that every industry or occupation with enough political power will use the state to control entry and retard the growth rate of competitors.[78] The constitutive impact of public policy in other policy areas has been less recognized but is no less pervasive. Social programs also have an extensive constitutive impact. For instance, Meyer has argued that federal intervention in public education during the 1960s shifted influence over educational programs from local groups to organizations and professionals who were able to wield influence at the national level.[79] Esping-Andersen has noted that the universal benefits offered by social programs have promoted the formation of broad-based coalitions of support for many social democratic governments, while in other countries, where social programs provide more narrowly targeted benefits, such coalitions have not arisen.[80]

The capacity of public policy to shape the interests and organization of social groups has important consequences for understanding the relationship between implementing agencies and their social environment. State leadership and the design of public policy may be used to encourage patterns of mobilization that reinforce the position of powerful social groups. Conceivably, they can also be employed to mitigate undue influence by the powerful and increase implementation responsiveness to the poor.

CONCLUDING REMARKS

Traditional perspectives stressing rationality or conflict illuminate important aspects of public policy implementation, but they are deficient in their conceptualization of relations between implementing agencies and actors in their societal environment. The Organizational Environment Perspective, with its focus on resource dependence and institutionalized rules, provides a better understanding of these relations. The resource dependence model generates useful propositions about the manner in which implementation is embedded in its societal environment. It submits that the dependence of government agencies on actors in their environment will be a function of the importance of the resources that those actors control, the extent that control over important resources is concentrated in the environment, and the uncertainty of the supply of resources from the environment. Traits of state agencies also affect dependence relations. Agencies with centralized control and abundant resources are likely to be more autonomous from their environment. The relatively broad definition of resources provides considerable latitude for strategic maneuver in the exchanges that occur during implementation.

Resource dependence can guide our analysis to implementation only so far as strategic choice can be understood to the exclusion of cultural context. The Organizational Environment Perspective supplements the resource dependence model by showing that institutionalized rules and the institutional authorities that sanction them shape both the rational and the conflictual aspects of implementation. While drawing heavily from organization theory, the perspective also highlights the deficiencies of its application to the study of policy implementation. It stresses that organization theory's generic treatment of organizations fails to take into account the distinctiveness of government agencies. These agencies have capabilities that are not available to other organizations. The Organizational Environment Perspective highlights the need to develop a better appreciation of these capabilities. With regard to policy implementation, the constitutive impact of public policy is especially important.

In contrast to some analysts, who seem to regard state autonomy as a means of freeing state agencies from societal constraints, the Organizational Environment Perspective suggests that neither autonomy nor dependence is intrinsically beneficial for policy implementation. By highlighting the fact that both implementing agencies and actors in their environment possess resources, it suggests that the prospects for achieving policy objectives are likely to improve when environmental actors can be induced to deploy their resources in ways that contribute to effective implementation. Such arrangements may well reduce agency autonomy while enhancing the efficacy of implementation. When should they be given priority over autonomy?

There is always a need for mechanisms to ensure responsiveness, since government agencies may advance their own interests instead of society's. Yet it is also necessary to ensure latitude for agencies to exercise their discretion and expertise. What is required is an "embedded autonomy," where the scope for exercising expertise is constrained to a greater or lesser extent by mechanisms to ensure responsiveness.[81]

The optimum balance between autonomy and responsiveness differs with the nature of the policy task and the conditions under which it is implemented. Autonomy should increase when technical expertise provides relatively clear decision rules; administration is performed by dedicated professionals; and the agency controls the economic, political, and informational resources necessary for effective implementation. The advantages of autonomy decline as the technical criteria for decision making become ambiguous and the staff less professional. Moreover, as disparities between the agency's resources and those necessary for achieving policy objectives increase, motivating environmental actors to use their resources in ways that advance implementation objectives becomes more essential.

Social environments are enabling as well as constraining. Relations between agencies and actors in their environment will always be strategic, but they need not be adversarial. Concern for autonomy should not divert attention from the importance of developing incentives that motivate social actors to act in ways that promote implementation objectives.

The Organizational Environment Perspective provides useful insights concerning the evolution of state-society relations. Its relational focus highlights the ways in which social groups shape state agencies and the manner in which agencies affect society. According to the Organizational Environment Perspective, resource dependence affects the distribution of power within a state. Those agencies, and units within agencies, that are responsible for coping with more important dependencies acquire greater power. Resource dependence also conditions the selection of officials by enhancing the prospects of those whose qualifications and views are attractive to powerful environmental actors. Finally, powerful actors are privileged in the selection process that creates institutionalized rules that condition the action of states. As a consequence of all of these factors, state agencies are likely to develop institutional biases that privilege the position of powerful actors at the expense of less powerful ones.

States, of course, are not passive objects of society. They are active participants in the construction of state-society relations. The Organizational Environment Perspective highlights the importance of the state's control over economic, political, and information resources. Perhaps more important, it stresses that states structure the organization of society through the constitutive impact of their policies.

While social structure constrains state agencies in any conjuncture, its effect is mediated by the strategies employed by state and societal actors. The strategic nature of state-society relations suggests that actors can alter constraints that confront them. Structural constraints are, after all, constituted by the historical accumulation of previous exchanges. Though they constrain action at any conjuncture, they are also subject to change. We need to develop a better understanding of continuity and change in state-society relations. This book is especially concerned with the constraints that social structure places on policies designed to increase the equity of social structures. How does social structure limit the prospects for these policies? What strategies for promoting social equity are most viable in light of these constraints? In order to better understand these issues, we now examine the implementation of three rural poverty alleviation programs.

CHAPTER 2

Rational Success, Political Failure

Programs to Benefit the Rural Poor during the New Deal

My final advice to those who are thus moved by injustices and human needs, and who think they perceive better possibilities through social organization, is to go ahead. Fail as gloriously as some of your predecessors have. If you do not succeed in bringing about any permanent change, you may at least have stirred some slow consciences so that in time they will give support to action. And you will have the satisfaction, which is not to be discounted, of having annoyed a good many miscreants who had it coming to them.

Rexford G. Tugwell

The American state is generally regarded as a liberal, laissez-faire state, and American policymakers are quick to prescribe "the magic of the marketplace" as the key to economic development. The history of American agriculture, perhaps the country's most internationally competitive sector, sharply contradicts this view. The economic and technological vitality of this sector has resulted from a history of extensive state intervention. This chapter explores the dynamics of state intervention in American rural development during a critical period of its evolution—the Great Depression. It focuses on New Deal programs to alleviate rural poverty during this period. The evolution and ultimate fate of these programs cannot be understood without reference to other state interventions in American agriculture that either preceded them or occurred simultaneously. To comprehend the impact of state intervention on the rural development in the United States, we must grasp not only its economic consequences but also its political and cultural repercussions.

The federal programs to alleviate rural poverty during the New Deal were without precedent. The economic dislocation caused by the Great Depression incited new interventions, such as the Agricultural Adjustment Administration (AAA), into the rural sector. The New Deal interventions to bolster the commercial farmers' economic solvency inadvertently created incentives for the mobilization of the rural poor and directed officials' attention to problems of rural poverty. These developments helped bring about the poverty alleviation programs.

The Rational Process Perspective illuminates how officials in the Roosevelt administration fashioned and refashioned the New Deal rural poverty programs under the Farm Security Administration (FSA) and achieved a remarkable degree of effectiveness. But if the programs were so effective, why were they terminated in the mid-1940s? The Conflictual Process Perspective shows how the administrators of the New Deal poverty alleviation programs became enmeshed in a conflict with the network formed by the American Farm Bureau Federation, the Extension Service, and the land-grant colleges. The administrators of New Deal rural poverty programs remained defiant even as the AFBF was finding allies among increasingly powerful congressional opponents of the New Deal. Their programs became natural prey for the conservative coalition.

The Organizational Environment Perspective illuminates important factors that shaped the outcome of the conflict over the FSA. Specifically, the transition from a crisis of overproduction to wartime shortages enhanced the power of commercial farmers. In addition, the AAA enhanced the political power of the AFBF and increased its conservatism by dramatically expanding its membership in the South. State interventions during the New Deal had ideological repercussions, which also bolstered the power of the commercial elites. The accommodations that government officials reached with local elites promoted "grassroots democracy": local committees, dominated by rural elites, that would monitor implementation and select local beneficiaries. FSA administrators attempted to insulate their programs from these local elites while promoting the participation of the poor. In fact, many of the measures that enhanced the effectiveness of the FSA's programs antagonized commercial farmers, especially in the South. Although the agency used its autonomy to fashion efficacious programs, it failed to maintain sufficient support to defend itself from the conservative on-slaught. In this sense, it was a rational success and a political failure.

THE ROOTS OF RESETTLEMENT: PROGRAMS
TO HELP THE RURAL POOR, 1933–1935

After its first century and a half, the federal government finally discovered the problem of rural poverty. Depression conditions made poverty an inescapable problem. At the beginning of the New Deal, few federal officials were well informed about the plight of the rural poor. Concern among many grew largely as a consequence of their experiences in implementing programs whose objectives were at best indirectly related to helping the rural poor. Throughout the New Deal, the rural poverty alleviation programs remained marginal to the Department of Agriculture's primary mission: to revive the nation's commercial agriculture. They emerged from four separate streams of policy development: the Agricultural Adjustment Administration, the Federal Emergency Relief Administration, experimental communities, and land-use planning.

The Agricultural Adjustment Administration

The Agricultural Adjustment Act of 1933 was passed in response to the protracted depression that had plagued the country's agricultural sector since 1920. Farmers had prospered from the demand stimulated by World War I, but after the war production far exceeded demand. Annual farm income dropped from its peak of $19 million in 1919 to less than $9 million in 1921, and it remained at less than $12 million for the rest of the decade. The depression of the 1920s was seriously aggravated by the economic collapse of 1929, which greatly reduced domestic and international demand. Under these circumstances, farmers fared far worse than industry because they lacked the organizational means to reduce production and maintain prices. From 1929 to 1932, the index for farm commodity prices dropped by more than 50 percent while the prices for commodities purchased by farmers dropped by only 32 percent. During the same period, the net income realized by farm operators plummeted to less than one-third of what it had been three years before.[1]

Although tenants and sharecroppers may have suffered even more than farmers, the first New Deal agricultural policies were predominantly concerned with ameliorating the plight of the farmers.[2] As Skocpol and Finegold point out, the Roosevelt administration's action to buoy the farmers was a consequence of its political dependence on the strategic electoral bloc that they comprised.[3] Implementation of the Agricultural Adjustment Act reflected the economic dependence of the administration on the larger commercial farmers.

The act was an omnibus bill combining a number of policy demands made by the farm bloc during the 1920s. The Roosevelt administration quickly selected production controls as the policy mechanism to revitalize the agricultural sector. Under the production control program, the Agricultural Adjustment Administration (AAA) would pay farmers for keeping their fields fallow. This policy was intended to reduce the volume of farm commodities reaching the marketplace and increase prices.

The plan for production controls was initially more popular among social scientists than farmers.[4] But the AAA had to enlist farmers' support, since they controlled the volume of production. In particular, it had to reach an accommodation with commercial farmers, since the owners of large farms controlled more production than small farm owners did. The AAA's dependence on large commercial farmers was also a consequence of the administrative means available to reach the farmers. Prior to the New Deal, the only direct link between the federal government and farmers was the Extension Service, which came into contact primarily with more affluent farmers. It provided the impetus for their organization into the American Farm Bureau Federation (AFBF). Thus, when implementation of production controls necessitated local planning and oversight, the AAA relied on the Extension Service to organize county committees of prominent farmers to perform these functions. This devolution of responsibilities gave the Extension Service, as well as the AFBF, a shot in the arm. The control of the prominent farmers over local implementation ensured that they would reap at least their share of AAA benefits.

In 1929, approximately seven million people lived in farm operator households with an annual income of less than $600. In addition, there were an estimated six million members of farm laborer families, most of whom had income below this level. One study concluded that more than thirteen million persons were living in the equivalent of rural slums.[5]

The AAA worked to the detriment of many of the rural poor. Its production controls restricted the amount of land under commercial production and lowered the demand for rural labor. Thousands of laborers and tenants were displaced as a consequence. The deleterious impact was particularly apparent in the South. The AAA awarded cotton landlords 4.5 cents for each pound of cotton not grown. The AAA's Cotton Division decided that landlords should compensate cash tenants at the full rate, while self-managing share tenants were to receive only 2.5 cents per pound and sharecroppers just 0.5 cents. This scale gave the landlords incentive to downgrade the status of their tenants. Since checks were mailed only to the landlords, some gave their tenants less than their due or nothing at all. One United States Department of Agriculture (USDA) study showed that even those tenants and sharecroppers who received federal funds through AAA production controls received a disproportionately low share.[6]

The disparities created by production controls caused considerable political unrest, especially in the South. Antagonism was most intense in the delta country of Arkansas, where tenant evictions led to the formation of the Southern Tenant Farmers' Union (STFU). The STFU struggled against evictions and the poverty-stricken conditions with a series of well-publicized strikes, demonstrations, and litigations. In the spring and summer of 1935, it suffered through what historian David Campbell described as a "reign of terror" perpetuated by local plantation owners. The STFU soon became a cause célèbre for a coalition of left liberals and socialists led by Norman Thomas and Gardner Jackson. Both used their personal ties with members of the Roosevelt administration to pressure the AAA into addressing the consequences of production controls for tenants.[7]

The political pressure exerted on the Roosevelt administration by advocates for the tenants sensitized it to the problems of the poor and contributed to the creation of the Resettlement Administration (RA). According to Gilbert and Howe, the STFU's struggle to gain a fair deal from the AAA precipitated the 1935 purge of liberals from the AAA.[8] But the history of the AAA suggests a more complex interpretation than a simple societal pressure–state response model.

Implementation of the AAA brought the problems of tenants and agricultural laborers under the scrutiny of USDA officials long before any political disturbance. As early as autumn 1933, a high-level debate raged within the AAA concerning the legal status of tenants in the provisions of the 1934–35 production control contracts. Alger Hiss, principal attorney of the AAA's Legal Division, and Jerome Frank, general counsel of the AAA and head of its Legal Division, advocated provisions that would give greater protection from displacement to tenants and authorize direct payments from the government to tenants. Hiss and Frank lost the dispute to Cully Cobb (head of the AAA's Cotton Division) and Chester Davis (head of the Production Division), who was soon to replace George Peek as the AAA administrator.[9]

In early 1934, the AAA sponsored a study of the impact of production controls on tenants. It hired Calvin B. Hoover, an economics professor at Duke University and a former AAA official, to conduct the investigation. He found "strong and definite" evidence that the AAA program had caused evictions and recommended that landowners be required to declare the number of their tenants before receiving AAA checks and that they be forced to account for the distribution of AAA payments to tenants. Hoover shrank from arguing that landlords be compelled to retain tenants who were no longer needed. Instead, he suggested that those who were displaced be resettled on subsistence plots and that collective farming communities be established on land purchased by the government. The Hoover study and subsequent corroborating studies by Harold Hoffsommer and William Amberson left little doubt that implementation of AAA production controls had displaced considerable numbers of tenants.[10]

In addition to its study of the tenants' plight, the AAA aroused further concern by creating a forum for tenants to voice their complaints. As early as August 1933, the Legal Advisory Committee (LAC) was established to hear tenant grievances. The Committee on Violations of Rental and Benefit Contracts replaced the LAC in January 1934. By February 1935, it had a backlog of more than 1,655 cases. Members of the committee complained that they were unable to keep up with the work load because of a "lack of adequate personnel to handle the great mass of complaints received."[11] In the spring of 1934, Chester Davis set up an Adjustment Committee (AC) to help conciliate disputes between tenants and landlords. The AC was composed of eight district agents from the Extension Service, who traveled through counties adjudicating disputes. Members of the Legal Division felt that the AC circumvented the authority of the Committee on Violations and accused it of favoring the landlords. Jerome Frank pressured Chester Davis into convening a conference on July 3, 1934, to set up a committee on landlord-tenant policy. At the meeting, it was agreed that once the new committee had enunciated a policy, it should create a subcommittee to investigate and adjudicate cases. The subcommittee was never convened, because Cully Cobb withdrew his support, insisting that responsibility for landlord-tenant relations in the cotton program should remain within his Cotton Division. Once again, the advocates of tenant interests succeeded in increasing awareness of the tenants' predicament but failed to institutionalize their concern within the AAA.[12]

The dispute between the AAA's Legal and Cotton Divisions led D. P. Trent, assistant director of the Commodities Division and Cully Cobb's immediate superior, to propose a resolution to the conflict. In addition to urging the inclusion of tenants in cotton contracts, Trent, like Hoover before him, urged measures that foreshadowed the RA. These included the establishment of farming colonies for displaced tenants and laborers and a program for helping tenants purchase their own land. Trent's proposals met with no response. He soon gave up his efforts to resolve the conflict and resigned from the AAA.[13]

The conflict reached its denouement in February 1935, when Jerome Frank's Legal Division issued a reinterpretation of cotton contracts that protected tenants from eviction. Chester Davis was so furious with Frank's reinterpretation that he threatened to resign. Henry Wallace, the secretary of agriculture, was not unsympathetic to Frank, but decided the matter in favor of Davis. Wallace feared the impact of losing Davis, a man with considerable popularity in agricultural circles.[14] He wrote in his diary that had he allowed the Legal Division's position to become AAA policy, it "would endanger the whole agricultural program" and he might have been forced to resign "to make way for someone who could get along better with the men from the South in Congress."[15]

In sum, the AAA contributed to the establishment of the Resettlement Administration by enhancing popular awareness of the tenants' problems as well as concern among officials of the Roosevelt administration. But the AAA never took measures to deal with the problem itself, because the prevailing coalition within it gave priority to fostering the recovery of the nation's commercial agriculture. Ultimately, the AAA refused to assume responsibility for improving the plight of tenants because it was unwilling to antagonize Southern commercial farmers, on whom the agency depended for successful implementation and political survival. The victory of Chester Davis and the conservative coalition clarified the limitations of the AAA as an agent of policies to benefit the rural poor. Concerned New Dealers turned their energies to creating an agency better suited to dealing with rural poverty.

The Federal Emergency Relief Administration

The FERA initiated the rehabilitation program that was to be an important feature of the RA. The FERA's establishment of its Rural Rehabilitation Division (RRD) and its development of the rural rehabilitation program illustrate the process of dynamic rationality. Initially, the FERA adopted a policy of undifferentiated relief for rural as well as urban residents. In October 1933, it conducted a survey of its clientele and found that more than one-third of the families on relief, about 1,150,000 in number, resided in rural areas.[16] On March 24, 1934, the FERA administrator, Harry Hopkins, announced that civil works and direct relief programs in rural areas would be replaced by a rural relief program whose objective was to enable "destitute persons eligible for relief in such areas to sustain themselves through their own efforts."[17] The rural rehabilitation program ingeniously combined Hopkins's concern to maintain the self-respect of the beneficiaries with the need for economy.

Getting more relief for the buck became a high priority with the shutdown of the Civil Works Administration. According to Lawrence Westbrook, head of the FERA's new RRD, "An analysis of our rural case load indicated that there were many thousands of destitute farmers receiving relief at a cost to the government of $10 to $30 per month who could be made self-sustaining by an investment in equipment and supplies which would not exceed the cost of extending relief over a period of several months."[18] The economic objective of the rural rehabilitation program was even more explicitly stated in an article by Paul V. Maris, the RRD's supervisor of field service. He wrote that relief clients should be eligible for the rural rehabilitation program even if the program would not make them self-sufficient but would merely reduce their need for relief.[19]

Many errors were committed in implementing the early rural rehabilitation program. Loans were often made to people with no means of repayment, and little progress was made in helping farmers plan and carry out improved farm practices.[20] Nevertheless, by creating a program that combined credit, planning, and supervision to fit the needs of individual farm families, the FERA established an innovative program whose implementation was refined later in the New Deal.

Experimental Communities

From the times of the pilgrims, the United States has been the site of numerous experimental communities, but the New Deal period marked the first time that the federal government sponsored experiments in community living. The New Deal community programs were inspired by Jeffersonian agrarian ideals and were supported by the president and two of the country's most powerful business leaders—Averill Harriman and Bernard Baruch. Nevertheless, no sooner were the New Deal experimental communities initiated than they became embroiled in controversy.

Legal authorization for the subsistence homesteads program was achieved when Senator John H. Bankhead attached Section 208 to the National Industrial Recovery Act. Section 208 gave the Roosevelt administration a broad mandate. It provided $25 million "to the President, to be used by him through such agencies as he may establish, and under such regulations as he may make, for making loans for and otherwise aiding in the purchase of subsistence homesteads." [21] Roosevelt allocated the new program to Harold Ickes' Department of Interior. On August 23, 1933, Ickes established the Subsistence Homesteads Division (SHD) and acceded to the president's request that M. L. Wilson be placed in charge.

While director of the Rural Economics Division at Montana State Agricultural College, Wilson had worked to establish Fairway Farms, an experimental corporation whose objective was to resettle tenants, supervise their production, and ultimately enable them to purchase their own land. His views on subsistence homesteads were congenial with Roosevelt's, and soon after his arrival in Washington he became a social acquaintance of the president and the first lady.[22] Wilson viewed subsistence homestead communities not as an immediate remedy to the urgent problems of the Depression but as a long-term resolution to problems brought upon society by the modern industrial age. He was not a reactionary agrarian but a man who valued decentralization, democracy, and the growth of a new cooperative attitude. Wilson believed that "somehow, or in some way, attitudes and lives of the families who occupy these communities must be integrated so as to provide a new and different view of life and a new and different set of family values." [23] Such a transformation would not be easy. According to Wilson, "Finding a recipe for success will take considerable experimentation." [24]

Wilson announced that the SHD would concentrate on three types of projects: (1) communities of part-time farmers located near industrial employment; (2) all-rural communities for resettled submarginal farmers; and (3) villages with new decentralized industry. The Federal Subsistence Homesteads Corporation was to be the financial agent of the program. Consistent with Wilson's belief in decentralized decision making, each project was to administer its affairs by forming a subsidiary corporation. A number of projects were begun under this admin-

istrative structure, but before any were completed, the solicitor general
issued a ruling that limited the subsidiaries' authority to make financial
decisions independent of the Department of Interior.

Eleanor Roosevelt and FDR's crony Louis Howe played an active
role in the subsistence homesteads program, especially in its highly publicized first project—Arthurdale. Mrs. Roosevelt became interested in
the project after touring several of West Virginia's impoverished mining
communities. Her vision of Arthurdale was controversial. She wanted
it to be a model community with the best of everything—including cop-
per plumbing and a progressive school system with six buildings for
only four hundred children. Such extravagance in the midst of West
Virginia's economically devastated mining towns brought ridicule on
the idyllic hamlet. Extravagance aside, the project's greatest shortcom-
ing was its failure to attract private industry to provide its residents
with employment.[25]

On May 12, 1934, penurious Harold Ickes, embarrassed by the ad-
verse publicity given to Arthurdale and lacking confidence in Wilson's
administrative ability, issued an order abolishing all authority of the
local corporations. Wilson left the SHD the following month. His replacement, the businessman Charles E. Pynchon, attempted to reduce
project costs and expedite implementation. Despite Pynchon's efforts,
delays in the planning and construction of SHD projects proliferated.
By the time the SHD was transferred to the RA, on May 15, 1935, it
had placed only 466 families on eleven projects. Most SHD projects
were still in the planning stage. Only $8 million of the division's $25
million had been spent. Various planning and administrative snafus had
made the SHD a bureaucratic nightmare. Almost as dismaying was its
tendency to select relatively well-off persons to become homesteaders
on its projects. It soon became obvious that the SHD was not accom-
plishing much in the way of relief.[26]

The Rural Rehabilitation Division of the FERA also tried its hand at
creating community projects. When Harry Hopkins asked Lawrence
Westbrook, then the administrator of the Texas Emergency Relief Administration, to come to Washington to head the RRD, he was asking
a man who had already initiated the experimental community of Wood-
lake, about one hundred miles north of Houston. Though the FERA
was obligated to let state organizations formulate their own programs,
Westbrook used his influence to encourage the state agencies to build
experimental communities.

Westbrook's view of experimental communities was different from that of Wilson and Eleanor Roosevelt. He saw them less as a step toward utopia than as a practical relief measure. Westbrook insisted that by using work relief to construct these communities, the government could absorb nearly half of their cost from funds that would have been spent anyway in extending relief to workers. The occupants of the communities were to be able-bodied, unemployed workers who had little chance of being reemployed in their present location. These "stranded workers," emphasized Westbrook, were public charges who would likely remain so unless they moved to a new community. Westbrook contended that these experimental communities would enable workers to "rehabilitate themselves and become self-sustaining citizens at less cost to the government than the cost of direct and work relief." [27]

Westbrook optimistically hoped to build from 100 to 150 communities with up to 100 families residing in each.[28] Unlike the SHD projects, which attempted to create employment opportunities by attracting private industry, the FERA communities provided jobs through cooperative farming and related agro-industries or cooperative handicrafts. In comparison to SHD communities, the FERA's rural-industrial communities were usually constructed with greater speed and economy, largely because the state corporations provided local control and were able to avoid red tape.[29] Because of their relatively late start, only two of the twenty-five communities planned had been completed by the time they were transferred to the RA.

Land-Use Planning

The stream of policy development that culminated in the land-use planning component of the RA began as a response to an undesired consequence of New Deal relief programs. In the summer of 1933, Secretary of Agriculture Henry Wallace, Assistant Secretary Rexford Tugwell, and Mordecai Ezekiel, economic adviser to Wallace, became alarmed because the scope of land reclamation likely to be undertaken by public works programs would increase the country's productive land and contradict the objectives of the AAA production controls.[30] Wallace urged President Roosevelt to establish a committee, made up of officials from the USDA and the Department of Interior, to iron out this inconsistency. Roosevelt—an enthusiastic advocate of land-use planning during his term as governor of New York[31]—authorized the creation of the National Land Use Planning Committee. The committee urged that for every dollar the federal government spent on land reclamation, it spend a dollar to purchase submarginal land. On December 28, 1933, the Public Works Administration allocated $25 million to the FERA for this purpose. This was the first time ever that the federal government had authorized funds to purchase submarginal land.[32]

Drawing on the USDA's growing expertise in land-use planning, the Land Policy Section of the AAA was responsible for selecting the submarginal land to be purchased. The FERA actually made the purchase and was responsible for resettling displaced persons. The Land Policy Section was also ordered to develop a long-term national land-use plan.

Twenty-five million dollars was a small amount to begin a national land-use program, and the supporters of land-use planning considered it just the beginning. The head of the Land Policy Section, Lewis C. Gray, worked with Rexford Tugwell and Mordecai Ezekiel to develop legislative proposals for more comprehensive, long-term land planning. The director of the budget, Lewis Douglas, quashed their proposals because he believed that such a policy would be too expensive for the federal government to support.

Though Roosevelt deferred to the advice of his budget adviser, in June 1934 he established the National Resources Board and asked it to submit a report on the nation's resources by December 1, 1934. The section of the report drawn up by the NRB's Land Planning Committee recommended that the federal government acquire 75 million acres of submarginal farm land in the next fifteen years. In all, the committee projected that its proposals would affect 454,000 families. It stressed that their resettlement was meant to improve their condition as well as to withdraw land from cultivation.[33]

The NRB report was well received, but problems still remained in the implementation of land-use planning. They stemmed from difficulties in coordination. Purchase of land and resettlement of displaced persons proved time-consuming. They created a bottleneck as the FERA was unable to keep pace with the recommendations of the AAA's Land Policy Section. The amount of land reclaimed vastly exceeded the acreage of land withdrawn from production. Though $21 million of the $25 million allotted for land retirement had been used by June 1935, L. C. Gray estimated that land worth an additional $50 million would need to be purchased to keep pace with reclamation.[34]

The need for coordination of land-use policy was an important impetus for the establishment of the RA. The traditional distrust plaguing relations between the Department of Agriculture and the Department of Interior made it highly unlikely that coordination among agencies such as the Land Policy Section, the FERA, and the SHD could be successful. In the spring of 1934, Rexford Tugwell, discouraged with the possibilities of working in a Department of Agriculture that he considered to be dominated by the interests of large farmers, suggested to Franklin Roosevelt that something needed to be done about the lack of coordination among land-use policies. By August 1934, Tugwell had convinced the president. Roosevelt suggested the possibility of using an executive order to establish a coordinating agency with emergency funds. Talks progressed through the following months, and by the spring of 1935 Tugwell's suggestion for creating a single federal agency to rehabilitate poor people and poor land had become a reality.[35]

CREATION OF THE
RESETTLEMENT ADMINISTRATION

More than any other individual, Rexford Tugwell was responsible for setting the course of the RA and its descendant, the Farm Security Administration. Tugwell established their institutional character and organizational mission.[36] Though he left the RA after less than two years, his protégés controlled the FSA well into the 1940s. For better or worse, the agencies were wedded to Tugwell and his controversial public image.

An economics professor from Columbia, Tugwell brought weighty intellectual baggage to the RA. An adherent of Simon Patten's institutional economics, he believed that major social problems emerge because social institutions are slow to adjust to technological developments. For Tugwell, an economy is a "concert of interests," which must be kept in harmony in order to preserve social welfare. He argued that the Depression had occurred because institutions had failed to adjust to the increases in productivity that had taken place during the 1920s. In their pursuit of profits, businessmen had appropriated a disproportionate share of the gains in productivity and invested in what quickly became excess capacity. The consequent crisis of underconsumption and overproduction caused the Depression. The crisis could be remedied if the laissez-faire regime were replaced with economic planning.[37]

Tugwell's intellectual pedigree placed him outside the realm of orthodox discourse concerning the nation's agricultural problems. His critics frequently attempted to discredit his views on agriculture by declaring that he had no practical experience in the area.[38] However, critics leveled these charges only by ignoring Tugwell's studies of agricultural problems in the United States and Europe during the 1920s.[39] As the member of the "brain trust" most concerned with the agricultural sector, Tugwell had helped to introduce Roosevelt to many of the ideas behind early New Deal agricultural policy and to many of the people who implemented them. Indeed, Henry Wallace was initially so deferential toward Tugwell that he was reluctant to ask Tugwell to be his assistant secretary because he felt that *he* should be working under Tugwell.[40]

Tugwell remained an outsider to the traditional USDA bureaucracy during his term as assistant and under secretary of agriculture. In particular, Tugwell distrusted the Extension Service, because he felt that it was dominated by large commercial farmers. On one occasion, in the middle of a meeting of federal and state extension officials, he announced publicly to Henry Wallace that he did not have "a damn bit of confidence in the Extension Directors." [41]

Tugwell assumed his post as administrator of the RA with well-defined opinions. He insisted that the RA's role could be properly understood only in the broader context of increasing agricultural productivity and what he viewed as "the inevitable movement from farm to city." Tugwell believed that the RA should provide "a more orderly pattern" for this transformation.[42] As it was, mechanization and increased production had intensified competition and resulted in a growing number of foreclosures, higher rates of farm tenancy, and a proliferation of rural poverty.[43] These developments were undesirable from an economic as well as a humanitarian perspective, because the rural poor constituted a drag on the economy. Relief for the rural poor was only a stopgap measure from Tugwell's perspective. The most important tasks were land-use planning; resettling of the rural poor; and the development of new social institutions, such as cooperatives and suburbs, that would enable the poor to secure viable livelihoods.

Tugwell established a centralized organizational structure for the RA. The RA's Washington office had fourteen divisions of two types: program divisions formulated policy and procedure for RA implementation; technical divisions (such as the Personnel, Business Management, Legal, Special Skills, and Construction Divisions) provided administrative services and technical support. The RA had four program divisions. The Division of Land Utilization implemented the agency's two-part program for planned land use. The first part was the development of national land-use planning. To pursue this objective, the planning staff of the AAA's Land Policy Section and the regional and state land-planning consultants of the National Resources Board were combined into the division's Land Use Planning Section. The second part of the land-use program involved federal land acquisition to retire submarginal farmlands and convert them to more appropriate uses, such as pasture, wildlife refuges, recreation areas, and additional land for Indian reservations. Since approximately one-third of the families whose land was acquired by the RA needed help in resettling,[44] the land acquisition program inherited thirty-three resettlement projects from the Division of Subsistence Homesteads and the Rural Rehabilitation Division of the FERA.[45] Tugwell was critical of the subsistence homesteads program because he disagreed with its premise that industry would relocate to rural areas to avail itself of the labor of such communities.[46] The Rural Resettlement Division handled three types of projects. Community projects placed farmers on a common settlement. The members of these projects worked either contiguous plots of land or common land in a cooperative fashion. Infiltration resettlement projects settled individual families in scattered plots within an area. Finally, in December 1935, the RA began an experimental tenant-purchase program, through which tenants were given loans to purchase the plots of land that they were working.

With the establishment of the Suburban Resettlement Division, Tugwell expanded the concept of resettlement from rural relocation to resettlement in metropolitan areas. Through suburban resettlement, workers would be relocated in communities planned to integrate residences with the wholesome attractions of nature while maintaining access to industrial employment. Tugwell hoped that his "greenbelt towns" would demonstrate the advantages of urban planning and the design of towns according to garden principles. Construction of suburban resettlement projects had the additional advantage of providing employment to thousands who were on relief.

The fourth RA program division was the Rural Rehabilitation Division. Its objective was to provide potentially viable farm operators with assets and advice, so that they could endure the hardships of the Depression and realize their potential profitability. The most important component of the program, the standard rural rehabilitation loans, continued the program of supervised credit established by the FERA. Low-interest, two-year loans were provided for the purchase of nonrecoverable goods, and five-year loans were provided for recoverable goods. Supervision usually took place through the formulation of annual farm and home management plans, which were supposed to help the farmers make optimal use of their assets and ensure high rates of loan recovery. The standard rehabilitation loan program was augmented by a program that provided grants to farm families in need of emergency assistance. Frequently these families were victims of natural calamities, but they also included standard loan clients who faced emergencies unprovided for by their farm and home plans. The RA also provided loans to finance community and cooperative services, so that these services and assets would be available to small farmers who otherwise could not afford them. Efforts were also made to finance purchasing and marketing cooperatives, to obtain better prices for inputs and products. Rural rehabilitation included a program for farm debt adjustment. Under this program, citizens' committees, appointed at the state and county levels, arbitrated negotiations between farmers and creditors to adjust debts in order to make repayments manageable. Finally, a program for tenure improvement endeavored to protect the rights of tenants by replacing oral lease agreements with written model leases.

RA AND FSA POLICY IMPLEMENTATION: A RATIONAL PROCESS PERSPECTIVE

Examining the RA and FSA from the Rational Process Perspective highlights the measures that the agencies took to maximize the effectiveness of their programs. Until fiscal year 1943, the agencies possessed extraordinary autonomy. They used it to alter their policy objectives so that they would meet the immediate needs of the rural poor and conform to the administrative and fiscal realities that confronted the agencies. They also devised innovative programs to combat the multifaceted nature of rural poverty. Implementation was not without its problems. Monitoring led to counterproductive outcomes, and funding limitations restricted the programs' impact. Even with these problems, the programs were reasonably effective in ameliorating the plight of their beneficiaries.

The RA was created by Executive Order 7027,[47] which gave the agency the mandate to resettle rural and urban low-income families, initiate and administer projects to conserve national resources, and finance loans to farmers and laborers to purchase farm land and equipment. The FSA replaced the RA a few months after the passage of the Bankhead-Jones Farm Tenant Act in 1937. The act offered guidelines for tenant-purchase loans, and it restricted the resettlement program to operations necessary for the completion and administration of projects for which funds had already been allocated. It imposed no serious restrictions on the flexibility of rural rehabilitation, the largest program under the FSA.[48]

Congress often limits the action of federal agencies through annual appropriation bills that place restrictions on the agencies' activities. Funds for the rural rehabilitation program were provided through emergency relief appropriation acts until fiscal year 1942, when they began to be included in the agricultural appropriation acts. These appropriations allowed great freedom in the use of funds. For example, the Emergency Relief Appropriation Act for fiscal year 1937 provided the RA with funds "for such loans, relief, and rural rehabilitation for needy persons as the President may determine," and the act for the following year allocated funds "for administration, loans, relief, and rural rehabilitation for needy persons." With the exception of the Emergency Relief Appropriation Act for fiscal year 1941, which prohibited loans to enable recipients to join cooperative associations, the first real restrictions on rural rehabilitation appropriations appeared in the Agricultural Appropriation Act for fiscal year 1943. Until then, rural rehabilitation had never been precisely delimited, nor was there any effort to allocate funds among its different components. The extraordinary autonomy enjoyed by the RA and the FSA enabled them to fashion their organizational structure, revise their policy objectives, and follow a series of innovative approaches to rural poverty alleviation.[49]

The establishment of the RA can be considered a step in the process of dynamic rationality. The RA consolidated the diverse array of rural poverty programs previously housed in the FERA, the SHD, the AAA, and the Farm Credit Administration. This consolidation enhanced the effectiveness of New Deal rural poverty programs in four ways. First, it combined similar programs (for example, the subsistence homesteads program with the FERA's rural community projects), thereby reducing administrative overlap and increasing economies of scale. Second, it reduced inefficient interorganizational transactions and facilitated coordination by bringing related programs (such as land-use planning and resettlement) together in one agency. Third, the RA increased the rationality of implementation by standardizing what had grown to be an unwieldy array of programs and accounting procedures under the forty-eight state relief corporations.[50] Fourth, combining these programs into one agency enhanced the effectiveness of implementation because it minimized conflicting priorities. Antipoverty efforts had been constrained by the AAA's dependence on the resources of larger farmers. Implementation of the subsistence homesteads program had been hindered by Harold Ickes' skepticism and (not unfounded) worry that it would turn into a boondoggle. Combining New Deal rural poverty programs under a single agency gave them a firmer institutional base. Tugwell himself declared, "Our organization was really an attempt by the President to rationalize one function of the government. . . . It brought together efforts formerly made by separate agencies to do something about our land and the people on it. . . . We have tried to put these activities together in a logical and economical way, to finish up the tasks begun by them and to give studied direction to all these efforts." [51]

Given the RA's multipurpose mandate and the mixed bag of programs that it inherited, the working out of a set of priorities was an important part of its rational processes of implementation. Tugwell had strong opinions about the RA's priorities. According to Lawrence Hewes, an RA regional administrator, "Tugwell took no pride in conducting a first aid program; our real job was to cure the deeper malady." [52] For Tugwell, curing the deeper malady called for an emphasis on land-use planning and resettlement. [53] He wanted to deemphasize the rural rehabilitation loan program. He considered rural rehabilitation a temporary part of the RA's work, which would grow progressively less important as resettlement gained momentum. Tugwell once told a meeting of RA staff, "We want to get out of this loan business anyway. We do not want to make it particularly attractive. In other words, we are interested in resettlement, not loans." [54] An indication of the minor role Tugwell envisioned for rural rehabilitation is that he initially authorized its administration by a section within the RA's Rural Resettlement Division.

Despite Tugwell's intentions, rural rehabilitation became the linchpin of the RA program. Arthur Schlesinger notes that rural rehabilitation was one of the most important policy commitments inherited by the RA. He contends that the administrative inheritance of the RA had a momentum of its own, which prevented Tugwell from establishing his priorities. [55] It would be wrong to argue simply that the RA's administrative inheritance foiled Tugwell's designs. Although the legacy of programs, financial provisions, and personnel imposed constraints on Tugwell's capacity to pursue his priorities, the process of dynamic rationality determined the RA's priorities.

The Roosevelt administration's desire to counteract the widespread destitution caused by the Depression with swift relief shaped the adaptation of RA priorities. When Roosevelt authorized the initial funding for the RA, he reportedly told Tugwell, Ickes, and Hopkins that the future allotment of funds among relief agencies would depend on how quickly the agencies could spend their funds.[56] Thus, from the beginning, an important priority of the RA was to transfer its funds to its clients as quickly as possible.

Resettlement was notoriously slow in providing client benefits. Projects had to be planned, land had to be acquired, and basic infrastructure had to be constructed before resettlement communities could begin to deliver benefits. In addition to the long gestation periods, resettlement projects had high administrative costs, so that a relatively smaller percentage of expenditures reached the clients' pockets. Finally, the RA lacked the administrative and legal capacity to implement a resettlement program that would be extensive enough to aid the vast numbers in need of help. Rural rehabilitation loans and grants had a much quicker impact. All that was needed was to select deserving clients, gain approval for annual farm and home management plans, and transfer credit. Administrative costs of rural rehabilitation were much lower. One county supervisor could provide guidance to many clients within his jurisdiction. Finally, the RA quickly developed the capacity to deliver loans and grants to farmers and tenants throughout the country. In sum, despite Tugwell's initial preferences, the priorities of the RA shifted toward rural rehabilitation simply because it met the perceived exigencies of the Depression far better than resettlement did.

To say that rural rehabilitation was better suited to meet the needs of the situation does not mean that the RA was inexorably driven to adopt it. There is no dearth of bureaucratic pathology. The record shows that soon after the RA was constituted, its officials began to reevaluate the resettlement program. As early as August 1935, the Land Use Planning Section of the Division of Land Utilization issued a preliminary report strongly recommending that resettlement be carried out on an infiltration basis rather than on a community basis. The community concept in conjunction with cooperative enterprises had been an important precept of the resettlement programs inherited by the RA. The Planning Section suggested that the RA's program settle individual farmers on scattered plots because (1) farmers would be assimilated into the locality more easily, (2) reliance on cooperative enterprises had proved a disappointment, and (3) the RA would not have to provide infrastructure and public services.[57]

Reconsideration of the resettlement program continued at the January 1, 1936, Regional Directors' Conference. One regional director, Jonathan Garst, advocated that the resettlement program be replaced by the use of rehabilitation loans to enable farmers to purchase plots to relocate themselves on. Garst's proposal was rejected, but there was considerable support for the position that the RA need not resettle everyone; rather, it need only provide an array of opportunities for displaced families.[58] Disenchantment with resettlement communities among RA officials was undoubtedly intensified by the controversy they had raised in Congress and among the public. By autumn of 1937, the FSA agreed not to establish any more resettlement communities. At the same time, the drought of the summer of 1936 called for expansion of the rural rehabilitation program. The Rural Rehabilitation Division distributed $22.7 million in emergency grants to rural families in drought-stricken areas, another $6 million to refugees from the drought, and more than $17 million in emergency crop and feed loans. For fiscal year 1936–37, drought expenditures increased the rural rehabilitation budget by 31 percent, to $195 million. They added more than 15 percent to the RA budget.[59]

The importance of resettlement rapidly diminished. Its share of the RA's budget dropped from 25 percent for fiscal year 1936–37 to 7 percent two years later. By September 1, 1937, the name Resettlement Administration was changed to Farm Security Administration (FSA) because, as Henry Wallace observed, the agency "was now carrying out a program which involves resettlement activities as only a minor part of its functions."[60] After 1942, resettlement constituted no more than 1 percent of the FSA's budget (see table 1).

The innovations put in place by the FSA and the RA to make their programs more effective also reflect rational processes of implementation. While implementing the rural rehabilitation program, the agencies' personnel found it necessary to reduce the debt and increase the security of many of their clients before rural rehabilitation loans could provide effective help. The RA acquired a program to adjust the debts of farmers from the Farm Credit Administration in August 1935. By 1946, the agencies had negotiated reductions in the debts of 111,979 clients for an average of $984 per case, or by 21.7 percent of the initial amount outstanding.[61]

Agency officials found that tenants' insecurity curbed their investment in land and equipment. To enhance the security of tenants, agency officials conducted a campaign to encourage written rather than oral

TABLE I
RESETTLEMENT ADMINISTRATION AND FARM SECURITY ADMINISTRATION FUNDS OBLIGATED BY FISCAL YEAR
(in thousands of current dollars)

Year	Total	Rural Rehabili- tation	Farm Tenant Purchase	Resettle- ment	Migratory Labor	Other	Technical Services and Adminis- tration
1936–37	340,547	194,957	0	85,895	919	0	58,776
1938	156,542	89,825	8,914	32,907	1,331	0	22,603
1939	206,827	136,730	23,249	14,729	5,909	0	27,173
1940	200,320	116,790	36,007	9,387	6,886	20	31,730
1941	227,018	122,593	45,677	16,675	5,550	64	36,459
1942	242,032	135,333	45,247	8,789	6,287	3,881	42,495
1943	180,347	103,960	29,246	2,168	7,302	400	37,271
1944	128,999	74,692	21,922	954	0	420	31,010
1945	114,760	73,903	11,777	1,431	0	658	26,991
1946	158,451	101,076	28,070	711	0	60	28,533
Total[a]	1,995,843	1,149,860	250,109	173,646	33,634	5,503	343,041

Percentage Distribution

Year	Total	Rural Rehabili- tation	Farm Tenant Purchase	Resettle- ment	Migratory Labor	Other	Technical Services and Adminis- tration
1936–7	100	57	0	25	—[b]	0	18
1938	100	57	6	21	1	0	15
1939	100	66	11	7	3	0	13
1940	100	58	18	5	3	—[b]	16
1941	100	54	20	7	3	—[b]	16
1942	100	56	19	4	3	1	17
1943	100	58	16	1	4	—[b]	21
1944	100	58	17	1	0	—[b]	24
1945	100	64	10	1	0	1	24
1946	100	64	18	—[b]	0	—[b]	18
Total[a]	100	59	13	9	2	—[b]	18

SOURCE: James G. Maddox, "The Farm Security Administration," Ph.D. diss., Harvard University, 1950, p. 88.

[a]Excludes $95,208,468 for the purchase of submarginal land and $47,141,413 for the construction of war housing projects.

[b]Less than 0.5 percent.

leases. The improvements to land and buildings that their loans and grants provided gave the agencies leverage on most landlords. By 1938, the FSA required landlords to extend written leases to their tenants before the tenants became eligible for rehabilitation loans. The FSA also promoted model leases that protected tenants' rights. It encouraged landlords to give their tenants multiyear leases. In 1944, 31 percent of all rehabilitation loan borrowers had leases extending over a minimum of two years.[62]

Implementation experience revealed that rural poverty was a complex phenomenon with multiple roots. This discovery led FSA authorities to formulate a more comprehensive approach to poverty alleviation. An example was the development of the agencies' public health program. In 1935, the RA surveyed rehabilitation borrowers who had failed to meet their loan payments on schedule. The survey disclosed that almost half were suffering from some illness. Many of them had been unable to afford proper medical care, and some had used what money they had to pay medical bills.[63] The discovery of the deleterious effect of poor health on rural rehabilitation induced the RA to establish a Public Health Section, which developed a program to meet the health needs of rehabilitation clients. These clients became members of newly formed county health insurance societies. They paid a monthly fee, calculated according to their financial capacity; those unable to pay were subsidized with grants. Funds were placed in the control of a bonded trustee and paid to participating physicians according to the services that they rendered. The members of the societies were free to call on any of the participating doctors. This health maintenance program became an important component of rural rehabilitation. Farm and home plans included payments to health insurance societies. By 1942, 142,074 families were members of 787 medical societies and 221 dental societies in forty-one states.[64]

Although the collection of information concerning the results of implementation is an important aspect of rational processes of implementation, the way that the FSA monitored implementation had counterproductive consequences—because of the discrepancy between quantitative indicators used to measure program performance and the outcomes actually desired. One such quantitative indicator was a good loan collection record. Since poor farmers and tenants were poor credit risks, there was a tendency to authorize rehabilitation loans to more affluent farmers. Indeed, a 1940 study by the Planning and Analysis Section of the Rural Rehabilitation Division showed that, from 1935 to

1939, the average net income of new borrowers increased from $217 to $442, and the average net worth rose from $442 to $945; from 1935 to 1940, the average size of new borrowers' farms had grown from 75 to 134 acres.[65]

The feedback collected by the Planning and Analysis Section alerted the FSA to this tendency to "skim the cream." In an effort to reverse the trend, the FSA liberalized the provision of grants to low-income rehabilitation borrowers. Grants were made available for ordinary family expenses, so that low-income borrowers could balance their farm and home plans. These grants, when combined with grants for health and sanitation, often fulfilled the cash needs of the low-income recipients and enabled them to channel their regular farm income toward paying farm operating expenses, accumulating working capital, and repaying FSA loans. Of the total of $25.9 million in grants given to standard rehabilitation loan recipients, $20.9 million was given in 1941 and 1942.[66] The grants were curtailed in 1943 because of the opposition of Congress and the resignation of C. B. Baldwin, the FSA administrator who initiated the grant program and was its staunchest supporter.

Rational processes of implementation also included efforts to resolve personnel problems. A 1939 FSA study committee reported that most of the field staff, although they possessed adequate formal qualifications for their work, lacked a proper understanding of the rural scene. Field personnel sometimes took paternalistic attitudes toward the clients under their supervision. The FSA hired Harold Lasswell to study relations between FSA officials and their clientele. Lasswell found that officials often were insensitive to their clients' views. The FSA could improve the implementation of its programs, he suggested, by promoting better communication between field personnel and clients.[67]

Concern for the shortcomings of FSA personnel led the agency to initiate a campaign to improve FSA training. It included talks by high-level FSA administrators, to infuse lower-level personnel with an organizational mission, as well as in-service training programs for field personnel. Although the training programs by no means eliminated all problems, by August 1941 ten of the twelve FSA regional directors responded to an inquiry about personnel problems by stating that they did not have important problems with their field staff. Seven of these ten said that the training programs had contributed to the eradication of such problems.[68]

The FSA's success in training its personnel and establishing its "organizational character" was an important factor in the evolution of its organization. The history of the RA and FSA's organizational structure is one of gradual decentralization, in response to the exigencies of efficient implementation across a large and diverse country. For instance, the FSA's twelve regional offices were initially authorized to approve borrowers for rehabilitation loans, but this procedure caused an administrative bottleneck. By July 1, 1940, district rural rehabilitation supervisors were authorized to approve all except unusually large loans. But before initiating a decentralization program, the FSA ensured that its organizational character was established and its personnel adequately trained. This strategy contrasted with the "grass-roots democracy" approach to decentralization followed by the TVA. The leaders of the FSA most likely shared the sentiments of Rexford Tugwell, who—along with his coauthor, Edward Banfield—wrote in 1950, "The way to get democratic administration is to begin organizing a central government strong enough to eliminate those conditions which make much of our national life grossly undemocratic." A strong government did not necessarily mean a centralized one. Tugwell approved of fellow New Dealer Paul Appleby's maxim "Nothing can be decentralized properly which has not first been centralized." This seems to have been the approach followed by the RA and the FSA.[69]

Despite many problems, the RA and FSA succeeded in implementing a set of programs that were reasonably effective within the limits of their administrative capacity. The rural rehabilitation program had widespread impact and a remarkable rate of loan recovery. From the inception of the RA until June 1946, $967 million in loans were made to 892,760 borrowers. More than one out of seven farm operators in 1940 had received rural rehabilitation loans. Including FERA loans, a total sum of $1.047 billion was advanced to individuals and cooperative associations. By June 30, 1946, the agencies had collected 88 percent ($704.7 million) of all matured principal and 87 percent ($97.2 million) of all interest due. Only 2 percent ($22 million) of the principal had been written off as uncollectible.[70] True, rising farm prices increased the rate of recovery. Nevertheless, considering that most of the borrowers were believed to be poor credit risks, this recovery rate is remarkable. Given that the alternative to rural rehabilitation was to spend millions of dollars in relief, rural rehabilitation loans saved the government a large sum of money while saving the dignity of thousands of farm operators.

Studies show that the rural rehabilitation program succeeded in ameliorating the conditions of its borrowers. One FSA study found that the average net family income of standard rural rehabilitation borrowers rose 80 percent (from $480 in the year before they received their FSA loan to $865 in 1941). The average net worth of borrowers increased by 43 percent (from $871 to $1,242), and the value of production for home consumption increased by 101 percent (from $163 in value to $327).[71] Almost all beneficiaries improved their position in the agrarian structure. Eighty-eight percent of sharecroppers who received loans improved their position, with 83.2 percent becoming tenants and 4.4 percent becoming landowners. Of the landless laborers who received loans, 96.4 percent improved their status; 89.6 percent became tenants, and 6.8 percent purchased land.[72]

Data for tenant-purchase loans show similar progress. The program's more conservative lending policy resulted in an even more favorable record of loan recovery. Of the 47,104 tenant-purchase loans made through June 30, 1947, only 9.7 percent—accounting for 8.1 percent of total loaned—had to be liquidated. The amount lost was estimated to be a negligible 0.02 percent of the total loaned.[73] Borrowers substantially improved their economic position. At the end of 1945, the average annual gross cash income of borrowers in real terms had increased by 71 percent (from $1,038 to $1,776 in 1935–1939 constant dollars). The average net worth of these borrowers almost tripled (from $1,819 at the time of the loan to $5,393 at the end of 1945).[74]

In addition to providing loans to individuals, the rural rehabilitation program also helped to create institutional change. Having experienced the failures stemming from the unbridled ambition of the resettlement program, the FSA set more modest objectives for this program. First of all, it awarded loans to group service associations—associations composed of two or more farmers who agreed to pool their resources and purchase working capital, whose profitable use necessitated a scale of operation in excess of that controlled by any individual. There were 29,797 in all; FSA loans were awarded to 25,543. More than 90 percent provided either farm machinery or sire services. By the end of June 1946, 63 percent of those who had received loans had repaid them in full. Twenty-one percent still owed money but had made their payments on schedule. Only 16 percent were inoperative or liquidated.[75]

The FSA also financed larger-scale cooperative associations, either with direct loans or indirectly through membership loans to individuals. Sixty-three percent of the cooperatives were for purchasing and marketing. Nine percent operated grain elevators. Of 2,064 FSA-financed cooperatives, 451 received direct loans amounting to $7.7 million. As of June 30, 1946, 52 percent had been repaid. Less than 10 percent of the amount due had been declared unrecoverable. James Maddox, former head of the Rural Rehabilitation Division, estimated that no more than 16 percent of such loans would be lost to the government.[76]

Finally, the FSA established cooperative leasing associations. These associations used FSA loans to lease large tracts of land from farmers—often plantation owners—who were operating at a loss. They then subleased lots to their members—usually agricultural laborers, sharecroppers, or tenants. By 1942, there were forty-five associations with a membership of 1,913 families. By the end of June 1948, twenty-three of these societies had repaid their loans in full. Fourteen had been liquidated, with debts totaling $45,174. The eight associations that had not been liquidated by the government still owed $149,912 in unpaid principal and interest. The maximum loss to the government was 12 percent of the total amount loaned.[77]

It is true that FSA programs had only a limited impact on rural poverty. Rural rehabilitation loans reached only one in seven farmers, and in 1940 the FSA administrator for the southeastern region estimated that only 35 to 40 percent of those needing loans received them.[78] The impact of the tenant-purchase loan program was even more limited. The FSA granted loans to only 2 percent of all tenants in 1940. Criticism of the limited impact of the FSA programs, however, is less a commentary on the way the FSA implemented programs than on its inability to attract more funding.

The data above suggest that the FSA developed effective programs to combat rural poverty. This conclusion is supported by the report of an independent committee commissioned by the war food administrator, Chester Davis, to investigate FSA programs. Though Davis expected that the study would provide him with evidence supporting the removal of FSA administrator C. B. Baldwin and the need to reorganize the agency, the secret report gave a positive assessment of the FSA. Indeed, one consultant wrote Davis that the rehabilitation program "begins to look like one of the most significant social inventions developed in the field of agriculture in recent decades."[79]

Since the FSA implemented effective programs to combat rural poverty, the agency's abolition demands an explanation. The Rational Process Perspective suggests that programs will be terminated only when they are ineffective or when their objectives are no longer considered important. Changes in the policy objectives of the Roosevelt administration contributed to the demise of the FSA. The inception of World War II fostered a need to maximize agricultural production. It also revived the economy by providing jobs for millions and inducing widespread migration from rural areas. Important as these changes were, they do not sufficiently explain the FSA's liquidation. For one thing, FSA officials made a credible claim that their programs provided efficient means to increase the country's agricultural production.[80] For another, data show that, despite the economic recovery engendered by the war, rural poverty was still considerable. In 1949, economist D. Gale Johnson testified before Congress that the percentage of farm families living in poverty had changed little. He estimated that the share having less than $600 in total annual production decreased only from 47.5 percent in 1939 to 45.6 percent.[81] Theodore W. Schultz supported Johnson's testimony and stressed the need to do more to combat rural poverty.[82] Although the absolute numbers of the rural poor declined with the migration out of agriculture during the decades since 1940, the percentage of rural poor remained high for years. As late as 1959, according to a U.S. Bureau of the Census estimate, the poverty rate in rural areas was 33 percent.[83]

The impending mechanization of Southern agriculture and transformation of American agriculture from family farming into large-scale commercial agriculture offer another possible rationale for the termination of the FSA.[84] Such an ex post facto explanation, however, imposes a retrospective viewpoint that was not shared by FSA opponents. A thorough review of the series of congressional hearings that led to the agency's demise shows that the attacks on the FSA had little to do with the future of American agriculture. Instead, they fell into three categories: inefficiency, ideology, and legality. Those who criticized the FSA for its inefficiency charged that the agency had high overhead, duplicated the work of other bureaus, and made wasteful expenditures by financing "luxurious homes" with electricity and potable water, medical care, sewage disposal plants, and irrigation systems.[85] They were appalled that the FSA publicized the availability of its loans, and they charged that the agency provided loans to unworthy people who would never be able to repay their debts.[86] These critics also charged that FSA programs made the agricultural sector less efficient by increasing the wages of agricultural laborers and creating labor shortages.[87] Ideological attacks were based on the alleged "communistic" tendencies of the FSA's cooperative projects and C. B. Baldwin, its administrator.[88] Legal charges centered on the agency's defiance of congressional orders to liquidate its cooperative projects and end its purchase of land.[89]

Ultimate vindication of the FSA came from Congress—the very institution that legislated its abolition. Four years after Congress passed legislation winding up the FSA, the congressional Subcommittee on Low-Income Families presented a report recommending that funds for the Farmers Home Administration, the watered-down replacement of the FSA, be increased to provide for more farm purchase and supervised production loans.[90] It urged the federal government to encourage the development of new industry in underdeveloped rural areas, to find suitable means for moving families to areas of better opportunity, and to improve the social welfare of agricultural laborers. The report reaffirmed the very policy agenda set by the FSA.

Any satisfactory explanation of the FSA's fate must go beyond the Rational Process Perspective. It must account for the conflicts that enveloped the agency. These were central to the agency's demise.

RA AND FSA POLICY IMPLEMENTATION: A CONFLICTUAL PROCESS PERSPECTIVE

Conflict between self-interested groups generated a set of dynamics that was important in shaping the evolution of the rural poverty alleviation programs. Conflict within the RA and FSA, including a difference in racial attitudes between top authorities and field-level personnel, created persistent tensions. Rivalry between the FSA and other agencies in the Department of Agriculture weakened its position within the department. The most important explanation for the FSA's demise, however, is that its policies antagonized Southern elites and the congressional opponents of the New Deal.

Intra-Agency Conflict

The creation of the RA reduced conflict within the Roosevelt administration. The growing concern among liberals for the plight of the rural poor had engendered disputes in the AAA, the Farm Credit Administration, and the Department of Interior. By consolidating rural poverty programs in the RA, Roosevelt was able to weed out the dissidents and give them a positive focus for their energies. Conflicts, however, did not disappear. One of the most striking consequences of the creation of the

RA and FSA was the displacement of conflict within agencies to conflict between agencies.

During the early days of the RA, there were considerable differences among upper-level administrators concerning policy priorities and the appropriate means of implementation. The RA's complex administrative structure bred conflict. Tensions among its four operating divisions and ten technical divisions caused problems at the regional as well as Washington offices. Antagonisms were exacerbated by the physical dispersion of the RA staff in Washington. Because no single location was available to house them, they were initially scattered in ad hoc arrangements in twenty-five different buildings. For the most part, RA officials in the upper levels of administration overcame these problems through Tugwell's leadership and their shared commitment to ameliorating the plight of the rural poor. By the time of Tugwell's departure in 1937, they had reached a consensus concerning the RA's priorities and institutionalized a division of labor among its divisions. Largely as a consequence of the commitment of its Washington staff, the FSA later developed a reputation for its "specialized zeal."[91]

Another area of conflict in the RA was reflected in the disparity between the implementation prescribed by upper-level officials and the practice of field-level personnel. The agency had inherited most of its lower-level personnel from other agencies, and initially these lower-level personnel lacked commitment to the agency. Many felt that their transfer had resulted in a loss of status and authority. There was also considerable confusion about the new agency's objectives. These problems were reduced as upper-level officials ordered the agency's priorities and began to articulate its organizational mission.[92]

Two other sources of conflict between upper- and lower-level administrators were more intractable. First was the contradiction between values necessary for effective implementation and the personal values of the field staff. Leaders in the top levels of the FSA were known for their commitment to racial equality, whereas lower-level officials, especially those in the South, tended to share local prejudices. Their resistance limited the capacity of upper-level administrators to attain racial equality in FSA programs. For instance, African-Americans comprised 23 percent of those receiving rural rehabilitation loans from 1935 to 1940. That this figure equals the share of African-Americans in the rural population reflects favorably on the FSA. However, African-Americans constituted 37 percent of the low-income farmers that the FSA sought to help. Similarly, African-Americans received 21 percent of tenant-purchase loans in the South but constituted 40 percent of Southern tenant families. African-Americans also constituted 25 percent of the families on resettlement projects, but FSA officials usually deferred to local customs and assigned them to all-black projects. Though implementation of FSA programs was blemished by instances of racial prejudice, historians generally agree that the FSA had the best record of all New Deal agencies in taking steps to reduce discrimination. This record was a consequence of the efforts of upper-level administrators to compel local authorities to avoid discrimination.[93]

Contradictory values were coupled with a discrepancy between the responsibilities given to field personnel and the time and resources at their disposal. The responsibilities were enormous. A county rural rehabilitation supervisor had an average of 173 clients who either borrowed or received grants from the FSA.[94] In addition to processing applications for new loans and grants, county supervisors had to formulate annual farm and home management plans and supervise their utilization. In discharging these responsibilities, the supervisors were required to make periodic visits to their clients' homes. With the addition of new programs—promoting, among other objectives, the organization of cooperatives, farm debt adjustment, and improved rural health—the supervisors' responsibilities dramatically increased.

Just as demanding as the array of responsibilities was the quality of the relationship with the clientele that field-level personnel were supposed to establish. They were not only responsible for providing government services; they were also supposed to develop personal relationships with clients in an effort to build their confidence, enhance their creativity, and improve their self-discipline. These duties required more time than many supervisors could spend on them. The problem was exacerbated because the records of field personnel were usually quantified in ways that overlooked the qualitative aspects of cases.[95]

Conflict between the FSA and Actors in Its Environment

In the process of establishing the agencies' institutional character and organizational mission, top officials of the RA and FSA encountered growing hostility in their environment. The organizational mission they elaborated was perceived to conflict with many of the established interests in the agricultural sector. Prior to the New Deal, the objectives of the USDA programs were primarily to fund agricultural research and disseminate technological advances to farmers through the Extension

Service. The AAA worked through the Extension Service and gained the support of established interests by providing them with financial benefits and creating local committees through which they could control local implementation. In contrast, the RA and FSA's programs distributed credit and other benefits directly to the poor. Their top administrators were suspicious of the motives of the Extension Service and affluent farmers, so they insulated the antipoverty programs from their influence.

Much of the early opposition to the RA and FSA came from the Extension Service. Although the RA and the Extension Service concluded a memorandum of understanding on June 7, 1935, relations between them were never good. Prior to the New Deal, the Extension Service had been the primary link between the Department of Agriculture and the public at large, and it resented incursions into its monopoly. The FSA was a particularly dangerous threat. Both organizations attempted to educate their clientele; but whereas the Extension Service emphasized self-help, the FSA provided direct access to grants and easy credit. Indeed, the FSA rural rehabilitation county supervisor was often called the "county agent with a checkbook." [96]

Antagonism between the agencies was exacerbated by their different organizational structures. The Extension Service was relatively decentralized, with managerial responsibility located in state offices that worked closely with land-grant colleges. The RA and FSA were more centralized. They had a direct line of command from Washington to county supervisors. Furthermore, regional and not state offices were made the important locus for direction of programs. Rexford Tugwell's order to transfer authority for approving loans, grants, and farm and home management plans from state to regional offices drew many protests from the Extension Service. Extension Service officials argued that this action removed decision-making authority from the best source of information about local agriculture. They charged that it disrupted coordination between the two organizations and violated their memorandum of understanding. [97]

The insulation of RA personnel from the influence of the Extension Service was intentional. Rexford Tugwell had expressed a lack of confidence in the Extension Service even before coming to the RA. After his first six months at the helm of the RA, he held an even lower opinion. He wrote to Franklin Roosevelt, "My greatest difficulty has been and will continue to be with the Extension Service which is arrogant, opinionated and largely Republican or reactionary." [98]

At times friction between the two organizations grew because they recommended different farming practices to their clients. The most efficient practices often varied with different-sized farms. The recommendations of the Extension Service were geared toward larger commercial farms; those of the RA were targeted for small and often subsistence farms.[99]

Despite their differences, the two agencies made efforts to cooperate. During 1937, the special assistant to the administrator of the FSA, Raymond Pearson, wrote to heads of the state Extension Services to suggest they help low-income farmers that the FSA could not reach. Essentially, the Pearson plan proposed that county agents make a special allocation of time to help poor farmers plan their production. It suggested that the Extension Services could recruit volunteers to visit and check the progress of the plans and then report back to the county agent. The reaction of the state Extension Service directors was a friendly but firm refusal. The response of O. B. Jesness, chief of the Division of Agricultural Economics at the University Farm in St. Paul, reveals much of the motivation behind the refusal: "There has been some suggestion that extension should shift its attention from the better to the poorer groups. However, is it not an important function of agricultural extension to assist in developing the most efficient agriculture possible? If so, the better farmers, who produce the bulk of the market supplies, should continue to receive attention. . . . A lessening of attention to the better farmers is not in the picture. An increase in work with the disadvantaged group apparently must come mainly from an expansion of the service." [100]

By the end of the New Deal, the Extension Service seemed more intent on maintaining its traditional programs than on competing with the FSA. The 1940 appointment of M. L. Wilson as national director placed the Extension Service under leadership that took a conciliatory attitude. On January 30, 1942, directors of the Extension Service in Southern states passed a resolution asking that Extension Service responsibilities be limited to educational work.[101] At a time when the FSA was under attack in Congress, Wilson wrote Representative John J. Sparkman of Alabama to deny charges that there was duplication of services provided by the Extension Service and the FSA. He added that the work of the FSA should be continued because its specialized zeal was essential for effective implementation of programs for low-income farmers.[102]

The Roosevelt administration greatly expanded the scope of the

USDA by establishing under its aegis agencies such as the FSA, the Soil Conservation Service, the AAA, and the Farm Credit Administration. Had the FSA been able to join forces with these agencies, it would have enhanced its viability. Instead, relations were largely competitive. The rivalry proved particularly damaging after Henry Wallace left the USDA. His successor, Claude R. Wickard, was not unsympathetic to the agency, but he was a weak administrator unable to command the department's sprawling bureaucracy. Wickard felt threatened by the Wallace loyalists who remained in the upper echelons of the USDA bureaucracy, and one of Wickard's first actions as secretary was to dismantle the secretariat that Paul Appleby, one of Wallace's closest allies, had assembled to help manage the vast department. The resulting isolation of Appleby diminished the power of one of the FSA's most capable allies.[103] It also left Wickard prey to manipulation by bureaucratic infighting among various agencies within the USDA.

Wickard's inability to take control over the agencies within the USDA had deleterious consequences for the FSA as well as for his own position. When he set up the Food Production Administration (FPA) at the end of 1942, he appointed Herbert W. Parisius as the FPA's first director. Parisius drew up a plan to reorganize the agencies related to food production, with the objective of integrating their operations. The plan was quite favorable to the FSA, since it placed FSA administrator C. B. Baldwin as deputy director. However, it was more reflective of Parisius's assessment of administrative capacities than the political realities within the USDA. The AAA, SCS, and FCA fought the plan. Wickard's executive assistant, Samuel Bledsoe, eventually convinced the secretary to veto it and replace Parisius with M. Clifford Townsend, a former official of the Indiana Farm Bureau. Wickard's muddled handling of the situation caused the president to lose confidence in him, and in March 1943 Roosevelt undercut much of the secretary's power by creating the War Food Administration and placing Chester Davis at its head. On June 16, 1943, Davis wielded his power to remove the wartime farm labor program from the FSA. With the loss of this program, the FSA lost an important responsibility in the war effort.[104]

The FSA's position in the Roosevelt administration steadily weakened during the 1940s. Roosevelt, an early supporter of the agency, increasingly directed his attention to the war effort. With Henry Wallace's departure, the FSA lost an influential voice in the administration; Claude R. Wickard never had the access of his predecessor and soon lost the president's respect.

An important cause of the FSA's decline within the USDA was the growing hostility to the agency from groups outside the government. One strategic group was composed of Southern rural elites. FSA programs struck at the root of the paternalistic control mechanisms that they employed to reduce the transaction costs required to discipline workers in labor-intensive Southern agriculture.[105] Rehabilitation loans curbed the dependence of tenants and sharecroppers on Southern planters for credit, and the supervision that accompanied these loans threatened the authority of the planters. The FSA's efforts to substitute more equitable, written leases for tenant farmers challenged the Southern planters' use of informal verbal agreements as a mechanism of control. The promotion of cooperatives providing goods and services undermined the landlords' control over credit and access to the local country stores, which they often used to promote dependence.

The AFBF, under the leadership of Edward O'Neal, was also at the forefront of the opposition. To some extent, O'Neal's hostility may have been a consequence of his interests as an Alabama cotton planter. But the AFBF also had broader institutional reasons to oppose the FSA. At a time when "grass-roots democracy" was the AFBF's panacea,[106] FSA officials took measures to insulate implementation from local elites. County and state rural rehabilitation committees possessed an ill-defined advisory capacity and were allowed to atrophy. Regionalization made management less susceptible to the power of the State Farm Bureau Federations. When the FSA decentralized its decision-making authority, it devolved responsibility on its district rather than county offices. Thus, it continued to insulate its implementation from the influence of the powerful county and state AFBF organizations.

The manner in which FSA programs distributed resources also antagonized members of the AFBF. They resented the fact that the FSA provided loans to tenants and sharecroppers at 3 percent interest when the lowest rate they could obtain from the Federal Land Bank system was 3.5 percent on an emergency basis and 4 percent for regular loans.[107] Leaders of the AFBF were particularly incensed when FSA officials appeared to be building a constituency relationship with the rival National Farmers Union.

Since the members of the AFBF were unable to exert much influence over FSA administrators, they directed their opposition through Congress. By the late 1930s, a conservative coalition in Congress—including fiscally conservative Republicans and Southern Democrats[108]—was increasingly asserting its power to roll back the New Deal. The FSA was a natural prey for the coalition. The Republicans targeted it as one of the most flagrant excesses of the New Deal. The FSA's potential for disrupting the racial relations that had been institutionalized since Reconstruction was an additional concern for the Southern Democrats.[109]

At the same time that the conservative coalition was emerging in Congress, the FSA was undertaking campaigns to infuse its personnel with its progressive ideology. After Will Alexander, the FSA's first administrator, was succeeded by C. B. Baldwin, FSA implementation began moving toward the left. The agency increased its use of grants to reverse the tendency to "skim the cream" and enable the very poor to take advantage of the rural rehabilitation program. It also conducted a drive to encourage FSA clientele to join cooperative purchasing and marketing societies. Despite congressional prohibition of new resettlement projects, the FSA continued to make loans to cooperative land-purchasing associations for developing new rural communities. It also established Defense Relocation Corporations to purchase land and develop it for farm families displaced by the expansion of the country's military establishment. From the perspective of FSA administrators, these measures were taken to make the agency's programs more effective in combating rural poverty. From the perspective of a growing number of people in Congress, they confirmed charges that the FSA was defying congressional authority and following imprudent credit policies.

Opposition to the FSA was centered in the agricultural subcommittee of the House Appropriations Committee. The subcommittee was chaired by Clarence Cannon, a Democrat from Missouri and a longtime opponent of the FSA. Everett Dirksen, a Republican from Illinois and an eloquent supporter of the AFBF, was especially influential among the committee's Republicans. Cannon and Dirksen soon succeeded in winning over many of their colleagues, including Georgia Democrat Malcolm Tarver, who took over chairmanship of the subcommittee in 1942.

Abolition of the FSA became a plank in the anti–New Deal coalition platform when the Joint Committee on Reduction of Non-Essential Federal Expenditures issued its preliminary report in December 1941. The committee was chaired by Senator Harry F. Byrd of Virginia, a staunch opponent of New Deal rural poverty programs ever since the days of the RA. He allowed the AFBF to give lengthy testimony on the shortcomings of the FSA, thereby enabling the AFBF to publicize its indictment of the agency. The indictment was based on charges generated with the assistance of six private investigators that the AFBF had hired to search for incriminating evidence.[110]

The budget process was the initial mechanism for dismantling the FSA. Though Clarence Cannon had been building a case against the FSA at least since 1940, when he succeeded in persuading the House to include a provision completely eliminating funds for the tenant-purchase program, FSA support remained firm in the Senate until 1942. In that year, FSA appropriations were slashed 27 percent. The following year, with the House Appropriations Committee urging that the FSA be abolished, Congress passed what FSA historian Sidney Baldwin described as the "death appropriation bill." [111] Though funds for the tenant-purchase program were reduced by only 8 percent, current appropriations for rural rehabilitation were curtailed by 43 percent. The bill also prohibited the use of funds for purchasing land and making loans for any cooperative activity.

The House Agricultural Committee responded to the Appropriation Committee's call to abolish the FSA by establishing the Select Committee to Investigate the Activities of the Farm Security Administration on March 18, 1943. The committee was headed by North Carolina's Harold D. Cooley. Cooley ultimately authored legislation calling for the abolition of the FSA and the continuation of the tenant-purchase program under a newly created Farmers Home Administration. His Farmers Home Administration Act was signed into law on August 14, 1946.

In contrast to the Rational Process Perspective, the Conflictual Process Perspective provides us with a plausible account of why the FSA met its demise. It shows that at a time when the FSA's support in the Roosevelt administration was on the decline, the agency's programs aroused the opposition of powerful groups in the private sector and Congress. These groups united to legislate the FSA's abolition. The Conflictual Process Perspective adds an important dimension of explanation necessary to understand the evolution of rural antipoverty implementation during the New Deal. However, its focus on political actors and their struggles for power overlooks important factors that shaped the final outcome—factors illuminated by the Organizational Environment Perspective.

RA AND FSA POLICY IMPLEMENTATION: AN ORGANIZATIONAL ENVIRONMENT PERSPECTIVE

Rational and conflictual processes of implementation are shaped by the structure of control over resources in an agency's environment. To understand the impact of the environment on the FSA, we must first examine the economic and political systems in that environment.

With the economic position of elites weakened by the Great Depression, farmers large and small welcomed New Deal interventions in the agricultural sector. Programs such as the AAA not only provided immediate relief but also helped initiate the great transformation of Southern agriculture. Their political impact strengthened the American Farm Bureau Federation's organization of large commercial farmers, especially in the South. World War II also enhanced the power of the country's commercial farmers by transforming the Depression-time crisis of overproduction into an imperative for increased production. As policy interventions and the war increased the power of the large commercial farmers, the constitutive impact of the FSA's policies alienated their support. The norms of "grass-roots democracy" created institutionalized rules that legitimated their attacks, and the structure of American political institutions enhanced their power while limiting that of the FSA's supporters.

The Economic and Political Environment

American agriculture during the 1930s was remarkably diverse. From the dairy farms of New England to the cornfields of Iowa and the commercial fruit farms in California, agriculture varied in the technology used, the amounts and types of labor employed, and the market dynamics that affected commodity prices. Here we will concentrate on the South, since the impact of the New Deal rural antipoverty programs was greatest there even though they were national in scope. The rural rehabilitation program, accounting for 59 percent of all Resettlement Administration and Farm Security Administration expenditures from 1936 to 1946, channeled 53 percent of its funds into the eleven Confederate states plus Oklahoma. The next-largest program, the tenant-purchase program, comprised 13 percent of all expenditures; 70 percent of its loans were made in fifteen Southern states.[112] Not only was the impact of the programs disproportionately large in the South, but the reaction to the programs was more vociferous there than in any other area of the country. Southern politicians and agricultural leaders dominated the political process that shaped and ultimately terminated the Farm Security Administration.

The economy of the South remained predominantly agricultural through the 1930s. In 1930, 68 percent of the people lived in rural areas, and 46 percent lived on farms.[113] Except for an area of subsistence farming encompassing southwestern Virginia, eastern Tennessee, and the Carolina piedmont, Southern agriculture was commercially oriented, with "King Cotton" as the preeminent crop. In 1929, 69 percent of all Southern farms planted cotton. The crop accounted for 41.7 percent of all cultivated area and contributed 46 percent of all cash earnings.[114] Much of the production was for export. From 1926 to 1929, an average of 58 percent was exported.[115] The commercialization and export orientation of Southern agriculture meant that the South suffered through the violent fluctuations of primary commodity cycles that had occurred since the end of the nineteenth century.

Though primarily a commercial economy, Southern agriculture operated on a small-scale, labor-intensive basis. In 1929, the average cropland harvested per farm was just thirty-five acres. If the arid states of Texas and Oklahoma are omitted, the average drops to only twenty-five acres. Only 7 percent of Southern farms possessed tractors in 1930. The average value of implements and machinery owned was only $215 (in 1930 dollars).[116]

Tenancy and sharecropping pervaded the South's agrarian structure. The end of slavery made it necessary to re-create the system of agricultural labor. Failure to provide freedmen with land and the other assets necessary for economic independence made African-Americans available for reincorporation into a system of domination by Bourbon elites. While freedmen sought to retain their independence, landowners wished to maintain control over their land and the management of production. A variety of arrangements evolved; but as the years passed, tenancy and sharecropping became most prominent. In 1930, tenants worked 59 percent of all farms in the South. This figure includes sharecroppers who labored on 26 percent of all Southern farms.[117]

The system of sharecropping was especially oppressive. Landlords selected the crops to be grown, the methods of cultivation, and the time and place for marketing the crops. They kept all records and determined their tenants' earnings. The cash incomes of sharecroppers were frequently insufficient to see them through the year. They turned to the landlord to provide them with the basic necessities of life. Landlords created a "furnishing system" in order to advance credit for commodities provided by their own commissary or a local merchant. Tenants and small farmers also suffered from shortages of capital and income. They frequently received credit from local merchants through the crop-lien system. Interest rates ranged from 25 to 50 percent per annum.[118]

The result of the system was extensive debt. According to a 1933 survey of 1,022 Alabama farm households, sharecroppers ended up taking a loss or breaking even 89 percent of the time.[119] Other studies found that 88 percent of African-American tenant farmers in Alabama broke even or suffered losses;[120] 43 percent of some 2,000 families interviewed in Mississippi, Texas, Alabama, and South Carolina were in debt before they planted the 1934 crop, and over one-third had debts of more than a year's standing;[121] and 80 percent of 3,000 Alabama sharecropper families surveyed had debts older than a year.[122]

The South's agrarian system engendered widespread poverty. Cotton monoculture and the agrarian structure led to a substantial depletion of soil fertility. The relative imbalance between rural population and land kept production units small and generated extensive underemployment. Southern industry failed to create enough jobs to relieve the situation; and migration to the North, stimulated by World War I, was limited by the industrial unemployment during the Great Depression.[123] Although labor was abundant, capital was scarce; as a result, agricultural practices that might have increased productivity and curbed poverty were not adopted.[124] Estimates are not available for the regional incidence of rural poverty, but national estimates are that 46 percent of farm families lived below the poverty line. Surely the figure for the South is considerably higher.[125]

In short, the South's agrarian system was a highly inequitable arrangement, with large numbers of tenants, sharecroppers, agricultural laborers, and small upland farmers and a much smaller class of landlords and planters. The tenants and sharecroppers were usually dependent on their landlord, who controlled land and credit. Smaller farmers in the upland areas were more independent, but they too often accumulated debts that rendered them dependent on credit merchants through the crop-lien system. The impact of New Deal policy interventions, the dissemination of new technologies, and the pull of jobs stimulated by World War II began to transform the rural South.[126] This transformation was shaped in important ways by the South's political regime.

Southern politics were characterized by elite domination, intraparty factionalism, and agrarian populism. Planters, local merchants, lawyers, and judges formed county rings that dominated local politics. Elite power was enhanced in no small measure by the use of literacy tests, the poll tax, and white primaries to disfranchise African-Americans and a large number of poor whites. Participation in general elections dropped from 64 percent of Southern adult males in the 1880s to an average of 30 percent in the decade following 1900. Although many view disfranchisement as racially motivated, there is substantial evidence to suggest that it was also sponsored by conservative black-belt elites to undercut the support of upland populists and Republicans. Support for populist and Republican opponents of the Democratic Party declined disproportionately after the 1890s. Between the 1880s and the first decade of the twentieth century, average support for Democrats decreased by 47 percent of adult males while that for their opponents dropped by 62 percent. By excluding African-Americans and poor whites and curbing political competition, disfranchisement reduced the political incentives to appeal for the support of the less affluent and limited the political salience of the South's economic disparities.[127]

The creation of the one-party South weakened party organization and increased factionalism. The reduction of partisan competition led to a weakening of party organization. Since elected representatives were, in effect, selected in the Democratic primary, the role of intra-party factions increased. As disfranchisement pushed economic disparities off the political agenda, politics became more concerned with personality, scandal, and reform. "Friends and neighbors" politics gave Democratic notables strong bases of support in their local bailiwicks. Extending this support usually required assembling an alliance of local county rings. Voter participation was slightly lower than in the general elections. From 1902 to 1910, winning candidates in elections with the highest turnout in each state received votes from an average of less than 15 percent of all voting-age males and 23 percent of all white males if we assume that no African-American voted. Low primary turnouts enhanced the importance of political organizations like the county rings.[128]

The domination of local politics by county rings and the electoral exclusion of African-Americans and many poor whites did not produce a monolithic outlook among Southern Democrats. For one thing, the populist tradition, while moribund outside the party, persisted within. Its colorful rhetoric continued to be used by conservatives like Eugene ("the Wild Man from Sugar Creek") Talmadge as well as radicals like Huey ("the Kingfish") Long. Despite their diverse positions on an array of issues, Southern senators and representatives stood united in protecting race relations in the South from federal intervention and defending Southern agrarian interests—especially those of cotton producers.

There was no consensus on the issue of rural poverty. Sentiments ranged from "Cotton Ed" Smith's implacable opposition to federal programs to the persistent support of John Bankhead and Hugo Black.[129]

The scarcity of agricultural commodities caused by World War II greatly enhanced the power of the commercial farmers. The crisis of overproduction in the 1930s had left most farmers dependent on federal intervention to curb their production. The scarcity of agricultural commodities during World War II made increasing production crucial, and the Roosevelt administration became wary of alienating the nation's large commercial farmers.[130] At the same time that the war enhanced the power of commercial farmers, it decreased the numbers of the rural poor and diverted attention from the problems of rural poverty. Though many remained mired in poverty, the onset of the war reduced their political salience and made the opposition of the country's agricultural elites to the FSA more difficult to resist. This opposition was intensified by the constitutive impact of the New Deal rural antipoverty programs.

The Constitutive Impact of Public Policy

The history of American agricultural policy provides a graphic illustration of how public policy can contribute to the political organization of social groups. State intervention in the agricultural sector has had a starkly disparate impact. Public policy enhanced the power of the more affluent farmers, while American political institutions diminished the power of the poor. Prior to the New Deal, the USDA used its county agents to organize larger farmers into the county committees that formed the basic unit of the AFBF. After the agricultural depression weakened the power of the AFBF membership, the AAA reinvigorated the organization by providing its members with control over the distribution of the funds that it was infusing into the agricultural sector. The repeated interaction between the state and the nation's farmers institutionalized a network of power that gave affluent commercial farmers political influence far beyond their collective votes.[131]

The AFBF became one of the staunchest opponents of the FSA, because its programs challenged the privileged position of the AFBF and the Extension Service in the agricultural sector. Unlike most other New Deal agricultural programs, FSA programs could be effectively implemented without the cooperation of affluent farmers. Programs such as rural rehabilitation directly linked the RA and FSA to the rural poor. The large farmers' control over a preponderant share of land and agricultural production gave them little direct power over implementation, especially since the RA and FSA authorities insulated program administration. The independence of the FSA programs became perceived as a threat to the AFBF, since it enabled the FSA to provide its rivals with political resources. The FSA's efforts to establish a constituency relationship with the National Farmers Union during the early 1940s was especially objectionable to the AFBF.

RA and FSA policies structured the political cleavages that ultimately brought about the FSA's demise. FSA implementation targeted its resources exclusively for the rural poor. Its rural rehabilitation loans, tenant-purchase loans, financing of cooperative societies, and the like, not only alleviated poverty but also threatened to reduce the dependence of the poor upon the dominant groups in rural society. Gunnar Myrdal singled out the educational facets of FSA programs—for example, teaching the poor to plan their budgets, understand their leases, and organize themselves cooperatively—as their most significant aspect. "By actually changing people," he wrote, New Deal programs such as the FSA became "a dynamic factor undermining the *status quo* in the South." [132] Combined with the FSA's successful insulation of its program implementation from the influence of affluent rural groups, its educational activities proved particularly threatening to dominant groups in the rural South.

The impact of the FSA's policy mandate and implementation procedures can be seen in the coalitions that formed to support or oppose the agency. Organizations representing the dominant interests of the agricultural sector—including the National Cotton Council, the Irrigated Cotton Growers, the Associated Farmers of California, and the National Council of Farmers Cooperatives—joined the AFBF's opposition to the FSA. The FSA's allies stood in stark contrast to these organizations of affluent producers. The agency's clientele numbered 800,000 by 1942, but these low-income agriculturalists were scattered and lacked organizational strength. The membership of the Southern Tenant Farmers' Union and the National Farmers Union reaped benefits from the FSA and became staunch defenders of the agency. The NAACP and the Urban League gave their support. The CIO was a consistent FSA backer. Finally, the FSA garnered support from a variety of religious organizations, including the National Conference of Catholic

Charities, the Catholic Rural Life Council, the YWCA, and the Federal Council of Churches of Christ in America.

The AFBF did not initially oppose the RA or the early FSA. What explains its transformation into the agency's archenemy? The AFBF's initial acquiescence was in part attributable to the weakened position of commercial farmers during the Depression. While they struggled to get back on their feet, they were in no position to fight the federal government. Southern elites, in particular, had the most to lose from FSA policies, since they threatened to undermine their paternalistic labor control. However, these elites, along with an overwhelming majority of farmers from all sections of the country, welcomed the initial wave of relief provided by the New Deal, since it reduced the burdens of supporting their tenants and croppers at a time when they themselves faced dire economic straits.[133] As programs such as the AAA helped Southern planters regain their economic viability, the threats posed by the FSA became more menacing.

Another reason for the AFBF's increasingly strident opposition was that it expanded its membership in the South during the 1930s and 1940s. Its Southern base had been weak in large part because, prior to the New Deal, the Extension Service had emphasized organizing cotton cooperatives rather than farm bureaus. With the help of the influence that its members gained over the AAA's cotton program, the AFBF multiplied its membership more than eighteen times, to 366,554, between 1931 and 1946. The share of the South in total AFBF membership increased from 7 percent to just under 30 percent.[134] The rapid expansion of the AFBF's Southern membership occurred just as the protestations of Southern elites against the FSA became increasingly vehement. It was only natural that the leaders of the AFBF would be responsive to the demands of such a formidable bloc.

Despite its growing membership, the AFBF's influence over the USDA waned during the late 1930s. After the 1936 election, Henry Wallace refused to promise AFBF president Edward O'Neal that he would not make any major decisions without consulting the AFBF. Wallace later approved appointments to top positions that the AFBF vehemently opposed.[135] In 1938, George Tolley, head of the AAA, took its administration at the state level out of the hands of the Extension Service and set up separate state and county offices. Moves within the USDA to enhance the authority of the Bureau of Agricultural Economics over the department's programs and their budgets, along with efforts by the bureau to promote land-use planning, further reduced the authority of the Extension Service and threatened AFBF power.[136]

The AFBF's dissatisfaction with these developments spurred it to demand that the USDA be reorganized. It advocated that implementation of all action programs should be placed under the control of an independent five-person board selected from the "nation's agricultural leaders." The Extension Service was to take charge of implementation in the field. The AFBF's attack on the FSA was a battle in its larger campaign to enhance its power over the USDA.[137]

Institutionalized Rules and the Evolution of the FSA

Institutionalized rules, as widely accepted prescriptions for public policy, can help to legitimate the actions of a government agency. The history of the New Deal poverty alleviation programs shows that an agency's failure to conform to institutionalized rules can undermine its political support. The FSA's programs appeared to contradict two norms considered basic to effective rural development: the sanctity of the family farm and the practice of "grass-roots democracy."

The ideal of the family farm has been enshrined in American culture at least since Thomas Jefferson espoused the virtues of the yeoman farmer. Agricultural programs that appear to undermine the family farm do so at great political risk. The FSA was at times portrayed with considerable effect as an opponent of this important value. Its resettlement projects were the source of much of the controversy. The House Select Committee to Investigate the Activities of the Farm Security Administration concluded that the FSA was financing "communistic resettlement projects where families could never own homes."[138] Despite repeated congressional demands that the resettlement projects be wound down, the FSA continued to fund them, and it initiated cooperative land-lease projects that appeared equally objectionable to congressional critics. The rural rehabilitation program also did not escape unscathed. It was charged with having "kept [some families] 'on the government' indefinitely" and "supervising its borrowers to the extent of telling the borrower how to raise his children, how to plan his home life, and, it is strongly suspected, how to vote."[139] There is more than a little irony in the effectiveness of these attacks, since the most important FSA programs—rural rehabilitation and tenant-purchase loans—were designed to bolster the family farm.

The New Deal established new linkages between state and society,

especially in the agricultural sector. As federal programs penetrated local politics, the need to legitimate the administration of these new programs became a pressing issue. Observers as far back as Alexis de
Tocqueville have observed that Americans relish participation in public
affairs and resent outside control. Such values have been vehemently
supported by local elites when their domination has been threatened by
outside intervention. As a consequence, most New Deal programs
strove to work out an accommodation between federal intervention and
the defenders of these widely shared political values.

The new accommodation, popularized under the rubric of "grass-
roots democracy," involved decentralizing administrative authority to
the local level and incorporating local sentiments into the implementation process. Frequently, local committees including representatives
from local organizations were established. These committees were intended to sensitize officials to local needs, promote local initiative, and
in many cases strengthen political support. By 1939, largely through
such committees, more than 892,000 private citizens participated in the
implementation of programs under the U.S. Department of Agriculture,
the Department of Interior, and the Tennessee Valley Authority.

The FSA leadership was for the most part skeptical of this new orthodoxy, but it was nevertheless obliged to create local committees. The
commitment of top FSA officials to the poor led them to question the
advantages of elite-dominated local committees for poverty alleviation
programs. The attitudes of most of the top FSA leaders are reflected in
the observation later made by Rexford Tugwell that local committees
represented the interests of the "grass tops," not the "grass roots." [140]
Their remedy for this problem was more, not less, participation. The
FSA promoted the organization of neighborhood action groups who
were encouraged to discuss their common problems and take collective
action to alleviate them. By 1944, the FSA had helped to establish some
4,000 neighborhood groups. [141]

Rural elites along with their representatives in Congress were not
enamored of the FSA's approach to local participation, and they compelled the agency to incorporate more of the "grass-roots" democracy
of the orthodoxy. In 1937, overruling Will Alexander's objections that
local committees would open the door to amateur incompetence, local prejudice, and favoritism, Congress wrote provisions into the
Bankhead-Jones Farm Tenant Act requiring the FSA to empower
county committees with mandatory approval over tenant-purchase
loans and advisory functions concerning disputes between clients and

supervisors and foreclosure proceedings.[142] The FSA leadership was also obliged to create local committees to supervise rural rehabilitation loans and the debt adjustment program as well as state committees to provide advice on the allocation of funds. The state committees initially had only a marginal impact. As congressional attacks against the FSA mounted, however, an important charge was that the agency had neglected its local farmers' committees. By 1943, FSA administrator C. B. Baldwin was compelled to enhance the power of local committees by ordering their consolidation into unified county committees consisting of three members nominated by the county supervisor for a three-year term. These committees not only retained power over the tenant-purchase program but also exercised the right to approve all rural rehabilitation loans and evaluate the progress of all rural rehabilitation clients.

In his classic study of the Tennessee Valley Authority, Selznick argues that administrators develop ideologies such as "grass-roots democracy" in order to legitimize the accommodations that their agencies must make with powerful actors in their environment. The experience of the FSA illustrates that the accommodations made by some organizations contribute to the creation of institutionalized rules, if not coherent ideologies, to which other organizations may be obliged to conform. FSA administrators made concessions to the prescriptions of grass-roots democracy only grudgingly, since they believed that such concessions would dilute their program's ability to serve the poor. The availability of the grass-roots democracy ideology to the rural elites legitimated their attacks against the FSA and ultimately helped them to gut the agency.

The demise of the FSA seems to support Selznick's contention that the choice confronting the leadership of agencies like the FSA often lies between accommodation of vested interests and organizational suicide.[143] Not only were the agency's defiant leaders forced to leave the FSA, which was ultimately dismantled, but the only program to survive intact was the tenant-purchase program—the only one over which local committees exerted extensive control. The survival of the tenant-purchase program is strong testimony to the importance of conformity to institutionalized rules, since the program potentially threatened to eliminate the primary means of labor control utilized by the FSA's arch-enemies—Southern agricultural elites. By compelling the FSA to devolve control over the program to county committees, whose members were appointed by the FSA county supervisor and the county extension officer, Southern Congressmen transformed the tenant-purchase program from a threat to local domination into a buttress.[144] One should not make sweeping generalizations from the experience of the FSA, however, since the institutional idiosyncrasies of the American political system during the 1930s and 1940s were important factors in determining the FSA's fate.

The Effect of American Political Institutions

The fragmentation and decentralization of authority within American political institutions make it easier to introduce innovations but more difficult to sustain them. The president is the sole authority controlling the different agencies of the executive branch, and the size and diversity of the executive agencies make it virtually impossible for him to impose a single point of view. On the contrary, the fragmented authority structure within the executive branch enables officials to create specialized niches, and the authority of agency heads to recruit their top staff promotes the infusion of new ideas. Perhaps more than any other modern president, Franklin D. Roosevelt used his presidential authority to encourage widespread experimentation with new ideas and programs by setting up an array of ad hoc advisory bodies and emergency agencies within his administration. The separation of powers characteristic of the federal government means that legislative and judicial branches can also provide the impetus for innovation. In addition, the federal system enables state governments to serve as a source of new ideas. The fragmentation of authority provides multiple points for opposition to new policies as well as opportunities for innovation. Executive branch initiatives are often rejected by Congress and the judicial system. Coalitions that lose a battle at one point can regroup and try again at another.[145]

Although state institutions reinvigorated the AFBF, they ignored and—in the South—actively discouraged the political organization of the poor. The poor were at an initial disadvantage because their spatial isolation and more itinerant lifestyle impeded their political organization. In the South, the education made available to them was often inferior. African-Americans attended segregated schools, if they went to school at all, and poor whites lived in isolation. Moreover, the legal rights of the rural poor were not protected; legal institutions often tolerated and abetted the repression of any efforts to organize them. Finally, a large number of the Southern poor—black and white—were effectively disfranchised through poll taxes, discriminatory registration qualifications, and the white primary.[146]

Even in the face of such institutional biases, the FSA might have fared better had the federal government been organized differently.[147] Unlike a parliamentary system, the doctrine of balance of powers governing relations between the legislature and the executive branch provides Congress with a tradition of independence and the means to oppose the executive. After a period of extraordinary quiescence during the first years of the New Deal, Congress began to reassert its prerogatives. The FSA fell victim to this reassertion.

The combination of state intervention and the congressional committee system fostered a pluralistic congressional politics that worked to the detriment of the FSA. The expansion of the federal government during the New Deal strengthened the committee system by enhancing the resources under committee control while simultaneously increasing the opportunities for reciprocity and logrolling among the committees.[148] Although this development strengthened the heterogeneous New Deal coalition by enabling diverse interests to dominate different policy domains, it enabled the AFBF to establish close ties with congressional agricultural committees. These links underpinned the alliance that brought about the FSA's demise.[149]

While the committee system enhanced the AFBF's ability to dominate agricultural policy, seniority rules—in combination with the lack of political competition in the South—placed more power in the hands of the FSA's congressional opponents. The appointment of chairs on the basis of seniority provided Southern Congressmen with disproportionate influence, since the South's one-party system enabled Southern politicians to remain in office for longer periods than Congressmen from other regions. Southerners chaired nine of the fourteen major Senate committees and twelve of the seventeen major House committees in 1933.[150] Though the FSA continued to receive support from Southern supporters of the New Deal, conservative Southern Democrats—such as Harry F. Byrd of Virginia, Malcolm Tarver of Georgia, and Harold D. Cooley of North Carolina—used their positions as committee chairs to spearhead the attack on the FSA.

CONCLUDING REMARKS

The experience of the FSA shows that administrative autonomy can have paradoxical consequences. The very measures that made the FSA's programs more effective contributed ultimately to its demise. The commitment of upper-level administrators antagonized powerful rural groups and Congressmen. The administrative steps that FSA leaders took to improve implementation exacerbated the antagonism because it insulated implementation authority. The FSA's elaboration of its organizational mission alienated powerful groups in the agricultural sector because it dramatized the conflict between its objectives and their interests. Although implementation of FSA programs was not without its problems, by most standards the agency was reasonably effective. But the effectiveness of its programs did not ensure the agency's survival. In this instance, autonomy proved to be a political liability. One of the strongest indictments of the agency was that it construed its enabling legislation with "great liberality and administrative ingenuity," and its officials "did just about everything under the sun they wanted to do."[151] Its failure to build congressional support at a time when the president became increasingly preoccupied with World War II was an important factor in its demise.

The FSA's demise occurred in an environment structured by previous state interventions and political institutions. These shaped the outcome. The USDA possessed extraordinary administrative capacity in comparison with that of other departments of the federal government.[152] It effectively intervened to increase agricultural production during World War I. It successfully organized producers to end the overproduction that plagued the agricultural sector during the 1920s and early 1930s. It was also effective in increasing production to meet the needs of the war effort in the 1940s. However, administrative capacity to do some things often impedes the capacity to do others.[153] Effective program implementation generally entails the creation of networks, including state agencies and social groups that often constrain the possibilities for future state activity.[154]

The USDA's success in spreading modern techniques of production through its county agents spurred the creation of the AFBF. The AAA's organization of production bolstered the AFBF and secured its position as the preeminent farm organization. Thus, USDA programs were in large part responsible for the AFBF's leading position in the agricultural sector. The AFBF's hegemony was an important factor in the demise of the FSA.

Nonetheless, despite their premature demise, the New Deal rural poverty alleviation programs bequeathed an important legacy to American political development. Their beneficiaries became wealthier and healthier than comparable nonbeneficiaries.[155] More of their children went into professional, technical, and managerial occupations. African-American beneficiaries became mainstays of the organizational life in their communities and later provided critical support for the civil rights movement.

The historical experience of the United States appears to offer a pessimistic lesson for developing countries. It seems to support the contentions of analysts who argue that rural elites cannot be dislodged from local power without "massive societal dislocation." [156] These arguments are supported by an array of studies showing the difficulties facing programs that threaten the power of a rural elite already bolstered by programs to increase agricultural production.[157] Nevertheless, the experience of New Deal programs to alleviate rural poverty does not provide sufficient evidence for a definitive answer to this question, since their fate cannot be understood without reference to the idiosyncrasies of American political institutions. The AFBF and its allies might not have succeeded in bringing down the agency were it not for the opportunities presented to them by the congressional committee system. Even with the congressional system, the Southern Congressmen who spearheaded the attack on the FSA might not have been so aggressive if they had been obligated to represent constituencies where African-Americans and poor whites actively cast their votes.

CHAPTER 3

Making Employment an Entitlement

Maharashtra's Employment Guarantee Scheme

The larger landowners complain that the EGS attracts
workers away from them. They ask us to close down the
EGS projects. But we can't listen to them since the poor are
in greater numbers.

> *Sabhapati, Parner Panchayat Samiti*
> *(Chairman, Parner Block Council)*

Entitlement programs are generally associated with the welfare states
of advanced industrial countries. Their expense and administration
usually are considered too burdensome for Third World countries. This
chapter discusses an entitlement program in the state of Maharashtra
in India: the Employment Guarantee Scheme (EGS). The EGS entitles
any adult residing in the state's countryside to a job and fulfills this
guarantee by creating a system of public works designed to promote
rural development. Implementing such an ambitious program in a state
whose population is larger than that of France, and whose area approximates that of Germany, presents many problems. Public works projects
must provide employment to 600,000 workers dispersed throughout
the state. Implementation must be made responsive to sizable fluctuations in the demand for employment occurring over time and across
space. In addition, corruption must be kept in check.

In spite of many problems, making employment an entitlement generates unexpected benefits. By guaranteeing jobs to the unemployed, the
EGS creates an incentive that shapes behavior. It politicizes the rural
poor by inciting them to demand employment from the state. Politicians
and government officials are also affected. Though it provides opportunities for patronage and corruption, the EGS facilitates mobilization
of the rural poor and encourages politicians and bureaucrats to be more
sensitive to their needs. Changing the micro incentives of such groups

results in a surprising macro outcome. Greater responsiveness on the part of politicians and government officials to the less privileged sections of society ultimately produces a redistribution of developmental expenditures to backward areas.

THE POLITICAL ECONOMY OF MAHARASHTRA

Maharashtra has one of the fastest-growing economies of any state in India. From 1970–71 to 1987–88, the net state product for Maharashtra grew in constant prices by 114 percent while that for all of India increased by only 82.4 percent. Real per capita income showed even greater disparities. India's per capita income increased by just 25.6 percent, while Maharashtra's grew by 48 percent. In 1987–88, per capita income in Maharashtra was 37 percent higher than that for India as a whole.[1]

The impetus for economic growth in Maharashtra was unevenly distributed. Much of it came from the manufacturing sector, which grew in real terms by 162 percent from 1970–71 to 1987–88. Manufacturing's share in Maharashtra's net state product grew from 26.5 percent to 32.5 percent. Most of the industrial growth has been concentrated in three districts: Greater Bombay, Thane, and Pune (see Map 1). Though these districts account for 25 percent of the state's population, they produce 81 percent of its industrial output. The agricultural sector, in contrast, has been much less dynamic. Its 60 percent real growth meant that its share in Maharashtra's net domestic product declined from 27.0 percent to 20.2 percent.

Agriculture in Maharashtra's rural hinterland is characterized by considerable diversity. The Ghat mountain range divides the state into two geographical zones: a narrow coastal strip running no more than 50 miles between the ocean and the mountains and the Deccan plain extending from the mountains almost 600 miles to the east. The monsoon winds drop plentiful rainfall as they rise over the Ghats, but they are depleted by the time they have traversed the mountains, creating an arid rain shadow on the other side. While paddy cultivation pervades the coastal strip, peasants in the rain shadow eke out a livelihood through dry-land agriculture based upon coarse foodgrains, except in limited areas near river basins that benefit from surface irrigation. Rainfall gradually picks up to the east, and commercial crops become viable in the central regions of the state. Paddy is the main crop in the easternmost districts of Bhandara and Chandrapur.

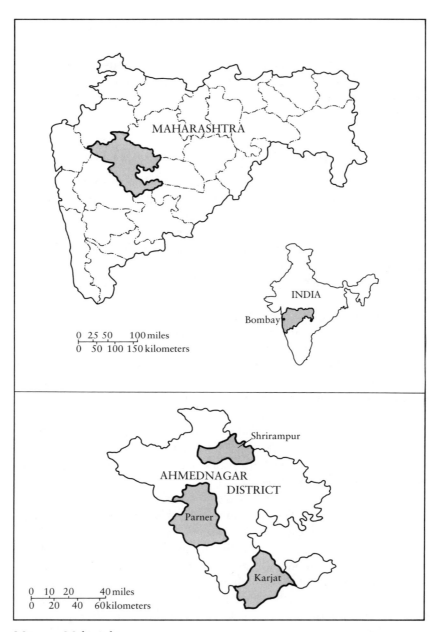

Map 1.   Maharashtra.

TABLE 2

DISTRIBUTION OF LANDHOLDINGS IN
MAHARASHTRA, 1980–81

Size of Operational Landholdings (in acres)	Percentage of Holdings		Percentage of Area Operated	
	Maharashtra	*India*	*Maharashtra*	*India*
Marginal (less than 2.5)	29.4	56.6	4.8	12.1
Small (2.5 to 5)	22.6	18.0	11.0	14.2
Semimedium (5 to 10)	24.0	14.0	22.8	21.2
Medium (10 to 20)	19.6	9.0	39.8	29.7
Large (over 20)	4.4	2.4	21.6	22.8
Total	100.0	100.0	100.0	100.0

SOURCE: Government of India, Director of Economics and Statistics, Department of Agriculture and Cooperation, Ministry of Agriculture, "Agricultural Census: All India," *Agricultural Situation in India* 40, no. 5 (August 1985): 410–11.

Maharashtra's average agricultural holding of 2.95 hectares is significantly above the 1.82 average for India as a whole. The share of landholdings comprised of marginal tracts, at 29.4 percent, is smaller than the all-India average of 56.6 percent (see table 2). The state's share of semimedium and medium holdings—24.0 percent and 19.6 percent, respectively—is considerably higher than the all-India figures of 14.0 and 9.0 percent.[2] Nevertheless, arid climate and relatively infertile soils ranging over much of the Deccan plateau have limited agricultural productivity, and rural poverty is higher than one might expect given the state's agrarian structure. In 1983, 51.3 percent of the state's rural households were estimated to live below the poverty line, whereas the all-India figure was 48.4 percent.[3]

Growth within the agricultural sector has been uneven. From the triennium ending in 1966–67 (that is, 1964–65, 1965–66, and 1966–67) to the one ending in 1986–87 (1984–85, 1985–86, and 1986–87), the average annual production of sugarcane grew by 128 percent while production of foodgrains increased by only 45 percent.[4] The lack of growth and productivity in foodgrain production is cause for concern, because most of the 65 percent of the state's workers employed in agriculture depend on foodgrain cultivation for their livelihood. Annual average foodgrain production per hectare in Maharashtra was 35 percent below the national norm for the period from 1982–83 to 1986–87. Furthermore, rates of increase of foodgrain productivity in Maharashtra have lagged behind those of the country as a whole. Average foodgrain productivity from the five-year period ending in 1965–66 to the five-year period ending in 1985–86 increased by 57.4 percent in India but by only 43.6 percent in Maharashtra.[5]

The relative stagnation of foodgrain production is in part a consequence of the low percentage of gross cropped area under irrigation. Only 12.2 percent of Maharashtra's gross cropped area is irrigated, whereas the rate for the country as a whole is 34.5 percent.[6] To some extent, this disparity occurs because Maharashtra's arid countryside has less irrigation potential. Nevertheless, the state has hardly approached the 30 percent of its gross cropped area estimated to be irrigable, and it lags behind most other states in this area.[7] A large share of the benefits from irrigation has been absorbed by water-intensive sugarcane cultivation. Sugarcane cultivators' appropriation of a disproportionate share of irrigation has become a matter of controversy as other cultivators have demanded a more equitable distribution.[8]

Uneven economic development has promoted an uneven distribution of political power in the state. Despite the buoyancy of the industrial sector, political leaders in Bombay have succumbed to the political logic dictated by the fact that 87 percent of the state's residents live outside the city. In fact, leaders of the state's dominant Maratha caste developed into a powerful political elite through the experience they acquired in the anti-Brahmin movement of the 1920s and the Samyukta (United) Maharashtra movement of the 1950s. One of the most striking political developments during the postindependence era in Maharashtra has been the "deurbanization" of political life, in which an urban-dominated political leadership was displaced by rural leaders.[9]

The Maratha political elite come from an agricultural caste that constitutes approximately 40 percent of the population and whose leaders were the traditional village (*patilki*) and regional (*deshmukhi*) elites of rural Maharashtra. The Marathas have gained control over the new institutions of rural power, including cooperatives, schools, and local government. Their control over sugar cooperatives, in particular, has enabled the Marathas to gain control over other institutions.[10] Since the

1960s, the "sugar lobby" has become one of the dominant factions in the state's legislative assembly. In 1977–78 and 1983–85, it succeeded in placing its leader, Vasantdada Patil, as chief minister of the state despite the reservations of Prime Minister Indira Gandhi.[11]

The Marathas' dominance has been especially resilient because of their knack for cementing their support with patronage and co-optation of potential rivals.[12] These skills were epitomized by Y. B. Chavan. From 1956 to 1975, Chavan became the dominant figure in the state's politics by fashioning a complex system of alliances and patronage that incorporated virtually all factions of the rural elite within the Congress party.[13] Because of Chavan's political craftsmanship, the Congress Party dominates state politics. Its dominance is plagued with factionalism because the bonds of patronage that hold it together are easily upset by ambitious individuals striving to improve their standing.

Why should Maharashtra's fractious state legislature, one that astute observers have described as a "kulak lobby," overwhelmingly support the EGS when the program threatens to raise agricultural wages and reduce the dependence of laborers on the cultivators?[14] One might answer this question by noting that the right to employment is an entitlement recognized by the Indian constitution. But why has Maharashtra established a program to provide this entitlement while other Indian states have failed to do so?[15] The most cogent answers to this question lie in the distinctive nature of the state's political economy. The state's thriving industrial sector makes it better able to afford the EGS. The program is funded by taxes whose incidence falls predominantly on Bombay, the center of the state's industrial dynamism. Urban political leaders support the program because they hope that it will curb migration of rural laborers to their already overcrowded metropolis.[16] At the same time, Maharashtra's rural Maratha elite makes concessions to subordinate groups in order to protect the legitimacy of its political and economic dominance.[17] By creating an abundant source of patronage, the EGS favors the interests of rural politicians even if it contradicts the interests of their most powerful supporters.

It has been argued that, contrary to initial appearances, the EGS actually favors the interests of cultivators. By providing supplementary employment to agricultural laborers at times when there is no work in the fields, the EGS frees cultivators from their traditional obligations to maintain their workers in slack agricultural seasons.[18] It also provides assets that increase the productivity of their cultivation and enhance the value of their land.[19]

In sum, the EGS offers something for everybody. The rural poor receive employment. Cities reduce overcrowding. Cultivators profit from the creation of agricultural infrastructure and freedom from traditional obligations. Politicians benefit from EGS because it provides them with a progressive image, not to mention an abundant source of patronage. The industrial dynamism of the state makes financial support for the program tolerable. As a result, the EGS enjoys widespread support and immense popularity.

THE ADMINISTRATIVE STRUCTURE OF THE EGS

Implementing the EGS requires a major commitment of resources. The EGS generated an annual average of 154 million person-days during the 1980s: approximately nine days of employment for each worker in the rural labor force, or a 300-day work year for 513,000 workers—3 percent of the rural work force. EGS expenditures totaled Rs. 2.46 billion in the fiscal year ending March 1, 1987—12.5 percent of all expenditures budgeted for Maharashtra's annual plan. As of December 1989, EGS projects completed 22,766 irrigation works, 117,461 soil conservation and land development projects, 17,350 road works, and 9,987 afforestation projects.[20]

This extensive public works program, with its diverse array of projects, is implemented through a complex administrative structure incorporating seven different agencies.[21] At the state level, the Planning Department manages the EGS fund and budgets EGS expenditures for each of the state's twenty-nine districts outside of Greater Bombay. It also encourages coordination between the EGS and other state programs. The Revenue Department is in charge of the EGS at the divisional and district levels, with the commissioner of the Revenue Division and the district collector exercising the ultimate authority over all EGS projects under their jurisdiction. The structure of EGS administration at the district level can be depicted as a spoked wheel. The Revenue Department is at the hub. Situated at the ends of the spokes are five technical departments in charge of implementing EGS projects: the Irrigation Department, the Public Works Department, the Agriculture Department (Soil Conservation), the Forestry Department, and the elected district councils known as the zilla parishads. Panchayat institutions have three levels: the district (i.e., the zilla parishads), the tahsil (subdistrict), and the village levels. Members from each level may serve on the committees that coordinate the activities of the technical departments.

Tahsil-level officers in the technical departments plan EGS projects. Wages must account for a minimum of 60 percent of project expenditures. Plans are reviewed and given technical sanction by departmental superiors at the district level. The senior Revenue Department official at the tahsil level, the tahsildar, collects the plans and assembles them into what is known as a "blueprint." Blueprints are supposed to contain a "shelf" of project plans sufficient to supply two years of EGS employment for the tahsil. Tahsil blueprints are then forwarded to the district collector, who assembles them into a district-level blueprint and submits them for approval of the district EGS committee and finally for review by the Planning Department.

People desiring work on the EGS are supposed to register with the village registering authority (i.e., the *talathi* or *gramsevak*). After their registration, they may ask for EGS employment either through the village registration authority or through the tahsildar. The tahsildar can either assign them to an ongoing work site or—when the absorptive capacity of ongoing projects is exhausted—begin a new project after receiving at least fifty requests for employment. To initiate a new project, the tahsildar selects a project from the blueprint and then submits it to the district collector for review and administrative sanction. After giving his or her sanction, the collector selects a technical department to implement the project and allocates the necessary funds.

Revenue Department officials are encouraged to provide work in projects located not more than eight kilometers from a laborer's residence. The statutory guarantee of employment, however, requires only that workers be given employment in the district where they live. The tahsildar must assign them to a project within fifteen days. If a worker appears at the site of the assigned project within seven days after receiving notification and is not provided with employment, that worker is legally entitled to unemployment compensation of Rs. 2 for every day that he or she goes without work.

The district collector possesses the ultimate authority over EGS implementation in a district. The collector and his or her subordinates in the Revenue Department monitor the progress of EGS implementation in the district. They collect data concerning labor attendance, expenditures, etc., from the departments, and they make periodic (and sometimes unannounced) inspections of projects.

EGS IMPLEMENTATION: A RATIONAL PROCESS PERSPECTIVE

The administrative structure of the EGS took shape during the late 1960s and early 1970s. The idea for the EGS was introduced and promoted by V. S. Page, a Gandhian politician who served as chair of Maharashtra's Legislative Council from 1960 to 1978. A pilot employment security program was introduced as part of the experimental Integrated Area Development Scheme (known as the Page Scheme) in Tasgaon tahsil of Sangli district in 1969. As part of the Page Scheme, elected village councils known as panchayats were made responsible for providing employment and loans so that those below the poverty level could purchase productive assets.

With the beginning of the extended drought in 1971, the need for widespread employment relief became painfully apparent. The Congress Party made implementation of the EGS on a statewide basis part of the fifteen-point campaign program during the 1972 state elections. It promised to integrate the EGS with the central government's Crash Scheme for Rural Employment (CSRE). However, the state government considered the EGS supplemental to the drought relief works, and the tremendous expansion of the relief effort during the scarcity period preempted efforts to implement the EGS.[22]

The legacy of the drought shaped the future of the EGS. From 1970 to 1973, the employment relief program was supervised by the Revenue Department and administered by the departments concerned with rural development. The relief effort was conducted under the slogan *Magel tyaala kaam* (Work to all who want it).[23] The state government's success in fulfilling this promise during the drought period enhanced its confidence in the administrative structure that had implemented the relief program. When it initiated the EGS on a statewide basis in 1974, virtually the same structure was retained. The idea of implementing the EGS through panchayats was discarded.[24]

The drought period provided the state administration with experience in planning labor-intensive public works projects and supervising the construction of these projects across the state. This experience also helped the state administration overcome practical logistical barriers, such as paying wages to large number of workers spread across the rural hinterland. Finally, the large number of projects left incomplete after the drought relief effort was terminated made early planning of projects for the EGS a less demanding task.

Effective administration of the EGS calls for decentralized planning, since administrators must provide employment over large areas and respond to the fluctuations in demand for employment that occur across Maharashtra's 39,354 villages and through its different agricultural seasons. They also must try to provide jobs within five to seven kilometers of workers' residences.

Planning of EGS works takes place primarily in the state's 303 tahsils.[25] Since the technical officers come mainly from outside the tahsil and lack a politician's familiarity with the localities, local politicians usually suggest EGS projects and their location. They make suggestions at the tahsil EGS committee meetings or under more informal circumstances—at the offices of technical officers or at EGS project sites. Politicians add to the administration's planning capacity by serving as sources of information about local conditions and needs.[26] Decentralization of planning at the tahsil level makes the planning process accessible to them.

The EGS combines two appealing objectives. It attempts to alleviate poverty by providing employment, and it promotes rural development by creating productive infrastructure. Achieving these objectives simultaneously is not without contradictions. Alleviating poverty through public works requires that projects generate employment for people with limited skills and in locations accessible to these people. These two conditions restrict the types of projects that can be undertaken and the return on the resources invested.

To reconcile the contradictions that arise in the pursuit of the program's two objectives, the EGS has created a matrix structure of authority at the district and tahsil levels—that is, two hierarchies of authority and a system of coordination between them. Research shows that matrix structures are particularly suitable when an organization has important competing objectives.[27] When each hierarchy is identified with a particular objective, the matrix structure of authority ensures that one objective will not be subordinated to the other. In the EGS, one hierarchy of authority runs through the Revenue Department, and the other is located in the technical departments. Responsibility for coordination resides largely with the Revenue Department and the EGS committees. The technical departments are responsible for making certain that EGS projects create productive assets while the Revenue Department makes certain that the program remains responsive to changes in demand for employment.

Achieving the dual objectives of the EGS requires technical expertise for project design, flexibility to respond to changes in demand for employment, and coordination among different technical departments. The matrix structure of EGS administration facilitates these tasks.[28] The technical departments apply their expertise in the design of projects. In periods of particularly high demand, they can shift personnel from regular departmental works to the EGS. The role of Revenue Department officers also enhances flexibility. When one department has insufficient personnel to meet demand for employment, the collector is authorized to shift some of the burden to other departments even if the work he assigns differs from these departments' normal functions.[29] Tahsildars also maintain discretion over which projects are initiated and can use their discretion to make efficient use of the available personnel. They may also select complementary projects that enhance development. As the impact of various decisions cumulates, however, the balance between different objectives becomes difficult to sustain. Many of the adjustments that have occurred during EGS implementation have been measures to preserve the balance of authority within the administrative matrix.[30]

The Government of Maharashtra has attempted to maintain that balance by issuing numerous government directives. During the first seven years of EGS implementation, no fewer than 506 directives were issued. Many of these dealt with relationships between the Revenue Department and the technical agencies. For instance, relations between the collector and officers in the technical departments were defined, redefined, and reiterated in at least 22 orders during the period. In an effort to clearly delimit the important roles in the EGS administrative structure, the government has compiled its directives into a 991-page compendium and distributed it to officers throughout the state.[31] To promote coordination, the government also requires the technical departments to provide the Revenue Department with detailed information on the progress of the EGS projects under their supervision. In addition to accounting for EGS expenditures, local departmental officers must furnish the Revenue Department's tahsildar biweekly reports on the potential for labor absorption and the number of workers attending the projects under their control.

The creation of boundary-spanning units at each important level of EGS administration is another measure employed to maintain the balance within the matrix. At the state level, the EGS committee of the state legislature and the Maharashtra State Employment Guarantee Council were established on August 20, 1975, and April 6, 1979, respectively. These committees enable members of the state legislature and experts on rural development to evaluate the progress of EGS implementation. At the divisional level, a special EGS unit was set up that incorporates a divisional-level officer of a technical department into the Revenue Department. Formally, this officer inspects individual works, to see whether they meet technical standards, and reviews tahsil-level blueprints to ensure their viability. Informally, the officer's status as a senior technical officer in the commissioner's office enables him or her to mediate disputes between officials in the technical departments and the Revenue Department.[32] Committees of officers from all departments and elected officials were created to coordinate the matrix at the district and tahsil levels. In Ahmednagar district, the collector established another means to coordinate implementation. For each of the district's thirteen tahsils, he assigned a district-level officer in a technical department to help supervise EGS implementation. These "monitors" were appointed to help resolve technical problems, promote coordination between technical agencies, and represent the perspective of the technical departments in the distribution of EGS projects.

A third way in which the Government of Maharashtra has attempted to maintain the efficacy of the EGS matrix has been through enhancing the superior authorities' ability to monitor implementation. In addition to creating EGS cells at the divisional level, the government has established a state-level Vigilance Committee, chaired by the secretary of the Revenue Department, and a special "audit squad" in the collector's office. Monitoring also takes place through inspections by Revenue Department officers and superior authorities in the technical departments. To enhance feedback to senior authorities, the government requires that laborers be given identity cards and wage books that record attendance and wages received. These materials also are intended to encourage laborers to take recourse if they feel that their wages have been manipulated.

While the government uses EGS projects to complement regular projects, it has found the program especially useful in fashioning responses to natural disasters. In 1979, after widespread flooding occurred in the Vidharbha region, encompassing the eight easternmost districts of the state, EGS labor and funds were used to repair damaged *bunds* (dams), terraces, and buildings; reclaim land; and clear debris. When an onslaught of paddy stemborers caused heavy losses to *kharif* crops in Kulaba (Alibagh) and Thane districts in 1978, the government called on EGS labor in its campaign to eradicate the pests. In times of natural disasters, the use of EGS labor and funds not only helps to repair the destruction suffered but also provides income to those who have lost their source of livelihood.

The Revenge of the Rational Peasant

The guarantee of employment causes special problems for the planning of implementation, since it makes the preferences of the workers an important factor in determining the location and size of EGS projects. The demand for EGS employment can be volatile. Droughts, natural disasters, or even seasonal changes cause dramatic shifts in demand. For instance, in the district of Ahmednagar, the dry 1982 monsoon caused average daily labor attendance to jump 64 percent, from 54,250 to 89,234, between July and August. Even with the relatively flexible administrative structure of the EGS, it is difficult to make adequate adjustments. Sudden increases in demand usually require rapid initiation of projects. New projects may have to be implemented without sufficient time for proper planning. In order to meet the demand for employment in the vicinity of the workers' residences, Revenue Department officers sanction projects that may be of little productive value. Sudden increases also overload administrative personnel and resources.

Administrative stress in extraordinary circumstances is to be expected. Less expected is the stress that arises from the individual preferences of EGS laborers. Despite government regulations requiring preliminary registration with the tahsildar or a designated village official, laborers prefer to appear at project sites and ask for employment. Because of the guarantee, project supervisors feel obliged to accept them. Local laborers thus have considerable autonomy in determining when and where they will work. The freedom allowed to workers creates problems for administrators supervising EGS projects. They are unable to predict how many workers will attend various projects. A project with a steady labor attendance of 100 may suddenly have 200 additional workers asking for work; similarly, projects that have 150 laborers one day may have fewer than 10 the next.

Though such volatility perplexes administrators, it is easy to explain from the workers' perspective. Rational decision criteria cause the fluctuations. Workers will leave projects en masse if another EGS project opens up closer to their village. The difficulty of the work is another factor entering into their calculus. The bulk of their work on projects such as road construction and soil conservation involves digging and transporting dirt. The effort required for such work increases considerably after the laborers have removed the topsoil and reached the compacted base below. Some workers are unable to exert the necessary physical effort; others feel that wage rates do not provide adequate compensation. When projects reach this stage, those with an excess of laborers often experience a sudden exodus and are left with an insufficient number to complete the project.[33]

Unanticipated fluctuations cause administrative turmoil. Sharp increases in labor attendance may cause projects to be completed before new projects are ready to take their place and may render locally available funds insufficient to pay wages. As the ratio of workers to supervisors grows, proper oversight becomes difficult. The number of workers may grow to the point where the productivity of their labor decreases. As a result, wages that are based on piece rates fall, the workers become discontented, and the quality of work declines. At the same time, project costs increase, and superior officers become displeased. In Ahmednagar district, project supervisors have closed down EGS work sites when labor attendance exceeds a project's estimated capacity to absorb workers.[34] In contrast, precipitous drops in labor attendance may mean that projects are not completed before the onset of the monsoon halts work and damages incomplete construction.

The Government of Maharashtra has reduced the problems arising from the volatility of labor attendance in four ways. First, project supervisors have been ordered to direct excess workers to other EGS works. Second, the supervisors have been authorized to shut down works when labor attendance falls below a necessary minimum. Third, the government has required laborers to commit themselves to a minimum of one month's work to be eligible for the EGS. Finally, the government has attempted to secure better estimates of the demand for employment. Directives have called for tahsil "manpower budgets," which estimate the demand for EGS employment in each village by month of the year and by the distance workers are willing to travel for EGS employment; but these budgets are rarely computed and put to use.[35] The government has also issued orders for updating the registration of workers desiring EGS employment. Despite these efforts, registration records are not kept up to date, and registration bears little relation to actual labor attendance.[36] In the absence of effective planning to anticipate demand for EGS employment, limiting the number of laborers on a project erodes the effectiveness of the employment guarantee, since other projects may not be available near the homes of the excess workers.

EGS planners feel that they are running out of viable projects in some areas. In the early years, minor irrigation projects were emphasized, but the potential for such projects and for traditional soil conservation works has been exhausted in some areas. The initiation of the Comprehensive Watershed Development Programme in 1984 was intended to alleviate the problem by stressing land development projects and encouraging more projects on private holdings.

Another weakness of EGS planning is the limited developmental impact of its projects. Usually, only a fraction of the potential benefits from EGS projects is realized. One problem is that desirable complementary investments—such as the construction of wells, land development, and the increased application of fertilizer—often are not made. A joint study by the Planning Commission and the Government of Maharashtra found that complementary investment was made in only 23 percent (thirteen of fifty-six) of the EGS projects where it was needed to realize optimum benefits. A related problem is that EGS projects are not well integrated with other ongoing developmental projects. In addition, the assets created by EGS projects are often poorly maintained. Maintenance usually becomes the responsibility of the zilla parishads, but the budget of these bodies usually does not increase in proportion to these additional responsibilities. As a result, nearly 25 percent of EGS works are poorly maintained.[37]

The limited developmental impact of the EGS makes it more difficult to justify the program's growing expenditures. The Government of Maharashtra had hoped that the EGS would eventually wither away as the productive assets created under the program promoted economic growth and generated employment opportunities for everyone. After fifteen years, Rs. 23 billion in expenditures, and the completion of 172,201 projects (as of December 1989), the demand for EGS employment generation shows little sign of subsiding. In June 1989—in an effort to improve the developmental impact of the EGS and encourage innovative projects that move beyond the traditional public works— the Government of Maharashtra initiated the Rural Development Through Labor Force program (RDLF). This component of the EGS attempts to increase the developmental impact of projects by creating village-level plans that will integrate EGS projects with local needs and other developmental programs. The scope of EGS works has also been expanded to include projects such as the development of horticulture, fish tanks, and *khadi* and village industries—in the hope that these projects will be more successful in reducing the demand for employment on the EGS. As of May 1990, however, the RDLF has yet to get off the ground.[38]

In sum, implementing the EGS is a formidable task requiring the administrative capacity to generate employment and respond to fluctuations in demand throughout Maharashtra's 39,000 villages. The Government of Maharashtra has responded to the challenge by creating a complex administrative structure that decentralizes planning while using a matrix system of authority to maintain coordination. Agency theory (discussed in chapter 1) posits two instruments for securing cooperation from the officials involved in EGS implementation: a system of monitoring that generates feedback on the agent's activity and/or program outcomes and a set of incentives motivating the desired behavior. The Rational Process Perspective shows that the government has tried to establish systems for monitoring the actions of those who implement the EGS; however, relatively little concern has been given to creating incentives to produce the desired behavior. In fact, the matrix system that was established to accomplish the dual objectives of the EGS actually interferes with the creation of a system of incentives that would properly motivate implementation authorities. As a result, conflicting interests within the administrative network have influenced EGS implementation.

EGS IMPLEMENTATION: A CONFLICTUAL PROCESS PERSPECTIVE

Conflicting interests abound in EGS implementation. Workers are often indolent and undisciplined. Administrators frequently lack commitment. These attitudes contribute to corruption. The interests of different departments in the administrative network also conflict. Tensions between the Revenue Department and the technical departments limit the ability of authorities to curb corruption. The demands of various social groups also create conflicts. Workers demand that EGS administrators be more responsive to their needs. Cultivators exhort administrators to limit EGS employment and locate projects in favorable positions. Politicians also urge that administrators implement the EGS in an advantageous manner.

Conflict between Individual Values and Implementation Objectives

V. S. Page, founder of the EGS and president of the Maharashtra State Employment Guarantee Council, has observed, "A major problem of the EGS is the lack of discipline. Laborers need more discipline in applying for work, coming to work daily, and in showing up on time. The administration needs discipline to avoid corruption."[39] This lack of discipline, Page believes, is the result of a conflict between the attitudes of individuals and the objectives of the EGS. Fifty percent (seventeen of thirty-four) of the project supervisors interviewed complained of the workers' indolence or lack of discipline.[40] Many EGS workers—for instance, the elderly and women, overworked from their other responsibilities, who are driven to the EGS by their need to supplement their incomes—simply do not have the energy to do vigorous work. Most of the problem, however, stems from habits developed by the workers: they arrive late for work, take inexcusably long lunch breaks and other work breaks, and often leave work early. Few of the officers lay the blame on the workers' inherent laziness but, rather, on the circumstances in which they work.

One problem is the manner in which workers are organized. Because of the indivisibility of tasks and the shortage of personnel to measure their work, laborers are usually grouped into gangs. Their wages are based on a piece-rate schedule designed to give them incentive to work industriously. Under the gang system, the departmental officers measure the work of gangs and calculate individual wages on the basis of the collective work performed. When gangs are formed by four or five friends or relatives, this is no problem. But often the gangs number more than twenty people. One engineer reported measuring work in gangs with more than one hundred members. The larger the gang, the greater the incentive to free-ride, and the less work gets done.[41]

Supervision of EGS workers presents another problem. The EGS regulations require that the technical departments directly supervise EGS laborers, whereas in regular departmental works supervision is generally assigned to private contractors. The departments usually hire muster assistants to perform daily supervision of EGS projects.[42] These low-paid positions (Rs. 300 per month) are filled on an ad hoc basis by a diverse range of persons, including unemployed youths and local notables. They often cannot maintain discipline. A junior engineer for the Public Works and Housing Department in Shrirampur describes this tendency as follows: "Muster assistants are lazy. They do not stay at the work site the entire day. . . . Some don't even take daily attendance." Irresponsible muster assistants set a bad example for the workers. Another problem with muster assistants is that those who take the low-paying position sometimes have dishonest motives. Muster assistants can parlay their control over the records of labor attendance into an illicit source of income. The relatively lucrative opportunities for corruption make the position attractive to the unscrupulous.[43]

The junior departmental officers also have difficulty disciplining workers. Though these project-level officers visit EGS works only two or three times a week, they have primary responsibility for the projects. Their duties include measuring the work performed, paying the workers, and ensuring that the work meets technical standards. In some cases, EGS laborers show disrespect for the officers; sometimes they intimidate them. One junior engineer recounted:

> Once I had to supervise a thousand laborers working on a road site. When I would go to measure their work, many of them would surround me. This makes taking measurements difficult. . . . Sometimes the workers would change the markings we made from previous measurements to make it appear that they did more work. If we complain, they get angry and protest. If we continue to confront them, they threaten to form a *morcha* [demonstration] and protest to the tahsildar. We get scared because we fear that if many people complain, the tahsildar will believe them even if their accusations are false.

More than a quarter of the field-level officers surveyed (nine of thirty-four) reported difficulties in trying to discipline EGS laborers. The guarantee of employment prevents them from withholding benefits—an important sanction that lower-level government officials employ to control their clientele. Furthermore, the officers' efforts are hindered because workers retaliate by placing them under political pressure, either directly, through demonstrations and delegations to their superiors, or indirectly, through politicians.[44]

Field-level supervisors are in an unusually difficult situation, although their problems are not insuperable. Their position is made more difficult because many of them are young. The average age of those reporting difficulties with laborers was twenty-eight. Their formal training is in engineering rather than labor management, and usually they are not prepared to manage hundreds of laborers. Their departments do not provide them with labor management training, nor is there much reward for developing such skills because the departments normally hire contractors to supervise construction. Experience is the primary means through which field-level officers learn to cope with their difficulties.

Not surprisingly, most field-level workers do not like working on the EGS: 79 percent (twenty-seven of thirty-four) of the officers said that they preferred working on regular departmental works to working on the EGS; only 6 percent (two of thirty-four) preferred the EGS. The officials have good reasons to prefer departmental works. Antagonism on the part of workers can result in verbal and physical abuse.[45] A number of the officers expressed dislike of the EGS because it placed them under greater public pressure. Others complained of the political pressures it subjected them to. Professional pride also dictates disdain. One official said that the EGS devalued his professional status because it compelled him to listen to the advice of everyone, "no matter how ignorant." Some officers complained about the excessive paperwork and meetings. They felt that their skills could be put to better use in other ways. Other officers said that they preferred regular departmental works because the quality of labor was better and they were able to complete projects properly. Finally, one ambitious engineer voiced a widespread sentiment: that departmental works enabled him to improve his relations with superiors in his department who were crucial to his promotion.

Most senior officials in the technical departments also disliked the EGS. The minutes of the Shrirampur tahsil EGS committee show that many tahsil- and district-level officials avoided attending the committee's meetings even after being reprimanded by the member of the legislative assembly (MLA) who served as chair. In an attempt to get district-level officials more involved with EGS implementation, the district collector of Ahmednagar asked them to help coordinate the efforts of the technical departments by serving as monitors of their implementation of the EGS in a tahsil. In at least four of the district's thirteen tahsils, officers wrote back requesting to be excused from these responsibilities. They stated that they were too busy to take on the extra work.[46] When I asked the collector about this problem, he insisted that technical officers at the district level shun involvement with the EGS because they wish to avoid the political pressure that accompanies it.

Dislike of the EGS extends even higher up departmental hierarchies. In a surprisingly frank interview that no doubt reflects widely held attitudes, a senior official in the Agriculture Department stated that he was "totally against schemes like the EGS," because "the EGS is more concerned with providing employment and amenities for workers," thereby diverting concern from "the quality of work." He charged that the politicians and collectors who demand more projects "have very short time horizons." He added, "Ultimately, we would like to reduce and even eliminate EGS funding, so that funds could be diverted to our regular plan work." [47]

Albert Hirschman suggests that corruption often occurs after a government official's first flush of enthusiasm for public service gives way to a more jaundiced assessment. "Losses in the satisfaction that is yielded by action in the public interest are made up by material gain." [48] From this perspective, it is not surprising that corruption flourishes among those who implement the EGS. Estimates of the extent of corruption on the EGS vary, but virtually everyone who has seriously looked into the matter has found it extensive. [49]

Corruption occurs at two levels. First, muster rolls recording the attendance and wages given to laborers can be manipulated. The complex wage-rate schedule utilized in computing wages often prevents workers from calculating their earnings and makes them susceptible to corruption. [50] Officials can add apocryphal names to pad the list, and they can overstate wages in order to pocket the surplus. [51] At the second level, project expenditures can be falsified, giving a misleading impression about the expenditures incurred. For example, according to the EGS committee of the state legislature, a percolation tank that had been reported to cost Rs. 2.8 million should have cost only Rs. 226,000. [52] Such corruption often involves collusion. Partners in corruption include muster assistants, local politicians, and even workers. [53]

EGS corruption is a serious problem and has received extensive publicity. However, proper evaluation should compare it with corruption in the implementation of other programs in India. Programs designed to ameliorate rural poverty—for example, the Integrated Rural Development Programme—also have serious problems with corruption. [54] The construction and operation of regular assets by government departments are also plagued with corruption. [55] Given the nature of the problem, rigorous comparisons are virtually impossible. Nevertheless, two factors that limit corruption on the EGS are not present on regular department works.

First, the decisions of EGS officers are more open to scrutiny by the public and by officers of the Revenue Department. Theories of corruption observe that the more likely the exposure of corruption, the less likely officials are to commit it. [56] Corruption on the EGS is more difficult to conceal than on regular departmental works. Planning of regular department works is done primarily within the technical departments, though politicians may have influence over the planning process. Selection of contractors to carry out projects often takes place behind closed doors and can be a source of payoffs. In contrast, on the EGS, project sites are selected mainly in tahsil committee meetings; project plans are subject to review, not only by senior officers in the technical depart-ments but also by the tahsildar and the collector as well as by tahsil- and district-level committees; and contractors are hired only for the capital-intensive component of these projects.

Second, the EGS provides more means to make officers accountable than regular department works. In India, a major form of corruption results from illicit attempts to influence public officials. "Speed money" is used to circumvent bureaucratic bottlenecks, and political clout and payoffs are often used to secure a favorable distribution of assets. Even if such corruption becomes apparent on regular departmental works, frequently the only way the public can change the situation is to up the corruption ante with even greater political influence or payoffs. Most departments are insulated from outside review, and superiors are often reluctant to reprimand their subordinates in such matters. The court system is notoriously slow. Any attempt to redress grievances outside the "corruption game" may elicit retaliation when the next round is played. The EGS, in contrast, opens a number of channels through which pressure can be brought to bear on corrupt officers. Workers' committees for projects with more than one hundred workers have been set up to hear grievances. The public can make complaints to tahsil committees, the state legislative committee, and various officials in the Revenue Department.

Conflictual Processes in the Administrative Network

Although implementation of the EGS involves seven different depart-ments, there is only one basic line of cleavage among them. Little con-flict occurs among the five implementing agencies because they are linked through pooled interdependence. The activities of one depart-ment do not have immediate consequences for the others. Their activi-ties are coordinated by the Revenue Department. Indeed, sometimes officials in these departments make common cause against the Revenue Department.

To understand the conflict between Revenue Department officers and those of the technical departments, it is useful to place their relations in historical context. Because the primary functions of administration during the colonial era were the extraction of revenue and the maintenance of law and order, the Revenue Department was the most power-ful department in district administration, and the collector was the su-preme district official. The emphasis on promoting rural development since independence has provided increased resources to those depart-ments concerned with rural development.[57] These departments are now filled with technical experts—usually engineers—who possess consid-erable professional pride and are united by their department's organi-zational mission. The Revenue Department may be first among equals in district administration, but the increasing expertise and power of technical department personnel make them less willing to countenance intervention by the generalist Revenue Department officers. In spite of this trend, implementation of the EGS is based on an administrative arrangement that was created to combat famines during the colonial era. It restores the preeminence of the Revenue Department and, as a consequence, incites the resentment of technical department officers.

In addition to such historical conditions, the very division of labor that engages the technical departments and the Revenue Department is a source of antagonism. Revenue Department officials are responsible for seeing that employment is properly provided. They are also respon-sible for auditing EGS expenditures and ensuring that the project su-pervisors provide adequate facilities for EGS workers. Technical de-partment officers are more concerned with ensuring that EGS projects are well designed and promote development. Contradictions between these two objectives become manifest in implementation and are a source of tension.

Tension and antagonism are especially apparent at the tahsil level, where most of the coordination between the Revenue and technical de-partments occurs. Half of the technical department officers interviewed (sixteen of thirty-two) responded affirmatively when asked whether they had any problems in their relations with Revenue Department of-ficials during the course of EGS implementation. They said that tahsil-dars assigned them too many projects, sent them more workers than their projects could absorb, and sometimes pressured them to begin works before they were properly planned. Tahsildars and other Reve-nue Department officials had complaints of their own. They charged that technical deparment officials refused to obey their orders. Another objection was that the technical departments were chronically late in submitting reports to them. Yet another was that technical department officers sometimes refused to take up works that they had sanctioned.[58]

The problems stemming from the antagonism between Revenue Department and technical department officers might not have such negative consequences if the collector possessed enough authority over technical department personnel to supervise them effectively. The collector's authority is circumscribed in ways that reduce his capacity to ensure effective implementation. First, the collector cannot add comments to the "confidential reports" used to evaluate the technical officers for promotion. Second, collectors cannot prosecute officers they discover to be involved in corruption. Third, the departments possess enough allies within the government to protect them from zealous collectors.

A dramatic illustration of the constraints a collector encounters is the controversy over Arun Bhatia, the crusading collector of Dhule district. Shortly after his appointment in 1981, Bhatia began an investigation into EGS corruption. He ordered his staff to verify 315 muster rolls randomly selected from the 44,500 that had been prepared in Dhule from September 1980 to August 1981. They detected 42 cases of misappropriation involving Rs. 43,000. Bhatia estimated that total corruption in the district was at least Rs. 860,000—some 13.5 percent of all EGS expenditures in Dhule in 1980–81.[59]

Public disclosure created a stir. The state legislature voted to establish a special commission headed by R. S. Gawai, chair of the Legislative Council, to investigate the matter. Bhatia was given orders to expand the scope of his investigation under the supervision of the Gawai Committee. Misappropriations of Rs. 190,000 were found after inspection of 1,490 musters.[60] Bhatia's investigation inspired the formation of the Dhule Zilla Rozgar Hami Bhrashtachar Nirmular Kruti Samiti (Action Committee for Eradication of Employment Guarantee Corruption in Dhule District), which investigated another avenue for corruption. It discovered eight projects where officials had made "excess payments" of more than Rs. 200,000 to contractors.[61]

The power of the technical departments shaped the final outcome of the revelations. The target of the investigation, the EGS project supervisors, organized a "bullet *morcha*" (a procession of their Enfield Bullet motorcycles) against Bhatia's actions and then refused to take up new EGS works.[62] Realizing that any attempt to get action through an appeal to technical department superiors would be futile, Bhatia attempted to prosecute the offenders through the police. However, the police aligned themselves with the technical departments. On June 25, 1982, Dhule's superintendent of police issued an order instructing his subordinates not to accept any more FIRs (charge sheets) from the Revenue Department concerning EGS corruption.[63] Despite a request from the Gawai Committee that Bhatia be allowed to complete his investigation, the collector was transferred in June 1982, shortly after the second phase of the investigation had begun. Bhatia alleged that technical department officers raised Rs. 500,000 to pay the minister in charge of the district to transfer him.[64] It was officially acknowledged in the state legislature that he had been transferred because he had passed on details of his investigation to the press before reporting it to the government.[65] The investigation's final result was that nine muster assistants were dismissed. Not one officer from the technical departments was prosecuted.[66]

From the Conflictual Process Perspective, the cleavage between the Revenue Department and the technical departments is a serious problem for EGS implementation. It impedes information flows and obstructs coordination. The power of the technical departments prevents Revenue Department officials from effectively auditing the EGS for corruption. These problems, combined with widespread disaffection for the EGS among technical department officers, create an atmosphere that breeds corruption.

Conflict between the Administration and Environmental Groups

Agricultural workers, cultivators, and politicians all attempt to pressure administrators to implement the EGS to their benefit. Workers try to increase opportunities for employment in EGS. Obtaining EGS employment may not be difficult if there is an ongoing project near their residence, but problems arise when no project exists within feasible walking distance. This has been a growing problem ever since the Planning Department issued directives instructing Revenue Department officers to finish incomplete works before taking up new ones.[67] Workers must often deploy persistent pressure to make the guarantee of employment effective. For example, a representative from the Rozgar Hami Kaamgaar Sangh (Employment Guarantee Workers' Union) in Haveli tahsil of Pune district gave me a memorandum stating that from December 12, 1983, through January 18, 1984, his organization had sent representatives from six villages to meet with the tahsil's subdivisional soil conservation officer (sub disco) from the Agriculture Department, the tahsildar, the deputy collector (EGS), and the deputy development commissioner (EGS). Even though the organization's members had filled out work applications and its representatives had made a list of suggested projects, their efforts to initiate a project in their locality failed.[68] When representations to government officials fail, workers often organize demonstrations and sometimes take the administration to court. In 1983, the Ahmednagar Zilla Shet Majoor Union (Ahmednagar District Agricultural Workers' Union) presented a petition to the High Court in Bombay, in an effort to have projects initiated in Shrirampur tahsil. On March 26, 1984, approximately 2,000 workers demanding more EGS projects staged a *dharna* (sit-in demonstration) at the Flora Fountain Park in downtown Bombay. The demonstration succeeded in obliging the chief minister to hear the demands of a delegation representing the workers.

Despite precautions built into EGS regulations, the guarantee of employment often interferes with agricultural production. Revenue Department officials are directed not to assign laborers to EGS projects when work is available in a farmer's fields. Wage rates were also established so that they would not draw laborers away from the employ of cultivators. Nonetheless, implementation of the EGS often contradicts cultivator interests. Many laborers prefer EGS work to working in a farmer's fields. Workers—especially women—can often earn more on the EGS because the wages paid by cultivators are sometimes less than the minimum wage. Even when agricultural wages are higher, some workers prefer the EGS because cultivators are more demanding taskmasters than EGS supervisors. As a consequence, cultivators often ask Revenue Department officials to close down EGS works so that they are assured an adequate supply of labor.

Cultivators also attempt to influence the decisions of EGS administrators concerning the location of EGS projects. An irrigation tank in the village may be a boon, but one in a cultivator's own field is a disaster. Resentment against the EGS is particularly high because proceedings for compensation are notoriously slow. As a result, EGS projects are often delayed by recalcitrant cultivators who refuse to give up their land.

Politicians stand between cultivators and workers. The EGS provides them with a source of patronage to build support among both cultivators and workers. They curry favor with local cultivators by using their influence to situate EGS projects in advantageous locations. Providing EGS jobs is a way of building support among large numbers of workers. For instance, the *sabhapati* (chairman) of Parner panchayat samiti (block council) proudly remarked that the EGS enables him to claim to have helped 15,000 workers get jobs in the preceding year.[69]

The EGS is an particularly important resource for MLAs. Since state laws exclude them from involvement with zilla parishads, they benefit little from that munificent source of patronage. Their political rivals often use zilla parishad patronage to build support in order to unseat them. As heads of the tahsil EGS committees, MLAs exert more control over EGS patronage than other politicians do. The EGS, thus, helps them fortify their position.

MLAs have been particularly generous to EGS workers. They have ensured that EGS wages keep pace with inflation. From 1974 to 1985, the basic daily wage doubled from Rs. 3 to Rs. 6. In 1985, EGS wages were made equal to the minimum wage, and by April 1, 1988, the Government of Maharashtra had increased minimum wages to Rs. 14 per day. The state legislature has also passed rules that on-site child care be provided for EGS workers with children aged three years or less. It has ordered that compensation be given to workers injured on the EGS or to the families of those who may have died as a result of injuries suffered while working on the program. The MLAs have provided EGS workers with a thirty-day maternity leave allowance at Rs. 6 per day, and some have advocated giving workers a Diwali holiday bonus.[70]

MLAs extend their generosity to EGS workers on their own terms. In addition to using the EGS to build worker support, some have used their control over the EGS to discourage independent organizations. In Pune and Sholapur districts, local social workers have alleged that the MLAs of their tahsils have used their influence to prevent the initiation of EGS works demanded by independent worker organizations.[71]

In sum, the Conflictual Process Perspective shows that implementation of the EGS suffers from serious problems. Poor supervision and the gang system of paying wages encourage indolent attitudes among workers. Project supervisors from the technical departments show a lack of commitment to the program's success. The EGS suffers from the liability of being a tacked-on program in the sense that it is a diversion from the main mission of the technical departments, whose personnel consequently lack dedication to its objectives. Revenue Department officials do not possess the authority necessary to effectively monitor the technical departments' implementation of the EGS. These circumstances produce widespread corruption.

Despite (and in some cases because of) this corruption, the EGS is sustained by widespread support from workers and cultivators as well as politicians. These observations lead to the conclusion that the EGS is a pork barrel—good for the individual interests of various groups in the short term but bad for society's interests over the long term. In arriving at such a conclusion, the Conflictual Process Perspective neglects some of the redeeming facets of the EGS. The Organizational Environment Perspective illuminates these facets.

EGS IMPLEMENTATION: AN ORGANIZATIONAL ENVIRONMENT PERSPECTIVE

The Organizational Environment Perspective suggests that rational and conflictual processes of implementation are shaped by the manner in which implementing agencies are embedded in their social environment. Specifically, institutionalized rules or cultural norms conditioned the development of the EGS administrative structure; the structure of control over important resources gave the technical departments relative autonomy from cultivators and politicians; and the EGS created a political market that encourages the organization of the rural poor and alters the incentives of administrators and politicians so that they have become more responsive to their constituents' needs.

The Impact of Administrative Culture on the Founding of the EGS

The EGS was shaped in important ways by the administrative culture that predominated in Maharashtra. V. S. Page, the Gandhian politician who is generally regarded as the founder of the EGS, originally made village panchayats the administrative agency for his prototype of the EGS. In fact, village panchayats and block-level panchayat samitis were responsible for implementing the Pilot Employment Guarantee Scheme created in the summer of 1969.[72] Yet by 1974, they played virtually no role in implementing the program. Why was authority over the EGS transferred from the local panchayats to the Revenue Department, technical departments, and zilla parishads? Exploration of this issue is particularly interesting in view of the later efforts by other states, such as West Bengal (see chapter 4), and most recently by the Government of India through the Jawahar Rozgar Yojana to implement comparable public works programs through village panchayats.

The local panchayats' role diminished as the scope and funding of the EGS increased. By 1972, when the Government of Maharashtra committed itself to implementing the EGS statewide, the program was viewed as supplementary to the public works implemented by village panchayats. The funding made available to the village panchayats, however, was so limited that they never were able to absorb more than a small share of the unemployment, and the EGS quickly dwarfed their efforts. The longstanding practice of using the technical departments to implement relief works made it "common sense" that they should be key agencies in implementing an extensive public works program. Furthermore, the technical departments and zilla parishads had gained valuable experience in planning local public works through the drought relief efforts and had proven capable of planning and implementing such works throughout the state.

Instead of transferring the EGS to the departments, why didn't the government transfer the departments' expertise to the panchayats? One reason is that, in the state government's view, the panchayats were not prepared to implement a program that would give them discretion over substantial funding. The state government showed a general reluctance to transfer programs to the panchayats, and it strictly circumscribed their discretion over those that it did transfer by earmarking their funding and elaborating strict guidelines. In addition, most technical department officials resented being placed under the authority of panchayat representatives, especially the less educated ones who predominated in the localities. They would have resisted the changes necessary to enhance the village panchayats' role. Finally, giving panchayats control of the EGS would have made many MLAs uneasy. Maharashtra was one of the few states to prohibit MLAs from participating in the tahsil- and district-level panchayats, and most MLAs had ambivalent attitudes toward them. While they supported the general principles of decentralization, they were wary of giving away control over resources and patronage, which might enable political rivals to build up a base of support. Partly because of this apprehension, the EGS committees set up at the tahsil and district levels enable MLAs to play an active role in guiding implementation.[73]

The Impact of the Structure of Control over Environmental Resources

Observers of the EGS have argued that its implementation is biased in favor of medium and large cultivators. Given the importance of these groups in Maharashtra's rural politics and the role of politicians in the planning of EGS works, these arguments seem plausible. The basis for such contentions is that the assets created under the EGS largely benefit

TABLE 3

DISTRIBUTION OF EGS BENEFITS
AMONG CULTIVATORS

Category of Landowner (in acres)	Percentage of Household Beneficiaries to Total Households	Percentage of Total Households	Percentage of Total Land Benefited	Percentage of Total Land
< 5	21.45	34.32	9.06	7.56
5–12.4	38.62	30.69	26.22	21.06
12.5–25	25.65	21.05	33.05	28.98
> 25	14.28	13.94	31.67	42.40
Total	100.00	100.00	100.00	100.00

SOURCES: Government of India, Programme Evaluation Organisation, Planning Commission, and Government of Maharashtra, Directorate of Economics and Statistics, *Joint Evaluation of Employment Guarantee Scheme of Maharashtra* (New Delhi: Controller of Publications, 1980), pp. 31–32; Government of Maharashtra, Department of Agriculture, *Report on Agricultural Census, 1970–71: Maharashtra State* (Bombay: Central Government Press, 1976), pp. 122, 158, 177, 223.

medium and large cultivators. According to a survey of eight tahsils conducted by the Planning Commission and the Government of Maharashtra, 91 percent of the households benefiting from assets created by the EGS were cultivator households, whereas only 6 percent were households of agricultural laborers. Furthermore, the distribution of the benefits from EGS assets favored medium and large cultivators at the expense of small ones. As table 3 shows, cultivator households owning less than five acres of land composed only 21.45 percent of the cultivator households benefiting from EGS assets, even though they constituted 34.32 percent of all households. Medium cultivators, owning from 5 to 25 acres, fared much better. Though they formed 51.74 percent of all cultivator households, they comprised 64.27 percent of those benefiting from EGS assets. Large farmers did not fare quite so well. They accounted for 13.94 percent of all cultivator households and 14.28 percent of the cultivator households benefiting from EGS assets.

The bias is less prominent when one considers the shares of land benefited. Small cultivators with less than five acres owned 7.56 percent of the land in the eight tahsils and 9.06 percent of the land benefiting from EGS assets. Middle-sized cultivators continued to fare disproportionately well. While their holdings amounted to 50.04 percent of the land, they accounted for 59.27 percent of the land benefiting from EGS projects. Cultivators with more than twenty-five acres owned 42.40 percent and large cultivators only 31.76 percent of the land benefiting from EGS projects.

My study of the EGS in three tahsils in Ahmednagar found that conflicts between workers and landed interests tended to occur less often in underdeveloped areas than in more advanced ones. In the less developed tahsils of Karjat and Parner, the prevalent dryland agriculture means that demand for labor is low, and in the off-season small and sometimes middle-sized landowners work on EGS projects. Another factor is that the assets created by the EGS have more value to cultivators in less developed areas that lack infrastructure. In the more developed Shrirampur tahsil, basic infrastructure of the kind normally constructed by EGS projects already exists. Cultivators feel that they have little to gain from the EGS.

Shrirampur's large share of gross cropped area under surface irrigation fosters conditions that further exacerbate the tensions. Surface irrigation promotes labor-intensive forms of agriculture such as sugarcane cultivation. Despite the demand for labor, agricultural workers sometimes prefer the less demanding work provided by the EGS because harvesting sugarcane is especially strenuous. At the same time, the concentrations of agricultural laborers and small cultivators that form in these areas are more amenable to organization. The conflicts between workers' organizations demanding EGS work and cultivators demanding that EGS projects be shut down place the administration in Shrirampur under more stress.

One of the most striking features of EGS implementation is the relative autonomy of the technical departments. Their control over resources provided by the state to promote rural development has made them powerful actors on the rural scene. The technical departments' claim to a monopoly of technical expertise and their authority over the distribution of the costs and benefits of rural development often provide them with so much power that it is difficult for other groups to make them accountable.

The technical departments' role in land acquisition for EGS projects illustrates the scope of their power. EGS projects such as irrigation tanks and roads often necessitate that landowners forfeit possession of their land to the state. Technical officers are required to collect the signatures of affected landowners on consent forms before beginning the projects. Approximately 80 percent of the landowners turn over their land only after "private negotiations" with technical department officers have preceded formal land acquisition proceedings.[74] Other landowners often attempt to forestall the acquisition of their land, causing delays in the initiation of projects. Resistance on the part of these landowners occurs because they often fail to receive timely and adequate compensation. According to a 1983–84 report of the state legislature's EGS committee, lands were taken from 15,082 owners but compensation had been provided to only 7,200. Not only were cultivators deprived of their land, but the committee noted that many were also compelled to pay land revenue tax even after they had lost possession.[75]

The responsibility for the landowners' predicament lies primarily with the technical departments. In many cases, they take possession of the land but do not inform land acquisition officers in the Revenue Department,[76] thereby delaying the initiation of compensation proceedings and preventing those responsible for the collection of taxes in the Revenue Department from knowing who has lost land to the EGS. The problem persists despite a campaign headed by the chief minister in 1978–79 and repeated complaints to the administration by the state legislature's EGS committee.

The EGS illustrates the remarkable autonomy of the technical departments even in relation to leading state politicians. The state legislature's EGS committee has repeatedly recommended that the authority of the collectors over the technical departments be strengthened.[77] Following the Arun Bhatia controversy, the Gawai Committee also urged that the collector's power over the technical departments be enhanced. The technical departments have succeeded in resisting such moves. According to V. S. Page, the longtime chairman of the state EGS council, they exercise too much political power to allow a diminution of their authority.[78]

The Constitutive Impact of the EGS on Local Politics

The EGS has given the rural poor greater incentive for political activism and organization.[79] In the first place, it creates a factory-like effect similar to that which has historically promoted the organization of trade unions.[80] It concentrates large numbers of workers in one place, places them in similar conditions, and increases their interaction. As a result, it helps to break down social differences and counters the effect of the caste system, which creates divisions among people occupying similar economic positions.[81] It also breaks down gender barriers. The EGS provides employment opportunities for women outside their households (at least 40 percent of EGS workers are women) and thus encourages them to be more active in public life. The fact that wage rates are equal for men and women helps to promote equal rights among the sexes.

By gathering workers in a single place, the EGS reduces spatial impediments to their organization. It places workers under a single employer rather than under multiple and dispersed ones. The state is a more benign employer than most cultivators. It does not actively repress worker organizations as cultivators have been known to do. The availability of alternative employment by the EGS provides a measure of security, so that workers employed in the private sector are less dependent on local elites and therefore can exercise more political independence.

The EGS has promoted a limited but not inconsiderable growth of organization among the rural poor. Some of these organizations focus exclusively on EGS workers, but most are multipurpose voluntary organizations whose activity is not exclusively limited to the EGS. The resources generated by the EGS have created opportunities for politicians as well as for independent organizers. Opposition parties have established organizations that take advantage of the opportunities provided by the EGS. The Janata Party's Shet Majoor Panchayat (Agricultural Workers' Assembly) claims a statewide membership of 24,000 and has used the EGS as an important component in its strategy to expand its membership.[82] In Ahmednagar, the Lal Nishan (Red Flag) Party has supported the organization of the Ahmednagar Zilla Shet Majoor Union. Its leaders claim a membership of 5,000. Three thousand of these members were organized as EGS workers.[83]

Politicians in the ruling Congress Party have probably benefited most from the EGS. EGS constitutive policies, however, have changed their position in the terrain of Maharashtra's rural politics. Even though the Congress Party has dominated rural politics, the political system remains highly competitive because elites vie for power within the party. In the past, success in politics has required support from rural institutions dominated by elites—e.g., sugar cooperatives, District Central Cooperative Banks, and private educational associations. The avail-

ability of the EGS as an alternative resource enhances the potential autonomy of rural politicians from other rural elites.

The EGS alters the political calculus of those politicians who come
to rely on it as a source of support. This point was made clear by the
sabhapati of the Parner panchayat samiti when he remarked that the
EGS sometimes placed him in the middle of a conflict of interests between many workers wanting EGS employment and a few landowners
who want to shut down EGS projects. It compelled him to weigh the
potential gain from the votes of the workers against the losses he would
incur if he defied the fewer but more powerful landowners. By doing
so, the EGS gives the numbers of the workers added weight in his calculations.[84]

The existence of the EGS enables politicians to build independent
political organizations similar to political machines. But—unlike machine organizations, which usually monopolize the distribution of benefits to their popular base of support—the EGS, with its guarantee of
employment, prevents such a monopoly. It facilitates the activation and
organization or workers by opposition parties and voluntary organizations as well as by ruling party politicians. As a result, multiple channels are available to represent workers' interests and increase the opportunities for workers to make politics more responsive to their
perceived needs.

The Impact of the Reconstituted Environment on EGS Implementation

By enhancing the rural poor's incentives for collective action and simultaneously altering the calculus of politicians, the guarantee of employment alters the environment of the government officials responsible
for EGS implementation. It creates pressures on EGS administrators to
respond to the needs of the poor by encouraging them to demand EGS
jobs. In effect, the employment guarantee embeds EGS administrators
in a political market that pressures administrators to respond to different levels in the rural poor's demand for EGS employment. In comparison to the misguided implementation and leakages that characterize
other poverty alleviation programs, the political market created by the
EGS incites administrators to be remarkably responsive to the needs of
the poor.

The EGS is not simply a pork barrel. While the aggregate expenditures on the EGS at the state level show a steady increase, the pattern

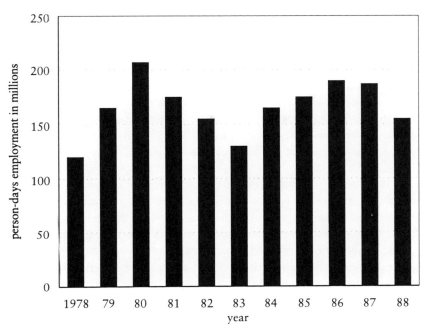

Figure 2.   EGS employment generation, 1978–88. *Source:* Data provided by Planning Department, Government of Maharashtra, Bombay.

of employment generation is much less consistent (see figure 2). EGS employment peaked at 205 million person-days in 1979–80 and then declined to 128 million in 1982–83 before peaking again in 1985–86 at 190 million. The explanatory power of the pork barrel model is further weakened when employment generation is disaggregated to the district level, since EGS employment declined in seven of twenty-four districts between 1975 and 1987.[85] The largest rates of decline were in Raigad and Thane, where EGS employment shrank at annual rates of 36 and 14 percent. Both are located close to Bombay and Maharashtra's industrial belt. In each district, considerable amounts of labor are absorbed through migration to the industrial metropolis. Kohlapur and Jalgaon experienced the next-largest declines. They possessed the first and fourth most productive agriculture of all districts in Maharashtra.[86] The variation in EGS employment generation among the districts suggests that pork barrel politics provides an insufficient explanation of the patterns of EGS employment generation and expenditures. It suggests that local labor market conditions also are important.

The political market created by the EGS makes program implementation remarkably responsive to the requisites of poverty alleviation. First, it effectively targets the poor, so that it efficiently utilizes resources to improve their conditions. Second, the EGS responds to gender inequities that contribute to poverty and exacerbate its social consequences for women. Third, it adjusts to crises (such as droughts and floods) that dramatically increase the need for poverty alleviation measures. Fourth, it responds to the temporal fluctuations in employment caused by the seasonal rhythms of agricultural production. Finally, the EGS responds to the spatial variation in the incidence of poverty.

Targeting the Poor   A program's effectiveness in targeting the rural poor is a function of two variables: the costs imposed on participants and the discretion given to administrators in selecting recipients among those who are willing to incur those costs.[87] The EGS requirement that participants perform manual labor at minimum wages acts as a mechanism for screening out the nonpoor. It seems more effective than other mechanisms, such as means tests, since an individual's willingness to work is less subject to manipulation than other criteria for eligibility. It also provides a more accurate indication of the needs of the rural poor, since it reflects the fluctuations in these needs that occur at different times and in different regions. While the costs imposed on participants screen out individuals not included in the target group, the stipulation guaranteeing employment circumscribes the discretion of administrators selecting EGS participants. Leakage to nontarget groups is relatively insignificant for the EGS. In their survey of 1,500 EGS participants, Dandekar and Sathe found that 90 percent of them lived below the poverty line. According to another survey, by Acharya and Panwalkar, the mean per capita income of households participating in the EGS was Rs. 790, almost 20 percent below the poverty line, and 77 percent had per capita incomes below the poverty line even after receiving EGS wages comprising 31 percent of their income. In still another study, Bhende and his colleagues found a strong inverse relationship between EGS participation and household wealth.[88]

Providing enough employment to absorb the rural poor is a more serious difficulty than leakage to nontarget groups. The guarantee under the EGS has been more effective than similar efforts, such as the Government of India's Rural Landless Employment Guarantee Programme, or its Jawahar Rozgar Yojana. EGS officials like to point out that the government has never had to make unemployment compensation payments to workers who do not receive EGS employment. Nevertheless, in many instances demands for EGS employment have not been met.[89] Workers frequently complain that projects are suddenly shut down when the number of laborers does not meet minimum levels; furthermore, administrative discretion can be utilized to exclude workers by assigning them to distant projects that make the costs of participation prohibitive.[90]

Reducing Gender Inequities   The EGS helps to reduce gender inequities. By giving women an independent source of income, it has lessened their social dependence. In the fiscal year ending in March 1985, 738,000 women worked on the EGS, accounting for 38 percent of all EGS workers.[91] As reported by Acharya and Panwalkar, who compared ninety-four households participating in the EGS and ninety-eight non-participants, the average female contribution of income in participating households was 56 percent, while that in non-EGS households was only 18 percent. In half of the latter households, women were confined to domestic work and did not earn any wages at all.

In contrast to agricultural wages in most areas in Maharashtra, EGS wage rates do not discriminate between genders.[92] Equal pay for women on the EGS enhances their bargaining power in labor markets. Acharya and Panwalkar found that in areas where the EGS was not present, average wages for women were 19 percent less than for men. In EGS areas, the mean for men and women was virtually equal.[93]

Responsiveness to Crises   EGS responsiveness to the demands created by crises was most apparent in 1979–80, when Maharashtra suffered from a sequence of natural disasters. Labor attendance rose sharply after a drought disrupted sowing operations during the 1979 monsoon in western Maharashtra and in the Marathwada region in central Maharashtra. Disaster then hit the eastern region of Vidharbha when August flooding destroyed the paddy crop in many areas. In response, EGS employment increased dramatically. EGS labor attendance from June through August jumped by 56 percent over the average of the preceding and following years for the same period.[94]

Crises can occur at the micro as well as the macro level when local conditions disrupt the income flow of particular households. The EGS helps to stabilize the income of agricultural laborers. According to a survey by Walker, Singh, and Asokan, the households in two villages where the EGS operated had income streams 50 percent less variable than those in a third village where there were no public works.[95]

Acharya and Panwalkar also found that households benefiting from access to the EGS had a much narrower distribution of per capita incomes than comparable households that did not benefit from the EGS. The standard deviation for the income distribution of EGS households was Rs. 543, while that for non-EGS households was Rs. 1901. The major reason for this disparity was that 41 percent of the non-EGS households had annual per capita incomes less than Rs. 250, while only 4.3 percent of the EGS households had incomes at this crisis level.[96] The performance of the EGS has led economist Martin Ravallion to commend the program for its social insurance benefits, which protect the poor from precipitous drops in their income.[97]

Responsiveness to Seasonal Fluctuations in the Demand for Labor
The EGS also appears to adjust to seasonal fluctuations in the demand for labor. Although Maharashtra is a diverse state, the predominant pattern in agricultural production is a single *kharif* crop beginning in July and ending in November or December. Winter cropping is less extensive in most areas, and late spring is the slack point in the agricultural year. According to the National Sample Survey for 1983, unemployment in Maharashtra peaked in the April–June quarter and was lowest in the October to December quarter. EGS employment roughly conforms to the seasonal pattern of unemployment. During April–June 1983, it averaged 798,000 person-days per day—5.1 percent of the total available person-days of employment. From October to December, EGS employment dipped to 348,000 and accounted for only 2.1 percent of the total person-days of employment available.[98]

EGS responsiveness to temporal fluctuations in the demand for labor is even better reflected at the district level, where—according to one study—variations in the seasonal pattern of EGS employment correspond to differences in the cropping patterns among districts. Thus, districts such as Bhandara, whose agriculture is based on a single cropping pattern, have greater variation in EGS employment than districts such as Sangli and Satara, which have more multiple cropping and larger areas under sugarcane—a crop that increases the demand for labor in slack periods.[99]

The EGS and Spatial Differentiation of Poverty in Maharashtra   The EGS is remarkably responsive to the spatial distribution of poverty in Maharashtra—largely because of the political market created by its implementation. Areas with a high incidence of poverty tend to have surplus labor and high rates of underemployment and unemployment. Districts with high underemployment tend to have greater demand for work on the EGS, and administrators create more jobs in these locales. Areas with less underemployment tend to have lower demand, and EGS administrators generate less employment in these areas.

These observations are based on a study that compares the incidence of EGS employment generation in twenty-five districts with thirteen socioeconomic variables that offer plausible hypotheses for explaining the variation in EGS employment. (For details, see the statistical appendix.) The dependent variable is based on data showing monthly EGS employment generation for each of the state's districts from July 1975 through December 1989.[100] The data on EGS employment were summed and divided by the rural labor force, to create a standardized dependent variable. The study's findings show that EGS labor attendance is most highly correlated in districts with high levels of traditional, dryland agriculture. Levels of employment generation are negatively correlated with various indicators of agricultural productivity. Multiple regression analysis also supports these findings. The equation explaining the most variation in EGS labor attendance is one that includes the share of the gross cropped area under dryland agriculture, the percentage of the labor force that is from scheduled tribes, and the percentage of the labor force that is accounted for by scheduled castes. Each variable has a significant positive relation to EGS employment generation. Together they account for 72 percent of the variation in EGS employment among the state's districts. Channeling EGS expenditures to areas with high levels of dryland agriculture, scheduled tribes, and scheduled castes contributes to poverty alleviation, since dryland agriculture is associated with underemployment and poverty while scheduled tribes and scheduled castes represent the most underprivileged groups in the state.

CONCLUDING REMARKS

Our examination of EGS implementation from the Rational Process Perspective revealed ways in which EGS administrators responded to the formidable problems confronting the program. EGS planners attempted to surmount these problems by creating a complex administrative apparatus that promotes decentralized planning and flexibility in response to fluctuations in the demand for employment. An important feature of this apparatus is its matrix structure of authority. The matrix helps to maintain the dual objectives of the program by assigning the Revenue Department responsibility for providing employment to laborers and the technical departments responsibility for ensuring that EGS projects are properly designed and constructed. During the course of implementation, a number of measures have been taken to improve coordination within the matrix.

While the matrix structure of authority seems beneficial from the Rational Process Perspective, it appears disastrous from the Conflictual Process Perspective. Largely because of the cleavage in its administration, administrators lack commitment to EGS objectives. The administrative division of labor generates antagonism between officials from the Revenue Department and the technical departments. Field officers' alienation from the EGS is reinforced by the pejorative attitude toward the program that is pervasive among their departmental superiors. The Revenue Department lacks the means to monitor and supervise the technical officers effectively. All these circumstances foment extensive corruption. From the Conflictual Process Perspective, prospects for resolving these problems are dim. The political clout of the technical departments seems too strong, and politicians appear to have little incentive to bring about changes.

Profuse corruption, the enhancement of the power of ruling party politicians, and the bias in creating assets that favor medium and large cultivators have led many scholars to be highly critical of the EGS.[101] Viewing the program from the Organizational Environment Perspective reveals some positive outcomes that are often unappreciated. By making employment an entitlement, the EGS encourages political mobilization of the rural poor and provides incentives for politicians to be more sensitive to their needs. These changes have incited EGS administrators to be more responsive to the demand for EGS employment throughout the state. Since demand tends to be associated with economically less developed areas, the EGS redistributes expenditures to these areas. In a state that is characterized by uneven development, this is a significant achievement.

The causes of uneven development, corruption, and elite domination in rural Maharashtra are deeply rooted in the state's political economy. In itself, the EGS alters their dynamics only marginally. Nevertheless, making employment an entitlement enhances the political capabilities of less privileged groups and alters the political terrain in a manner that improves the prospects for more equitable development.

CHAPTER 4

Politics Takes Command

Implementation of the National Rural
Employment Programme in West Bengal

In bourgeois parliamentary democracy, the common man has
no political role once he has cast his vote in the election. We
are determined to give him a continuing role in rural
development. When the common villager has realized this
role, he will be able to acquire self-confidence, and take
collective initiative to change the life of the rural poor and
middle class.

> *Promode Das Gupta, General Secretary,*
> *Communist Party of India (Marxist),*
> *West Bengal*

Does public participation in policy implementation enhance or reduce
the effectiveness of programs to help the rural poor? Contentions concerning this question can be grouped into three hypotheses. The Greater
Responsiveness Hypothesis is based on the premise that a substantial
gap exists between government bureaucracy and the poor. Public participation, according to the hypothesis, helps to surmount these problems by creating opportunities for the poor to communicate their needs
to officials. Participation is also said to have an educational impact. It
transforms the poor from objects of development into knowledgeable
subjects of progress. Perhaps most important, popular participation
transfers authority to the public and enhances the ability of the poor to
oblige government officials to respond to their needs.[1]

The Elite Domination Hypothesis posits that increasing the opportunities for public participation reinforces the power of social elites.
Unless political equality is accompanied by measures to establish a
more egalitarian economic order, those who exercise predominant control over economic resources remain socially dominant. In a dialectical
fashion, social elites will employ their power to gain control over the

political space opened by opportunities for public participation; then they will use their political power to reinforce their other modes of social domination.[2]

The Political Patronage Hypothesis is premised on the assumption that public participation is mediated by political parties, nongovernmental organizations (NGOs), and other organizations, whose interests do not necessarily coincide with those of the public. Political parties, for instance, may be more concerned with enhancing their campaign funds and building electoral support than with advancing the interests of the poor. The leaders of parties and NGOs alike can become more interested in advancing their careers and increasing their personal incomes than representing the public interest. Proponents of the Political Patronage Hypothesis contend that enhancing the role of public participation usually increases the opportunities for various forms of political patronage, which leads to corruption of the implementation process and ineffective public policy.[3]

To assess the strengths and weaknesses of these arguments, we need to examine two components of public participation: *the opportunity structure for public participation* and *the process of interest representation*. The opportunity structure refers to the matrix of incentives and disincentives that condition an individual's decision to participate in policy decisions.[4] Reforming state institutions is the most common approach to enhancing the opportunities for public participation. Interest representation includes efforts to influence policy decisions as well as electoral mobilization to affect the selection of representatives with authority over public policy. The nature of interest representation is important because in virtually all cases there is no obvious public interest but, rather, a discourse among competing actors, each striving to take advantage of opportunities to advance his own interests. Disproportionate control over economic, political, and information resources privileges some actors in this discourse, but its nature is also shaped by the opportunity structure for participation and the strategies that different actors employ.

The Greater Responsiveness Hypothesis assumes that altering state institutions to create opportunities for public participation will make antipoverty programs more effective. Advocates of this hypothesis, however, rarely give adequate consideration to the nature of interest representation and the limits it places on the ability of the poor to advocate their interests. The Elite Domination Hypothesis is more cognizant of these limits. By pointing out that elites are privileged in the process of interest representation because they control a preponderant share of economic and political resources, it offers a much less sanguine view of the benefits of popular participation for the poor. Its tendency to equate control over economic resources with control over politics, however, underestimates the potential autonomy of the political process. The Political Patronage Hypothesis provides more scope for the independent impact of politics. Its implications do not necessarily contradict the Elite Domination Hypothesis, since political patronage often occurs within the parameters of elite domination.

Together, the Elite Domination Hypothesis and the Political Patronage Hypothesis suggest a "paradox of participation." Using public participation to make policy responsive to the needs of the poor requires a political process that represents their interests. But as long as the poor remain poor, they are disadvantaged in securing equitable representation. This chapter examines factors that might assist in resolving this paradox. Employing the conceptual framework elaborated in chapter 1, it also examines the evidence for and against these three hypotheses about public participation.

THE SETTING

West Bengal provides a distinctive context for our study of the National Rural Employment Programme (NREP). It spans territory greater than that of Austria and encompasses a population larger than that of France (see Map 2). Although metropolitan Calcutta dominates the state's commercial, political, and cultural life, 74 percent of the state's residents live in its rural hinterland. Situated on the western edge of one of the world's largest river deltas, much of West Bengal is low-lying alluvial soil used largely for paddy cultivation. As one proceeds westward away from the delta, the terrain becomes undulating and the soil is increasingly less fertile laterite. Northern West Bengal ascends to the Himalayan foothills, where commercial crops such as jute and tea become important.

High population density and scarce land combine to make poverty pervasive in rural West Bengal, even by Indian standards. Its rural population density of 466 persons per square kilometer is more than two and a half times greater than the all-India rural average and more than seventeen times greater than the urban and rural average of the United States.[5] More than 30 percent of all households in rural West Bengal are without land.[6] Of the landed households, 89.3 percent had marginal

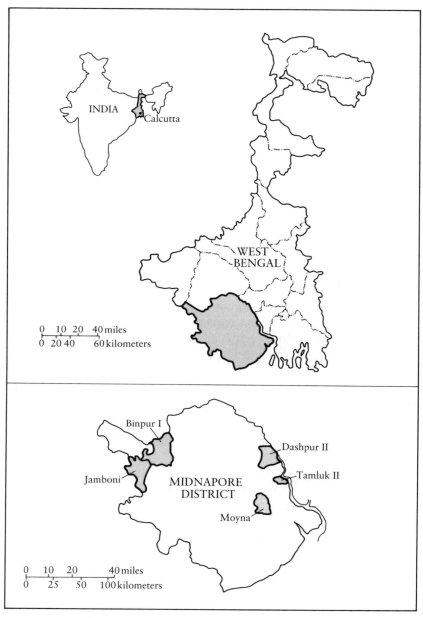

Map 2.   West Bengal.

TABLE 4
DISTRIBUTION OF LANDHOLDINGS
IN WEST BENGAL, 1980−81

Size of Operational Landholdings (in acres)	Percentage of Holdings		Percentage of Area Operated	
	West Bengal	*India*	*West Bengal*	*India*
Marginal (less than 2.5)	69.7	56.6	29.2	12.1
Small (2.5 to 5)	19.6	18.0	31.2	14.2
Semimedium (5 to 10)	8.8	14.0	25.2	21.2
Medium (10 to 20)	1.9	9.0	10.7	29.7
Large (over 20)	0.0	2.4	3.7	22.8
Total	100.0	100.0	100.0	100.0

SOURCE: Government of India, Director of Economics and Statistics, Department of Agriculture and Cooperation, Ministry of Agriculture, "Agricultural Census: All India," *Agricultural Situation in India* 40, no. 5 (August 1985): 410–11.

or small holdings (less than five acres). These holdings cover 60.4 percent of the area operated (see table 4). These figures are considerably higher than the all-India averages of 74.6 percent and 26.3 percent, respectively. The average size of landholdings in West Bengal, at .94 hectares, is just half the all-India average of 1.82 hectares and second lowest of all Indian states.[7] More than 44 percent of all workers in agriculture are employed as agricultural laborers.[8] Sixty-eight percent of West Bengal's rural population lived beneath the poverty line in 1983.[9] In this respect, the state ranks far above the all-India average of 48.4 percent and is second only to Bihar in the incidence of rural poverty.

West Bengal has been ruled by the Communist Party of India (Marxist), or CPI(M), and its allies since 1977. This state of 67 million people is the world's most populous political unit to be ruled by a democratically elected Communist party. The CPI(M) has also established what may well be a record for the duration of a democratically elected Communist government.

With more than 70 percent of the population of West Bengal residing

TABLE 5

SEATS WON BY MAJOR PARTIES IN THE WEST BENGAL ASSEMBLY ELECTIONS, 1967–1991

	1967	1969	1971	1972	1977	1982	1987	1991
Communist Party of India (Marxist)	43	80	111	14	178	174	187	187
Forward Block	13	21	5	0	25	28	26	28
Revolutionary Socialist Party	6	12	3	3	20	19	18	19
Communist Party of India[a]	16	30	13	35	2	7	11	7
Congress (I)	127	55	105	216	20	49	40	43
Janata Party	—	—	—	—	29	—	—	
Others	75	82	40	12	20	17	11	10
Total seats won by Left Front govt.					230	238	251	245
Total assembly seats	280	280	277[b]	280	294	294	293	294

SOURCES: Anjali Ghosh, *Peaceful Transition to Power: A Study of Marxist Political Strategies in West Bengal, 1967–1977* (Calcutta: Firma K. L. Mukhopadhyay, 1981), pp. 89, 145, 167; Election Commission of India, *Report on the General Elections to the Legislative Assemblies* (New Delhi: Controller of Publications, 1979), p. 64; Election Commission of India, *Report on the General Elections to the Legislative Assemblies* (New Delhi: Controller of Publications, 1984), p. 29; Indranil Banerjie, "West Bengal: A Startling Sweep," *India Today,* April 15, 1987, p. 80; and "Tally," *The Telegraph* (Calcutta), June 19, 1991, p. 1.
[a]The CPI has been a member of the Left Front since the 1982 elections.
[b]Elections were countermanded in three constituencies.

in rural areas, political success in Bengali politics requires building a rural constituency. The CPI(M) was largely an urban-based party through the 1960s. Its efforts to cultivate rural support began in earnest in the late 1960s, when it organized militant agitations for agrarian reform. However, the extension of the CPI(M)'s organization into rural areas was limited by a wave of repression unleashed by the central and state governments under the Congress Party during the 1970s.

Despite its success in 178 of West Bengal's 294 state legislative assembly seats in 1977, the CPI(M) faced the task of consolidating its position (see table 5). For one thing, many of the votes it garnered reflected popular protest against Indira Gandhi's authoritarian rule rather than solid support for the CPI(M). Another reason for the insecurity of the party's position was that its success in 1977 came about at least partly because the newly organized Janata Party cut into the constituency of the CPI(M)'s traditional rival, the Congress Party.[10] In short, the CPI(M)'s victory, in alliance with several smaller leftist parties, presented it with the opportunity to consolidate its position as the state's leading party by augmenting its rural support. In this context, implementation of rural poverty alleviation programs like the National Rural Employment Programme gave the CPI(M) a chance to demonstrate its commitment to ameliorating rural poverty and expand its electoral support.

In his incisive analysis of poverty alleviation programs in India, Atul Kohli contends that the regime established by the CPI(M) in West Bengal offers greater promise for effective poverty alleviation than do the conditions established by any other party in his study.[11] Kohli names four factors central to the CPI(M)'s success: its pragmatic approach, coherent leadership, ideological commitment to poverty alleviation, and disciplined organization. These traits, argues Kohli, have enabled the CPI(M) to penetrate the countryside without being co-opted by the landed classes; to institutionalize a reformist orientation in state institutions, primarily through the activation of the panchayats; and to mobilize the poor to buttress state power as an instrument of social reform. If Kohli's analysis is correct, then the CPI(M) has created conditions that are especially favorable for effectively implementing the NREP in West Bengal. Our study will explore some of the implications of Kohli's arguments.

The NREP has two basic objectives. First, it is designed to provide work to unemployed laborers residing in rural areas. To improve the standard of living and nutrition of the rural poor, it pays workers in cash and foodgrains. The program's second objective is to construct durable assets that will improve the infrastructure of rural areas. The assets created by the program are supposed to promote economic growth that will eventually curtail unemployment and poverty. In a country with large amounts of surplus labor and extensive underdeveloped rural areas, the NREP relies on public works to utilize surplus labor to promote economic development.

The NREP has been an important component of the Government of India's campaign to eliminate poverty. It provided a Rs. 24.87 billion outlay for the program during the Seventh Five Year Plan (1985–86 to

1989–90). The NREP was targeted to create 290 million person-days of employment annually during the Seventh Plan. In the first four years of the plan, it created 1,476 million person-days of employment, exceeding its target by 27 percent.[12] In 1986–87, NREP projects built 39,000 kilometers of rural roads. They created minor irrigation works covering 55,000 hectares. NREP projects afforested 215,000 hectares and constructed 159,000 community buildings.[13]

In 1989, the program was given new impetus when the government combined it with the Rural Landless Employment Guarantee Programme (RLEGP) into the Jawahar Rozgar Yojana (JRY). This program was designed to concentrate employment generation in 120 backward districts with acute poverty and unemployment. Funding was almost double the combined previous levels of the NREP and RLEGP in 1989–90, and it was budgeted to remain at approximately this level in 1990–91.[14] This reorganization of India's public works programs makes the experience of the NREP in West Bengal particularly relevant. The Government of India has authorized gram panchayats (village councils) to be the primary implementing agency of the JRY. Because gram panchayats have exercised authority over the NREP and its predecessor programs in West Bengal since 1978, examination of the experience in West Bengal is likely to hold valuable lessons for the new national program.

Shortly after the CPI(M)-dominated Left Front came to power, it began to rejuvenate the state's panchayat system. In 1978, elections for new panchayat officers were held for the first time in fifteen years. Whereas the panchayats had previously served as advisory bodies to local government authorities, the CPI(M) placed local government officials under the authority of the panchayats. The panchayats' power to levy taxes was enhanced, and their incentive to do so was increased by the state government's offer of matching funds. The panchayats' authority was further increased under the Left Front's 1985–86 initiative to decentralize the planning by creating a bottom-up process that enabled each panchayat to propose projects for its constituency. Finally, the Left Front symbolized its commitment to the panchayats by elevating the Department of Panchayats and Community Development to cabinet status.

The panchayat system rejuvenated by the CPI(M) has three tiers. *Gram* (village) panchayats are at the lowest level. Their jurisdiction includes between 8,000 and 15,000 people. Members of gram panchayats are elected from constituencies of approximately 500 voters. The representatives elect a *pradhan* (chairman) from among themselves. The powers of the gram panchayat are largely delegated to the pradhan. Pradhans oversee the financial, record-keeping, and executive activities of the gram panchayats and supervise the staff.[15] There are 3,242 gram panchayats with 45,237 members throughout the state of West Bengal.

Panchayat samitis constitute the middle tier. Their jurisdiction is co-terminous with developmental blocks—the lowest administrative unit of the state government. They encompass 60,000 to 250,000 people and from seven to fifteen gram panchayats. Members of panchayat samitis include representatives elected from constituencies of approximately 2,500 voters, the pradhans of all gram panchayats within the block, and all members of parliament and the state legislative assembly residing in the block. Panchayat samiti members elect a chair, or *sabhapati*. The authority of the panchayat samiti is largely delegated to this office and to eight permanent committees elected from the members. The top government official at the block level, the block development officer (BDO), serves as ex officio executive officer of the panchayati samiti. There are 324 panchayat samitis in West Bengal.

The *zilla parishads* are at the top tier of the system. Their jurisdiction is coterminous with the districts of the state. They include populations of 1.24 million to 11 million. Members of a zilla parishad include representatives elected from two constituencies per block, the *sabhapatis* of all panchayat samitis in the district, and all members of parliament and members of the state legislative assembly that reside in the block. Members of the zilla parishad elect a chair, or *sabhad hipati,* and eight permanent committees to carry out most of its business. The state government's top official at the district level, the district magistrate, serves as executive officer of the zilla parishad. There are fifteen zilla parishads in West Bengal.

Each of the three tiers of West Bengal's panchayat institutions is involved in implementing the NREP. When the program was first initiated, authority over planning and implementation was vested with the gram panchayats. Since October 1982, NREP funding has been divided so that 20 percent is placed under the control of the zilla parishads. The 80 percent of the funding remaining with the gram panchayats is commonly called "small NREP"; the funds used by the zilla parishads are referred to as "big NREP." This distinction reflects the difference in the scale of projects undertaken at the different levels. Panchayat samitis play a relatively minor role. They suggest large NREP projects to the zilla parishads. Their office provides technical assistance to the gram panchayats, and they coordinate small NREP projects that span the borders of single gram panchayats.

The analysis in this chapter is based on intensive fieldwork in Midnapore district, in addition to interviews with government officials, politicians, and members of the public at the state and national levels and examination of official records and the relevant secondary literature. Midnapore is the second-largest district in West Bengal, with a population of 6.74 million. It is a rural, agricultural district. Ninety-two percent of its population resides in rural areas, and 76 percent of its "main workers" are engaged in agriculture.

Poverty is widespread. Sixty-three percent of all landholdings are one hectare or less. Nearly 75 percent of the families engaged in agriculture are dependent on wage labor as a source of income. Agriculture, however, is not a lucrative occupation. Because of technological backwardness and lack of infrastructure, the agricultural sector generates an average of less than 120 days of employment per worker. The average daily wage is estimated to be ten rupees (less than one dollar). Midnapore's district planning officer estimates that a member of the average family of agricultural laborers consumes an incredible daily average of 300 grams of foodgrain; their estimated minimum daily requirement is 800 grams.[16] In short, Midnapore is a district where the NREP has the potential for dramatic impact.

NREP performance in Midnapore was slightly above average by West Bengal standards. The percentage of budget allotments that were used in Midnapore from fiscal year 1981–82 through 1983–84 was 108.6 percent—slightly above the average of 104.5 percent for all districts in West Bengal. It placed Midnapore fifth out of the state's fifteen districts. The average cost of generating a person-day of employment in Midnapore from 1981–82 to 1983–84 was 8.31 rupees. This amount was lower than the 8.80-rupee average for all districts and ranked Midnapore fourth out of fifteen.[17]

An important reason for choosing to study NREP implementation in Midnapore is that the district includes considerable variation in ecology and economic development. It is divided into two major ecological zones. The major ecological division is the state highway running from Garbheta in the north to Danton in the south. West of this divide is the undulating extension of the Chota Nagpur plateau. The soil is a laterite, often sandy loam. Erratic monsoons make agriculture somewhat uncertain, and the limited scope of irrigation restricts double cropping. East of the divide lies the relatively more fertile alluvial deposits of the

Hoogli River and its tributaries. The black alluvial soil is well suited for paddy cultivation. The climate is humid, and the average rainfall is abundant (154 centimeters). The area's major ecological problem is that it is subject to natural catastrophe. Its lowlands suffer periodic flooding when monsoon rains overflow from silted riverbeds. The littoral in the extreme south of the eastern region constitutes an ecological subregion. The soil and groundwater of this tract are susceptible to problems with salinity.

Levels of agricultural development roughly parallel these ecological zones. Comparison of data from the Tamluk and Ghatal subdivisions in eastern Midnapore with the Jhargram subdivision in western Midnapore dramatizes the difference. Productivity of *aman* (July to October) paddy is 1.85 metric tons per hectare in the east as opposed to 1.36 in the west. Productivity of *boro* (February to May) paddy is 3.14 metric tons per hectare in the east as opposed to 2.94 in the west. The eastern subdivisions consume 185 kilograms of fertilizer per hectare, whereas Jhargram subdivision consumes 108 kilograms per hectare. Cropping intensity is also greater in the east than the west. The percentage of gross cropped area to net cropped area is 148 percent in the eastern subdivisions. In western Midnapore, it is 127 percent.[18]

The present study was designed to take advantage of this diversity. Intensive research was conducted in five of Midnapore's blocks, which were selected on the basis of two variables. Since the purpose was to investigate whether different levels of agricultural development had an impact on NREP implementation, each block was ranked according to an index of agricultural development.[19] The second variable explored was whether the dominance of different political parties over a block's panchayat institutions was significant. District blocks were divided by the political party that controlled a majority of the gram panchayats and the panchayat samitis.

Combining the two variables creates a fourfold grid (see figure 3). Blocks to fill each of the table's quadrants were selected. Moyna and Tamluk II were chosen because they ranked first and second on the index of agricultural development. While these relatively developed blocks share common agricultural conditions, they are under the political control of different parties—the Congress (I) and the CPI(M), respectively. Binpur I and Jamboni were selected because they were less developed blocks. They ranked 30 and 38 on the index of agricultural development. Though similar agricultural conditions characterize these contiguous blocks, they are under the control of different political par-

	Party in Power	
	---	---
	CPI (M)	OPPOSITION
More Developed	Tamluk II Dashpur II	Moyna
Less Developed	Jamboni	Binpur I

Figure 3.   Selection of blocks in Midnapore.

ties. The panchayat institutions in Binpur I are largely controlled by the Jharkhand Party. The CPI(M) dominates those in Jamboni. The fifth block chosen was Daspur II, a relatively developed block (ranked eleventh) also under control of the CPI(M). Its inclusion provides more representative weightage for the CPI(M) in the total sample.[20]

Research in each block was divided into three parts. First, survey interviews were conducted with the pradhans and secretaries of the gram panchayats in the block. In total, thirty-six pradhans and forty-four secretaries (67 percent and 80 percent of the total number of all pradhans and secretaries in the blocks) were interviewed. Each came to the block office and provided written responses to a schedule of sixty-four structured and unstructured questions. Second, block development officers and members of their staff involved in implementing the NREP were interviewed. The third phase included interviews with local political leaders and members of the program's attentive public.

NREP IMPLEMENTATION:
A RATIONAL PROCESS PERSPECTIVE

Proponents of the Rational Process Perspective contend that implementing agencies exemplify the process of "dynamic rationality." That is, they make periodic, if not continuous, adjustments to ensure that their programs become more effective means for obtaining policy objectives. Planning and monitoring implementation are the important components of dynamic rationality. Planners design organizational structure to maximize efficiency, taking into account implementation technologies, information processing needs, transaction costs, and environmental contingencies. Monitoring, of course, is the source of information providing the basis for adjusting implementation to improve its effectiveness.

In planning for the NREP and its predecessor programs, officials of the Government of West Bengal concluded that they could make implementation more effective by altering the opportunity structure for participation. They therefore decided to incorporate panchayat institutions into the administrative network responsible for implementing the program. This move extended the network in two dimensions. It extended it vertically to include gram panchayats, a more basic level of administration. Government planners felt that if public works programs like the NREP were to be successful, planning and implementation would have to be performed at a level below the block.[21] By incorporating gram panchayats into the administrative network, they created a more localized unit. The inclusion of panchayat institutions also extended the administrative network by including politicians and the general public. The literature on relations between bureaucrats and politicians in India usually stresses the tensions that arise.[22] In this case, in contrast, bureaucrats repeatedly told me that incorporation of panchayats facilitated implementation for those who were able to make the necessary adjustments. According to these officials, block development officers had to adjust from having the final word to being more like a captain of a team. The preeminent district official, the district magistrate, was also obliged to adjust. He told me, "Decisions are less individual and more collective. . . . I now have a symphony to work with. I have to conduct it." [23]

Not all bureaucrats have made the transition, but those who have find that working with panchayat institutions provides an array of advantages. At the block level, they often act as a buffer between the public and the block development officer. They seem to have reduced the number of disruptions of the administration. A survey by the Home Department of the Government of West Bengal found that since the rejuvenation of the panchayats in 1978, the number of *gheraos* (demonstrations) against block development officers has declined throughout the state.[24] Jamboni's block development officer told me that gram panchayat members are helpful because they can use social pressure to dissuade recalcitrant individuals from interfering with NREP implementation. Midnapore's district planning officer observed that panchayati raj institutions improve the performance of block development officers by providing them with "detailed knowledge of the needs of their block." [25]

Similarly, panchayat institutions facilitate the work of district-level administrators. A former district magistrate, then serving as director of the Department of Panchayats, stated that the district magistrate "can use zilla parishad politicians to control 'their people' and prevent law-and-order problems.[26] Midnapore's district magistrate related that he prefers to work through panchayat institutions because of the way they structure his relations with politicians. Previously, members of the legislative assembly and parliament would unexpectedly appear and make demands. The existence of the zilla parishads regularizes interaction with politicians. The district magistrate often finds the zilla parishad a useful organizational buffer because he can refer other politicians to it.[27] Panchayat institutions even provide a means for the district magistrate to keep other district officials in line. Conflicts between the magistrate and departmental engineers can arise just as they do between any generalist and technocrat. District magistrates can use their influence over the zilla parishad to curb the opposition of technocrats.[28]

The incorporation of panchayats into the implementation process increases government officials' administrative capacity. By serving as a focus for interest representation, they simultaneously increase the flow of information to officials and serve as buffers insulating them from disturbances. They also enhance the government's capacity for social control. This increase in power has positive and negative consequences. On the positive side, government officials have used the panchayats to collect unpaid irrigation taxes and help detect power theft.[29] At the same time, corporatist collusion between government officials and panchayat officials can insulate decision making from popular demands and render authorities less accountable to the public. This repressive aspect of the new institutional arrangements was illustrated by the comments of a block development officer from Purulia district, who observed that with the incorporation of the panchayats into the policy process, government personnel or panchayat officials could get away with actions that previously would have caused a riot.[30]

Extension of the implementation network to the gram panchayat level was intended to improve the planning of projects. The members of the gram panchayats, being elected representatives of local communities, are presumed to have an intimate knowledge of local needs. They are more familiar with local problems than officials such as the block development officer, who are usually outsiders posted for relatively short periods. Furthermore, decentralization to the gram panchayats neutralizes the shortcomings of decision-making authorities, since it makes them more accessible to the public at large.[31] It was hoped that gram panchayats would use their superior knowledge to design projects more suitable to local needs and devise more efficient ways of constructing the projects.

After devolving authority over NREP implementation, in 1985–86 the Left Front attempted to improve the implementation of rural development programs by creating a system of decentralized planning.[32] Gram panchayats were authorized to prepare a "needs statement" for their constituency. Panchayat samitis were ordered to incorporate these statements into block-level plans describing ongoing and proposed developmental projects. These plans were then assembled into district plans by District Planning Committees (DPCs), whose membership included the *sabhapatis* of the district's panchayat samitis, the chairs of all municipalities in the district, the *karmadhyakshas* (executive committee) of the zilla parishad, and officials from the government departments. The DPC was chaired by the *sabhadhipati* of the zilla parishad. The district plan was then vetted by the District Planning and Coordination Council, which, in addition to the members of the DPC, included the district's members of Parliament and the state legislative assembly. The DPCC was chaired by a minister in the state government.

This system of decentralized planning was intended to improve the system of planning in three ways. First, the new system was designed to take into account the diversity of developmental needs among different localities. It was also hoped that the bottom-up process would encourage popular participation in planning. Finally, by increasing the input from the grass roots, the decentralization of planning was intended to improve coordination among various programs, since localities were better positioned to see their complementarities and conflicts.[33]

Implementing the NREP through panchayat institutions has achieved these objectives to at least some extent. Critics often allege that planning in India has an institutional bias favoring the creation of new assets rather than the maintenance and improvement of old ones. As a result, the country suffers from increasing capital-output ratios. Rural inhabitants experience this phenomenon in their everyday life through the inefficient disrepair of irrigation canals, roads, buildings, embankments, and tubewells. NREP planning through panchayat institutions overrides this bias by making planning more accessible to the everyday experience of rural inhabitants. Examination of the plans for 453 projects in thirty-seven of forty-four gram panchayats in four blocks in Midnapore shows that 55 percent of all projects and 45 percent of allocated expenditures were for the maintenance and repair of

TABLE 6

PERCENTAGE DISTRIBUTION OF NREP
EXPENDITURES IN 1984–85 FOR THIRTY-SEVEN
GRAM PANCHAYATS IN FOUR MIDNAPORE BLOCKS[a]

Category	New Projects	Maintenance of Existing Assets	Improvement of Existing Assets	Total
Roads	45.4	45.8	8.8	100
Schools and community buildings	41.7	52.1	6.2	100
Irrigation and drainage	63.1	29.9	6.9	99.9
Drinking water and tubewells	26.8	73.2	—	100
Forestry	100			100
Scheduled caste and scheduled tribe development	63.1	29.9	—	100
Total	48.8	44.9	6.3	100.00

SOURCE: Annexure A forms collected from the block offices of Jamboni, Binpur I, Tamluk II, and Dashpur II, Midnapore district, West Bengal.
    [a]These figures do not include all expenditures made by the gram panchayats, since Annexure A forms were unavailable for all allotments. The total expenditures included in this table are Rs. 949,478. This total excludes Rs. 44,865 in miscellaneous expenditures.

existing assets. In addition, 6 percent of the projects and 6 percent of allocations were for improvement of assets (see table 6).

Despite the advantages, implementing the NREP through the panchayats creates substantial problems. Although public participation at the local level is supposed to improve coordination between the NREP and other programs, most authorities did not know how to coordinate the programs. When I asked Midnapore's *sabhadhipati* about coordination between the NREP and the Integrated Rural Development Scheme (IRDP), he replied, "How can there be? The NREP creates collective assets while the IRDP distributes loans to scattered individuals." In addition to the lack of coordination between the NREP and other antipoverty programs, the *sabhadhipati* told me that there had been little coordination between the NREP and the work of the state government departments. The district planning officer stated that there had been no linkage between the NREP and the district plan.[34] Even Benoy Chowdhury, minister for Rural Development, Land Reform, and Panchayats, admitted that there was a lack of coordination.[35] It was precisely this problem that the initiative for decentralized planning was intended to change. One of the main advantages of the new system is that it places the NREP within the framework of a district plan.[36]

Planning at the gram panchayat level suffers many problems. Some are attributable to the irregular provisions of NREP funding. Gram panchayats usually are notified that they are to receive a certain sum for the following fiscal year. They are asked to formulate plans on the basis of this amount. Rarely, however, is this amount made available to them over the year. For instance, although gram panchayats were supposed to receive between Rs. 50,000 and Rs. 60,000 in fiscal years 1983–84 and 1984–85, the funds actually made available to the gram panchayats in Jamboni block amounted to only Rs. 27,000 and Rs. 30,000. According to Jamboni's block development officer, "Previously, gram panchayats made ambitious plans and were disappointed when they got inadequate funds. Subsequently, they wait until allotments are made and then submit plans."[37]

The tendency to neglect advance planning in favor of last-minute planning once funds are in hand is widespread. In my survey of eighty pradhans and secretaries, 68 percent (fifty of seventy-four) of the respondents said that they wait until allotments are physically available before they plan their usage. The problem appears to be statewide. On January 7, 1983, the secretary of the Government of West Bengal wrote a letter to *sabhadhipatis* and district magistrates complaining about his lack of information concerning plans for NREP projects.[38]

For a number of reasons, the gram panchayats tend to take up very small projects; the average cost of one project in the plans of the thirty-seven gram panchayats that I examined was less than Rs. 2,000. Since they delay their planning until funds are physically available, they have only small amounts—usually around Rs. 15,000—to begin with. Funds are further dispersed because political considerations encourage each member of the gram panchayat to secure projects for his or her own constituency. In addition, if a gram panchayat decides to take up a large project, it faces bureaucratic disincentives. It must secure governmental sanction for any project costing more than Rs. 5,000. To circumvent this requirement, gram panchayats deciding to take up more costly projects often divide them into phases.[39] The lack of technical expertise available to gram panchayats also encourages them to take up small projects. Their members usually lack the necessary technical training, and—despite government training programs—the job assistants provided for each gram panchayat usually do not have the expertise necessary to plan sophisticated projects. Subassistant engineers at the block office have the expertise, but they are often preoccupied with other responsibilities.[40] The result is that gram panchayats tend to avoid technically complex projects, and they sometimes make mistakes in project construction.[41]

Implementing the NREP through the panchayats has attenuated administrative accountability. According to a survey conducted by the Government of West Bengal, at least 25 percent of the gram panchayats did not maintain proper records concerning public works programs. Another study of panchayat institutions in Midnapore found that official supervision of gram panchayat finances was inadequate because extension officers for panchayats were overworked and unable to carry out necessary audits.[42] Delays in the collection of utilization certificates are another manifestation of the erosion of the panchayats' accountability. Upon spending NREP funds, gram panchayats are required to submit utilization certificates to the block development officer, who collects them for the entire block and sends them to the district. The same process occurs at the district and state levels until utilization of NREP funds is certified by the central government. States must certify utilization of 50 percent of their installments before the central government will provide another. Delays at different levels of the administrative hierarchy can accumulate and prevent the state from acquiring the funds authorized to it by the central government. Such delays have contributed to West Bengal's relatively low rate of NREP fund utilization. As table 7 reveals, West Bengal's rate of utilizing available NREP resources has been among the lowest for all Indian states with a population greater than five million. Its 74.4 percent average rate of utilization during the 1980s is the second lowest of all states.

Government officials gave four reasons for the delays. First, an extension officer (panchayat) told me that some gram panchayats have trouble keeping records according to government guidelines.[43] Second, since responsibility for NREP projects is often divided among different members of the gram panchayat, information must be collected from different members.[44] Also, the larger the number of members involved in project supervision, the greater the likelihood that irresponsible

TABLE 7

NREP RESOURCES UTILIZED AS A PERCENTAGE OF RESOURCES AVAILABLE ANNUALLY BY STATES WITH POPULATIONS OF MORE THAN FIVE MILLION[a]

State	1981–82	1982–83	1983–84	1985–86	1986–87	1987–88	1988–89	Average 81–82 to 88–89
Andhra Pradesh	72.9	73.3	70.1	101.2	91.6	77.1	108.0	84.9
Assam	50.1	63.6	47.4	67.3	102.6	67.2	67.3	66.5
Bihar	52.1	70.2	65.1	97.3	83.7	106.2	106.0	82.9
Gujarat	39.8	76.1	96.0	73.9	85.4	112.6	85.2	81.3
Haryana	74.9	72.8	77.2	102.0	97.6	88.9	104.5	88.3
Jammu and Kashmir	83.1	65.7	80.4	67.5	87.4	109.8	93.1	83.9
Karnataka	57.1	73.2	75.1	90.5	65.4	90.8	117.8	81.4
Kerala	96.7	72.2	76.7	81.7	106.0	74.6	119.0	89.6
Madhya Pradesh	100.0	93.0	84.9	71.6	101.3	94.2	112.8	94.0

TABLE 7 (continued)

State	1981–82	1982–83	1983–84	1985–86	1986–87	1987–88	1988–89	Average 81–82 to 88–89
Maharashtra	100.0	52.7	60.8	100.3	104.9	94.8	78.8	84.6
Orissa	61.1	48.4	46.6	106.8	103.5	93.1	127.8	83.9
Punjab	100.0	94.0	98.3	100.0	100.0	81.7	94.9	95.6
Rajasthan	74.3	72.2	71.6	83.6	103.6	111.2	92.1	86.9
Tamil Nadu	71.6	84.9	90.3	88.7	112.0	84.9	130.5	94.7
Uttar Pradesh	67.8	73.3	78.1	98.6	85.3	73.3	123.9	85.6
West Bengal	42.8	62.8	66.1	72.3	114.0	87.0	74.4	74.2
Average for states above	71.5	71.8	74.0	87.7	96.5	90.5	102.3	84.9

SOURCE: Computations from data provided by the Government of India, Ministry of Agriculture and Rural Development, Department of Rural Development, Report on the National Rural Employment Programme (New Delhi: Government of India Press, 1985), Annexures II–IV, and Annual Report, 1989 (New Delhi: Government of India Press, 1989), Annexures XIII–XVI.
[a]Data for 1984–85 are not available.

members will gain authority. A third reason is that delays in submitting utilization certificates are increased because gram panchayats create a lot of paperwork by taking up so many small projects.[45] Finally, some say that the delays are caused because the gram panchayats are understaffed. Pradhans fulfill their responsibilities on a part-time basis only. And despite the fact that gram panchayats maintain two full-time employees, I was told, "If a gram panchayat office was a government office spending the equivalent money, it would have at least five staff to fulfill its responsibilities."[46]

Given the scope of poverty in West Bengal, the inability of the panchayats to absorb more NREP funding is a blemish on their poverty alleviation record. The annual average of employment generated in West Bengal from 1985–86 to 1988–89 was 16.6 million person-days; each year, some 664,000 persons—17 percent of the state's agricultural laborers—received twenty-five extra days of employment through the NREP.[47] According to a study of India's fourteen largest states, West Bengal had by far the greatest disparity between its share of NREP employment and its share of the "ultra-poor"—i.e., those whose incomes are at most 80 percent of the level of income specified as the poverty line. It generated only 3.1 percent of NREP employment while it included 12.7 percent of the ultra-poor.[48]

Another reason for West Bengal's low rate of utilization is that distribution of NREP funds does not take adequate account of the economic disparities within districts. Funds are allocated among West Bengal's fifteen districts on the basis of a formula that provides 75 percent weightage to the number of agricultural laborers in the district and 25 percent to the population of scheduled castes and tribes. Zilla parishads then distribute small NREP funds to gram panchayats in equal shares. The rationale for allocating equal shares is to facilitate the public's evaluation of the performance of their gram panchayat relative to that of others.[49] Conditions confronting the gram panchayats, however, vary considerably.

Level of agricultural development is a good indicator of need for NREP projects. Since agricultural development in West Bengal is usually achieved through labor-absorbing technology (such as irrigation, increased application of fertilizer, and higher-yielding varieties of seeds), relatively less developed areas are likely to have more underemployment and unemployment. The rudimentary assets created by NREP projects are also likely to be more highly valued in less developed areas, where there is less basic infrastructure. In Midnapore, the areas with the highest levels of agricultural productivity and development also tend to be those with limitations on the extent to which the NREP can be implemented. The *sabhapati* in Moyna told me that in areas like his block the intensity of cultivation and frequent floods make NREP implementation all but impossible for ten months out of the year.[50] The same is true to a lesser extent in Dashpur II and Tamluk II blocks. In contrast, blocks like Jamboni and Binpur I faced no such limitations.

In view of these circumstances, it is plausible to hypothesize that utilization of NREP funds will be higher in blocks with relatively less agricultural development. The data from Midnapore support this hypothesis. The five least developed blocks utilized 90.1 percent of their NREP funding from April 1, 1983, to February 20, 1985, while the most developed five utilized only 64.4 percent.[51]

The differences in rates of utilization suggest that, rather than allotting funds equally among the gram panchayats within a district, the Government of West Bengal might use NREP funds more effectively by allowing different allocations for the gram panchayats of different blocks within a district. Funds would thereby be given to blocks with the most need and the greatest capacity to absorb them. Increasing the rates of utilization by gram panchayats would increase the utilization rates reported by the districts and, in turn, the state's utilization rate.

My fieldwork uncovered a troublesome gap in monitoring processes of implementation. The government lacks a mechanism to verify whether expenditures made on paper have properly materialized in the field. Overreporting of physical achievement has been a common form of corruption in other public works programs. Projects may not meet specifications, or at times they may not exist at all. The absence of mechanisms for monitoring expenditures encourages corruption.

In sum, the Rational Process Perspective shows the consequences of implementing the NREP through panchayats to be a mixed bag. Devolving administrative responsibilities onto the democratically elected panchayat members has promoted a cooperative relationship between bureaucrats and politicians. By decentralizing authority over implementation, it has made decision making more accessible to the public at large. There is considerably greater public involvement in NREP planning and implementation than in other programs, although the difference is difficult to measure. In addition, the delegation of authority over developmental expenditures to the panchayats has encouraged a parallel decentralization of the activities of political parties and related organizations. As a result of these changes, NREP projects appear to better conform with local needs.

The consequences of popular participation also have a downside. The development of cooperative relations between local politicians and bureaucrats can degenerate into collusion that insulates these authorities from popular accountability. Gram panchayats plan projects that are too small. They lack the technical expertise to implement sophisticated projects. Their ability to absorb available funds was disappointing. Many gram panchayats failed to keep adequate records—an especially troublesome problem given the absence of systematic bureaucratic checks on their performance. However, because of the constraints placed on them by the process of interest representation, the performance of the panchayats was better than what one might expect given the paucity of bureaucratic controls. To understand these constraints more fully, we must take into account the insights of the Conflictual Process Perspective.

NREP IMPLEMENTATION:
THE CONFLICTUAL PROCESS PERSPECTIVE

The Conflictual Process Perspective contends that implementation is shaped primarily by conflicts. With regard to policy implementation, conflicts arise from three sources: (1) conflict between values and goals of individuals in an administrative network and the objectives of implementation; (2) organizational conflict in an administrative network; (3) conflicts between actors in the administrative network and their social environment.

The attitudes and actions of NREP workers often conflict with the program's objectives. Forty-five percent of pradhan and secretary respondents (thirty-one of sixty-nine) said that supervisors of NREP projects encountered problems with workers. Specifically, laborers would demand full wages even though they had not performed the required amount of work; they asked for higher wages; they became unruly when there were more workers present than available jobs; and they became hostile when funds ran out and they could no longer be employed. Some workers lack the motivation for hard work. One pradhan in Jamboni observed, "It is difficult to get the required amount of work done because many people confuse NREP work with relief."

The problems with workers are concentrated in the less developed blocks. Forty-seven percent of the respondents in these blocks said that they had problems with workers, while only 33 percent had problems in the developed blocks. Similarly, when asked to name "the two most important problems that arise during the implementation of the NREP," 47 percent (fifteen of thirty-two) in the less developed blocks listed labor problems, while only 6 percent (three of forty-eight) did so in the developed blocks.

Lack of worker motivation is detrimental to everyone involved with the program. Workers lose self-esteem. The public gets short-changed because the works projects do not produce productive assets, and the program becomes discredited. Measures to ensure that laborers work hard would help to maintain the developmental advantages of the program and prevent it from becoming a burdensome dole.

The corruption that arises as a consequence of using program resources for private benefit is an even more serious problem. Leakage of NREP funds takes many forms. Grain dealers were accused of providing substandard and short-weighted foodgrains. Panchayat samiti members were accused of attempting to implement a "big NREP" project through a contractor, so that they could enrich themselves by receiving kickbacks. A subassistant engineer reported that he was asked to add nonexistent workers to the payroll of a big NREP project.[52] And all too frequently members of gram panchayats were alleged to have appropriated NREP funds for their personal use.[53] The manner in which responsibilities are allocated among gram panchayat members creates circumstances conducive to corruption and patronage. Gram panchayats frequently give individual members responsibility for implementing projects in their constituencies. They also provide funding for the project in advance. This system creates opportunities for corruption that members often find irresistible.[54]

The extent of corruption cannot be gauged with any precision. In my study of the panchayat institutions in five blocks for the seven years since 1978, I found that gram panchayat members were expelled from office because of alleged corruption in eleven of fifty-five panchayats. Midnapore's district magistrate reported instances of corruption in sixteen of the panchayats that he investigated from 1983 to 1985.[55] These findings suggest that nearly one out of five gram panchayats is guilty of corruption. To put this rough indication in context, however, one would need answers to several questions: How does corruption in the panchayats compare to corruption in the government bureaucracy? (Serious charges were leveled against one of the block development officers in the five blocks that I studied.)[56] To what extent is panchayat corruption more vulnerable to detection because of the more open nature of implementation by the panchayats? Is the corruption in panchayats being reduced over time?

The design of NREP implementation in West Bengal reduces conflict in the administrative network to a large extent; implementation of small NREPs is left exclusively to the gram panchayats, and there is virtually no need for cooperation between different agencies. Conflicts between actors in the administrative network occur mainly along party lines in the gram panchayats. In Midnapore, more than 90 percent of gram panchayat members have party affiliations.[57] Theoretically, the party that controls the gram panchayat can implement the NREP accordingly to its will. Indeed, I came across a case where cooperation between the two parties with representatives in the gram panchayat had completely broken down after opposition members began to boycott panchayat meetings. Representatives from the majority party were able to continue operating the panchayat on their own.[58] Matters become more delicate when party majorities are insecure. Pradhans must take care to maintain their majorities. Midnapore's district panchayat officer told me that in the twenty months following the 1983 panchayat elections, as many as 25 pradhans and *upa-pradhans* (vice-chairmen) have lost their majority. Thus, control over approximately 5 percent of Midnapore's 516 gram panchayats changed hands. These changes usually result when gram panchayat members defect from one party to another. Political loyalty is weaker at the gram panchayat level than at any other level of the panchayat system. As a result, panchayats with insecure majorities take longer to reach decisions and are more susceptible to dividing up funding to satisfy the members' demands for patronage.[59]

Outside of the administration, political parties are by far the most important actors that influence NREP implementation. The CPI(M), in particular, exerts considerable influence over how the NREP is implemented. Its organization parallels that of the panchayats. For every gram panchayat, there are branch committees. Local committees and panchayat samitis usually function at the block level. Zilla parishads and district committees operate at the district level. Though the specific nature of relations between party and NREP implementation varies with the people involved, I have gathered sufficient information to provide a general overview.

The CPI(M)'s organization plays an important role in planning. When the availability of NREP funds is announced, local committees convene meetings that include CPI(M) pradhans and members of the party's branch committees. Everyone is instructed to hold meetings with villagers to discuss local needs. The local committee secretary convenes a second meeting to discuss the information gathered and set priorities. The pradhans and other party members then present the decisions reached at the meetings for approval by their respective gram panchayats.[60]

The party also plays a supervisory role in NREP implementation. Party officials frequently visit NREP projects to investigate their progress. They are sometimes called on to help resolve disputes. Eighty-one percent of my survey respondents (sixty-five of eighty) said that those responsible for supervising implementation included either party members or panchayat members, most of whom have a party affiliation. One party official claimed that the CPI(M) local committee in his block performs an internal audit of the gram panchayats.[61]

CPI(M) officials also exert considerable influence over the zilla parishads. Once a week, members of the district committee meet with the party's zilla parishad members. They review the performance of the various programs under the zilla parishad's purview and reach collective decisions on how performance can be improved.[62]

In sum, the stated objective of the CPI(M)'s role in NREP implementation is to guide the process. The party's cadres encourage members of the public to voice their opinions on matters of implementation. The party also evaluates implementation performance and monitors implementation to improve its effectiveness. The party serves as an important means of curtailing corruption. In the five blocks that I studied, at least six of the ten CPI(M) pradhans who left office on charges of corruption were forced to do so because the party had expelled them. I was also told that between 1978 and 1985 the district committee of the CPI(M) expelled five of the party's zilla parishad members for corruption.[63]

Although political parties enhance the capacity of the administrative network, their role is mediated by their organizational interests. As a consequence, implementation is shaped by party interests. The disparity between the limited economic opportunities offered by the NREP and the employment and infrastructural needs of rural West Bengal makes the temptation to favor supporters virtually irresistible. I came across charges that employment was given to supporters of the party in power while others were excluded.[64] Party workers agitated for payment of higher wages than those sanctioned by the official wage schedule; they attempted to secure payment of *mate* (wages) for supervision of projects even though such work was superfluous.⁶⁵ Project sites were selected to benefit party supporters while the land of others went neglected.⁶⁶ Allegations were made that program funds were siphoned off into party coffers.⁶⁷ In short, the NREP presents parties with the opportunity to secure resources to strengthen their organization and build support. There is a general consensus that all parties avail themselves of the opportunities for patronage to some extent, though the degree to which implementation is distorted is difficult to measure.

While the political process provides avenues for corruption, it also creates mechanisms to constrain its scope. Voters have frequently used electoral sanctions against panchayat members with a reputation for corruption. In Moyna block, the CPI(M) has dominated local politics ever since 1977. It won the panchayat elections in 1978. It defeated the Congress (I) Party in the 1982 state legislative assembly elections for the Moyna constituency by 10,000 votes. It stemmed the tide in favor of Rajiv Gandhi by winning 2,000 votes more than the Congress (I) Party in the parliamentary elections in 1984. Yet it lost the panchayat elections in 1983 when the Congress (I) Party won control over seven of the block's eleven gram panchayats. What is the cause of this anomaly? The most persuasive explanation is that three CPI(M) pradhans became mired in charges of corruption. These charges created a popular backlash against the party at the local level and caused its defeat.⁶⁸

A similar situation occurred in Binpur I. The CPI(M) had won control over all ten of the gram panchayats in the block in the 1978 elections. Corruption became an issue in the 1983 campaign. Binpur I is divided by the Kasai River. Four gram panchayats are located east of the Kasai and six to the west. The CPI(M) was criticized for channeling funds and benefits to the four eastern gram panchayats and neglecting the six in the west. This tendency was encouraged by the fact that there are two CPI(M) local committees for the block—one for the east and one for the west. The *sabhapati* of the block's panchayat samiti was also secretary of the local committee for the east. By channeling disproportionate benefits to his home base, he alienated the six panchayat constituencies to the west. In the 1983 elections, the opposition defeated the CPI(M) in all six of the western gram panchayats, while the CPI(M) retained control over three of the four gram panchayats in the east.⁶⁹

Corruption was a less potent issue against the CPI(M) in Jamboni block even though it appeared more pervasive among CPI(M) pradhans. In the 1978 elections, the party won seven of ten gram panchayats. Four of its seven pradhans and the *upa-sabhapati* (vice-chairman) of the panchayat samiti were implicated in corruption. The CPI(M) voted to remove them from office and expel them from the party, thereby losing control over two gram panchayats. The CPI(M)'s discipline paid off. It won control over all ten of Jamboni's gram panchayats in the 1983 elections.[70]

In conclusion, the Conflictual Process Perspective shows that two types of conflict are important in shaping NREP implementation. Conflicts between individual values and policy objectives are a source of considerable corruption. Policy objectives also come into conflict with the organizational interests of political parties. Shifting authority over NREP implementation to panchayats has greatly increased the power of political parties, especially the CPI(M), which controls a vast majority of panchayat seats and maintains a parallel organization that closely monitors and frequently intervenes in implementation. The importance of political parties in NREP implementation means that conflict between implementation objectives and party interests has the potential for serious distortion of implementation. In implementing the NREP through panchayats, the Government of West Bengal has in essence relied on political feedback to limit corruption. There is evidence that political feedback—e.g., elections and internal party discipline—places constraints on corruption. At the same time, the importance of political parties in the feedback process raises concern that political feedback may be attentuated because partisan organizational interests may distort it. Enthusiasts of panchayats contend that the electoral process will limit this distortion to tolerable levels. Experience with political machines in the United States or one-party dominant systems in other Third World countries such as Mexico leads to more pessimism, because it shows that corrupt parties can maintain themselves in power through a combination of repression, patronage for their constituencies, and control over access to information.

NREP IMPLEMENTATION: THE ORGANIZATIONAL ENVIRONMENT PERSPECTIVE

According to the Organizational Environment Perspective, the relations between government agencies and their environment affect policy implementation in four ways. First, the culture shared by individuals in the agency and in its environment conditions their perceptions and values. It influences their understanding of what is plausible and desirable.

Second, the structure of control over resources in the environment constrains the possibilities for successful implementation. Third, public policy can shape the manner in which exchanges of resources occur between state and environmental actors. Finally, political institutions limit how resources can be used in exercising power.

In implementing programs through panchayat institutions, the Left Front government employed an "institutionalized rule" with widespread public acceptance. (The concept of "institutionalized rules" is discussed in chapter 1.) Village panchayats have existed far back into the history of rural India. Mahatma Gandhi proposed them as an important level of government in his vision of a decentralized Indian polity. Panchayats are included in the directive principles of the Indian constitution, and the Government of India has sponsored two major commissions that have advocated their extensive use in promoting rural development.[71] In West Bengal, under the leadership of the Congress Party, the state government passed legislation mandating the creation of panchayats in 1957. Had resort to this widely accepted "institutionalized rule" not been available, or had the Left Front government been inclined to invoke a more alien label, such as "soviets," its substantial enlargement of popular control over implementation would not have been so readily accepted. Since panchayats enjoy widespread legitimacy, there is little ideological space available to oppose them.

The CPI(M)'s interest in panchayats is ironic. It contradicts the orthodox Marxist faith in central planning by state bureaucracies. It also presents a political paradox, since the panchayats were established by its rival, the Congress Party; and yet, despite its initial enthusiasm, the Congress allowed the panchayats to become inactive in West Bengal and virtually every other state where it retained power.[72] Why did the Left Front revive the panchayats?

The answer to this question has two parts. First, Benoy Chowdhury, minister for Rural Development, Land Reforms and Panchayats, the second most powerful member of the Left Front government, is a strong supporter of panchayats. Decentralized development and democratic participation in implementation are important values for Chowdhury and his party, the CPI(M). Chowdhury considers panchayats an effective means of implementing rural development programs and increasing support for the party. Thus, he has repeatedly taken initiatives to revitalize West Bengal's panchayat system.[73]

The commitment of political leaders is frequently insufficient to ensure the success of their initiatives. The second factor explaining the

CPI(M)'s revival of panchayats in West Bengal concerns differences in the organization of the Congress (I) and the CPI(M). Ever since the Atulya Ghosh gained control over the state party organization through his Hoogly political machine in the early 1950s, the Congress Party in West Bengal has lacked a unifying ideology and has been riven with factionalism.[74] The CPI(M), with its requirements for the ideological commitment of its members and its organization on the basis of democratic centralism, has relatively more discipline within its ranks.

Efficacious panchayat institutions take on disparate meanings in these different contexts. Within the faction-ridden Congress Party, they become threats to members of the state legislative assembly (MLAs).[75] These MLAs spend considerable periods of time in the capital away from their constituency. They attempt to maintain local support by using their access to top authorities in the state government to provide government services. Their access to top government officials gave them an incentive to avoid decentralizing authority over services. To the extent that panchayat institutions become an alternative source of services, one more accessible than an MLA, they can potentially erode an MLA's support and provide political resources for his rivals. In West Bengal, as in other states, Congress-led state governments enacted legislation creating the panchayats but simultaneously reduced this threat by minimizing their funding and circumscribing their authority. Decentralizing decision-making authority to the panchayats poses less of a threat to the CPI(M)'s MLAs. Party discipline curtails factionalism, and state leaders play a decisive role in allocating positions on the party ticket.

Many studies of public policy argue that economic structure limits the scope of poverty elimination.[76] For a proper understanding of the constraints of economic structure, one must recognize that it is embedded in a broader environment. In Midnapore district, as in most of rural India, the most important economic resource is land. Land ownership entails control over employment and income—and frequently, as a result, over political resources as well. The distribution of land in Midnapore approximates that for West Bengal as a whole (see tables 4 and 8). Both rank low on the dimension of abundance. In Midnapore, small and marginal landholdings (those up to five acres) account for 88.2 percent of all holdings. Control over land is not particularly concentrated. Holdings of less than five acres amount to 62.5 percent of the total area of land owned, while holdings of ten or more acres amount to only 14.2 percent of the total.

TABLE 8
DISTRIBUTION OF LANDHOLDINGS IN MIDNAPORE, 1984–85

Category of Landowner (in acres)	Number of Holdings	Percentage of Total Holdings	Area of Holdings	Percentage of Total Area
< 2.5	598,199	63.1	259,949	29.8
2.5–4.9	237,977	25.1	285,245	32.7
5–9.9	85,563	9.0	203,916	23.4
≥ 10	26,947	2.8	123,750	14.2
Total	948,686	100.0	872,860	100.1

SOURCES: *Annual Plan on Agriculture, 1984–85, Midnapore East* (Tamluk: Office of the Principal Agricultural Officer, Midnapore East, 1984), p. 6; and *Annual Plan on Agriculture 1984–85, Midnapore West* (Midnapore: Office of the Principal Agricultural Officer, Midnapore West, 1984), pp. 5–8.

The impact of this agrarian structure on the politics of the district is less clear than what many observers have presumed. Given the tremendous scarcity and the fact that almost 75 percent of the families engaged in agriculture are dependent on wage labor as a source of income, it seems plausible that those with little or no land would be highly dependent on those who own enough land to be a source of employment. Such dependence could have considerable impact on local politics and on implementation. For instance, writing in 1968, Marcus Franda observed,

> The existing man/land ratio and the short supply of land in relationship to demand reinforce an economy of high rents and a high rate of tenancy, and encourage attitudes of acquiescence on the part of landless and tenant farmers. This accounts for the fact that conflicts between landholders and peasant cultivators have not developed to any significant degree in the countryside, [and] for the failure of the Communist Party to promote a "class struggle" in the rural areas.[77]

And indeed, rural politics in West Bengal in the 1950s and 1960s was dominated by "key men" whose political power was largely derived from their control over land and the consequent dependence of those lacking land and viable independent livelihoods.[78] Yet it would be myopic to argue that this is the exclusive outcome of such an agrarian structure. The large numbers of smallholders and agricultural laborers constitute a potential constituency for a politics serving as a vehicle for their independence rather than their dependence. Advocates for the rural poor have long searched for the means to bring about such a transition. The transformation of rural politics in West Bengal from one dominated by local economic elites and the Congress Party to one dominated by the CPI(M) provides some clues.

The impact of public policy is an obvious key. The rejuvenation of the panchayats was an important step. More often than not, however, the panchayats have reinforced the dominance of rural elites. The early experience with panchayats in West Bengal is typical:

> In West Bengal, about two-thirds of anchal Pradhans were either jotedars [big landowners] or businessmen; only in a small number of cases, a teacher or a service holder was found to have been elected a Pradhan. . . . In the rural economy, the moneylending activities of a jotedar and/or businessman, when coupled with powers of a Pradhan, usually helped him to exercise effective leadership and play a domineering role in the locality.[79]

Even where panchayats were dominated by economic elites, they engendered some changes that had positive consequences for the poor. In his anthropological study of politics in the Midnapore village of Torkotala, Marvin Davis observed that the establishment of a gram panchayat in the village promoted a factional politics that differed from other forms of village politics in that it was based on voluntary rather than ascriptive terms. The support of nonelites was contingent on the receipt of benefits in return. The benefits from these exchanges included recognition of claims to higher social status; projects that advanced the interests of the village as a whole; a means for the development of leadership among subordinate groups; and the introduction of the notion of politics as a means for progress to a better world, as opposed to the previously dominant attitude of politics as a means to restore traditional social order.[80] These benefits are not inconsiderable, though they were delivered within the parameters of elite domination.

How did the CPI(M) end the rural elites' control over the panchayats? After coming to power in 1977, it altered the opportunity structure for public participation in their affairs. First, political parties have been allowed to play an active role in panchayat elections. Prior to 1978, parties were proscribed from participating in elections. All too frequently, these nonpartisan elections were perfunctory, and local elites actually selected panchayat members prior to the elections.[81] Inclusion of parties has promoted public interest and more competition. The greater electoral competition for control over the panchayats is manifest in the large number of candidates who campaign for office. In 1983, 134,583 candidates contested for 45,237 gram panchayat seats; 25,058 candidates competed for 8,660 panchayat samiti seats; and 2,160 candidates campaigned for 678 seats in West Bengal's fifteen zilla parishads.[82] Another indication of the competitiveness is the violence that accompanies the elections.[83]

An important reason for this competition is that control over panchayats means control over development funds, patronage, and positions of authority that enhance electoral prospects for the state assembly and the national parliament.[84] Since 1978, the Government of West Bengal has allocated enough funding to panchayats to make them sites of power. It was estimated that for 1983–84 Rs. 4 billion were given to the panchayat system; between Rs. 500,000 and Rs. 800,000 went to each gram panchayat.[85]

The revival of panchayats in West Bengal began with the 1978 elections—the first in fifteen years. The partisan electoral contests provided the CPI(M) with an opportunity to dislodge the Congress (I) and its large landowning allies from their domination of the rural sector. A good indication of the change brought about can be gathered by the social backgrounds of the pradhans who chair the gram panchayats and exercise predominant control over programs like the NREP (see table 9). In contrast to earlier gram panchayats, my survey found that most of the pradhans were not members of the traditional elite. Sixty-five percent (twenty-three of thirty-five respondents) were white-collar employees. Fifty-seven percent (twenty of thirty-five) were schoolteachers. The overrepresentation of schoolteachers is apparently characteristic of the district and the entire state. Midnapore's district panchayat officer conducted a survey of the district's pradhans and found that 42 percent (217 out of 515) were schoolteachers.[86] According to a survey of 100 gram panchayats throughout the state, 29 percent of all pradhans were teachers.[87]

The pradhans were remarkably young. Half were younger than forty. Their mean age was 39.1 years. Most came from the middle castes. The largest share belongs to the Mahishyas—a *sat sudra* cultivating group that is the largest caste in Midnapore.

The background of the fathers of the pradhans was relatively modest. Eighty-three percent (twenty-nine of thirty-six) were cultivators. Information concerning the amount of land their fathers owned was

TABLE 9
SOCIAL BACKGROUNDS OF PRADHANS
IN SELECTED BLOCKS IN MIDNAPORE DISTRICT

A. Occupations of All Pradhans

Cultivators	8
Businessmen	1
Teachers	20
Social workers	2
Service workers	1
Tenant farmers	1
Unemployed	2
Not available	1
Total	36

B. Occupations of Pradhans' Fathers

Cultivators	29
Businessmen	1
Teachers	1
Doctors	1
Service	2
Agricultural laborers	2
Total	36

C. Castes of All Pradhans

Superior castes	
Brahmin	4
Middle castes	
Jaishal Banik	1
Mahato	2
Sadgop	2
Mahishya	15
Goala	1
Karmakar	1
Khatriya	1
Scheduled castes,	
scheduled tribes,	
and minorities	
Rajbanshi	1
Bhogta	1
Santal	4
Muslim	1
Not available	2
Total	36

D. Years of Education
Attained by Pradhans

Years	*No. of Pradhans*
7	1
8	1
9	1
10	10
11	6
12	0
13	0
14	6
15	8
16	0
17	3
Total	36
Mean	12.4 years

TABLE 9 (*continued*)

E. Age of All Pradhans

< 30	2
30–39	16
40–49	15
50–59	3
> 60	0
Total	36
Mean	39.1

collected from seventeen pradhans. Sixty-five percent (eleven of seventeen) owned less than one hectare. The median amount of land owned was 2.6 acres. Most of the pradhans had availed themselves of education to achieve occupational mobility. Their mean level of education was 12.4 years, with 47.6 percent (seventeen of thirty-six) having obtained at least a B.A. (fourteen years of education).

In short, the social background of pradhans differed from that of the traditional rural elite. Most of the pradhans were members of a new rural middle class.[88] CPI(M) party documents stress the importance of forming an alliance with "middle peasants," since "they are an effective weapon in building up public opinion."[89] The CPI(M)'s efforts to extend its organization into the countryside have created opportunities for this emerging class. For instance, the Left Front government has expanded West Bengal's educational system. According to Kanti Biswas, the Left Front's minister of education, it has opened 12,000 schools and appointed 46,000 new teachers since 1977.[90] Many of the new teachers are CPI(M) members or sympathizers. Indeed, one of the CPI(M)'s tactics for expanding its rural base has been to recruit rural youth who attended institutions of higher education in urban areas before they returned to their rural homes—often as schoolteachers.[91] There is strong evidence that the CPI(M) is using the position of schoolteacher as a patronage sinecure for party workers.[92] The sympathies and affiliations of many teachers with the CPI(M), coupled with the large numbers of teachers elected as panchayat officials, seem to support a hypothesis that the CPI(M) has accommodated the new middle class and institutionalized its power in the panchayats.[93]

The political ascendance of this group has parallels throughout rural

India. Social and political change has increased the power and assertiveness of a middle social stratum usually identified as the "backward classes." The political systems of different Indian states have incorporated them in different fashions.[94] In West Bengal, the collective political power of this group has been relatively weak—in large measure because West Bengal's middle castes are much more fragmented than the middle castes of other states.[95] No middle caste is able to assert political power on a statewide level. There is no dominant middle-caste group comparable to the Marathas in Maharashtra, the Jats in Haryana, or the Reddys in Andhra Pradesh. The consequence has been a lower salience of caste-based politics and the middle castes' greater dependence on the CPI(M) to organize their political power.

The competitiveness of gram panchayat elections, their greater funding, and their control over developmental activities have also made people more aware that panchayats are a potential source of benefits. This awareness has incited frequent contact between pradhans and members of the public. My survey found that 96 percent of the pradhans reported frequent contact with members of the public while planning NREP projects. Eighty-nine percent reported frequent contact during implementation. Significantly, the rates of contact for categories of the poor were close to the rates of the highest categories. For instance, 81 percent of the pradhan respondents said that they had frequent contact with agricultural laborers during the planning of NREP projects. This is just below the two higher rates—91 percent for cultivators and 89 percent for political workers. Eighty-one percent of the pradhans reported frequent contact with agricultural laborers while implementing the NREP. This is just less than the 88 percent for cultivators and 86 percent for political workers.[96] Of course, one must treat these data with some skepticism, since the pradhans might well exaggerate their consultation with the public. At the minimum, it reflects the widespread legitimacy of public participation among the pradhans. My informal discussions with the public have convinced me that it is also a product of their increased interest in programs implemented by the panchayats.

Ever since Max Weber's *Protestant Ethic and the Spirit of Capitalism,* scholars have argued that people's attitudes are an important factor in promoting economic development.[97] Implementation through panchayats has helped to instill attitudes that promote economic development. It forces panchayat members and to some extent members of the public to consider development issues. This is a beginning of an educational process through which they learn the consequences of different alternatives. But just as important, panchayat members learn organizational and managerial skills that in one way or another promote development. Finally, implementation through panchaya institutions has built popular commitment to development and greater confidence that personal effort can bring about change. One panchayat samiti clerk told me, "With the inception of NREP schemes, the rural people have gotten the taste of doing their own work. This has increased their understanding and developed their self-confidence." [98]

While parties have made panchayats more responsive to popular needs, panchayats have brought parties into closer contact with the people. For example, the secretary of the Tamluk II Krishak Samiti (Peasants Association) believes that implementing the NREP through gram panchayats has strengthened his party (the CPI(M)) because the party must keep in close contact with villagers in order to plan and implement the program. [99] Decentralized authority over development has required higher party officials and MLAs to keep in closer contact with their constituencies. Prior to the revival of panchayats in 1978, MLAs often stayed in Calcutta and paid only infrequent visits to their constituencies. If they wanted to get something done for their constituency, they approached the minister or the secretary of the appropriate department in the capital. With the devolution of authority over development to the panchayats, an MLA often must go to the zilla parishad or even the gram panchayat to initiate a project. Thus, there is considerable disincentive for MLAs to behave in the stereotypical fashion of returning to their district only at election time. [100]

Implementing the NREP through the panchayats has elevated the importance of political resources relative to economic ones. Nonetheless, economic resources, especially control over land, remain important, since the resistance of landowners can cause problems for implementation. Sixty-two percent of the pradhans and secretaries (forty-seven of seventy-six) encountered problems acquiring the land or soil necessary to complete NREP projects. [101] These encounters are not surprising, since the NREP provides no funds for compensation. However, only 11 percent of the pradhans and the secretaries (nine of seventy-nine) named land acquisition as one of the two most important problems arising in NREP implementation. One explanation—as was pointed out by four of the pradhans who said they faced problems with land acquisition—is that such problems are often quickly resolved after the issue is brought into the open and public pressure is directed to those delaying the project.

Political parties also dominate the process of interest representation. In Midnapore, as in most of rural West Bengal, the CPI(M) is paramount. From 1983 to 1988 it controlled almost 70 percent (359 of 518) of the district's gram panchayats, 89 percent (48 of 54) of its panchayat samitis, and 89 of 108 seats in the zilla parishad. In his insightful appraisal of the role of the CPI(M), Atul Kohli stresses the ideological commitment and disciplined organization of the party as an important factor in its success in rural poverty alleviation.[102] There is much evidence to support this position. Nevertheless, this study points to a less sanguine conclusion concerning the virtues of the CPI(M).

The CPI(M) has grown considerably since it came to power in West Bengal. Party membership stood at 43,342 in February 1978. It grew to 136,980 in 1985 and 189,732 in 1991.[103] Party organization has expanded into new areas. With the Left Front coming into power, the party's responsibility has been extended to include overseeing the state government as well as party affairs. The resuscitation of the panchayats has been especially demanding. In 1978, the CPI(M) took it upon itself to come up with 47,000 reliable candidates at a time when its party membership was just over 40,000. Between elections, it must oversee the work of 3,305 gram panchayats.

The tremendous growth of the CPI(M)'s membership and responsibilities strained the capacity of the party's organization. New members frequently lack adequate political training. They often strive to advance their personal ambition instead of the public welfare or even party interests. The influx of opportunists into the party and the rapid extension of its organization have caused gaps in the party's network of control and communication. CPI(M) members heading the panchayats are not always subject to party discipline. Party members in branch and local committees who lack experience and dedication often lose touch with the public.[104] Furthermore, those who control popular support can often secure CPI(M) backing even if they have been tainted by corruption.[105] Since the party has gained control over the state government, party membership has become a valuable commodity, and branch and local committee secretaries have become susceptible to bribes for helping people get into the party after they have been denied membership.[106] Finally, gaps in the party's communication network make it difficult for cadres at the district and state levels to keep in touch with public sentiment and to monitor the activity of party members.[107] As a result, senior officials become less effective in assessing public sentiment and maintaining party discipline.

Increasingly, the will of party leaders to curtail corruption and patronage has been called into question. Allegations of corruption have reached the highest levels of the government. Chief Minister Jyoti Basu has been accused of ordering preferential treatment for a company whose top executives include his son and of overriding previous legislation and the objections of top civil servants to approve exorbitant compensation for the British-owned Calcutta Tramway Company.[108] There is also mounting evidence that CPI(M) officials, in a fashion reminiscent of Communist Party officials in the Soviet Union or China, are coming to identify the interests of the state with those of their party apparatus. A letter—on record in the state legislative assembly—written by the Chief Minister's special assistant on the letterhead of the Chief Minister's secretariat provides a remarkable example. In response to the complaints made from a farmer in Hoogly district that he was being harassed by criminals, the official wrote, "The complaint cited in your letter dated 31.8.87 has been investigated on the CM's instructions. We have learned that the dispute could not be resolved because you [the farmer] failed to respond to the summons of the CPM's district committee."[109] Other examples of the identification of party interests with state interests include the state government's stifling of the efforts of its own Vigilance Commission to prosecute government officials who allegedly were involved in corruption worth hundreds of thousands of rupees;[110] the insistence of Jyoti Basu that CPI(M) cadres be deployed alongside police at a Congress (I) demonstration where CPI(M) cadre allegedly beat up Congress (I) leader Mamata Banerjee;[111] and the growing number of allegations of collusion between party officials, the police, and criminal elements.[112]

In sum, the Organizational Environment Perspective helps us understand the CPI(M)'s accomplishments. Since coming to power in 1977, the CPI(M) has endeavored to transform the linkages between the state and society in rural West Bengal. The party's class rhetoric has altered the terms of political discourse and increased the political consciousness of the poor relative to the era of Congress Party rule. The CPI(M) has transformed the opportunity structure for participation by empowering the panchayats and decentralizing authority over the implementation of programs such as the NREP. As a result, decision makers and information about implementation have become more accessible to the public at large. These changes have helped the CPI(M) create a new network of political support that stands as an alternative to that of the Congress (I). In the process, it has enhanced the responsiveness of the state government.

Though the changes brought about by the CPI(M) have increased government responsiveness to the rural poor, this responsiveness is limited by certain constraints. West Bengal's emerging rural middle strata are at the center of the CPI(M)'s political network. Why did the CPI(M), a party avowedly committed to the rural poor, come to rely on this emerging middle class? The CPI(M) quickly became dependent on this group's political resources. The social status and influence possessed by the middle classes enhanced their ability to garner support from the various strata of West Bengal's social hierarchy. They also can relate more comfortably with government officials, whose caste and social status are usually comparable if not higher. There is an even more pragmatic reason. Implementing programs such as the NREP requires a minimum level of educational training. The middle strata have greater access to education than the poor. Ninety-eight percent of West Bengal's agricultural laborers have no more than a primary school education and 80 percent are illiterate.[113]

The impact of the CPI(M)'s dependence on these middle strata is difficult to measure in precise terms. Kohli contends that the party has been able to inculcate its members with a commitment to the poor and that the class backgrounds of its cadres and sympathizers have had only a minimal impact.[114] Others have argued that lack of representation of the poor in the panchayats has diluted the party's commitment.[115] The opportunism that characterizes a significant segment of the CPI(M)'s supporters raises reservations about Kohli's position, but the determinism of extrapolating political attitudes from class backgrounds fails to account for the admirable dedication among a substantial segment of CPI(M) functionaries. The Organizational Environment Perspective suggests that each position misses an important factor in explaining the level of responsiveness of the state to the rural poor. Responsiveness will vary with the degree of competition among parties and leaders and the importance of support from the rural poor for maintaining political power.

CONCLUDING REMARKS

The first of the three hypotheses stated at the beginning of this chapter, the Greater Responsiveness Hypothesis, posits that increasing the opportunities for public participation will enhance implementation effectiveness. We have seen considerable evidence to support this proposition. Public participation through the panchayats has resulted in the devolution of implementation authority to those better acquainted with local needs. It has also made decision makers more accessible to the public and has resulted in the planning of projects more appropriate to local circumstances. At the same time, the usefulness of the projects has been limited by their small size and the shortage of technical expertise available to panchayat authorities. Panchayat officials have also contributed to West Bengal's low utilization rate of NREP funds. Although implementing the NREP through panchayats has reduced accountability through bureaucratic channels, it has heightened accountability through electoral sanctions. The net outcome of this change in modes of accountability is difficult to measure. In fact, it is likely to depend on the process of interest representation that characterizes local politics.

Although, as Atul Kohli contends, the CPI(M) has made substantial strides in poverty alleviation, he neglects important problems inherent in the CPI(M)'s regime. Specifically, the panchayats still need greater access to technical expertise if programs such as the NREP are to provide effective solutions to the problems that confront equitable rural development. Resolving this problem will take more than allowing elected officials to become full-time office workers, as Kohli suggests.[116] To some extent, the problem is a consequence of the historical limitations of West Bengal's technical departments, which have failed to provide adequate services to levels of government below the district and subdivisional level. But the problem is also manifest in the CPI(M)'s need to make better use of the technical expertise already available. By decentralizing planning and attempting to make the state bureaucracy more responsive to the panchayats, the party has shown that it is aware of the need for better integration of the departments' technical expertise. Such integration is absolutely essential if public works programs like the NREP are to create assets that contribute to increased production. Given the scarcity of resources in rural West Bengal relative to the state's sizable population, increasing production, as opposed to merely redistributing scarce resources, must play a central role in poverty alleviation.[117] Kohli's work, despite its stress on the importance of political regimes, provides little help in discerning the institutional arrangements most effective in delivering the technical expertise necessary for increasing production.

The Elite Domination Hypothesis contends that increasing the role of public participation in implementation enhances the control of local elites, who distort implementation to benefit their own interests. Our findings in this regard differ from the views of those who view the CPI(M) regime as a captive of "its landlord base" and the "dominant elite." [118] They also diverge from the views of those who stress the CPI(M)'s dedication to uplifting the plight of the rural poor.[119] By allocating substantial resources to the panchayats and subjecting them to partisan elections, the CPI(M) has made success in democratic competition decisive for controlling NREP implementation. In its effort to build its rural support and dislodge the Congress (I) and its elite supporters, the CPI(M) has established a base of support among the emerging rural middle classes. In spite of the party's ideological commitments, the rural poor are for the most part junior partners in the CPI(M)'s coalition. Rather than giving direction to the CPI(M), the rural poor become dependent on its largesse in the form of the patronage that is made available through programs like the NREP.

It is important to keep in mind the distinctiveness of the setting in West Bengal. Few parties can claim the dedicated leadership and ideological commitment to the poor possessed by the CPI(M). Few parties show as much concern for maintaining party discipline as the CPI(M), even with its recent problems. The party's relative success in dislodging traditional landed elites is unlikely to be replicated in less favorable circumstances. And even the CPI(M) was obliged to align with the emerging middle classes as well as the poor in order to maintain political power. Social structure leaves its imprint on public participation even though altering the opportunity structure for public participation can change the parameters under which social groups represent their interests.

The Political Patronage Hypothesis asserts that public participation distorts policy implementation by providing political organizations with opportunities to control policy outputs. Our study has shown that elevating the role of the panchayats has given political parties, especially the CPI(M), a prominent role in guiding development. They provide local authorities with information about local circumstances. They also monitor the performance of panchayat members and weed out those engaged in corruption. At the same time, their potential for distorting implementation is considerable. Even the ideologically committed CPI(M) is guilty of patronage and corruption. In the short term, patronage and corruption limit the impact of the program and may discredit it; over the longer term, the use of programs such as the NREP for patronage creates political dependence, which limits the public's capacity for autonomous collective action.[120]

Public participation has both positive and negative consequences for poverty alleviation programs such as the NREP. Implementation has become more efficient because authority has been transferred to those with more knowledge about local problems and the poor are encouraged to participate in implementation decisions. Although a lack of technical expertise and inattentive record keeping have presented problems, they do not seem insuperable if the proper administrative resources and training are made available. More intractable problems arise as a consequence of the process of interest representation. These problems are summarized by the paradox of participation. If public participation is to make policy responsive to the needs of the poor, their interests must be equitably represented, but as long as the poor remain poor, their position in the process of interest representation is disadvantaged.

How can the paradox be resolved? Kohli's stress on party discipline offers one alternative.[121] However, he overestimates the CPI(M)'s discipline and understates the need for democratic competition. Admittedly, the CPI(M)'s commitment and organizational discipline were important to the effectiveness of its poverty alleviation efforts. And Kohli does recognize the impact of democratic politics on the CPI(M); in fact, he perceptively observes that it caused some dissipation of power among the various wings of the CPI(M)'s leadership and reduced likelihood for authoritarian commandism.[122] He fails to stress, however, that democratic competition is essential to maintaining party commitment and discipline over the long run.

The declining competitiveness of politics in West Bengal suggests that there may be a reduction in responsiveness to the rural poor.[123] There is also evidence that the CPI(M) has taken measures to discourage organizations of the rural poor that are independent of the party.[124] The Congress (I) Party is in an unprecedented state of disarray. Its disorganization enabled 4,939 Left Front candidates to run unopposed in the 1988 panchayat elections.[125] The decline of the Congress (I) is even more clearly manifested in the deterioration of its electoral performance. The share of seats in the 1988 panchayat elections won by the Congress (I) declined from 33 percent in 1983 to just 23 percent in 1988. The performance of the Congress (I) in the West Bengal assembly elections has also been disappointing (see table 5). At the same time, the CPI(M) has steadily increased its dominance over its partners within the Left Front and the Congress (I). It now holds 66 percent of all elected panchayat positions (up from 55 percent in 1983) and 64 percent of all members of the state legislative assembly.

Drawing an analogy with communist societies is tempting. In both

China and the Soviet Union, the membership of the Communist Party, in many cases, was initially inspired by an ideological commitment to alleviate poverty and promote economic development. However, in each case, in the absence of democratic competition, there was no means of checking the influence of the party's institutional interests. And since the party monopolized the avenues of social mobility, it increasingly attracted careerists with less commitment to social equity and greater vulnerability to corruption.

Comparison with single-party dominant democratic systems is more appropriate. The CPI(M), like other parties that have dominated democratic systems, has embarked on a "virtuous cycle," where it uses its electoral victories to refashion public policy, political institutions, and political symbols to strengthen its political support.[126] The dominance of the Partido Revolucionario Institucional (PRI) in Mexico is a possible analogue. The era of Mexico's most progressive reform came at a time when Lázaro Cárdenas built an alliance with peasants and workers in order to break with the conservative Callista faction that had previously dominated the ruling party.[127] The history of the PRI from the Cárdenas era to the 1980s is characterized by the decline of the party's social responsiveness and the spread of corruption. The PRI's monopoly over political power, the absence of an autonomous civil service, and the party's growing control of economic resources through the expansion of the public sector all contributed to these outcomes. On the other hand, greater degrees of political competition in one-party dominant systems such as Sweden and Japan help to limit the spread of corruption and encourage responsiveness to social needs.[128]

Political competition can assume many modes. As their number increases, political parties tend to compete by fashioning and refashioning alliances with one another rather than by expanding their constituencies to include those previously excluded from power. Pressures to outflank the opposition by mobilizing new groups, according to Huntington, is stronger in a two-party system. Furthermore, he argues that competition in a two-party system strengthens internal party organization.[129] Enhancing popular responsiveness also requires that members of the public be given the opportunity to formulate and signify their own preferences.[130] They can most easily express their preferences when competition takes place between programmatic parties competing for support by offering the public a coherent set of policies.

Of course, competition also can take place within political parties.

Some measure of intraparty competition may help to stymie the Mich-elsian "iron law of oligarchy" and maintain the party's popular respon-siveness. For instance, intraparty competition within the "Congress sys-tem" helped to maintain the Congress Party's responsiveness, if not to the poor, at least to different factions of social elites.[131] Yet, as the de-cline of the Congress Party in West Bengal illustrates, excessive com-petition based on personal factions can undermine a party's efficacy.[132]

Geddes' game-theoretical model of administrative reform offers a good starting point for understanding which forms of partisan compe-tition are likely to enhance the representation of the poor.[133] According to this model, reform is most likely to occur when there is a limited number (usually two) of evenly matched parties, and where party lead-ers exercise close control over the selection of party candidates. Evenly matched parties in search of electoral advantage have greater incentive to reform than dominant parties. As the party system becomes more fragmented, partisan concerns are diverted from appeals to new con-stituencies to the construction and maintenance of coalitions. Open ac-cess to partisan candidacies reduces the incentives for reform, since it gives incumbent legislators greater incentive to bolster their position by maintaining their access to patronage. Legislators will be more willing to sacrifice their patronage prerogatives when their career prospects are dependent on party leaders. This observation parallels Kohli's advocacy of disciplined parties as an important means for poverty alleviation. However, the parallel seems strongest when legislators have little con-trol over policy and therefore compete primarily by offering patronage. Our study suggests that decentralizing authority over policy to local officials may elevate its importance in local political competition.

Partisan competition may be insufficient to ensure responsiveness to the poor. Efforts to garner majority support often motivate parties to assume middle-of-the-road positions on policy issues. Parties assume cautious postures in order to avoid offending powerful groups. Their aggregation of interests impedes them from responding to all social groups. As we have seen, decentralizing state authority can encourage parties to be more responsive to local needs. Still, partisan interests create tensions between the requisites for local responsiveness and the requirements of political success at the provincial and national levels. When parties suppress conflict within their ranks, they reduce their re-ceptiveness to societal pressures. Instead of responding to popular in-terests, party leaderships may "re-present" them in ways that advance their personal and partisan interests. By establishing patronage networks, parties often create dependence rather than the capacity for independent collective action.

NGOs (nongovernmental organizations working in the interests of the poor) and social movements are often viewed as alternatives to political parties.[134] Free of the requisites of majoritarian politics and partisan interests, they create political spaces that empower individuals and communities to define their interests and articulate their politics in ways that are more reflective of local needs. Yet the strengths of NGOs and social movements can also be their weakness. Their local focus and political independence may result in broader political insignificance.[135]

Political parties, NGOs, and social movements stand in a complementary if often antagonistic relationship.[136] While parties are indispensable for aggregating diverse social interests in electoral systems, NGOs and social movements can play an important role in enabling the poor to articulate and act on their interests. They can empower the poor to curb political parties' tendency to allow partisan interests to reduce their popular responsiveness. Promoting political competition among programmatic political parties and a vibrant NGO and social movement sector may be the best way to surmount the paradox of participation.

CHAPTER 5

The Politics of Rationality
and the Rationality of Politics

The beauty of the social democratic strategy was that social
policy would also result in power mobilization. By
eradicating poverty, unemployment, and complete wage
dependency, the welfare state increases political capacities
and diminishes the social divisions that are barriers to
political unity among workers.

Gøsta Esping-Andersen

By combining organization theory with political economy, this book
creates an analytical framework that uniquely illuminates the implementation of public policy. The framework includes three perspectives.
The Rational Process Perspective stresses that planning and monitoring
shape implementation by improving the correspondence between
means and ends. The Conflictual Process Perspective, in contrast, contends that conflict is endemic to implementing agencies and largely determines the course of implementation. Finally, the Organizational Environment Perspective proposes that exchanges of resources between
implementing agencies and their environment, as well as the institutionalized rules that mold these exchanges, are crucial factors shaping implementation.

This framework has been applied to three cases. While each case
involves the implementation of a rural poverty alleviation program,
each has a distinct administrative network. The Roosevelt administration implemented its rural poverty programs through a single agency
during the New Deal. The Employment Guarantee Scheme (EGS) in
Maharashtra employs a complex administrative network incorporating
seven different departments. Implementation of the National Rural Employment Programme (NREP) in West Bengal occurs through democratically elected local governing institutions. By observing the variations in these programs, one can test the propositions advanced by the

conceptual framework and note the advantages and disadvantages of the different types of administrative networks, albeit in a preliminary way.

Each perspective generates important insights about the cases, but none provides sufficient explanations of the policy outcomes. The Rational Process Perspective, with its focus on planning and monitoring of implementation, captures an important implementation dynamic. However, it underestimates the resilient impact of conflict between actors, and its analytical tools are inadequate for examining state-society relations. There is no gainsaying the role of conflict in shaping implementation, as highlighted by the Conflictual Process Perspective. However, the perspective pays inadequate attention to the ways in which planning and monitoring can shape this conflict. Furthermore, it lacks a rigorous conceptualization of various sources of power that state agencies and social actors use to shape implementation. It also has little to say about the ways in which culture may mold relations between agencies and social actors. The Organizational Environment Perspective, in contrast, offers a more sophisticated understanding of state-society relations. Without the insights of the Rational and Conflictual Process Perspectives, however, it offers limited insight into the internal dynamics of state agencies. Since each perspective portrays a particular logic of implementation, they can be regarded as ideal types that supply relatively parsimonious models to make sense of complex circumstances. As with any intelligent use of ideal types, application of the three perspectives reveals their limitations as well as their strengths. Moreover, each perspective helps to explain deviations from the predictions of the others.

By combining the insights of the Organizational Environment Perspective with those of the Rational Process Perspective, we can see more clearly how rationality shapes implementation. Effective planning must account for important environmental contingencies—most notably, the societal distribution of resources. In addition, institutionalized rules structure the bounded rationality of decision makers by shaping their selection of alternatives for resolving problems and their "logic of appropriateness." [1]

The Organizational Environment Perspective also illuminates the conflictual processes of implementation. Resource dependence shapes conflict by conditioning the distribution of power in state agencies. Those agencies (and units within agencies) that are responsible for coping with more important dependencies acquire greater power. Resource dependence also shapes the selection of authorities by enhancing the prospects of those whose qualifications and views are congenial with powerful environmental actors. By delimiting the sources of power and the nature of exchanges between state agencies and social groups, the Organizational Environment Perspective improves the Conflictual Process Perspective's understanding of relations between state and society. It transforms that perspective's concept of conflict into a fuller depiction of the politics of conflict.

Although the insights from the Organizational Environment Perspective enhance our understanding of the rationality and politics of implementation, major issues remain unexamined. What is the relationship between the rationality and politics of implementation? Most analysts emphasize the negative impact of politics on implementation. Some contend that one way to limit this negative impact is to increase the autonomy of state agencies from external political influences. What are the consequences of enhancing state autonomy for poverty alleviation? Finally, what lessons does our study teach for fashioning administrative structures and programs that will promote more effective poverty alleviation? This chapter examines these questions.

THE POLITICS OF RATIONALITY

The essential elements of the Rational Process Perspective are planning and the monitoring of implementation. The proponents of this perspective emphasize that organizational structure must be made to fit various contingencies in order to achieve effective implementation. Monitoring implementation provides the basis for adjustments that improve the correspondence between policy outcomes and objectives. However, proponents of the Rational Process Perspective often analyze planning and monitoring outside of their political context, even though each is conditioned by politics in important ways.

How do policymakers design the administrative networks that implement public policy? Our cases suggest that their decisions are frequently shaped by bounded rationality and incrementalism. A common result is that the design of administrative networks is usually limited to alterations of existing institutions—partly because existing institutions constrain the imagination of policymakers and partly because ideas for new programs come from personnel in these agencies. For example, early rural poverty alleviation programs during the New Deal were implemented by the diverse array of agencies where they originated. The creation of the Resettlement Administration (RA) and its successor, the Farm Security Administration (FSA), highlights the importance of political factors in shaping the design of administrative networks.[2] The impetus for consolidating the New Deal's rural poverty alleviation programs into a single agency came largely from the conflict between advocates of the rural poor and defenders of other interests in agencies such as the AAA and the U.S. Department of Agriculture.

Comparing the ways in which the administrative networks of the Employment Guarantee Scheme and the National Rural Employment Programme were designed provides further insights into the impact of political factors. The EGS and the NREP attempt to alleviate poverty in similar ways, but the programs are implemented by starkly different administrative networks. These differences are difficult to explain solely in terms of administrative rationality. The impact of institutionalized rules and politics was probably even more important.

In Maharashtra, planners of the EGS were presented with two alternatives. The program could be implemented through panchayat institutions or by the technical departments that operate in rural areas. Both of these procedures were accepted as institutionalized rules in the sense that they were legitimate prescriptions for solving the administrative problems of rural development programs. Even though the EGS was initially designed to be implemented through panchayat institutions, it was transferred to a network of technical departments in 1974. Part of the explanation lies in the impact of the drought relief programs in the early 1970s, when the state's technical departments were pressed into service to implement the extensive system of public works in rural areas. The EGS is implemented through virtually the same administrative arrangement as the relief programs. This arrangement was chosen in order to take advantage of the administrative experience that the departments had accumulated, but political factors reinforced the decision. Use of panchayat institutions was undesirable from the perspective of the state legislators who sanctioned the EGS. Confronted with a competitive political environment where rivalries within the Congress Party as well as between parties made their security tenuous, the state legislators were wary of giving authority over the EGS to panchayat institutions, since such authority would provide their rivals with a major source of patronage. Instead, they decided to implement the program through state bureaucracies and to establish tahsil-level committees, which they headed. These committees enabled them to control EGS patronage for themselves.

The NREP was initiated in West Bengal under very different circumstances. After the CPI(M)'s election in 1977, party leaders wished to consolidate power by extending and institutionalizing its support in the countryside. It began to rejuvenate the state's panchayat institutions to do so. On one level, it is ironic that the CPI(M) turned to the panchayats to accomplish its objective. Panchayat institutions were, after all, a creation of its archenemy the Congress Party. Yet on another level, the CPI(M)'s resort to the panchayats makes perfect sense. Although the Congress Party never provided the panchayats with the resources necessary for them to play a vital role in rural development, it succeeded in establishing the state's political culture as an institutionalized rule offering a legitimate solution to the problems of rural development. This institutionalized rule was readily available for the leaders of the CPI(M) to adopt for their own purposes.

Panchayat institutions performed different political functions for the Congress and the CPI(M). For the former, it provided a populist appeal. This appeal was rather hollow, however, since the panchayats reinforced the domination of the traditional elite, and the resources allocated to them were never substantial. For the CPI(M), the panchayats provided an efficacious means for ousting the traditional elite and building support among the poor and emerging middle classes. Since the CPI(M) had a disciplined organization with much less factionalism than the Congress (I), its state legislators had less to fear from this source of patronage. They acquiesced to the organizational needs of the party.

Political parties are not the only important actors that condition the politics of administrative structure. As the experience of the New Deal shows, government bureaucracies were also powerful actors. Bureaucratic conflict led to the establishment of the RA. Moreover, power was concentrated in the national offices of the RA and the FSA, and strong regional offices were created, because Rexford Tugwell and his protégés wanted to insulate decision-making authority from the influence of the Extension Service and the American Farm Bureau Federation. In the case of the EGS, even though the departments in charge of implementing the EGS are unenthusiastic about this responsibility, they resist placing such a lucrative program outside their authority.

In sum, while the perception of social needs generally provides stimulus for institutional development and policy initiatives, rationality and institutionalized rules establish constraints that condition policy responses. They do so at two levels. First, they limit the responses under consideration, since the alternatives must plausibly correspond to the needs created by situational contingencies and the "logic of appropriateness" derived from institutional rules. Second, rationality and institutionalized rules shape the procedures and structures of state institutions involved in determining a policy response. Within these parameters, however, politics plays a crucial role.[3] The impact of politics, most immediately, arises from the pursuit of interests by particular politicians, bureaucrats, and social groups. Although cultural norms and institutions constrain and facilitate the strategies of these conflicting actors, the norms and institutions are themselves usually the product of earlier conflicts.

Politics also shapes the monitoring of implementation. Since organizational resources are limited, the number of indicators an agency can use to monitor implementation is restricted.[4] The selection of feedback indicators is frequently influenced by political considerations. Powerful actors can impose their interests on the selection process, and everyone provides information strategically in order to advance his or her own interests. Estimates of local demand for employment are essential in the EGS. The Government of Maharashtra has issued directives ordering the calculation of tahsil "manpower budgets," which estimate demand for EGS employment. However, these budgets are rarely calculated and used.[5] The government has also ordered that the registration of workers desiring EGS employment be updated. Nevertheless, registration records remain outdated, and registration bears little relation to labor attendance.[6] These shortcomings occur in part because those wanting to work on EGS projects prefer simply to show up on project sites and ask for work. But another reason why better indicators of demand for EGS employment have not been developed is that the personnel of the technical departments are more concerned with project supervision. Moreover, local politicians are not keen on developing such indicators because their control over such information would thereby be reduced.

Monitoring of the NREP is also shaped by political factors. The supervision of NREP projects is often divided among different gram panchayat members. According to one survey, 73 percent of the public works projects implemented by the panchayats are supervised by panchayat members or nonofficial residents of the locality.[7] This fragmentation contributes to delays in communicating data from the field and results in inadequate records.[8] A survey by the Government of West Bengal found that more than 25 percent of the West Bengal's gram panchayats do not keep proper records.[9] Perhaps even more worrisome, the

Government of West Bengal does not have an adequate mechanism to verify whether expenditures reported on paper by the panchayats have properly materialized in the field.[10]

Politics may also limit the learning process that derives from monitoring implementation—especially where programs are "tacked on" to agencies with well-defined organizational missions that have little relevance to the program.[11] In the EGS, for instance, few senior officials in the technical departments ever monitor EGS implementation. Even fewer devote energies to overcoming the problems of the EGS.[12] As a result, the technical departments are virtually never a source of policy innovation. District collectors show more concern for monitoring the EGS, because they are held responsible for its implementation by their superiors in the Revenue and Planning Departments. More often than not, however, collectors are absorbed by their other responsibilities. They are hard pressed just to smooth over the most obvious problems. The collectors' lack of time and expertise limit their role in improving EGS implementation.

When actors in an administrative network pursue different objectives, the effectiveness of implementation usually depends on the establishment of incentives that harness self-interested behavior to implementation objectives.[13] In the EGS, there are few incentives for technical department officers to become proficient in their responsibilities. Promotions depend on the recommendations of superiors, who care little and sometimes show disdain for the EGS. Field-level workers evince a notable lack of enthusiasm for the program. Working in their department's regular projects was the obvious path to career advancement, and the field-level workers particularly disliked the EGS requirements that they supervise laborers themselves rather than delegate the responsibility to contractors. In fact, field-level personnel are ill prepared for their EGS responsibilities. Their training as engineers gives them little preparation for managing labor relations and dealing with the public. Their lack of commitment to EGS objectives is a likely source of corruption.

To combat the lack of commitment by lower-level personnel, the FSA provided training programs and institutionalized an organizational mission that articulated the agency's objectives and identified the appropriate means to achieve them. No such measures were taken by the EGS. Even though the field-level personnel faced difficulties that they were ill prepared to deal with, training for the special problems that they confronted was not a consideration. The field-level personnel belonged to departments that considered the EGS peripheral to their primary objectives. Furthermore, while articulation of an organizational mission helped to resolve the problems of the FSA, it is part of the problem for the EGS. One reason for the lack of commitment among lower-level personnel is that the EGS has no place in the organizational missions of their agencies. Working on the EGS entails methods that are thought to be inferior by departmental standards, and most officials consider it to be a diversion from agency goals.

Like the FSA, the NREP experienced little interagency conflict, because gram panchayats retained most of the authority over implementation. Political factors still played an important role in conditioning implementation. Gram panchayat representatives generally prefer to distribute funds among their constituencies, even though larger projects with a greater potential for contribution to the area's development are not implemented as a result. The disparity between the limited economic opportunities offered by the NREP and the employment and infrastructural needs of rural West Bengal makes the temptation to favor their political supporters virtually irresistible, even when program expenditures could have a larger developmental impact if used in a nonpartisan fashion. Also, because the government lacks the means to verify whether expenditures made on paper have properly materialized in the field, funds can be siphoned off through substandard project construction and other forms of corruption.[14]

If implementing the NREP through panchayati raj institutions seems to open the door for political considerations to shape implementation, it also suggests that politics might be a factor curbing corruption and making implementation more responsive to social needs. In West Bengal, the dominant CPI(M) party frequently expelled members who were popularly associated with corruption. As discussed in chapter 4, parties that did not take such action were voted out of power with surprising frequency. Perhaps, then, implementation becomes more effective when it is embedded in a political process that pressures authorities to respond to social needs.

THE RATIONALITY OF POLITICS

Is politics always an impediment to effective implementation? Advocates of state autonomy argue that insulating state agencies from the political power of social groups is essential to effective implementation.[15] Does empowering state agencies to formulate independent goals and overcome the resistance of social groups necessarily make implementation more rational? A preoccupation with building state autonomy, in my view, diverts our attention from a more important problem—the need to balance state autonomy with mechanisms that make state agencies responsive to social needs. In poverty alleviation programs, these mechanisms generally require the use of political resources.

The implementation of public policy is left to government agencies that are enmeshed in complex relations with society. Most analysts contend that such "embedded bureaucracies" maintain an elitist bias that is counterproductive for effective poverty alleviation.[16] Bureaucratic authorities are likely to share the ideology of social elites. The ranks of government agencies may be filled by patronage appointees lacking the requisite expertise and commitment.[17] Officials in lower echelons are generally underpaid and susceptible to the temptations of corruption. Powerful local elites usually outlast policy initiatives from above, and local officials tend to adopt conservative attitudes rather than risking the hostility of these elites. Most observers of public policy in the Third World would agree with Joel Migdal's contention that "triangles of accommodation" formed among bureaucrats, politicians, and local "strongmen" reinforce the existing power structures and curtail the capacity of the state for bringing about social change.[18]

It is in this context that increasing state capacity and autonomy appears so desirable. State capacities derive from the accumulation of bureaucratic expertise, the commitment of officials, the availability of sufficient financial resources, and the maintenance of appropriate policy instruments. Autonomy is often the fortuitous consequence of conjunctural events such as war, destabilizing crises, or foreign intervention. However, many argue that autonomy can be enhanced if a corporate identity is established among state officials—which, following Weber, generally necessitates that bureaucrats receive a distinctive social status. Finally, in order to represent societal rather than particularistic interests, officials must be insulated from the demands of political parties and parochial groups.

The New Deal agencies for rural poverty alleviation present us with the strongest case for making implementing agencies autonomous from politics. From the mid-1930s to the early 1940s, the Roosevelt administration succeeded in insulating them from external political pressures. During the early years of the New Deal, funding came from emergency appropriations controlled by the president; and the top officials of the

RA and the FSA distributed decision-making authority within the agency in a way that made it less vulnerable to outside pressure. The RA and FSA's efforts to monitor their programs and redress the problems that were revealed were relatively effective. Operating with an ambiguous policy mandate and in a context of environmental uncertainty, they also improved the rationality of their programs by retrospectively adjusting their objectives to correspond better with their means. Yet many of the measures that increased the rationality of implementation contributed to the growing opposition to the agency among powerful social groups. With the FSA unable to secure a powerful constituency either among the public or within the Roosevelt administration, the opposition to the agency ultimately established a budgetary stranglehold, which it used to bring about the agency's demise. The fate of the FSA clearly suggests that, at the minimum, autonomous agencies need to build enough political support to ensure their survival. Either the programs that they implement should not become viewed as detrimental by dominant social interests, or they must build a constituency that is sufficiently powerful to defend them.

The case of the EGS raises other questions about the relationship between state autonomy and policy implementation. The technical departments that were responsible for implementing the program were relatively well endowed with expertise and resources. Their autonomy from outside pressure, however, led to many detrimental consequences. The technical departments were able to confiscate land from landowners with impunity. They were virtually immune from the efforts of the Revenue Department to discipline them. They also defied the state legislative committee in charge of supervising the program and succeeded in overriding its order to allow Arun Bhatia, a district collector, to proceed with his investigation of their involvement in EGS corruption. The experience of the EGS is replicated in other parts of India and throughout the world, especially where government agencies monopolize control over resources—such as irrigation, credit, construction contracts, and licenses—highly valued by society. In such cases, predatory motives, rather than those arising from the rational processes of implementation, often guide the activity of state agencies.[19]

These illustrations lead to the conclusion that we need a closer analysis of the optimal relationship between state and society than is usually provided by advocates of state autonomy. These analysts generally define state autonomy as the state's ability "to formulate and pursue goals that are not simply reflective of the demands or interests of social groups, classes, or society."[20] They frequently point out that the state, in its efforts to implement policies, must overcome the resistance of societal interests. In the process, they sometimes attribute a "global rationality" to state authorities while ignoring their predatory tendencies.[21] Their efforts to discern sources of state autonomy divert attention from another key problem, the need for mechanisms to make state agencies responsive to social needs.[22]

The relative importance of autonomy and responsiveness varies with attributes of policies and the agencies responsible for implementing them. Emphasis on autonomy is more appropriate for agencies such as central banks, which have technical criteria to guide their policy decisions and need relatively little external cooperation for effective implementation. Agencies such as agricultural extension services and rural poverty alleviation programs, which often lack specific technical criteria to guide their programs and whose successful policy implementation generally depends on the cooperation of groups in their environment, are in a different situation. They face greater needs for gathering information at the point of program delivery—especially as the diversity of local conditions increases. For such agencies, excessive autonomy may be detrimental to effective implementation. As successful implementation becomes more dependent on the provision of resources and information by actors in an agency's environment, autonomy becomes less important, and the need for mechanisms to ensure agency responsiveness increases.

Although advocates of strong states argue otherwise, state capacity and autonomy are not necessarily complementary. Theda Skocpol, in her thoughtful discussion of the concept, argues that state capacity consists of four components: stable administrative and military control of a given territory, loyal and skilled officials, plentiful financial resources, and the availability of policy instruments appropriate for obtaining the policy objectives at issue.[23] This form of capacity is likely to be positively related to state autonomy, since its increase involves the accumulation of state resources that free the state from societal constraints. However, increases in another type of state capacity may reduce state autonomy. Enhancing the resources controlled by state agencies is not the only way to increase state capacity. A state can augment its capacity by enlisting other social groups to contribute the use of their resources for achieving policy objectives. State-society relations need not be viewed as zero-sum games where strong societies mean weak states.[24] Implementation of the NREP sheds some light on this possibility, since political parties enhanced the state's capacity to achieve its policy objectives through their assistance in the planning and implementation of the program. Similarly, the information about local conditions provided by politicians and the demand for work expressed by workers enhanced the capacity of EGS officials to implement their program effectively.

Augmenting state capacities by securing the cooperation of nonstate actors is especially attractive to resource-poor developing states. But it usually requires a process similar to what Richard Samuels has described as the "politics of reciprocal consent," which may limit state autonomy.[25] Samuels conceptualized the politics of reciprocal consent to explain the success of Japanese industrial policy. Success, in part, hinged on the Japanese state's ability to persuade industrial elites to employ their resources in ways that helped to achieve policy objectives. The efficacy of Japan's industrial policy also grew out of the negotiations that were required to secure private sector cooperation. During these negotiations, observes Samuels, "businessmen are invited to the interior processes of government and bureaucrats are invited into the interior processes of the market."[26] The politics of reciprocal consent not only gained the cooperation of powerful industrial elites but also fostered a process of dynamic rationality, which refined policy objectives and adjusted policy instruments in a way that made policy more effective.

This discussion of state autonomy and state capacity highlights the importance of examining the mechanisms (or absence of mechanisms) available to ensure that policy implementation by state agencies is responsive to social needs. As state capacity increases through the state's accumulation of resources, the power of the state relative to society increases. Without the creation of mechanisms to ensure that the state uses its power in socially responsible ways, state autonomy may lead to state predation. As the state increases its capacity by securing the cooperation of actors in civil society, its autonomy will be constrained. Whether these constraints will make policy implementation responsive to social needs depends on two factors. First, a balance must be struck that allows state authorities sufficient discretion to exercise their expertise while simultaneously leaving nonstate actors with enough power to veto misguided state initiatives. Striking this balance is what Peter Evans refers to as "embedded autonomy."[27] The second factor is the relationship between the objectives of policy and the process of interest representation in the policy domain. The success of Japanese industrial policy was greatly facilitated by the coincidence of its objectives with the interests of powerful industrial elites. Each desired industrial growth and international competitiveness. The relationship between the objectives of rural poverty alleviation programs and the representation of rural interests is likely to be more problematic.

The social context of rural poverty alleviation programs is, of course, much different from that of Japanese industrial policy. The Japanese state is dependent on private industry, whose control over important economic resources makes its cooperation imperative. Because Japanese industrialists maintained close links to politicians in the ruling Liberal Democratic Party, they acquired political resources that helped to ensure bureaucratic responsiveness. The high degree of formal and informal organization among Japanese industrial elites, along with the stability of relations between industry and the state, also facilitated effective policy. In contrast, implementing agencies for the antipoverty programs discussed in this book did not depend on the economic resources of actors in the private sector. In each case, the administrative networks' control over economic resources and information provided implementing officials with power over their constituencies and opportunities for corruption.

THE PARADOX OF PARTICIPATION

The limited ability of environmental actors to influence the implementation of these poverty alleviation programs through their control over economic and informational resources means that politics provides them with their most viable medium of influence. This reliance on political mechanisms presents a paradox to those interested in making poverty alleviation policies responsive to the needs of the poor. The responsiveness of poverty alleviation programs to the poor requires a political process that represents their interests. But as long as the poor remain poor, they are disadvantaged in securing equitable representation.

Underpinning the paradox of participation is the assumption that inequalities of power, stemming from the differences in individual resource endowments, mediate political representation. Although citizens may possess formal political equality, there are marked variations in their social power. These differences stem, in large measure, from their positions in the organization of economic production and in other social organizations, such as the family and the community. Finally, but not the least important, are the differences resulting from their relations with political parties and the state.

The constraints posed by the structure of social power present serious problems for designing successful poverty alleviation programs. In the short term, dominant groups will intervene to ensure that programs do not impinge on their fundamental interests. They will also use their power to exploit program resources for their personal economic and political benefit. Over the long term, the intervention of dominant groups is likely to shape trajectories for economic development and condition political institutions in ways that reproduce their social dominance.

Land reform is one measure commonly offered to overcome the structural constraints on poverty alleviation and equitable development.[28] According to its advocates, in a country such as India, where the distribution of resources is skewed, the powerful will inevitably corner a lion's share of any goods and services targeted for the poor. They will do so because of their ability to collude with local bureaucrats and appropriate poverty alleviation resources for themselves. Without a prior redistribution of the bases of political power, the state is unlikely to provide poverty alleviation programs with sufficient resources to improve their plight relative to other groups. Any effort to create countervailing bases of power through political organization will proceed only until the wealthy begin to perceive it as a threat. Ultimately, strategies for economic development are constrained to reproduce structural inequalities, since their success depends on the production decisions of those already in control over economic resources. Since public policy cannot alter the consequences of an iniquitous structure, land reform is viewed as essential for equitable development.

Persuasive as it may be, advocacy of land reform is vulnerable to a number of criticisms. Most fundamental is its lack of political viability. Advocates of land reform point out that more incremental reforms are ineffective because they are subverted by landed interests; yet they seem to disregard this constraint in advocating a policy that strikes at the heart of these interests. Another criticism in the South Asian context is that there simply may not be enough land to go around.[29] This objection in part is surmounted by Herring's advocacy of a land-to-the-tiller policy combined with very low land ceilings; but, as Herring himself concludes, even then a vast majority of India's burgeoning rural proletariat is likely to be excluded from the benefits.[30] Others have argued that land ownership is no longer as central to economic development as suggested by the advocates of land reform. M. L. Dantwala, for instance, points out that land redistribution does not exhaust the possibilities for resource redistribution.[31] He advocates a strategy of augmenting income flows to the poor through the development of ancillary industries such as animal husbandry, forestry, and fisheries. Dantwala contends that transferring resources to the poor in these areas is likely to meet with less political resistance, since making the poor the primary beneficiaries of the development of ancillary industries does not bring them into confrontation with established interests.

Prescriptions for land reform, like those for more incremental reforms, founder on their lack of political viability. Can the political process be made more supportive of equitable development? A second strategy advocated to resolve the paradox of participation is to enhance the political organization of the rural poor. This strategy is based on the proposition that political power can achieve a measure of autonomy from other sources of social power. Even if social structure conditions political power, the formal political equality intrinsic to democracy offers possibilities for making the distribution of political power more equitable than that of social power. As the poor enter into political associations, they employ their political resources in a manner that enables them to make the state more responsive to their needs. Ultimately, they can use their political power to promote equitable development.

Nongovernment organizations (NGOs) , it is often suggested, can be organized to represent the political interests of the poor. The desirability of NGOs raises the important question of whether top-down initiatives can assist in promoting bottom-up development.[32] What can public policy do to encourage the development of NGOs? For historical reasons, the Indian state has long recognized the contributions of NGOs and provided them with considerable funding.[33] In its Seventh Five Year Plan, for instance, the Government of India recognized the role of NGOs in "accelerating the process of social and economic development" and declared, "During the Seventh Plan, serious efforts will be made to involve voluntary agencies [i.e., NGOs] in various development programmes, particularly in the planning and implementation of programmes of rural development."[34] State funding has increased from Rs. 40 million during the First Five Year Plan to Rs. 2 billion in the Seventh.[35] According to a survey of 1,273 NGOs completed in 1988, 47 percent received some form of funding from the Indian government.[36]

The patronage of the Indian state has not been without controversy, especially in the 1980s, when the state took a series of measures that appeared to be part of a systematic campaign to co-opt and control the increasingly rambunctious voluntary sector.[37] In 1980, the Kudal Commission was convened to investigate the Gandhi Peace Foundation. Ultimately, it investigated allegations against 945 NGOs. The 1983 Financial Act made it more difficult for NGOs to raise funds independently of the government by eliminating the tax exemption for industries making donations for rural development.[38] A 1985 amendment to the Foreign Contributions Control Act empowered the Government of India to ban foreign contributions to selected voluntary organizations. Shortly thereafter, it announced a list of 142 voluntary agencies that would be ineligible to receive foreign funds. The inclusion of the People's Union for Civil Liberties and the People's Union for Democratic Rights—civil liberties organizations that had been highly visible critics of the government but had never before even applied for permission to receive foreign funds—among those prohibited from receiving foreign funds dramatized the desire of the government to rein in its critics. Finally, in 1985, the government introduced legislation to establish a national council of voluntary agencies and a code of conduct. The legislation met with vehement opposition from many quarters of the NGO sector, who perceived it as an effort to extend state control.

The evolution of India's NGO sector reflects the exquisite tension between the state's capacity to stimulate NGOs and the need of the NGOs to retain autonomy from the state if they are to maintain their efficacy. While the financial benefits of state patronage have served as a stimulus to the voluntary sector, they have also made it vulnerable to state co-optation and control. The potential contribution of a vibrant but autonomous NGO sector to promoting equitable development raises the issue of whether there are ways that public policy might stimulate the development of such a sector while reducing the dangers of state control. Before looking into this issue, we must briefly examine the other agent that potentially can make political processes more responsive to the poor: political parties.

In his comparative study of poverty alleviation programs in three Indian states, Atul Kohli notes that the "political regimes" created by parties are the most important variables explaining the different degrees in the efficacy of poverty alleviation.[39] Yet, while noting the desirability of strong parties, Kohli is also cognizant of the difficulties in their development. In fact, he argues that they develop only under exceptional circumstances.[40] Our study of the NREP provides considerable support for Kohli's understanding of the importance of disciplined parties, even if it is less sanguine about the CPI(M)'s organizational discipline and commitment to the poor. Given their desirability, is there any way to encourage the development of NGOs and strong parties committed to the poor? Answering this question requires a better understanding of the relationship between public policy and political development.

POLITICAL DEVELOPMENT AND PUBLIC POLICY

The literature on political development provides us with few clues to why NGOs and disciplined political parties come into existence. Through the mid-1960s, most of the literature was concerned with developing a general theory to explain how the transition from "tradition" to "modernity" affected political systems. Analysts investigated the relationship between socioeconomic variables associated with modernization and the evolution of public participation and political parties.[41] By the 1970s, the recognition that political development was a crisis-laden process led to a greater interest in history and state formation.[42] At the same time that the study of public policy spread in the United States, observers of the Third World began to explore public policy as a means of better understanding how to overcome barriers to development.[43] Public policy became an important variable in explaining the economic success of some countries. It became crucial, if highly controversial, in explaining the successful development of the resource-poor countries such as South Korea and Taiwan.[44] Despite this appreciation of the importance of public policy for economic development, there has been little study of the impact of public policy on political development.[45]

Public policy has profound consequences for political development. While this conclusion is rooted in the empirical findings of this book, it also draws theoretical inspiration from recent studies of the development of welfare states.[46] Analysts of political and economic development in the Third World are only beginning to digest and employ these insights.[47]

The political impact of public policy stems in large measure from the ways that it affects the incentives of different groups for collective action. Different policies promote divergent patterns of political mobilization. These, in turn, shape the viability of new policies and, over the long term, the evolution of political institutions. Thus, different sequences of public policies help to explain divergent patterns of political as well as economic development. It is important not to commit the state-centered fallacy of understating the constraints on public policy presented by the social structure in which the state is embedded. While the formulation and implementation of public policy are conditioned by social structure, public policy simultaneously shapes the reproduction of that structure. Marxists, among others, tend to argue that the impact of public policy reinforces the structure of class relations in its environment. There is much evidence to support this contention. However, social structure conditions but does not determine the outcomes of public policy. While we must take seriously the constraints of social structure on public policy, we must also examine the impact of public policy on social structure, since it can produce alternative trajectories of development.

The New Deal policies toward agriculture are highly instructive in this sense. As discussed in chapter 2, American agriculture was in a state of crisis during the 1930s. To resolve the crisis, the Roosevelt administration intervened in the agricultural sector in unprecedented ways. New initiatives—such as the Agricultural Adjustment Administration, the Soil Conservation Service, and the Tennessee Valley Authority—provided the state with policy instruments that enhanced the state's power within the sector. The effectiveness of these agencies, like that of the Extension Service before them, depended on the cooperation of the country's commercial farmers. And while state intervention improved the desperate economic straits of the country's commercial farmers, it also strengthened their political power. The farmers used their new political resources to increase their influence in later rounds of policymaking and in some cases roll back the intervention of the state.

India has experienced a similar pattern. Its efforts to promote agricultural growth through the subsidization of inputs, commodity pricing, and the extension of physical and institutional infrastructure have produced a capitalist agricultural class and encouraged its political mobilization. In fact, India's agricultural development policies have given rise to two of the country's most dynamic political forces over the last decade: the new farmers' movement and the backward castes.[48] Policies designed to increase agricultural production enhance the power of dominant agricultural classes in most countries.[49] The success of these policies increases the resources under the control of these classes. Mechanisms used to stimulate production increase the farmers' incentives for political mobilization, which, in turn, enhances their capacity to make the state responsive to their interests.

If policies to promote agricultural development increased the economic and political resources of capitalist farmers, what about the impact of rural poverty alleviation programs? The mobilization and political organization that develop as a consequence of poverty alleviation programs are shaped by the political incentives created by the programs. Charles Tilly's resource mobilization model is useful for explaining the dynamics of collective action among the rural poor. The model asserts that collective action is a function of four variables: interest, organization, mobilization, and opportunity.[50]

Tilly argues that collective action is more likely when people believe that they have common interests.[51] The stated objectives of poverty alleviation programs often encourage the perception of common interests among the poor. For instance, the FSA's implementation of poverty alleviation programs during the New Deal helped to spur a broad-based coalition to defend the agency from the attack of Southern conservatives and commercial agriculturalists. The EGS's guarantee of employment makes workers' common interest in employment security explicit. In addition, the program also assembles the poor in large numbers under common conditions, thus reducing many of their subjective social divisions (such as caste). At the same time, it dramatizes that they can acquire employment by making demands on government officials. The NREP promotes the realization of common interests among the rural poor by highlighting their need for employment security and reducing social divisions in a fashion similar to the EGS. In addition, by decentralizing authority over implementation in gram panchayats and involving the public in the decision-making process, it encouraged the development of a popular interest in program implementation. However, the absence of an employment guarantee has enabled politicians to use the program to reward loyal supporters and penalize their opponents. These actions have created new divisions among the rural poor.

The EGS and the NREP facilitated organization by reducing logistical barriers. For instance, prior to the program, most EGS workers were geographically dispersed on their own plots or on the farms of others. The EGS assembles workers in central locations and subjects them to a single employer and common working conditions. By coordinating the actions of workers to achieve a common objective, the projects promote interaction and cooperation. The social networks that spread among workers encourage collective action, just as the establishment of assembly line factories facilitated the unionization of factory workers. In contrast, the programs of the FSA did relatively little to enhance the organization of its beneficiaries. Its main program, the rural rehabilitation loans, did little to promote interaction among its beneficiaries. Although other FSA programs, such as cooperatives and neighborhood action groups, potentially could have promoted political mobilization, these programs were either limited in scope or their membership was small and scattered. They never coalesced into a potent political force.

Tilly's third variable, mobilization, refers to the acquisition of collective control over resources. He suggests that group loyalty promotes mobilization by increasing the probability of collective control.[52] Others stress the importance of entrepreneurs in resource mobilization.[53] By placing workers in situations where they cooperate in pursuit of common goals, programs like the EGS and the NREP encourage the development of loyalties among their constituencies. They also create conditions that facilitate the activity of entrepreneurs by providing them with resources—in this case employment—that they can deliver as rewards to workers for participation in collective action. Differences between the two programs, however, create important variations in the patterns of mobilization that develop. The employment guarantee in Maharashtra has contributed to the state's active NGO sector. In West Bengal, in contrast, implementation of the NREP through the panchayats without any work guarantee has enabled political parties such as the CPI(M) to control the distribution of the benefits. Party control has limited the ability of entrepreneurs outside the party to mobilize the poor, and it has made the poor more dependent on the CPI(M).

Opportunity, the final variable in Tilly's theory of collective action, has three components: repression, opportunity, and power. The EGS and the NREP encourage collective action by reducing the probability that it will be repressed. In rural India, larger farmers sometimes take violent measures to discourage mobilization of their workers. Government is a more benign employer. By making jobs available to the rural poor, the EGS and the NREP provide opportunities that reward collective action. Similarly, by protecting the interests of migrant workers and providing rehabilitation loans, the FSA often reduced the dependence of its clientele on local elites. This potential threat motivated agricultural elites to terminate the programs. Power is also likely to facilitate collective action. According to Tilly, the more powerful a collectivity, the more likely it is to realize opportunities and the greater propensity it will have to undertake collective action to obtain its opportunities. The EGS, in particular, enhances the power of its clientele. The employment guarantee legitimates the workers' claims for employment and mandates that the state respond positively. The program also facilitates collective action of the rural poor against their employers in the private sector by providing them with alternative sources of employment security. While the NREP has similar effects, they are diluted by the limited amount of employment made available under the program and the wider scope for political discretion in the distribution of employment.

In each of our cases, the implementation of poverty alleviation programs has important consequences for the political mobilization of the poor. Each program, to a greater or lesser extent, shaped the rural poor's perception of common interests, as well as their organization, mobilization, and opportunities for collective action. Yet there are important differences in the programs' political impact. The impact of the New Deal programs was constrained by the rural rehabilitation program's limited effect on the organization and mobilization of its clientele. Societal and institutional factors—such as the geographical isolation of clientele, their lack of education, racial divisions, and disfranchisement—also impeded collective action. The EGS promoted more pluralistic mobilization than the NREP. While the ruling Congress (I) probably was most able to take advantage of the opportunities for mobilization, the opposition and NGOs also benefited. Consequently, the poor were provided with a variety of avenues to advance their interests. In the NREP in West Bengal, the local party in power—usually the CPI(M) or a Left Front ally—monopolized the opportunities for mobilization. The NREP was used for patronage resources, which built up the party by benefiting party supporters while providing few benefits to those supporting other parties and NGOs.

Implementation of these programs also affected political parties. By generating benefits to distribute to the poor, they identify a new constituency and direct a party's attention in its direction. As parties take advantage of the opportunities provided by programs to mobilize support from the poor, they become less dependent on the support of other groups. To the extent that parties can gain access to power through the votes of the poor, as opposed to the resources of others, poverty alleviation programs help to make the political process more autonomous from other forms of social power. Although rural poverty programs do not radically transform parties, they may alter their strategic calculus.

All poverty alleviation programs are likely to have some impact on the incentives for collective action among the rural poor. However, distributive programs are more likely to benefit politicians and officials responsible for determining who gets the benefits; universalistic programs, in contrast, are less amenable to being monopolized in this fashion. They generate greater mobilization of the poor, since they create incentives for such mobilization by opposition parties and NGOs, in addition to the opportunities they provide to the party in power. Universalistic policies have facets that are especially desirable for encouraging the development of NGOs. By creating incentives for the mobilization of the poor without directly intervening in the process, they shape the political marketplace to stimulate the development of NGOs but do not interfere with the autonomy that is essential to their vitality. In generating incentives for NGOs and opposition parties to mobilize the poor, they spawn multiple avenues for pursuing the interests of the poor. Universalistic programs do not eliminate the patronage politics characteristic of the NREP in West Bengal, but they make the poor less dependent on the party in power by providing them with alternative avenues for securing program benefits. The programs, in turn, are likely to be more responsive to the needs of the poor because the organizational interests of a ruling party cannot completely supersede their interests.

ENHANCING CAPABILITIES, TARGETED UNIVERSALISM, AND EQUITABLE DEVELOPMENT

What types of policies are likely to produce more equitable development if one considers the political consequences of public policy? The answer to this question depends in part on the initial conjuncture of economic and political circumstances. Below, I pose the issue for India and the United States. Of course, the situations in the two countries are quite different. But even with these differences, there are some striking parallels.

While India's current economic problems make expensive new departures unlikely and cuts in expensive but ineffective programs attractive, changes in Indian society make new approaches to poverty desirable. India's rural sector has remained remarkably large after the country's first four decades. Although agriculture's share of the GDP dropped from 60 percent in 1950–51 to 33 percent in 1987–88, its share of the labor force remained substantial—falling only from 68.1

percent in 1951 to 66.5 percent in 1981. Population growth has placed growing pressure on the land. From 1970 to 1980, the number of operational farmholdings increased from 70.5 million to 89.4 million, while the area operated increased by only 0.67 million hectares. The percentage of marginal farmers (those owning less than one hectare) increased from 50.6 to 56.5 percent, and the portion of the rural labor force working as wage laborers rose from 34 percent in 1972–73 to 40 percent in 1983.[54]

At the same time that the number of marginal farmers and agricultural laborers is increasing, traditional patron-client relations are eroding.[55] In the process, the basis of social domination has been transformed.[56] Traditional forms of domination, embedded in the reciprocal obligations arising from primary production relations, are increasingly replaced by market relations, the legal system, political patronage, and coercion. Agricultural laborers and peasants increasingly look to the state for the social services and social safety net that were once provided by their patrons. The role of the state in providing these services has become an important issue in Indian politics. The growing numbers of small farmers and agricultural laborers provide a substantial constituency for social welfare programs.

India is in a period of intense political competition. The failure of the Congress (I) Party to win a majority in the 1989 and 1991 general elections signaled the end of its hegemony over Indian politics. While the Congress (I) remains in power as a minority government, opposition parties are engaged in a heated competition to fashion new political coalitions capable of capturing power. The Bharatiya Janata Party endeavors to build a new majority through its appeal to *Hindutva,* or Hindu nationalism. The Janata Dal is struggling to assemble a coalition from groups in the lower echelons of India's caste system: the "backward classes," the scheduled castes, and the scheduled tribes. The intensity of the competition increases the attractiveness of appealing to groups at the bottom of the social hierarchy, although, until now, efforts to incorporate these groups have been based more on symbolic gestures and populist appeals than on systematic programs.[57]

India, like most developing countries, cannot afford expensive poverty alleviation programs that do not contribute to economic growth. Instead, it needs strategies that increase production while laying the foundation for more equitable development. Such a strategy might link two current approaches to economic development: Amartya Sen's capability-enhancing strategy and Theodore Schultz's advocacy of investment in human capital.[58] A strategy for enhancing people's capabilities by creating a well-educated, healthy, and secure work force can lead to improved productivity and economic efficiency. By enabling people to replace "the domination of circumstances and chance" with their "domination over chance and circumstances" it also can help to make the political process more responsive to popular needs.[59]

While analysts like Sen make a persuasive case for a capability-enhancing strategy, they do not tell us how such a strategy might be implemented successfully in the sober realities of Indian public policy. The barriers to effective programs are formidable. Indian politicians have traditionally appealed to the poor with progressive rhetoric while allowing wealthy businessmen, government bureaucrats, and prosperous farmers to intervene in the policy process to protect their interests. As a consequence, poverty alleviation programs are underfunded and inefficiently implemented. Funding for primary education is inadequate, despite an impressive accumulation of evidence showing that greater spending would reap high social returns.[60] Spending for elementary education declined from 56 percent of all education expenditures in India's First Five Year Plan (1951–1956) to 29 percent in the Seventh Five Year Plan (1985–1990).[61] Public food distribution in India has poor rural coverage, and in fact functions more as an instrument for agricultural price supports.[62] Funding for public health is also in short supply, and preventive measures go neglected while less efficient curative medicine remains highly subsidized.[63]

The gravity of these problems leaves little room for optimism. There is a substantial gap between the progressive rhetoric that justifies new programs and the bleak reality of their implementation. Numerous studies show that, if these programs are to be efficient and socially responsive, the people they are designed for must pressure government officials to achieve policy objectives.[64] There is no simple recipe for achieving such political mobilization. It usually arises from a complex of historical, social, cultural, and political variables.[65] This study has suggested that the incentives for collective action established by public policy can also contribute to the political mobilization of the poor.

Recent advocates of social policy reform stress the importance of targeting program beneficiaries in order to maximize the benefits delivered to them within given financial constraints.[66] Rarely do they take into account the political repercussions of targeting. Reducing the scope of a policy also circumscribes its constituency. In the case of poverty alleviation programs, narrowing the target restricts the constituency to segments of society with traditionally the least political clout. Thus, such targeting increases the efficiency of expenditures but undercuts the programs' political viability. The impact of targeted programs is frequently limited from the beginning, because they fail to attract sufficient budgetary allocations. Such programs become especially vulnerable at times of fiscal stress. Programs that provide universal benefits, in contrast, create the potential for broad political coalitions that transcend classes, castes, and religious groups. Such coalitions are usually essential to long-term political viability.[67]

The cases discussed in this book illustrate these dynamics. The targeting of the rural poor by the New Dealers contributed to making the FSA one of the most vulnerable components of the New Deal legacy after mobilization for World War II changed budget priorities and placed fiscal pressures on the federal government. One might expect that targeting the rural poor in India would have greater political viability given the greater share of the country's population mired in poverty. Nevertheless, the impact of poverty alleviation programs such as the NREP remained limited because the Government of India failed to allocate sufficient funds. The EGS, on the other hand, with its universalistic entitlement and greater success at creating productive infrastructure, is supported by a broad-based popular coalition and has received more generous funding. Since May 1988, EGS employment and expenditures have been scaled back somewhat. That the government made these cuts through surreptitious administrative means, while ostensibly doubling EGS wages, illustrates the continued popularity of the program even in times of fiscal crisis.[68]

Developing countries such as India are unlikely to be able to afford universalistic social welfare programs at a time when even the welfare states of advanced industrial societies find the costs of such programs prohibitive.[69] Fortunately, policies whose benefits are distributed on universalistic principles need not exclude targeting. In fact, it is possible to reap some of the advantages of each principle through *targeted universalism*[70]—that is, through the strategic selection of policy tasks to which universalistic principles are to be applied. These tasks should be selected according to four criteria. First, the policies should be legitimated by values that have widespread social appeal. Second, the policy task should be within the administrative competence and financial capacity of the state; otherwise, the appealing rhetoric of a policy is transformed into hypocrisy by the state's inability to deliver on its promises. Third, the policy domain should be defined so as to include substantial potential for reducing poverty while distributing its benefits according to universalistic principles. Finally, the political impact of these policies should reduce the dependence of the poor, increase their political capacities, and help to establish a political configuration that would encourage the pursuit of more equitable developmental strategies.

Targeted universalism would require bridging the gap between rhetoric and reality in Indian social programs. Guarantees of employment would have to be fulfilled. Efforts to universalize primary education—first pledged by Article 45 of the Indian constitution for 1960, now proposed for 1995—would have to be pursued more systematically. Primary health centers would have to be made more viable. As it is now, a vicious cycle leads to the hollowing of many social welfare programs. Primary schools lack the facilities and resources to impart educational skills successfully.[71] The schools' failure to provide stimulation and skills make the option of leaving school to augment family income all the more attractive. Similarly, the lack of supplies and services at the primary health centers encourages their neglect by residents.

Targeted universalism offers the promise to reverse the vicious cycle of neglect by the government and clientele alike. The strategy involves creating new incentives for increasing popular demand for targeted services. It would do so in two ways. First, the government would limit the array of services supplied by the state and enhance their quality. Second, the social welfare programs would decentralize authority over implementation to permit greater popular participation. As our study of the EGS and the NREP illustrates, decentralizing the administrative level to block or gram panchayats encouraged greater interest in the administration of these programs. It also created incentives for parties and interest groups to keep in closer contact with the local scene. Political competition on the local scene among parties and NGOs promotes political mobilization and makes implementation more responsive.

The universalistic provision of employment security, primary education, and public health programs would help to break down the manifold divisions in Indian society by promoting broad-based coalitions in support of these programs. Castes and classes alike would acquire a common interest in sustaining and enhancing the services provided. History shows that when community institutions such as primary schools and primary health centers become vital centers of social activity, they also encourage community mobilization.[72]

Employment security, primary education, and public health programs would benefit everyone, but they would be especially beneficial in improving the plight of the poor. Landowners would be the primary beneficiaries of the infrastructure created through public works, but the poor would obtain immediate gains through the opportunities for supplementing their income. They would also secure secondary benefits as additional infrastructure augments their income-generating opportunities. While studies show that increased education has a significant positive effect on agricultural productivity,[73] the impact is greatest in backward regions characterized by poor environmental conditions and low technology. Furthermore, the social rate of return from education of backward castes is higher than for nonbackward castes.[74] In fact, numerous studies have concluded that higher levels of education contribute to a reduction in income inequality and in the incidence of poverty.[75] Similarly, an effective primary health care system would be especially beneficial to India's poor. Studies show that the poor suffer from relatively higher rates of illness than other segments of Indian society. Poor health translates into lost days of work and reduced earnings; better health means higher productivity, and more robust agricultural workers receive higher wages.[76]

A major advantage of the capability-enhancing strategy's emphasis on employment security, primary education, and primary health care is the complementarities that exist among these different fields. Parents with employment security will be less likely to encourage their children to miss school in order to supplement the family income. Their employment security is also likely to contribute to better nutrition and improved health. The spread of primary education and literacy has been shown to be positively related to higher earnings. Better education, especially among women, contributes to better health and nutritional practices. It also promotes greater receptiveness to family planning. Improved health increases one's earnings and one's ability to learn. Furthermore, as life spans grow longer, the incentives to invest in a child's education and training increase.

Applying the principle of targeted universalism to social policy will require a reorientation of fiscal and administrative priorities, but the strains that accompany these changes are likely to be less than anticipated. For instance, the costs of guaranteeing the right to work through manual labor on public works can be held down if wage rates are regulated to make employment attractive only to those truly in need. Such wage rates can act as a selection mechanism to increase the efficiency of expenditures on other poverty alleviation programs. For instance, recipients of India's Integrated Rural Development Programme loans could be required to provide labor on public works and contribute a share of their earnings as "sweat equity."[77] This arrangement would have the additional benefit of making the selection of IRDP beneficiaries the product of the choice of the beneficiaries themselves rather than the discretion of local politicians. In primary education, recent studies have shown that Karnataka's transfer of control over primary education to *mandal* (local) panchayats improved their effectiveness dramatically. In addition, the panchayats raised additional resources to improve facilities and hire more teachers.[78] In public health, India's vast array of programs might be reduced to a more manageable set of tasks.

Targeted universalism offers a way to make the implementation of capability-enhancing programs more effective. In targeting policy tasks (rather than beneficiary groups), policymakers can ensure that the ambitiousness of policy objectives does not exceed the available resources and bureaucratic expertise. As this study of the EGS and the NREP illustrates, decentralized authority also enhances implementation efficiency by encouraging local politicians and residents to provide valuable information about the best way to meet local needs. Although the decentralizing of authority may provide local officials and politicians with more opportunities for corruption, it discourages corruption in the more senior ranks. In fact, combining decentralized authority with targeted universalism creates mechanisms that curb corruption. Universal eligibility limits the discretion of authorities to select beneficiaries, while decentralization makes information about implementation more easily available to the public. The activities of local authorities are also more susceptible to public scrutiny, and the channels for pursuing grievances are more accessible. As this comparison of the EGS in Maharashtra and the NREP in West Bengal suggests, universalism also encourages the development of more pluralistic political mobilization. In Maharashtra, the universalism of the EGS provided incentives for the political organization of the poor by nongovernmental organizations and opposition parties as well as by the ruling party. In contrast, the NREP in West Bengal was used largely as a source of patronage by the CPI(M). Although no party in Maharashtra has demonstrated a commitment to the rural poor comparable to the CPI(M)'s, the availability of alternative avenues for representing the interests of subaltern groups clearly enhanced the responsiveness of the state.

Some critics will argue that these proposals are too expensive for a resource-poor country like India. However, India's allocation of resources in these areas frequently falls below that of other countries at comparable levels of development. Furthermore, the problem is not only one of allocating additional resources but also of improving the efficiency of current expenditures.[79] By forcing a reevaluation of policy, India's economic problems may well enhance the prospects for new policy departures rather than curtail them.[80] Ultimately, increasing expenditures in the policy domains that I have outlined is economically viable because it constitutes a good investment in growth as well as social equity.

Other critics will argue that these proposals are too modest and that more radical redistributive programs are needed. However, redistributional policies are much more difficult to implement than expanding-sum policies that simultaneously promote greater equity. Moreover, capability-enhancing policies can be instrumental in bringing about a context favorable to more radical reform. They can lay the basis for progressive policy sequences that establish the conditions for more equitable development in the future. Ultimately, these criticisms reflect the demanding task that confronts any policymaker: to advocate measures that maximize the achievement of policy objectives while not exceeding the limits of what is possible.

While rural poverty is an important item on India's political agenda, it remains one of the most striking silences of American public policy.[81] In contrast to India, the rural population of the United States has diminished to only 22.5 percent of the total population, and the consequent electoral demographics divert the attention of many politicians to other areas. But this sectoral trend has not prevented the federal government from subsidizing America's farmers with billions of dollars in annual price supports, even though farmers and farmworkers account for less than 2 percent of the nation's work force. A primary reason for American policymakers' inattentiveness to social welfare in rural America is that the patterns of political mobilization established the hegemony of the farm bloc over rural development policy.[82] This hegemony has been sustained by the continuing linkages between producer organizations and congressional subcommittees as well as by the continued resonance of "agricultural fundamentalism"—the belief that rural America is still a land of farms.[83] As we have seen, ever since the Extension Service helped to organize the local farm bureaus, public policy has promoted the organization of commercial farmers. The farmers' political mobilization, as well as their control over critical resources, shaped the development of state institutions such as the USDA in ways that protected their interests. The impetus to alleviate rural poverty during the New Deal was extinguished by the attack of farm organizations such as the American Farm Bureau Federation and weak support within the USDA. Farmers continue to dominate the rural agenda even though agricultural employment accounts for only 8 percent of the rural work force.[84]

Another important reason for the neglect of rural poverty in the United States has to do with the American version of the "urban bias" that is usually associated with the developing world.[85] Those concerned with poverty have tended to focus on more visible urban areas rather than on rural areas. The plight of the urban poor has been dramatized by protest and violent crime, whereas rural areas have remained relatively peaceful. It is simply more difficult to ignore poverty in the nation's political, cultural, and financial capitals than in peripheral areas such as Appalachia and the Mississippi delta.

Yet it can be argued that the problem of poverty is at least as serious in rural as in urban areas. Rural poverty has consistently remained at higher levels than poverty in metropolitan areas, and the gap increased during the 1980s.[86] In 1989, rural poverty (poverty in nonmetropolitan areas) reached 16.3 percent, significantly higher than the 12.7 percent for metropolitan areas. True, poverty in central cities reached a level of 19 percent; but the level of poverty in the rural South was 20.5 percent.[87]

The history of neglect has not made the problem less serious. Neither has the movement of the rural population out of agriculture. In 1989, only 8 percent of the rural work force was employed in agriculture. The service and trade sector employed 63 percent, and manufacturing employed 18 percent—slightly higher than the 17 percent of the urban work force in manufacturing. However, 72 percent of rural manufacturing jobs were in routine manufacturing industries, which employ low-wage laborers on semiskilled jobs.[88] Just as it seemed that rural America had integrated itself with American industry, albeit at the lower end, American industry began to lose or transfer its low-wage jobs abroad. During the 1980s, the United States economy continued to create new jobs at a rate that was the envy of other advanced industrial societies. As a study of job creation between 1979 and 1984 has shown, two-thirds of these jobs were in the service sector and over 80 percent of them were located in urban areas.[89] The result was a rural economy with a high share of low-wage jobs, if jobs were available at all.

A consequence of these trends is that the working poor make up a large share of the rural poor. In 1987, about 10 percent of the working households in rural America lived below the poverty line.[90] Of the rural poor, 46 percent worked either full-time or part-time during 1987. Some 72 percent of the working poor were unable to find full-time work while 28 percent worked full-time but for such low wages that they remained in poverty.[91] The high rates of underemployment and unemployment mean that much of the concern for individual motivation reflected in the Family Support Act of 1988 and much of the recent literature on poverty are far less relevant to resolving rural poverty than is the need to provide people with skills and viable jobs.

The rural economy is characterized by uneven development as well as low-wage jobs. Economic growth varied much more in rural than in metropolitan counties of the United States. While one in every five rural counties experienced a net loss of employment between 1977 and 1984, one in four created more jobs than the average metropolitan county. The fastest-growing counties were those where the service industry was fueled by an influx of retirees, the tourist industry, or government jobs. A series of studies by the USDA classified 206 of 2,443 rural counties as "persistently low-income counties"—counties with the lowest per capita income of all rural counties in the years 1950, 1959, 1969, 1979, and 1984. All but eighteen of these counties were located in the South, and most were in Appalachia, the Ozark-Ouachita Plateau, and the Mississippi delta. These economically backward counties were characterized by low levels of education. The share of persons over twenty-five years old who did not complete high school was 58.1 percent, versus 42.5 percent for all rural counties. They also possessed a disproportionate share of African-Americans—23.3 percent compared to 8.4 percent for all rural counties.[92]

Rural poverty manifests some important parallels with urban poverty. Recent studies have cogently argued that there is a rural as well as an urban "underclass." Like those who make up the urban underclass, members of the rural underclass tend to be concentrated in high-poverty areas and suffer from long-term poverty. Thirty-nine percent of the rural poor reside in high-poverty areas, while 52 percent of the urban poor live in such areas. Even a larger number of rural poor (7.8 percent) than urban poor (4.4 percent) are enmeshed in long-term poverty. In a meaningful sense, both rural and urban poor are caught in pockets that have become increasingly isolated from the economic mainstream as a result of economic restructuring. They suffer from the emigration of their most talented members. Those who are left behind lack education and skills and are economically marginalized.[93]

All these statistics clearly indicate that capability-enhancing programs such as job training, public service employment, and improved social services are needed in the United States just as they are in India. However, the political obstacles confronting the enactment of such programs are even more formidable in the United States. After all, the rural poor constitute a much smaller share of the American population— approximately 3.7 percent—and are even more marginalized. By the late 1960s, even the potent farm bloc was obliged to engage in logrolling by including the food stamp program in the same legislation with agricultural price supports in order to gain enough support to enact its program.[94] Designing policies that unite the interests of the rural poor with the urban poor and other segments of the American public will be essential to enacting a program that can ameliorate their plight.

CONCLUDING REMARKS

The politics of rationality—the political conditioning of rational processes of policy implementation—is generally viewed as detrimental to effective policy implementation. One measure often recommended for minimizing this problem is to enhance the autonomy of state agencies. I have made a qualified argument against this solution. Enhancing autonomy by augmenting the resources and expertise employed by an agency can increase the effectiveness of public policy to a point. Government agencies certainly need resources and expertise in order to achieve their policy objectives. In cases where state agencies use technical criteria as decision rules to guide implementation, and where they are involved in "stroke of the pen" implementation requiring little cooperation from others, building technical expertise and autonomy may suffice. In many cases, however, as resources and power become concentrated in state agencies, there is need to establish mechanisms to ensure responsiveness to societal needs in order to limit the predatory tendencies of the agencies.

Government agencies frequently depend on the cooperation of other actors to enhance state capacity and achieve policy objectives. Here, a process akin to "the politics of reciprocal consent" may act as a mechanism to secure responsiveness. However, enhancing the effectiveness of public policy in this way requires policy objectives to coincide with the interests of the most powerful actors in the implementation environment. But rural poverty alleviation programs are not designed to benefit "the most powerful actors." Thus, "the paradox of participation" comes into play: public participation is essential for making the implementation of poverty alleviation programs responsive to the needs of the poor; but since the poor lack political power, the participatory process inadequately represents their interests. Enhancing the power and representation of the poor is essential for resolving this paradox.

Some argue that, because political power is closely tied to social power, effective poverty alleviation can occur only after fundamental changes in the structure of social domination take place. In broader terms, they maintain that social structure limits the agency of public policy to courses of action that reproduce social domination. Others contend that the structural constraints on public policy can be transformed with the establishment of organizations—such as NGOs and disciplined political parties—that support the interests of the poor. While sympathetic to this approach, I have claimed that it is insufficient, since it does little to explain how such organizations will be created.

The challenge for policymakers interested in alleviating poverty and promoting more equitable development is to alter the constraints of iniquitous social structures by designing programs that enhance the incentives for political mobilization of the poor. Such programs will enable the poor to secure more equitable representation and will make public policy more responsive to their interests. Specifically, capability-enhancing programs implemented on the basis of targeted universalism can build political support for more equitable development. By improving the education of the poor, these programs increase their political awareness. By ameliorating their health, they lay the basis for a more energetic activism. By increasing their employment security, the strategy reduces their economic dependence on social elites. Providing the benefits of these programs on a universalistic basis enhances their political viability in the immediate conjuncture and helps to forge coalitions that are likely to promote more equitable development over the long run.

The argument here is not that capability-enhancing programs implemented on the basis of targeted universalism will radically transform the constraints of social structure. In fact, the specific content of capability-enhancing programs will have to be tailored to accommodate the constraints of a particular conjuncture if they are to be viable. At the same time, however, the impact of these programs will augment the political resources controlled by subaltern groups and increase their ability to make the policy responsive to their needs. This strategy is likely to produce incremental change, resulting in more equitable trajectories of development. Even though it is unlikely to produce radical change, it prepares subaltern groups to play a more efficacious role in periods when dramatic change becomes possible.

The political impact of public policy has important consequences whether or not it is properly evaluated. It can be an important factor in promoting more equitable development. Although social structure constrains the viability of policy alternatives, it often allows options that encourage the accumulation of political resources by the less privileged segments of a society. This accumulation process is likely to be slow and incremental. It may suffer reverses. The consequences of change in the political distribution of resources will continue to be shaped by social structure. Nevertheless, using public policy to augment the political resources of the poor is a viable strategy for generating the support necessary for more equitable economic and political development.

Statistical Appendix to Chapter 3

Relationships between Social Economic
Variables and the Spatial Distribution
of EGS Employment Generation

If, as I have argued, the guarantee of employment under the Employment Guarantee Scheme creates a political market, then areas within Maharashtra with relatively greater surplus labor should have greater demand for EGS labor, and implementation of the EGS should respond by generating more employment in these areas. To test this argument, I examined the relationship between the incidence of EGS employment and various socioeconomic factors in twenty-five districts throughout Maharashtra. The dependent variable is based on data provided by the Planning Department of the Government of Maharashtra showing monthly EGS employment generation for each of the districts from July 1975 through December 1989. Thirteen independent variables are socioeconomic indicators that I hypothesized should be related to the demand for EGS employment. These variables fall into four categories.

Category I includes indicators of agricultural development. If my hypotheses are correct, EGS employment will be negatively related to the level of agricultural development. DRYAG represents the average share of gross cropped area planted under *rabi jowar, bajra,* and pulses for each district for the years from 1976–77 through 1978–79. These crops represent traditional agriculture. They are rain-fed crops that are generally located in arid areas. They yield low productivity.[1] PROD is another indicator of agricultural development. It represents the average productivity per hectare of agricultural land from 1978–79 to 1980–81. AGINDEX is a composite measure of agricultural development that sums three indices: (1) the annual average percentage of a district's gross cropped area that is irrigated for 1976–77 to 1978–79, divided by the percentage of gross cropped area that is irrigated in the state as a whole during the same period; (2) a district's average fertilizer consumption in kilograms per hectare for 1980–81 to 1982–83, divided by the statewide average; (3) the share of normal area sown in cereals that was under hybrid and higher-yielding varieties of seeds in 1982–83, divided by the share for the entire state. LIT is also included as an indicator of agricultural development. It represents the share of the rural population that is literate.[2]

Category II includes indicators of labor-intensive agriculture. My hypothesis is that EGS employment should decline with increases in the labor intensity of a district's agriculture. The first variable is DBLCROP, the share of a district's net sown area that was double-cropped in 1978–79. The second variable is GROSSIR, the average percentage of a district's gross cropped area that was irrigated from 1976–77 through 1978–79. RAIN, the third variable, represents the average rainfall in each district over the fifty-year period from 1901 to 1950.[3]

Category III includes variables representing groups in the population that are thought to have a high demand for EGS employment. AGLAB indicates the share of a district's rural (main) labor force in 1981 that is composed of agricultural laborers. SCLAB represents the share of a district's rural labor force that is composed of members of scheduled castes in 1981. STLAB is the share of a district's rural labor force in 1981 that is composed of members of scheduled tribes. TWOHAS is an indicator of the prevalence of small farmers. It represents the share of the total number of operational landholdings in a district that were less than two hectares in 1970–71. Finally, HHIND represents the change in the percentage of the rural work force employed in household industries from 1971 to 1981.[4]

Category IV is based on the assertion that administrative capacity may affect EGS employment.[5] Increases in EGS employment may be associated with the greater availability of officials to administer the program. The sole variable in this category is ADMIN, the number of a district's Revenue Department and technical department officers in 1974, divided by its rural work force in 1981.[6]

DRYAG is the independent variable most highly correlated with LABATT (see table 10). Its .78 Pearson correlation coefficient is significant at the .001 level. Next, note the high negative correlation between LABATT and PROD. The −.58 coefficient is significant at the .01 level. PROD is probably the best indicator of agricultural development. This finding further supports the argument that the EGS redistributes expenditures to districts with relatively underdeveloped agriculture. Two other variables have significant correlations with LABATT. RAIN has a negative correlation of −.55. This is probably a function of its −.64 correlation with DRYAG. LIT also has a significant correlation coefficient of −.52. Literacy is often associated with development. Indeed, our data show that it has a .44 correlation with PROD—our measure of agricultural development. The significant negative relationship between LIT and LABATT supports our argument that the EGS tends to generate employment in relatively backward districts.

The correlation between AGINDEX and LABATT is negative, as we would predict, but its −.28 coefficient is not significant. The relatively weak association is probably a consequence of the unexpectedly high positive correlation between GROSSIR, one of AGINDEX's indices, and LABATT. Their .52 coefficient is the opposite sign from our predictions. It is significant at the .01 level.

There are two plausible explanations for this anomaly. One is that the correlation may be spurious. All districts have less than 20 percent of their gross cropped area under irrigation. Ten have less than 10 percent. These small shares may not be sufficient to drive the relationship. The small size of gross cropped area under irrigation explains how irrigation can be positively associated with dryland agriculture. The .52 correlation coefficient for GROSSIR and DRYAG is significant at the .01 level.

Second, the coincidence of high levels of EGS employment with the most extensive areas under irrigation in the Western Maharashtra districts may be the result of an underlying political dynamic. Western Maharashtra is usually considered to be the region of the state with the greatest political influence in the state government. The relatively high share of gross cropped area under irrigation and EGS employment and expenditures may be a consequence of the greater political influence exercised by the politicians of these districts.[7]

We can better understand the relationship of the variables to the incidence of EGS employment among Maharashtra's districts by using multiple regression to test the four categories (see table 11). Category I generates the highest adjusted R square statistic. Its adjusted R square of .66 is achieved largely through the relationship of DRYAG to LABATT. DRYAG's beta value of .60 is by far the most substantial of all variables in the category. Its t test is significant at the .001 level. It is the only variable of the category that is significant. Category II fares less impressively. Its adjusted R square is only .46. RAIN is the only variable that is significant.

Category III produces better results. Its adjusted R square is .51. It includes four significant variables. STLAB and SCLAB have substantial beta values with the predicted signs. TWOHAS is also significant, but its sizable beta value is the opposite sign of what is predicted. Since both its correlation coefficient and beta value are substantial but the opposite sign of what we expected, we are obliged to reinterpret our understanding of the relationship between TWOHAS and the EGS employment. If we look back at table 10, we see that TWOHAS is highly correlated with RAIN and PROD. It is likely that areas with better natural endowments support more intensive land use. While these areas have more small cultivators, they are not areas with high levels of EGS employment. AGLAB's substantial beta value is significant, but it is the opposite sign of our predictions. We hypothesized that those districts with the highest levels of agricultural laborers in the rural work force would have greater levels of EGS employment, since agricultural laborers would seem to be the most in need of EGS employment. The finding is corroborated by two other studies, which show that the percentage of agricultural laborers working on the EGS is unexpectedly low: 45 percent in a study by Dandekar and Sathe; 21 percent in a joint study conducted by the Government of India and the Government of Maharashtra.[8]

The unexpectedly small percentage of agricultural laborers working on the EGS has several explanations. Perhaps most important is the fact that surplus labor is greatest in areas where traditional dry land agriculture is most pervasive. These areas usually support one crop a year, thus absorbing labor for four to five months. During the rest of the year, many languish without work. As a consequence, cultivators comprise 74 percent of the households below the poverty line in rural Maharashtra.[9]

TABLE 10

PEARSON CORRELATION COEFFICIENTS OF EGS LABOR
ATTENDANCE (LABATT) AND SOCIOECONOMIC VARIABLES[a]

Correlations:	LABATT	DRYAG	PROD	AGINDEX	LIT	RAIN
LABATT	1.0000	.7774**	−.5756*	−.2754	−.5247*	−.5505*
DRYAG	.7774**	1.0000	−.4380	−.1811	−.3499	−.6411**
PROD	−.5756*	−.4380	1.0000	.7057**	.4420	.6949**
AGINDEX	−.2754	−.1811	.7057**	1.0000	.2586	.1306
LIT	−.5247*	−.3499	.4420	.2586	1.0000	.2749
RAIN	−.5505*	−.6411**	.6949**	.1306	.2749	1.0000
DBLCROP	.3864	.2568	−.0193	.1968	.0037	−.2107
GROSSIR	.5205*	.5188*	.1339	.3902	−.0281	−.2372
AGLAB	.0839	−.0211	−.6336**	−.2106	−.0806	−.6249**
STLAB	.0957	−.2112	−.1092	−.0114	−.1211	.0925
SCLAB	.4572	.4460	−.2170	.0661	−.3369	−.4678*
HHIND	−.3206	−.0794	.1949	−.1091	.1169	.2291
TWOHAS	−.4675*	−.4251	.8240**	.4600	.5503*	.6917**
ADMIN	−.1458	.0313	.0435	.0354	.1799	.1941

Correlations:	DBLCROP	GROSSIR	AGLAB	STLAB	SCLAB	HHIND
LABATT	.3864	.5205*	.0839	.0957	.4572	−.3206
DRYAG	.2568	.5188*	−.0211	−.2112	.4460	−.0794
PROD	−.0193	.1339	−.6336**	−.1092	−.2170	.1949
AGINDEX	.1968	.3902	−.2106	−.0114	.0661	−.1091
LIT	.0037	−.0281	−.0806	−.1211	−.3669	.1169
RAIN	−.2107	−.2372	−.6249**	.0925	−.4678*	.2291
DBLCROP	1.0000	.6625**	−.0499	−.0419	.1033	−.5914**
GROSSIR	.6625**	1.0000	−.3238	−.1319	.3437	−.2192
AGLAB	−.0499	−.3238	1.0000	.2258	.0317	−.2635
STLAB	−.0419	−.1319	.2258	1.0000	−.5081*	.2455
SCLAB	.1033	.3437	.0317	−.5081*	1.0000	−.2688
HHIND	−.5914**	−.2192	−.2635	.2455	−.2688	1.0000
TWOHAS	.1357	.2246	−.7009**	−.0347	−.2978	.2432
ADMIN	−.0508	−.1372	−.2243	−.0245	−.2710	−.0640

TABLE 10 (*continued*)

Correlations: TWOHAS ADMIN

	TWOHAS	ADMIN
LABATT	−.4675*	−.1458
DRYAG	−.4251	.0313
PROD	.8240**	.0435
AGINDEX	.4600	.0354
LIT	.5503*	.1799
RAIN	.6917**	.1941
DBLCROP	.1357	−.0508
GROSSIR	.2246	−.1372
AGLAB	−.7009**	−.2243
STLAB	−.0347	−.0245
SCLAB	−.2978	−.2710
HHIND	.2432	−.0640
TWOHAS	1.0000	.1012
ADMIN	.1012	1.0000

N = 25, One-tailed Significance: *p = .01, **p = .001.
[a]DRYAG = dryland agriculture; PROD = productivity per hectare; AGINDEX = index of agricultural development; LIT = literacy rate; RAIN = average rainfall; DBLCROP = percent of double-cropped area; GROSSIR = percent of gross area irrigated; AGLAB = agricultural laborers in labor force; STLAB and SCLAB = percent of scheduled castes and scheduled tribes in labor force; HHIND = change in percent of work force employed in household industries, 1971–81; TWOHAS = landholdings less than two hectares; ADMIN = administrative officers.

EGS regulations discourage the participation of agricultural laborers by stipulating that the program should not attract agricultural laborers from the employ of local farmers. Until 1985, wages on the EGS remained below the minimum wages for agricultural laborers. While the extent to which the minimum wage is effective in Maharashtra is open to question, agricultural laborers undoubtedly can generally earn more working for local farmers than on the EGS. Furthermore, working for local farmers may provide a more secure livelihood than the EGS. Rarely does the EGS provide year-round employment, and it may require laborers to travel a considerable distance to obtain work. The poorest agricultural laborers often need to receive their wages immediately. They have a strong preference for the daily wages available from cultivators rather than the weekly EGS wages, whose payment is sometimes delayed for lengthy periods.

Historical factors also help to explain the unexpectedly low share of EGS employment generation in districts with a large share of agricultural laborers. These districts are located in the Vidharbha region of eastern Maharashtra, whereas EGS employment generation is greatest in the dryland agricultural regions of western Maharashtra. Because the EGS was initiated in the wake of the public works programs that were the mainstay of Maharashtra's drought relief program from 1971 to 1973, government officials in drought-prone areas were better prepared to implement the EGS and tended to give it higher priority.

TABLE II

REGRESSION OF SOCIOECONOMIC VARIABLES WITH EGS
LABOR ATTENDANCE[a]

Category I	Unstandardized Regression Coefficient	Beta Value	t-ratio	Significance
PROD	− 1.141	−.280	− 1.428	n.s.
DRYAG	7.884	.595	4.301	$p < .001$
LIT	− 9.505	−.215	− 1.576	n.s.
AGINDEX	2.248	.086	.498	n.s.

$N = 25$, Adjusted R Square = .656, $df = 20$

Category II				
DBLCROP	.153	.031	.146	n.s.
GROSSIRR	16.636	.393	1.827	n.s.
RAIN	− 18.379	−.451	− 2.735	$p < .02$

$N = 25$, Adjusted R Square = .465, $df = 21$

Category III				
AGLAB	− 12.412	−.582	− 2.694	$p < .02$
TWOHAS	− 10.778	−.642	− 2.966	$p < .01$
STLAB	10.447	.518	2.932	$p < .01$
SCLAB	30.201	.461	2.556	$p < .02$
HHIND	− 85.780	−.321	− 2.042	n.s.

$N = 25$, Adjusted R Square = .514, $df = 19$

Category IV				
ADMIN	− 12.807	−.146	−.707	n.s.

$N = 25$, Adjusted R Square = −.021, $df = 21$

Combining the Significant Variables

DRYAG	9.521	.718	2.950	$p < .01$
RAIN	4.980	.122	.405	n.s.
AGLAB	−.762	−.036	−.122	n.s.
TWOHAS	− 2.474	−.147	−.697	n.s.
STLAB	8.609	.425	3.081	$p < .01$
SCLAB	24.060	.367	2.293	$p < .04$

$N = 25$, Adjusted R Square = .688, $df = 19$

[a]For explanation of abbreviations, see footnote to table 10.

Moreover, the drought relief programs left a legacy of incomplete projects and unimplemented plans that facilitated the initiation of EGS projects in these areas. Previous experience with drought relief programs also helped socialize the public to take advantage of the opportunities provided by the EGS.

Political factors also may have reinforced the dynamic. Because of western Maharashtra's political predominance, it has received a disproportionate share of developmental expenditures. The Vidharbha region, in contrast, has not been as well represented in the halls of power in the state. It has received a relatively low share of state expenditures. Despite the considerable need in Vidharbha, the EGS has not overcome this bias in the state's political economy.[10]

Category IV hypothesizes that those districts with greater administrative capacity will generate greater EGS employment. It has little explanatory power. Its adjusted R square is $-.02$. ADMIN's beta value of $-.15$ is the opposite sign of our prediction, but its t test is not significant. Administrative factors may still affect the EGS, but their impact is not captured by ADMIN.

Combining all the significant variables into a regression equation produces an interesting result. The adjusted R square for the equation is .69. DRYAG remains the most strongly related variable, and STLAB and SCLAB also remain significant. Their beta values are substantial, and they have the predicted signs. These three variables alone explain 72 percent of the variation in EGS employment among the state's districts.

Notes

INTRODUCTION

1. For perhaps the most elaborate statement of the transaction cost approach to institutions, see Oliver E. Williamson, *The Economic Institutions of Capitalism* (New York: Free Press, 1985), and *Markets and Hierarchies* (New York: Free Press, 1975). For overviews of agency theory, see Kathleen M. Eisenhardt, "Agency Theory: An Assessment and Review," *Academy of Management Review* 14, no. 1 (1989): 57–74; Daniel Levinthal, "A Survey of Agency Models of Organizations," *Journal of Economic Behavior and Organization* 9 (1988): 153–85; Terry Moe, "The New Economics of Organization," *American Journal of Political Science* 28, no. 4 (November 1984): 739–77; and John Pratt and Richard Zeckhauser, eds., *Principals and Agents* (Cambridge, Mass.: Harvard University Press, 1985).

2. See, for instance, Sven Steinmo, Kathleen Thelen, and Frank Longstreth, eds., *Structuring Politics: Historical Institutionalism in Comparative Analysis* (New York: Cambridge University Press, 1992); Peter Hall, *Governing the Economy: The Politics of State Intervention in Britain and France* (New York: Oxford University Press, 1986); Peter B. Evans, Dietrich Rueschemeyer, and Theda Skocpol, eds., *Bringing the State Back In* (Cambridge: Cambridge University Press, 1985); Stephen D. Krasner, "Approaches to the State: Alternative Conceptions and Historical Dynamics," *Comparative Politics* 16, no. 2 (January 1984): 223–46; Theda Skocpol, *States and Social Revolutions* (Cambridge: Cambridge University Press, 1978).

3. Walter W. Powell and Paul J. DiMaggio, eds., *The New Institutionalism in Organizational Analysis* (Chicago: University of Chicago Press, 1991); James G. March and Johan P. Olsen, *Rediscovering Institutions: The Organizational Basis of Politics* (New York: Free Press, 1989); Lynne Zucker, ed., *Institutional Patterns and Organizations: Culture and Environment* (Cam-

bridge, Mass.: Ballinger, 1988); James G. March and Johan P. Olsen, "The New Institutionalism: Organizational Factors in Political Life," *American Political Science Review* 78, no. 3 (September 1984): 734–49; John W. Meyer and W. Richard Scott, eds., *Organizational Environments: Ritual and Rationality* (Beverly Hills, Calif.: Sage, 1983); Paul J. DiMaggio and Walter W. Powell, "The Iron Cage Revisited: Institutional Isomorphism and Collective Rationality in Organizational Fields," *American Sociological Review* 48, no. 1 (April 1983): 147–60; and John W. Meyer and Brian Rowan, "Institutionalized Organization: Formal Structure as Myth and Ceremony," *American Journal of Sociology* 83, no. 2 (September 1977): 340–63.

4. For a provocative discussion of the ways in which different cultures shape rationality and the importance of adopting "ontological polytheism" as a consequence, see Richard A. Shweder, *Thinking through Cultures: Expeditions in Cultural Psychology* (Cambridge, Mass.: Harvard University Press, 1991). Friedland and Alford argue that even the economists' primary unit of analysis—the individual as rational-instrumental actor—is a contingent cultural construct. See Roger Friedland and Robert R. Alford, "Bringing Society Back in: Symbol, Practices, and Institutional Contradictions," in DiMaggio and Powell, *The New Institutionalism,* pp. 232–63. By contending that the "individual" identified as "homo economicus" is itself a social construct, Michel Foucault provides an even more radical critique. For a concise statement see Michel Foucault, "The Subject and Power," in *Michel Foucault: Beyond Structuralism and Hermeneutics,* trans. Hubert L. Dreyfus and Paul Rabinow (Chicago: University of Chicago Press, 1983), pp. 208–26. See also Karl Marx, "On the Jewish Question," in *Karl Marx: Early Writings,* trans. Rodney Livingstone and Gregor Benton (New York: Vintage, 1975), pp. 212–41 (originally published in 1843).

5. For criticisms of the economic approach to organizations along these lines, see Pranab Bardhan, "Alternative Approaches to the Theories of Institutions in Economic Development," in *The Economic Theory of Agrarian Institutions,* ed. Pranab Bardhan (Oxford: Clarendon Press, 1989), pp. 3–17; John R. Bowman, "Transaction Costs and Politics," *Archives Européenes de Sociologie* 30 (1989): 150–68; Charles Perrow, "Economic Theories of Organization," *Theory and Society* 15, nos. 1–2 (1986): 11–45; Karen S. Cook and Richard M. Emerson, "Exchange Networks and the Analysis of Complex Organizations," in *Research in the Sociology of Organizations,* vol. 3 (Greenwich, Conn.: JAI Press, 1984), pp. 1–30; and Charles Perrow, "Markets, Hierarchies and Hegemony: A Critique of Chandler and Williamson," in *Perspectives on Organization Design and Behavior,* ed. Andrew Van De Ven and William Joyce (New York: Wiley Interscience, 1981), pp. 371–90. For a work in this tradition that incorporates political power, see Margaret Levi, *Of Rule and Revenue* (Berkeley: University of California Press, 1988). For a work that begins to include the cultural dimension, see Douglass C. North, *Institutions, Institutional Change and Economic Performance* (Cambridge: Cambridge University Press, 1990).

6. Robert Grafstein, *Institutional Realism: Social and Political Constraints on Rational Actors* (New Haven, Conn.: Yale University Press, 1992), and

"The Problem of Institutional Constraint," *Journal of Politics* 50, no. 3 (August 1988): 577–99.

7. See, for instance, Bob Jessop, *State Theory: Putting Capitalist States in Their Place* (University Park: Pennsylvania State University Press, 1990), pp. 278–88.

8. Theda Skocpol, "Bringing the State Back In: Strategies of Analysis in Current Research," in Evans, Rueschemeyer, and Skocpol, *Bringing the State Back In*, p. 4. More recent analysis in this perspective is much less vulnerable to this criticism. Most would agree with Kathleen Thelen and Sven Steinmo, who argue that focusing on institutions "does not replace attention to other variables—the players, their interests and strategies, and the distribution of power among them. On the contrary, it puts these factors in context, showing how they relate to one another by drawing attention to the way political situations are structured." See Kathleen Thelen and Sven Steinmo, "Historical Institutionalism in Comparative Politics," in Steinmo, Thelen, and Longstreth, *Structuring Politics,* p. 13.

9. Akhil Gupta has made this point to me in personal communication. See also Friedland and Alford, "Bringing Society Back In," pp. 237–38.

10. Michael Lipsky, *Street-Level Bureaucracy* (New York: Russell Sage Foundation, 1980), p. xii. The emphasis is Lipsky's.

11. See Albert O. Hirschman, "Policy Making and Policy Analysis in Latin America: a Return Journey," *Policy Science* 6, no. 4 (1975): 385–402.

12. One of the first to make this argument is Gøsta Esping-Andersen in his *Politics against Markets* (Princeton, N.J.: Princeton University Press, 1985). He further develops his arguments in *The Three Worlds of Welfare Capitalism* (Princeton, N.J.: Princeton University Press, 1990). Despite its important implications, this observation has been applied to developing societies only recently. See, for instance, John W. Thomas and Merilee S. Grindle, "After the Decision: Implementing Policy Reforms in Developing Countries," *World Development* 18, no. 8 (August 1990): 1163–81; Robert H. Bates, *Beyond the Miracle of the Market: The Political Economy of Agrarian Change in Kenya* (Cambridge: Cambridge University Press, 1989); and John Echeverri-Gent, "Guaranteed Employment in an Indian State," *Asian Survey* 28, no. 12 (December 1988): 1294–1310.

13. Early works in this tradition include Howard Odum, *Southern Regions of the United States* (Chapel Hill: University of North Carolina Press, 1936); Rupert Vance, *Human Geography of the South* (Chapel Hill: University of North Carolina Press, 1932); and Walter Prescott Webb, *Divided We Stand: The Crisis of Frontierless Democracy* (New York: Farrar and Rinehart, 1937). During the New Deal, this view was given official support from the Roosevelt administration. See U.S. National Emergency Council, *Report on Economic Conditions of the South* (Washington, D.C.: U.S. Government Printing Office, 1938). For overviews of the early literature, see George Brown Tindall, *The Emergence of the New South, 1913–1945* (Baton Rouge: Louisiana State University Press, 1967), pp. 594–98, 605, and "The 'Colonial Economy' and the Growth Psychology: The South in the 1930's," *South Atlantic Quarterly* 44 (Autumn 1965): 465–77. See also Paul E. Mertz, *New Deal Policy and South-*

ern Rural Poverty (Baton Rouge: Louisiana State University Press, 1978), pp. 221–52. Later analyses in this tradition include C. Vann Woodward, *The Origins of the New South* (Baton Rouge: Louisiana State University Press, 1951), pp. 291–320; Richard Franklin Bensel, *Sectionalism and American Political Development* (Madison: University of Wisconsin Press, 1984): and Gavin Wright, *Old South, New South: Revolutions in the Southern Economy since the Civil War* (New York: Basic Books, 1986).

14. Testimony of D. Gale Johnson, in *Low-Income Families: Hearings before the Subcommittee on Low-Income Families of the Joint Committee on the Economic Report*, 81st Cong., 1st sess., December 12–22, 1949 (Washington, D.C.: U.S. Government Printing Office, 1950), p. 293.

15. For instance, see Charles L. Flynn, Jr., *White Land, Black Labor: Caste and Class in Late Nineteenth-Century Georgia* (Baton Rouge: Louisiana State University Press, 1983); Woodward, *The Origins of the New South*, especially 354–67; John Dollard, *Caste and Class in a Southern Town* (New York: Doubleday, 1957); Gunnar Myrdal, *An American Dilemma: The Negro Problem and Modern Democracy* (New York: Harper and Brothers, 1944).

16. Sidney Verba et al., *Caste, Race and Politics: A Comparative Study of India and the United States* (Beverly Hills, Calif.: Sage, 1971); Gerald D. Berreman, "Caste in India and the United States," *American Sociological Review* 66, no. 2 (September 1966): 120–27; Oliver Cromwell Cox, *Caste, Class and Race: A Study in Social Dynamics* (Garden City, N.Y.: Doubleday, 1948); Gunnar Myrdal, *Asian Drama: An Inquiry into the Poverty of Nations*, 3 vols. (New York: Twentieth Century Fund, 1968).

17. Louis Dumont, *Homo Hierarchus*, trans. Mark Sainsbury, Louis Dumont, and Basia Gulati (Chicago: University of Chicago Press, 1980), pp. 247–66.

18. In 1969, the Congress Party split into the Congress (O) and the Congress (R). The Congress (R) was frequently referred to as simply the Congress Party, since it remained in control of the central government while the strength of the Congress (O) dissipated. In January 1978, the Congress (R) was splintered as Indira Gandhi created the Congress (I) Party. In the text that follows, I will refer to the Congress Party through 1969 and the Congress (R) as simply the Congress Party. I will refer to the faction led by Indira Gandhi from January 1978 as the Congress (I) Party.

19. These generalizations hold in spite of the substantial diversity that characterized the politics of the rural South and India. For overviews of Southern politics, see V. O. Key, *Southern Politics in State and Nation* (New York: Knopf, 1949); and J. Morgan Kousser, *The Shaping of Southern Politics: Suffrage Restriction and the Establishment of the One-Party South, 1880–1910* (New Haven, Conn.: Yale University Press, 1974). The literature on factionalism in Indian politics is voluminous. For recent overviews see Atul Kohli, *Democracy and Discontent: India's Growing Crisis of Governability* (Cambridge: Cambridge University Press, 1990); and Paul R. Brass, *The Politics of India since Independence* (Cambridge: Cambridge University Press, 1990).

20. Key, *Southern Politics*, pp. 352, 356. For an account of the incorporation of Southern farmers into the farm bloc, see John Mark Hansen, *Gaining*

Access: Congress and the Farm Lobby, 1919–1981 (Chicago: University of Chicago Press, 1991), pp. 61–75. For a study of Southern Democrats in the formulation of agricultural policy in Congress during the New Deal, see Edward L. Schapsmeier and Frederick H. Schapsmeier, "Farm Policy from FDR to Eisenhower: Southern Democrats and the Politics of Agriculture," *Agricultural History* 53, no. 1 (January 1979): 352–71.

21. Myron Weiner, "Capitalist Agriculture and Rural Well-Being," in Myron Weiner, *The Indian Paradox: Essays in Indian Politics,* ed. Ashutosh Varshney (New Delhi: Sage, 1989), pp. 99–132; Ashutosh Varshney, "Organizing the Countryside: Peasant Mobilization in the 1980s," unpublished paper, Massachusetts Institute of Technology, 1989; Gail Omvedt, "New Movements," *Seminar* 352 (December 1988): 39–44; Lloyd I. Rudolph and Susanne Hoeber Rudolph, *In Pursuit of Lakshmi: The Political Economy of the Indian State* (Chicago: University of Chicago Press, 1987), pp. 312–32.

22. Jean Dreze and Amartya Sen, *Hunger and Public Action* (Oxford: Clarendon Press, 1989). See also Amartya Sen, *On Ethics and Economics* (Oxford: Blackwell, 1987), *Commodities and Capabilities* (Amsterdam: Elsevier, 1985), "Development: Which Way Now?" in *Resources, Values and Development,* ed. Amartya Sen (Cambridge, Mass.: Harvard University Press, 1984), pp. 485–508, and *Poverty and Famines* (Oxford: Clarendon Press, 1981). For a selection of Schultz's work on human capital, see *Restoring Economic Equilibrium: Human Capital in the Modernizing Economy* (Cambridge, Mass.: Blackwell, 1990), *Investing in People: The Economics of Population Quality* (Berkeley: University of California Press, 1981), *Investment in Human Capital: The Role of Education and of Research* (New York: Free Press, 1971), and *Transforming Traditional Agriculture* (New Haven: Conn.: Yale University Press, 1964).

23. For more on the relationship between the principles of targeting and universalism, see Theda Skocpol, "Targeting within Universalism: Politically Viable Policies to Combat Poverty in the United States," paper presented at the annual meeting of the American Political Science Association, San Francisco, August 31, 1990.

CHAPTER 1

1. For a discussion of the relationship between organizational structure and organizational technologies, see James D. Thompson, *Organizations in Action* (New York: McGraw-Hill, 1967). For more on organizational structure and informational processing needs, see Jay R. Galbraith, *Organizational Design* (Reading, Mass.: Addison-Wesley, 1977). The following works focus on organizational structure and environmental uncertainty: Arthur L. Stinchcombe, *Information and Organizations* (Berkeley: University of California Press, 1990), especially pp. 32–72; William G. Ouchi, "Markets, Bureaucracies and Clans," *Administrative Science Quarterly* 25, no. 1 (1980): 129–41; and Paul R. Lawrence and Jay W. Lorsch, *Organizations and Environment: Managing Differentiation and Integration* (Boston: Graduate School of Business Administration, Harvard University, 1967).

2. For the most elaborate statement of this position, see Oliver E. William-

son, *The Economic Institutions of Capitalism* (New York: Free Press, 1985), and *Markets and Hierarchies* (New York: Free Press, 1975). For a version of this argument that incorporates political considerations, see Margaret Levi, *Of Rule and Revenue* (Berkeley: University of California Press, 1988). Douglass C. North, in *Institutions, Institutional Change and Economic Performance* (Cambridge: Cambridge University Press, 1990), is one of the first to add a cultural dimension.

3. For recent discussions of bounded rationality, see Herbert Simon, "Human Nature in Politics: The Dialogue of Psychology with Political Science," *American Political Science Review* 79, no. 2 (June 1985): 293–304; and James G. March, "Bounded Rationality, Ambiguity and the Engineering of Choice," *Bell Journal of Economics* 9 (Autumn 1978): 587–608. Simon pioneered the concept in his *Administrative Behavior,* 2nd ed. (New York: Macmillan, 1961), especially 240–41; and in *Models of Man* (New York: Wiley, 1957).

4. Arthur L. Stinchcombe, *Creating Efficient Industrial Administrations* (New York: Academic Press, 1974), p. 20.

5. For a recent study highlighting feedback as an important variable for policy implementation, see Malcom L. Goggin et al., *Implementation Theory and Practice: Toward a Third Generation* (Glenview, Ill.: Scott, Foresman, 1990), pp. 152–70. A seminal work is James D. Steinbruner's *The Cybernetic Theory of Decision* (Princeton, N.J.: Princeton University Press, 1974).

For the liabilities of this form of organizational learning, see Barbara Levitt and James G. March, "Organizational Learning," *Annual Review of Sociology* 14 (1988): 319–40; S. R. Herriott, D. Levinthal, and J. G. March, "Learning from Experience in Organizations," *American Economic Review* 75, no. 2 (1985): 298–302; Lynne G. Zucker, "Institutional Theories of Organization," *Annual Review of Sociology* 13 (1987): 443–64. For similar concepts in theories of international policymaking, see the discussion of "irrational consistency" in Robert Jervis, *Perception and Misperception in International Politics* (Princeton, N.J.: Princeton University Press, 1976); and the discussion of "cognitive closure" in Richard Ned Lebow, *Between Peace and War: The Nature of International Crisis* (Baltimore: Johns Hopkins University Press, 1981).

6. See Douglas MacRae, *Policy Indicators* (Chapel Hill: University of North Carolina Press, 1985); March, "Bounded Rationality"; Aaron Wildavsky, *Speaking Truth to Power: The Art and Craft of Policy Analysis* (Boston: Little, Brown, 1979), especially pp. 139–40; and Giodominco Majone and Aaron Wildavsky, "Implementation as Evolution," in *Policy Studies Review Annual,* ed. Howard E. Freeman (Beverly Hills, Calif.: Sage, 1978), pp. 103–17.

7. For an excellent review of agency theory, see Kathleen M. Eisenhardt, "Agency Theory: An Assessment and Review," *Academy of Management Review* 14, no. 1 (1989): 57–74. Also see Daniel Levinthal, "A Survey of Agency Models of Organizations," *Journal of Economic Behavior and Organization* 9 (1988): 153–85; Terry M. Moe, "The New Economics of Organization," *American Journal of Political Science* 28, no. 4 (November 1984): 739–77; and Kenneth Arrow, "The Economics of Agency," in *Principals and Agents,* ed. John Pratt and Richard Zeckhauser (Cambridge, Mass.: Harvard University Press, 1985), pp. 37–51.

8. For discussions of these variables, see Jonathan Bendor, Serge Taylor, and Roland Van Gaalen, "Stacking the Deck: Bureaucratic Missions and Policy Design," *American Political Science Review* 81, no. 3 (September 1987): 873–96; B. Dan Wood, "Principals, Bureaucrats, and Responsiveness in Clean Air Enforcement," *American Political Science Review* 82, no. 1 (March 1988): 213–34; and Moe, "The New Economics of Organization."

9. James G. March and Johan P. Olsen, *Rediscovering Institutions: The Organizational Basis of Politics* (New York: Free Press, 1989), pp. 7, 50; and Martha S. Feldman and James G. March, "Information in Organizations as Signal and Symbol," *Administrative Science Quarterly* 26, no. 2 (June 1981): 171–86.

10. For instance, see Kenneth Shepsle and Barry Weingast, "Why Are Congressional Committees Powerful?" *American Political Science Review* 81, no. 3 (September 1977): 935–45; J. Demski, *Information Analysis* (Reading, Mass.: Addison-Wesley, 1980); and G. A. Ackerloff, "The Market for 'Lemons': Qualitative Uncertainty and the Market Mechanism," *Quarterly Journal of Economics* 84, no. 3 (August 1970): 488–500.

11. See Samuel B. Bacharach and E. J. Lawler, *Power and Politics in Organizations* (San Francisco: Jossey-Bass, 1980); and Jeffrey Pfeffer, *Power in Organizations* (Marshfield, Mass.: Pitman, 1981), especially pp. 68–71.

12. See, for instance, Michael Lipsky, *Street-Level Bureaucracy* (New York: Russell Sage Foundation, 1980); B. Guy Peters, "Bureaucracy, Politics, and Public Policy," *Comparative Politics* 11, no. 3 (April 1979): 339–58; Michel Crozier, *The Bureaucratic Phenomenon* (Chicago: University of Chicago Press, 1964); and Gordon Tullock, *The Politics of Bureaucracy* (Washington, D.C.: Public Affairs Press, 1965).

13. Pfeffer, *Power in Organizations,* pp. 79–96.

14. Edward J. Lawler and Samuel B. Bacharach, "Political Action and Alignments in Organizations," in *Research in the Sociology of Organizations,* vol. 2 (Greenwich, Conn.: JAI Press, 1983), pp. 83–107.

15. Regarding organizational structure and distribution of power, see Michel Crozier and Erhard Friedberg, *Actors and Systems,* trans. Arthur Goldhammer (Chicago: University of Chicago Press, 1980), especially p. 71. For organizational structure as an object of conflict, see Lawler and Bacharach, "Political Action and Alignments," especially pp. 86–87; and Pfeffer, *Power in Organizations,* p. 267.

16. Robert S. Montjoy and Laurence J. O'Toole, Jr., "Toward a Theory of Policy Implementation: An Organizational Perspective," *Public Administration Review* 39, no. 5 (September 1979): 466–67; Carl E. Van Horn and Donald S. Van Meter, "The Implementation of Intergovernmental Policy," in *Public Policy Making in a Federal System,* ed. Charles O. Jones and Robert D. Thomas (Beverly Hills, Calif.: Sage, 1976), pp. 49–50; Laurence J. O'Toole, Jr., and Robert S. Montjoy, "Interorganizational Policy Implementation: A Theoretical Perspective," *Public Administration Review* 44, no. 6 (November 1984): 491–503.

17. Eugene Bardach, *The Implementation Game: What Happens after a Bill Becomes a Law* (Cambridge, Mass.: MIT Press, 1977), p. 51.

18. Jeffrey L. Pressman and Aaron B. Wildavsky, *Implementation* (Berkeley: University of California Press, 1973), especially 87–124.

19. James Q. Wilson, *Bureaucracy: What Government Agencies Do and Why They Do It* (New York: Basic Books, 1989), pp. 72–89.

20. Jeffrey Pfeffer and Gerald R. Salancik, *The External Control of Organizations: A Resource Dependence Perspective* (New York: Harper and Row, 1978), p. 2.

21. Ibid., pp. 44–53. See Pfeffer, *Power in Organizations,* pp. 97–136, especially pp. 103–9, for a discussion of the discretion over supply resources as a source of power. Bates and Lien's finding that taxpayers with movable assets exercised greater bargaining power with British and French monarchs provides a good example of the power of discretion. See Robert H. Bates and Da-Hsiang Donald Lien, "A note on Taxation, Development and Representative Government," *Politics and Society* 14, no. 1 (1985): 53–70.

22. Ibid., p. 53.

23. Thompson, *Organizations in Action* (note 1 above); D. J. Hickson et al., "A Strategic Contingencies Theory of Intraorganizational Power," *Administrative Science Quarterly* 19, no. 1 (March 1974): 45–59; and, more recently, David M. Boje and David A. Whetten, "Effects of Organizational Strategies and Contextual Constraints on Centrality and Attributions of Influence in Interorganizational Networks," *Administrative Science Quarterly* 26, no. 3 (September 1981): 378–95.

24. Pfeffer and Salancik, *External Control of Organizations,* pp. 71–78, 225–45.

25. Ibid., p. 230. See also John Child, "Organizational Structure, Environment and Performance: The Role of Strategic Choice," *Sociology* 6, no. 1 (January 1972): 1–22; and Pfeffer, *Power in Organizations.*

26. David Jacobs, "Corporate Economic Power and the State: A Longitudinal Assessment of Two Explanations," *American Journal of Sociology* 93, no. 4 (January 1988): 858.

27. Ronald S. Burt, "Autonomy in a Social Typology," *American Journal of Sociology* 85, no. 4 (January 1980): 898–99, and *Toward a Structural Theory of Social Action* (New York: Academic Press, 1982), pp. 268–73.

28. Atul Kohli, *The State and Poverty in India* (Cambridge: Cambridge University Press, 1987).

29. Paul Burstein, "Policy Domains: Organization, Culture and Policy Outcomes," *Annual Review of Sociology* 16 (1991): 343.

30. Burdett A. Loomis, "Coalitions of Interests: Building Bridges in a Balkanized State," in *Interest Group Politics,* 2nd ed., ed. Allan J. Cigler and Burdett A. Loomis (Washington, D.C.: Congressional Studies Quarterly, 1986), pp. 258–74.

31. Robert H. Salisbury, "The Paradox of Interest Groups in Washington— More Groups, Less Clout," in *The New American Political System,* 2nd ed., ed. Anthony King (Washington, D.C.: AEI Press, 1990), pp. 203–30.

32. Charles E. Lindblom, *Politics and Markets* (New York: Basic Books, 1977), p. 172.

33. Levi, *Of Rule and Revenue* (note 2 above).

34. Barry Bozeman, *All Organizations Are Public* (San Francisco: Jossey-Bass, 1987), pp. 7–13.

35. Philip Selznick, *TVA and the Grass Roots* (Berkeley: University of California Press, 1980), p. 20 (reprint of 1949 ed.).

36. Ibid., pp. 171–79. I thank John F. Padgett for suggesting this point to me.

37. Paul Sabatier, "Social Movements and Regulatory Agencies," *Policy Sciences* 6, no. 3 (1975): 301–42.

38. Thompson, *Organizations in Action* (note 1 above).

39. For instance, see Crozier, *The Bureaucratic Phenomenon* (note 12 above); and Andrew M. Pettigrew, "Information Control as a Power Resource," *Sociology* 6, no. 2 (May 1972): 187–204.

40. John Mark Hansen, *Gaining Access: Congress and the Farm Lobby, 1919–1981* (Chicago: University of Chicago Press, 1991), especially pp. 12–17, 103–6.

41. John E. Chubb, *Interest Groups and the Bureaucracy: The Politics of Energy* (Stanford, Calif.: Stanford University Press, 1983), pp. 107, 144, 159–60, 198.

42. Denis Goulet, "Participation in Development: New Avenues," *World Development* 17, no. 2 (February 1989): 165–78.

43. Margaret Weir and Theda Skocpol, "State Structures and the Possibilities for 'Keynesian' Responses to the Great Depression in Sweden, Britain and the United States," in *Bringing the State Back In,* ed. Peter B. Evans, Dietrich Rueschemeyer, and Theda Skocpol (Cambridge: Cambridge University Press, 1985), pp. 107–63; and Hugh Heclo, *Modern Social Politics in Britain and Sweden* (New Haven, Conn.: Yale University Press, 1974).

44. J. Kenneth Benson, "The Interorganizational Network as a Political Economy," *Administrative Science Quarterly* 20, no. 2 (June 1975): 233; Hickson et al., "A Strategic Contingencies Theory," pp. 221–22; and Boje and Whetten, "Effects of Organizational Strategies," p. 379. For an important modification of this argument, see Karen S. Cook and Richard M. Emerson, "Exchange Networks and the Analysis of Complex Organizations," in *Research in the Sociology of Organizations,* vol. 3 (Greenwich, Conn.: JAI Press, 1984), pp. 1–30. Michael Mann (in "The Autonomous Power of the State: Its Origins, Mechanisms and Results," *Archives Européennes de Sociologie* 25, no. 2 [1984]: 185) asserts that "state autonomy . . . flows principally from the state's unique ability to provide a *territorially-centralised* form of organization" (italics in the original).

45. Salisbury, "The Paradox of Interest Groups."

46. Barry Bozeman and Jeffrey D. Straussman, "'Publicness' and Resource Management Strategies," in *Organizational Theory and Public Policy,* ed. Richard H. Hall and Robert E. Quinn (Beverly Hills, Calif.: Sage, 1983), pp. 75–91.

47. For example, Graham Wilson ("The Political Behavior of Large Corporations," paper presented at the annual meeting of the American Political Science Association, Chicago, September 3–6, 1987) found that dependence on government contracts, measured in total revenue, is by far the most important

factor explaining the scope of a corporation's political activity—as measured by the size of its PAC and its Washington office.

48. Gerald R. Salancik, "An Index of Subgroups' Influence in Dependency Networks," *Administrative Science Quarterly* 31, no. 2 (June 1986): 194–211; and Edward O. Laumann and David Knoke, *The Organizational State* (Madison: University of Wisconsin Press, 1987), pp. 343–73.

49. W. Richard Scott, "Introduction: From Technology to Environment" and "The Organization of Environments: Network, Cultural and Historical Elements," in John W. Meyer and W. Richard Scott, *Organizational Environments: Ritual and Rationality* (Beverly Hills, Calif.: Sage, 1983), pp. 14, 156.

50. North, *Institutions, Institutional Change and Economic Performance* (note 2 above), p. 8.

51. Our discussion of the relationship between the resource dependence model and cultural context here parallels recent work that explores the relationship between rational choice and social norms. See, for instance, John Ferejohn, "Rationality and Interpretation: Parliamentary Elections in Early Stuart England," in *The Economic Approach to Politics*, ed. Kirsten R. Monroe (New York: HarperCollins, 1991), pp. 279–305; Karen Schweers Cook and Margaret Levi, eds., *The Limits of Rationality* (Chicago: University of Chicago Press, 1990); March and Olsen, *Rediscovering Institutions* (note 9 above); and Jon Elster, *The Cement of Society: A Study of Social Order* (Cambridge: Cambridge University Press, 1989).

52. John W. Meyer, John Boli, and George M. Thomas, "Ontology and Rationalization in the Western Cultural Account," in *Institutional Structure: Constituting State, Society and the Individual*, ed. George M. Thomas et al. (Newbury Park, Calif.: Sage, 1987), p. 12. The term *institutionalized rules* was first used by John W. Meyer and Brian Rowan, in "Institutionalized Organizations: Formal Structure as Myth and Ceremony," *American Journal of Sociology* 83, no. 2 (September 1977): 340–63.

53. Pamela Tolbert and Lynne Zucker, "Institutional Sources of Change in Organizational Structure: The Diffusion of Civil Service Reform, 1880–1930," *Administrative Science Quarterly* 28, no. 1 (1983): 25–27.

54. For example, Feldman and March (in "Information in Organizations as Signal and Symbol," note 9 above) have shown that various practices of information collection become legitimized because they reflect cultural values stressing rationality, even though they may be inefficient from the standpoint of the immediate economic welfare of the organizations in which they occur.

55. Paul Sabatier, "Towards Better Theories of Policy Process," *PS: Political Science and Politics* 24, no. 2 (1991): 147–56, and "An Advocacy Coalition Framework of Policy Change and the Role of Policy-Oriented Learning Therein," *Policy Sciences* 21 (Fall 1988): 129–68. See also Hugh Heclo, "Issue Networks and the Executive Establishment," in *The New American Political System*, ed. Anthony King (Washington, D.C.: American Enterprise Institute, 1978), pp. 87–124.

56. Bob Hinings and Royston Greenwood, "The Normative Prescription of Organizations," in *Institutional Patterns and Organizations: Culture and Environment*, ed. Lynne G. Zucker (Cambridge, Mass.: Ballinger, 1988), pp. 53–

70. Meyer, Boli, and Thomas, in "Ontology and Rationalization," p. 13, go so far as to assert, "We see the 'existence' and characteristics of actors as socially constructed and highly problematic, and action as the enactment of broad institutional scripts rather than a matter of internally generated and autonomous choice, motivation and purpose."

57. Tolbert and Zucker, "Institutionalized Sources of Change."

58. Paul J. DiMaggio and Walter W. Powell, "The Iron Cage Revisited: Institutional Isomorphism and Collective Rationality in Organizational Fields," *American Sociological Review* 48, no. 1 (April 1983): 147–60. Property rights theorists argue that the ability to exchange ownership rights helps to evaluate efficiency. Such market evaluation is not feasible for government organizations, since rights of ownership in government organizations cannot be transferred. See Bozeman, *All Organizations Are Public* (note 34 above), pp. 51–55.

59. L. E. Lynn, *Managing the Public's Business* (New York: Basic Books, 1981), p. 119.

60. Meyer and Rowan, "Institutionalized Organizations," 349–50; and Brian Rowan, "Organizational Structure and Institutional Environment: The Case of Public Schools," *Administrative Science Quarterly* 27 (1982): 259–87. See also Lynne G. Zucker, "The Role of Institutionalization in Cultural Persistence," *American Sociological Review* 42, no. 3 (October 1977): 725–43.

61. Clause Offe ("The Divergent Rationalities of Administrative Action," in *Disorganized Capitalism* [Cambridge, Mass.: MIT Press, 1985], pp. 300–316) makes the interesting argument that, with the development of welfare states, "political rationality" has supplemented economic rationality as states increasingly resort to institutionalized rules to justify their activity.

62. Paul J. DiMaggio, "Interest and Agency in Institutional Theory," in Zucker, *Institutional Patterns*, pp. 3–21; Pamela S. Tolbert, "Institutional Environments and Resource Dependence: Sources of Administrative Structure in Institutions of Higher Education," *Administrative Science Quarterly* 30, no. 1 (March 1985): 1–13; Zucker, "Institutional Theories of Organization" (note 5 above).

63. John Kingdon (*Agendas, Alternatives, and Public Policies* [Boston: Little, Brown, 1984], pp. 122–51) describes a similar selection process for policy ideas, though he is somewhat less concerned with the impact of the social distribution of resources on the process. For a similar argument concerning the formation of culture in general, see Robert Wuthnow, *Meaning and Moral Order: Explorations in Cultural Analysis* (Berkeley: University of California Press, 1987).

64. Peter A. Hall, "Conclusion: The Politics of Keynesian Ideas," in *The Political Power of Keynesian Ideas: Keynesianism across Nations*, ed. Peter A. Hall (Princeton, N.J.: Princeton University Press, 1989), pp. 361–91.

65. Sabatier, "Towards Better Theories of Policy Process" and "An Advocacy Coalition Framework of Policy Change."

66. North, *Institutions, Institutional Change and Economic Performance* (note 2 above), pp. 73–82.

67. Margaret Weir, *Politics and Jobs: The Boundaries of Employment Policy in the United States* (Princeton, N.J.: Princeton University Press, 1992), and

"Ideas and Politics: The Acceptance of Keynesianism in Britain and the United States," in Hall, *Political Power of Keynesian Ideas,* pp. 53–86; and Weir and Skocpol, "State Structures and the Possibilities for 'Keynesian' Responses" (note 43 above).

68. Peter Gourevitch, *Politics in Hard Times: Comparative Responses to International Economic Crisis* (Ithaca, N.Y.: Cornell University Press, 1986). See also Peter Gourevitch, "Keynesian Politics: The Political Sources of Economic Policy Choices," in Hall, *Political Power of Keynesian Ideas,* pp. 87–106.

69. John W. Meyer, "The World Polity and the Authority of the Nation-State," p. 46, and Francisco O. Ramirez, "Institutional Analysis," especially pp. 318 and 323; both in Thomas et al., *Institutional Structure* (note 52 above). See also W. Richard Scott, "The Adolescence of Institutional Theory," *Administrative Science Quarterly* 32 (1987): 493–511.

70. Richard Ritti and Jonathan H. Silver, "Early Processes of Institutionalization: The Dramaturgy of Exchange in Interorganizational Relations," *Administrative Science Quarterly* 31, no. 1 (March 1986): 25–42. This article describes how the Pennsylvania Public Utility Commission's Bureau of Consumer Services transformed its potentially antagonistic relations with the utilities companies that it was responsible for regulating into mutually beneficial ones by developing rituals evoking institutionalized values. Participation in these rituals enhanced the legitimacy of the bureau as well as its regulatees.

71. The argument here is similar to the contention of Ann Swidler ("Culture in Action: Symbols and Strategies," *American Sociological Review* 51, no. 2 [April 1986]: 273–86) that the most important impact of culture is not on the ends that people pursue but, rather, on the actions that they take.

72. For an excellent example of the historical sedimentation of culture and conflicting rules, see Stanley Heginbotham, *Cultures in Conflict: Four Faces of Indian Bureaucracy* (New York: Columbia University Press, 1975). For an interesting argument about the sources of contradictory rules, see Roger Friedland and Robert R. Alford, "Bringing Society Back In: Symbols, Practices, and Institutional Contradictions," in *The New Institutionalism in Organizational Analysis,* ed. Walter W. Powell and Paul J. DiMaggio (Chicago: University of Chicago Press, 1991), pp. 232–63.

73. March and Olsen, *Rediscovering Institutions* (note 9 above), pp. 69–94.

74. Stephen D. Krasner, "Sovereignty: An Institutional Perspective," *Comparative Political Studies* 21, no. 1 (April 1988): 74–75.

75. Russell Hardin, "Groups in the Regulation of Collective Bads," in *Public Choice,* ed. Gordon Tullock (New Orleans: Public Choice Society, 1980), pp. 99–102.

76. This paragraph draws from the discussion of "governance structures" in Bozeman, *All Organizations Are Public,* pp. 72–76.

77. Chubb, *Interest Groups and the Bureaucracy* (note 41 above), pp. 93, 125, 259. See also p. 171 for similar consequences of decision-making procedures in the regulation of the oil industry.

78. George J. Stigler, "The Theory of Regulation," *Bell Journal of Economics and Management Science* 2, no. 1 (Spring 1971): 5.

79. John W. Meyer, "Centralization of Funding and Control in Educational Governance," in Meyer and Scott, *Organizational Environments* (note 49 above), pp. 192–93.

80. Gøsta Esping-Andersen, *Politics against Markets: The Social Democratic Road to Power* (Princeton, N.J.: Princeton University Press, 1985), and *The Three Worlds of Welfare Capitalism* (Princeton, N.J.: Princeton University Press, 1990). See also Peter Baldwin, *The Politics of Social Solidarity: Class Bases of the European Welfare State, 1875–1975* (Cambridge: Cambridge University Press, 1990). For a similar argument relative to the United States, see Margaret Weir, Ann Shola Orloff, and Theda Skocpol, eds., *The Politics of Social Policy in the United States* (Princeton, N.J.: Princeton University Press, 1988), especially pp. 3–27, 293–311.

81. Peter B. Evans, "The State as Problem and Solution: Predation, Embedded Autonomy, and Structural Change," in *The Politics of Economic Adjustment: International Constraints, Distributive Conflicts, and the State,* ed. Stephan Haggard and Robert R. Kaufman (Princeton, N.J.: Princeton University Press, 1992): 139–181; Peter B. Evans, "Predatory, Developmental and Other Apparatuses: A Comparative Political Economy Perspective on the Third World State," *Sociological Forum* 4, no. 4 (1989): 561–87.

CHAPTER 2

1. Richard S. Kirkendall, "The New Deal and Agriculture," in *The New Deal: The National Level,* ed. John Braeman, Robert H. Bremner, and David Brody (Columbus: Ohio State University Press, 1975), p. 184; Murray R. Benedict, *Farm Policies of the United States, 1790–1950* (New York: Octagon Books, 1966), pp. 168–72, 310–11; Kenneth Finegold, "From Agrarianism to Adjustment: The Political Origins of New Deal Agricultural Policy," *Politics and Society* 11, no. 1 (1982): 1–27; Arthur M. Schlesinger, Jr., *The Coming of the New Deal,* vol. 3 of *The Age of Roosevelt* (Boston: Houghton Mifflin, 1959), p. 27.

2. Aid to farmers was clearly the objective of the executive order creating the Farm Credit Administration on March 27, 1933; the Agricultural Adjustment Act of May 12, 1933; and the Farm Credit Act of June 16, 1933.

3. Kenneth Finegold and Theda Skocpol, "Capitalists, Farmers and Workers in the New Deal—The Ironies of Government Intervention," paper presented at the annual meeting of the American Political Science Association, Washington, D.C., August 31, 1980, pp. 18–24.

4. Richard Kirkendall, *Social Scientists and Farm Politics in the Age of Roosevelt* (Columbia: University of Missouri Press, 1966), p. 59.

5. Carl C. Taylor, Helen W. Wheeler, and E. L. Kirkpatrick, *Disadvantaged Classes in American Agriculture* (Washington, D.C.: U.S. Government Printing Office, 1938), pp. 8–9.

6. Paul E. Mertz, *New Deal Policy and Southern Rural Poverty* (Baton

Rouge: Louisiana State University Press, 1978), pp. 22–31; David Eugene Conrad, *The Forgotten Farmers: The Story of the Sharecroppers in the New Deal* (Urbana: University of Illinois Press, 1965), pp. 64–83; Donald H. Grubbs, *Cry from the Cotton: The Southern Tenant Farmers' Union and the New Deal* (Chapel Hill: University of North Carolina Press, 1971), pp. 17–28; Harold Hoffsommer, "The AAA and the Cropper," *Social Forces* 13, no. 3 (March 1935): 494–500; Raymond Wolters, "The New Deal and the Negro," in Braeman, Bremner, and Brody, *The New Deal,* pp. 172–73; and Mordecai Ezekiel, Memo to the Secretary, USDA, dated May 5, 1935, National Archives, Record Group (hereafter cited as NA, RG) 145.

7. Conrad, *The Forgotten Farmers,* pp. 83–104; Grubbs, *Cry from the Cotton;* M. S. Venkataramani, "Norman Thomas, Arkansas Sharecroppers, and the Roosevelt Agricultural Policies, 1933–1937," *Mississippi Valley Historical Review* 47, no. 2 (September 1960): 225–45; and Jerold Auerback, "Southern Tenant Farmers: Socialist Critiques of the New Deal," *Labor History* 7 (Winter 1966): 3–18.

8. Jess Gilbert and Carolyn Howe, "Beyond 'State vs. Society': Theories of the State and New Deal Agricultural Policies," *American Sociological Review* 56, no. 3 (April 1991): 212–13 especially.

9. Conrad, *The Forgotten Farmers,* pp. 54–60. The position of the victors was stated most succinctly by Davis. He contended that, regrettable and undesirable as some of the conditions were, it was not possible or advisable to undertake a definite and complete solution as part of the AAA—an emergency program designed to relieve an economic crisis.

10. See Calvin B. Hoover, Memo to the Secretary, USDA, March 7, 1934, NA, RG 16; Hoffsommer, "The AAA and the Cropper"; Committee on Minority Groups in the Economic Recovery, "Foreword and Conclusion of a Study of Agricultural, Economic and Social Conditions in the South," NA, RG 145. For the study by William Amberson, see *Plight of the Sharecropper,* ed. Norman Thomas (New York: League for Industrial Democracy, 1933), 33 and passim; and Grubbs, *Cry from the Cotton,* pp. 28–29.

11. Committee on Violations of Rental and Benefit Contracts, Memo to Administrator, AAA, February 15, 1935, in NA, RG 145.

12. Conrad, *The Forgotten Farmers,* pp. 126–33.

13. Trent to Extension Directors in Southern States, April 12, 1934, NA, RG 145; cited in Conrad, *The Forgotten Farmers,* pp. 133–34.

14. Mertz, *New Deal Policy,* p. 35.

15. Cited in Conrad, *The Forgotten Farmers,* p. 147.

16. Olaf F. Larson, ed., *Ten Years of Rural Rehabilitation in the United States* (Washington, D.C.: Bureau of Agricultural Economics, 1947), p. 28.

17. Ibid., p. 5.

18. Lawrence Westbrook, "The Program of Rural Rehabilitation of the FERA," *Journal of Farm Economics* 17, no. 1 (February 1935): 89.

19. Paul V. Maris, "Policy Interpretation," *Rural Rehabilitation,* February 15, 1935, p. 13. This journal was issued by the FERA and distributed to state relief administrations.

20. James G. Maddox, "The Farm Security Administration," Ph.D. diss., Harvard University, 1950, p. 17.

21. Title II, Section 208, National Industrial Recovery Act. Cited in Paul K. Conkin, *Tomorrow a New World: The New Deal Community Program* (Ithaca, N.Y.: Cornell University Press, 1959), p. 88.

22. Joseph P. Lash, *Eleanor and Franklin* (New York: Norton, 1971), p. 395.

23. M. L. Wilson, "How New Deal Agencies Are Affecting Family Life," *Journal of Home Economics* 27, no. 5 (1935): 227.

24. M. L. Wilson, "Place of Subsistence Homesteads in Our National Economy," *Journal of Farm Economics* 16, no. 1 (January 1934): 81.

25. Conkin, *Tomorrow a New World*, p. 250. For another account of Eleanor Roosevelt and Louis Howe's involvement in Arthurdale, see Lash, *Eleanor and Franklin*, pp. 394–412.

26. Conkin, *Tomorrow a New World*, pp. 126, 129.

27. Westbrook, "The Program of Rural Rehabilitation," p. 97.

28. Lawrence Westbrook, "Rural-Industrial Communities for Stranded Families," NA, RG 69.

29. Conkin, *Tomorrow a New World*, pp. 135–36.

30. Kirkendall, *Social Scientists and Farm Politics* (note 4 above), p. 74.

31. See, for instance, "A Message to the Legislature Formulating a Land Policy for the State," Albany, January 26, 1931, and "Address before the Conference of Governors on Land Utilization and State Planning," French Lick, Indiana, June 2, 1931, in Franklin D. Roosevelt, *Public Papers and Addresses*, vol. 1, (New York: Random House, 1938), pp. 480–85, 485–90.

32. Kirkendall, *Social Scientists and Farm Politics*, pp. 74–75.

33. M. L. Wilson, "Report on Land of the National Resources Board," *Journal of Farm Economics* 17, no. 1 (February 1935): 44.

34. Kirkendall, *Social Scientists and Farm Politics*, p. 87.

35. Bernard Sternsher, *Rexford Tugwell and the New Deal* (New Brunswick, N.J.: Rutgers University Press, 1964), pp. 264–65.

36. For a classic discussion of the role of administrative leadership in institutionalizing organizations, establishing "organizational character," and defining organizational missions, see Philip Selznick, *Leadership and Administration* (Evanston, Ill.: Row, Peterson, 1957), especially pp. 16–17, 37–40, 67–88.

37. See Sternsher, *Rexford Tugwell*, chap. 2, especially pp. 18–19, for a good summary of Tugwell's economic thought and his analysis of the Depression.

38. Hugh Johnson once charged, "Rex Tugwell knows as much about agriculture as Haile Selaissie knows about Oshkosh Wisconsin." See "The Cabinet: Flop, Mess, Tangle," *Time,* November 11, 1935, p. 11.

39. Prior to his appointment as assistant secretary of agriculture, Tugwell had published numerous articles and two books on agriculture. In 1928, he was asked to write a policy memorandum surveying the agricultural sector for Al Smith's presidential campaign. For a bibliography of Tugwell's works and papers, see Sternsher, *Rexford Tugwell*, pp. 413–24.

40. Raymond Moley, *Twenty-Seven Masters of Politics* (New York: Funk and Wagnalls, 1949), p. 81.

41. Russell Lord, *The Wallaces of Iowa* (Boston: Houghton Mifflin, 1947), p. 449.

42. Rexford Tugwell, "Down to Earth," *Current History* 44, no. 4 (July 1936): 38.

43. Rexford G. Tugwell, "Changing Acres," *Current History* 44, no. 4 (September 1936): p. 57.

44. Resettlement Administration, *First Annual Report* (Washington, D.C.: U.S. Government Printing Office, 1937), pp. 23–24.

45. Ibid., p. 3.

46. Rexford G. Tugwell, "Cooperation and Resettlement," *Current History* 45, no. 5 (February 1937): p. 74.

47. The executive order is reproduced in full in Resettlement Administration, *First Annual Report*, pp. 1–2.

48. Bankhead-Jones Farm Tenant Act, *United States Statutes at Large* (hereafter *U.S. Statutes*), vol. 50, pt. 1 (Washington, D.C.: U.S. Government Printing Office, 1937), pp. 522–23.

49. Emergency Relief Appropriation Act: fiscal year 1937, *U.S. Statutes*, vol. 50, pt. 1 (1937), pp. 353–54; fiscal year 1938, *U.S. Statutes*, vol. 52, pt. 1 (1938), p. 810; fiscal year 1939, *U.S. Statutes*, vol. 53, pt. 2 (1939), pp. 929–30; fiscal year 1941, *U.S. Statutes*, vol. 54, pt. 1 (1941), p. 615. Department of Agriculture Appropriation Act: fiscal year 1942, *U.S. Statutes*, vol. 55, pt. 1 (1942), pp. 438–41; fiscal year 1943, *U.S. Statutes*, vol. 56, pt. 1 (1943), pp. 695–97.

50. When the RA was created, Lawrence Westbrook, head of the FERA's Rural Rehabilitation Division, wrote Tugwell to suggest that the programs of the states be compared and evaluated. He urged that the best be chosen and combined into a standard program (letter from Westbrook to Tugwell, May 27, 1935, NA, RG 96). The fact that it took the RA more than a year just to audit the state programs is testimony to their variety and the confusing diversity of their accounting procedures (Resettlement Administration, *First Annual Report*, p. 17).

51. Address of Rexford Tugwell over NBC radio network, April 30, 1936, in NA, RG 96.

52. Sternsher, *Rexford Tugwell*, p. 265.

53. Schlesinger, *The Coming of the New Deal* (note 1 above), p. 369; Sidney Baldwin, *Poverty and Politics: The Rise and Decline of the Farm Security Administration* (Chapel Hill: University of North Carolina Press, 1968), pp. 104–5; and Marie Panor, "The Resettlement Administration: A Study in the Evolution of Major Purpose," M.A. thesis, University of Chicago, 1951, p. 34.

54. Minutes of RA staff conference, July 31, 1935, NA, RG 96; cited by Panor, "The Resettlement Administration," p. 38.

55. Schlesinger, *The Coming of the New Deal*, p. 369.

56. Minutes of RA staff conference, July 10, 1935, NA, RG 96; cited in Panor, "The Resettlement Administration," p. 28.

57. "Resettlement Policy and Procedures: Suggestions," preliminary report of Committee of Land Use Planning Section, Division of Land Utilization, August 1935, NA, RG 96.

58. Notes of Regional Directors' Conference, January 30, 1936, NA, RG 96; cited in Panor, "The Resettlement Administration," p. 44.

59. *Report of the Administrator of the Resettlement Administration, 1937* (Washington, D.C.: U.S. Government Printing Office, 1937), p. 5; and Maddox, "The Farm Security Administration" (note 20 above), p. 88.

60. Memo 732 from Secretary of Agriculture, Henry Wallace, dated September 1, 1937, NA, RG 96.

61. Maddox, "The Farm Security Administration," p. 219.

62. Ibid., p. 231.

63. *Report of the Administrator of the Farm Security Administration, 1939* (Washington, D.C.: U.S. Government Printing Office, 1939), pp. 9–11.

64. Baldwin, *Poverty and Politics,* p. 209.

65. Cited in Maddox, "The Farm Security Administration," pp. 152, 153. See also Larson, *Ten Years of Rural Rehabilitation* (note 16 above), pp. 113, 125; and Mertz, *New Deal Policy* (note 6 above), pp. 208–10.

66. Maddox, "The Farm Security Administration," p. 168.

67. Baldwin, *Poverty and Politics,* p. 314.

68. Letters from Regional Directors to C. B. Baldwin, FSA Administrator, all dated in August 1941, in NA, RG 96.

69. See R. G. Tugwell and E. C. Banfield, "Grass Roots Democracy—Myth or Reality?" *Public Administration Review* 10, no. 1 (1950): 54, for both the quote and the invocation of Paul Appleby, *Big Democracy* (New York: Knopf, 1945), p. 104.

70. Maddox, "The Farm Security Administration," pp. 175, 369–70.

71. "Progress in Income and Net Worth among Active Standard Rural Rehabilitation Borrowers Who Have Been in the FSA Program for More Than One Year," December 31, 1941, in NA, RG 96.

72. Larson, *Ten Years of Rural Rehabilitation* (note 16 above), pp. 313–421.

73. Edward C. Banfield, "Ten Years of the Farm Tenant Purchase Program," *Journal of Farm Economics* 31, no. 3 (August 1949): 469, 479.

74. Maddox, "The Farm Security Administration," pp. 465–66.

75. Ibid., pp. 267–69.

76. Ibid., pp. 294–99.

77. Ibid., pp. 241–77.

78. Cited in Mertz, *New Deal Policy,* p. 191.

79. Baldwin, *Poverty and Politics,* pp. 387–89.

80. The arguments of FSA officials received weighty support from an investigation conducted for the National Defense Advisory Commission in 1942. The study concluded that the importance of FSA programs to the success of the war food production program was "difficult to overestimate," and the money spent on FSA programs was effective in enhancing the productivity and welfare of their clients; therefore, it would be a "very unwise course of action" to cut

down on FSA expenditures (cited in Baldwin, *Poverty and Politics,* p. 383). A survey conducted by the Bureau of Agricultural Economics and the FSA of FSA rural rehabilitation standard loan clients provided further support. It showed that, in 1942, FSA clients increased their production proportionately more than the average farmer did. It found that FSA clients contributed more than their share to increases in seven of nine farm commodities. See P. G. Peck and James C. Jensen, "Contributions of Farm Security Borrowers to Agricultural Production Goals," *Journal of Farm Economics* 25 (February 1943): 101–4.

81. *Low-Income Families: Hearings before the Subcommittee on Low-Income Families of the Joint Committee on the Economic Report,* 81st Cong., 1st sess., December 12–22, 1949 (Washington, D.C.: U.S. Government Printing Office, 1950), p. 293.

82. Ibid., p. 319. See also Theodore W. Schultz, "Reflections on Poverty within Agriculture," *Journal of Political Economy* 58 (February 1950): 1–15.

83. See William P. O'Hare, *The Rise of Poverty in Rural America* (Washington, D.C.: Population Reference Bureau, 1988), p. 7, for a time series of the rural poverty rate from 1959 to 1986.

84. In the volumes of criticism of the FSA, I found only one reference to this argument. As one of their four criticisms of the FSA, Assistant Director John B. Blandford and Chief Budget Examiner James E. Scott of the Budget Bureau apparently told a committee headed by Representative John H. Tolan (Democrat from California) that "the small marginal farm was an anachronism"; that large-scale commercial farming was the wave of the future; and that the FSA "should not try to resist the inevitable" (Baldwin, *Poverty and Politics,* p. 346).

85. The inefficiency argument was a favorite of Edward O'Neal, president of the American Farm Bureau Federation. For his testimony, see *House Hearings,* Agricultural Appropriations (1942), 77th Cong., 2d sess., p. 607; *Senate Hearings,* Agricultural Appropriations (1942), 77th Cong., 2d sess., p. 728; *House Hearings,* Agricultural Appropriations (1943), 78th Cong., 1st sess., p. 1482. His argument was supported by Senator Harry F. Byrd in *Senate Hearings,* Agricultural Appropriations (1942), p. 722. Representative Malcolm Tarver criticized the FSA's "wasteful" expenditures on medical care in *House Hearings,* Agricultural Appropriations (1943), p. 1025. The criticism of expenditures on "hospitals, rest homes, sewage disposal plants, and irrigation systems" was also made in a 1944 report to the House of Representatives: Report no. 1430, *Investigating the Activities of the Farm Security Administration* (Washington, D.C.: U.S. Government Printing Office, 1944), p. 7; hereafter cited as the *Cooley Committee Report.*

86. Testimony of Judge Robert Greene, *House Hearings,* Agricultural Appropriations (1942), 77th Cong., 2d sess., p. 632; testimony of R. E. Short (president, Arkansas Farm Bureau Federation), *House Hearings* (1942), pp. 650–52; Rep. Malcolm Tarver, *House Hearings* (1943), 78th Cong., 1st sess., p. 743; testimony of Edward O'Neal, *Senate Hearings,* Agricultural Appropriations (1942), 77th Cong., 2d sess., p. 726; Sen. Harry F. Byrd, *Senate Hearings* (1942), p. 722; testimony of Earl C. Smith (vice president, American Farm Bureau Federation; president, Illinois Agricultural Association), *Senate Hear-*

ings (1942), p. 795; testimony of Ransom E. Aldrich (president, Mississippi Farm Bureau Federation), *House Hearings* (1942), p. 662.

A related charge of considerable political importance was that FSA loans paid for the poll tax of its clients. See testimony of Judge Robert Greene, p. 628; Rep. Malcolm Tarver, *House Hearings* (1942), pp. 195, 652; Sen. Kenneth D. McKellar, *Senate Hearings* (1942), p. 668; and *Cooley Committee Report*, p. 7.

87. The effect of the FSA on agricultural wages and the labor supply was a special concern of Malcolm Tarver and Everett Dirksen. See *House Hearings* (1943), pp. 974–1104, especially pp. 950, 1004, 1005, 1007.

88. Rep. Malcolm Tarver, *House Hearings* (1942), p. 740; Sen. Kenneth D. McKellar, *Senate Hearings* (1942), p. 692; testimony of Edward O'Neal, *Senate Hearings* (1942), p. 726; testimony of Oscar Johnston (president, National Cotton Council), *Senate Hearings* (1943), p. 954; *Cooley Committee Report*, p. 2.

89. Testimony of Robert H. Shields (solicitor, USDA), *Hearings before the House Select Committee to Investigate Activities of Farm Security Administration*, 78th Cong., 1st sess. (1943), pp. 655–60; *Cooley Committee Report*, pp. 11, 17. See also Baldwin, *Poverty and Politics*, p. 384.

90. U.S. Congress, Subcommittee on Low-Income Families of the Joint Committee on the Economic Report, *Low-Income Families and Economic Stability*, Senate Document 146 (Washington, D.C.: U.S. Government Printing Office, 1950), pp. 4–8.

91. For a good account of the early conflicts among RA staff, see Arthur W. MacMahon, John D. Millett, and Gladys Ogden, *The Administration of Federal Work Relief* (Chicago: Public Administration Service, 1941), pp. 261–68.

92. Ibid., pp. 28–29, 103.

93. Richard Sterner, *The Negroes Share: A Study of Income Consumption, Housing and Public Assistance* (New York: Harper and Brothers, 1943), pp. 295–309; Raymond Wolters, *The Negroes and the Great Depression: The Problem of Economic Recovery* (Westport, Conn.: Greenwood Press, 1970), pp. 60–77, and "The New Deal and the Negro" (note 6 above), pp. 176–78; Donald Holley, "The Negro in the New Deal Resettlement Programs," *Agricultural History* 45, no. 3 (July 1971): 179–93; Gunnar Myrdal, *An American Dilemma: The Negro Problem and Modern Democracy*, vol. 1 (New York: Harper and Brothers, 1944), p. 275; and Baldwin, *Poverty and Politics*, pp. 197, 200–203.

94. "Report of the Rural Rehabilitation Division, 1938–39," in NA, RG 96.

95. For instance, a memo dated February 10, 1942, from Carl N. Gibboney, acting director of the Rural Rehabilitation Division, to William F. Littlejohn, chief personnel officer of the FSA, complained that implementation effectiveness was being curbed because "our program is getting too complex and the burden of responsibility on the county supervisor too great" (NA, RG 96). See also Larson, *Ten Years of Rural Rehabilitation* (note 16 above), pp. 130–53.

96. Baldwin, *Poverty and Politics*, p. 252.

97. Letter from H. Umberger, director of Extension Service, Kansas, to R. Wharburton, RA director for Region VII, dated July 24, 1936, in NA, RG 96; and telegram from C. B. Smith, acting director of the Extension Service, cited in letter from Paul V. Maris to C. B. Smith, dated August 7, 1936, in NA, RG 96. See also Christiana McFadyen Campbell, *The Farm Bureau and the New Deal* (Urbana: University of Illinois Press, 1962), p. 167.

98. Rexford G. Tugwell to Franklin D. Roosevelt, November 18, 1935, cited in Conkin, *Tomorrow a New World*, p. 160.

99. Maddox, "The Farm Security Administration," p. 118.

100. Letter from O. B. Jesness to Raymond A. Pearson, dated November 13, 1937, in NA, RG 96.

101. Campbell, *The Farm Bureau*, p. 168.

102. M. L. Wilson to John J. Sparkman, dated April 17, 1943; cited in Baldwin, *Poverty and Politics*, p. 390.

103. Dean Albertson, *Roosevelt's Farmer: Claude R. Wickard in the New Deal* (New York: Columbia University Press, 1961), pp. 155–70.

104. Ibid., pp. 367–77.

105. For an excellent study of the impact of FSA programs on Southern paternalism, see Lee J. Alston and Joseph P. Ferrie, "Resisting the Welfare State: Southern Opposition to the Farm Security Administration," in *Emergence of the Modern Political Economy*, ed. Robert Higgs (Greenwich, Conn.: JAI Press, 1985), pp. 83–120. For an elaboration of this thesis in regard to the Social Security Act, see Lee J. Alston and Joseph P. Ferrie, "Labor Costs, Paternalism, and Loyalty in Southern Agriculture: A Constraint on the Growth of the Welfare State," *Journal of Economic History* 45, no. 1 (March 1985): 95–118.

106. For an explanation and critique of "grass-roots democracy," see Philip Selznick, *TVA and the Grass Roots* (Berkeley: University of California Press, 1980, reprint of 1949 ed.).

107. Orville Kile, *The Farm Bureau through Decades* (Baltimore: Waverly Press, 1948), p. 255.

108. For the most comprehensive analysis of the ascendance of the conservative coalition, see James T. Patterson, *Congressional Conservatism and the New Deal: The Growth of the Conservative Coalition in Congress, 1933–1939* (Lexington: University of Kentucky Press, 1967). See also Richard Polenberg, "The Decline of the New Deal, 1937–40," in Braeman, Bremner, and Brody, *The New Deal*, pp. 246–66.

109. The rest of this section is indebted to Sidney Baldwin's thorough legislative history of the FSA's demise. See his *Poverty and Politics*, pp. 335–404.

110. Ibid., pp. 349–50.

111. Ibid., p. 383.

112. Computed from Maddox, "The Farm Security Administration," pp. 88, 175–76, 424.

113. U.S. Bureau of the Census, *Fifteenth Census of the United States: 1930*, vol. 4: *Agriculture* (Washington, D.C.: U.S. Department of Commerce, 1932), pp. 40–41.

114. Ibid., pp. 40–41, 712–817. The estimate of cotton's share of cash

earnings is taken from George Brown Tindall, *The Emergence of the New South, 1913–1945* (Baton Rouge: Louisiana State University Press, 1967), p. 429.

115. According to Tindall (*Emergence of the New South,* p. 134), 40 percent of tobacco, the South's other major commercial agricultural commodity, was also exported. Exports also accounted for one-sixth of the petroleum, one-third of the sulfur, and half of the naval stores produced in the South.

116. Bureau of the Census, *Fifteenth Census of the United States,* pp. 58–59, 91–103, 536–37.

117. For an excellent description of the evolution of agricultural labor control in the South following the Civil War, see Harold D. Woodman, "Post–Civil War Southern Agriculture and the Law," *Agricultural History* 53, no. 1 (January 1979): 319–37.

118. Charles S. Johnson, Edwin Embree, and W. W. Alexander, *The Collapse of Cotton Tenancy* (Chapel Hill: University of North Carolina Press, 1935), pp. 25–32; Tindall, *Emergence of the New South,* pp. 410–11.

119. Tindall, *Emergence of the New South,* p. 410.

120. Johnson, Embree, and Alexander, *Collapse of Cotton Tenancy,* p. 12.

121. Ibid., pp. 11–12.

122. Harold Hoffsommer, "Landlord-Tenant Relations and Relief in Alabama," *Monthly Report of the Federal Emergency Relief Administration,* October 1935, pp. 1–4.

123. Gilbert C. Fite, *Cotton Fields No More: Southern Agriculture, 1865–1980* (Lexington: University of Kentucky Press, 1984), especially pp. xii, 101, 143.

124. Gilbert C. Fite, "The Agricultural Trap in the South," *Agricultural History* 60, no. 4 (Fall 1986): 38–50.

125. Testimony of D. Gale Johnson, in *Low-Income Families: Hearings before the Subcommittee on Low-Income Families of the Joint Committee on the Economic Report,* 81st Cong., 1st sess., December 12–22, 1949 (Washington, D.C.: U.S. Government Printing Office, 1950), p. 293.

126. Fite, *Cotton Fields No More,* especially pp. 139–206. See also Jack Temple Kirby, "The Transformation of Southern Plantations, c. 1920–1960," *Agricultural History* 57, no. 3 (July 1983): 257–76; Pete Daniel, "The Transformation of the Rural South, 1930 to the Present," *Agricultural History* 55, no. 3 (July 1981): 321–49.

127. The partisan motivation for disfranchisement is argued most cogently by J. Morgan Kousser, *The Shaping of Southern Politics: Suffrage Restriction and the Establishment of the One-Party South, 1880–1910* (New Haven, Conn.: Yale University Press, 1974), especially pp. 1–9, 83–103, 224–29, 238–65. V. O. Key suggests but does not ultimately endorse this position. See *Southern Politics in State and Nation* (New York: Knopf, 1949), pp. 509–663.

128. Kousser, *Shaping of Southern Politics,* pp. 224–37; Key, *Southern Politics,* especially pp. 11–18, 386–405.

129. In his examination of the voting records of Southern senators and representatives, Key (*Southern Politics,* pp. 345–82) found that Southern Democrats in general had only slightly greater solidarity than senators and represen-

tatives from other regions. However, the Southern senators and representatives showed remarkable solidarity in favor of positions on race, agriculture, and labor issues. For an excellent discussion of the attitudes of Southern members of the Senate and House of Representatives to New Deal rural antipoverty legislative initiatives, see Mertz, *New Deal Policy* (note 6 above), especially pp. 93–187.

130. See, for instance, David Brody, "The New Deal and World War II," in Braeman, Bremner, and Brody, *The New Deal* (note 1 above), pp. 277–78.

131. Grant McConnell, *The Decline of Agrarian Democracy* (Berkeley: University of California Press, 1953).

132. Myrdal, *An American Dilemma* (note 93 above), p. 465.

133. Alston and Ferrie, "Resisting the Welfare State" (note 105 above), pp. 94–95.

134. Kile, *The Farm Bureau* (note 107 above), p. 326. See also Robert L. Tontz, "Memberships of General Farmers' Organizations, United States, 1874–1960," *Agricultural History* 38, no. 3 (July 1964): 155.

135. Especially irksome to the AFBF was Wallace's appointment of A. G. Black as governor of the FCA in 1939. See Campbell, *The Farm Bureau*, p. 172; and Kile, *The Farm Bureau*, p. 258.

136. Gregory Hooks, "From an Autonomous to a Captured State Agency: The Decline of the New Deal in Agriculture," *American Sociological Review* 55 (February 1990): 33–34; Kirkendall, *Social Scientists and Farm Politics* (note 4 above), pp. 167–87; and Benedict, *Farm Policies of the United States, 1790–1950* (note 1 above), pp. 377–95.

137. The information from the previous two paragraphs is taken from Kirkendall, *Social Scientists and Farm Politics,* chaps. 10–11; Campbell, *The Farm Bureau,* p. 178; and McConnell, *Decline of Agrarian Democracy,* pp. 118–19.

138. *Cooley Committee Report,* p. 2.

139. Ibid.

140. Tugwell and Banfield, "Grass Roots Democracy" (note 69 above), p. 51.

141. Larson, *Ten Years of Rural Rehabilitation* (note 16 above), pp. 194–200; and Baldwin, *Poverty and Politics,* pp. 207–8.

142. See Baldwin, *Poverty and Politics,* pp. 183, 309, for documentation of Alexander's position as well as that of other top officials in the U.S. Department of Agriculture.

143. Selznick, *TVA and the Grass Roots* (note 106 above), p. 48.

144. Alston and Ferrie, "Resisting the Welfare State," p. 105.

145. For an insightful discussion of the impact of American institutions on policy innovation, see Margaret Weir, *Politics and Jobs: The Boundaries of Employment Policy in the United States* (Princeton: Princeton University Press, 1992), pp. 18–26.

146. Classic descriptions of the way in which institutions discouraged the political participation of the rural poor in the South include Kousser, *The Shaping of Southern Politics;* Key, *Southern Politics,* especially pp. 504–663; and Myrdal, *An American Dilemma,* pp. 474–504.

147. For a comparison of institutional structures in the United States, Sweden, and the United Kingdom during the Depression, see Margaret Weir and Theda Skocpol, "State Structures and the Possibilities for 'Keynesian' Responses to the Great Depression in Sweden, Britain and the United States," in *Bringing the State Back In,* ed. Peter B. Evans, Dietrich Rueschemeyer, and Theda Skocpol (Cambridge: Cambridge University Press, 1985), pp. 107–63.

148. Richard Franklin Bensel, *Sectionalism and American Political Development* (Madison: University of Wisconsin Press, 1984), pp. 149–50.

149. For a description of the development of the farm bloc under AFBF hegemony, see John Mark Hansen, *Gaining Access: Congress and the Farm Lobby, 1919–1981* (Chicago: University of Chicago Press, 1991), pp. 11–97.

150. George E. Mowry, *Another Look at the Twentieth Century South* (Baton Rouge: Louisiana State University Press, 1973), pp. 45–46.

151. *Cooley Committee Report,* p. 4.

152. Theda Skocpol and Kenneth Finegold, "State Capacity and Economic Intervention in the Early New Deal," *Political Science Quarterly* 97, no. 2 (Summer 1982): 255–78.

153. Claus Offe, "The Theory of the Capitalist State and the Problem of Policy Formation," in *Stress and Contradiction in Modern Capitalism,* ed. Leon N. Lindberg et al. (Lexington, Mass.: Heath, 1975), p. 135.

154. Dietrich Rueschemeyer and Peter B. Evans, "The State and Economic Transformation: Toward an Analysis of the Conditions underlying Effective Interventions," in Evans, Rueschemeyer and Skocpol, *Bringing the State Back In,* especially p. 69.

155. For a remarkably systematic study of the long-term impact of RA and FSA programs on Southern African-Americans, see Lester M. Salamon, "The Time Dimension in Policy Evaluation: The Case of the New Deal Land-Reform Experiments," *Public Policy* 27, no. 2 (Spring 1979): 129–83. For a study that focuses more on public health, see Richard A. Couto, *Ain't Gonna Let Nobody Turn Me Around: The Pursuit of Racial Justice in the Rural South* (Philadelphia: Temple University Press, 1991).

156. Joel Migdal, *Strong Societies and Weak States: State-Society Relations and State Capabilities in the Third World* (Princeton, N.J.: Princeton University Press, 1988), p. 269.

157. Merilee S. Grindle, *State and Countryside: Development Policy and Agrarian Politics in Latin America* (Baltimore: Johns Hopkins University Press, 1986); Richard H. Adams, Jr., *Development and Social Change in Rural Egypt* (Syracuse, N.Y.: Syracuse University Press, 1986); Francine R. Frankel, *India's Political Economy, 1947–1977* (Princeton, N.J.: Princeton University Press, 1978).

CHAPTER 3

1. The data in this and the following paragraph are based on computations from Government of India, Ministry of Planning, Department of Statistics, *Estimates of State Domestic Product, 1970–71—1987–88* (New Delhi: Control-

ler of Publications, 1989), pp. 9, 37; and Ministry of Finance, Government of India, *Economic Survey, 1989–90* (New Delhi: Government of India Press, 1990), p. S-3.

2. The data comparing Maharashtra's agrarian structure with the all-India averages are from Government of India, Director of Economics and Statistics, Ministry of Agriculture, Department of Agriculture and Cooperation, "Agricultural Census: All India," *Agricultural Situation in India* 40, no. 5 (August 1985): 410.

3. N. Kakawani and K. Subbarao, "Rural Poverty and Its Alleviation in India," *Economic and Political Weekly* 25, no. 13 (March 31, 1990): A-6.

4. Data computed from *Maharashtra Quarterly Bulletin of Economics and Statistics* 28, no. 4 (January–March 1988): 43; 10, no. 4 (January–March 1970): 48; and 8, no. 3 and no. 4 (October 1967–March 1968): 140.

5. Computed from *Maharashtra Quarterly Bulletin of Economics and Statistics* 28, no. 2 (July–September 1987): 95; 26, no. 4 (January–March 1986): 187; 8, no. 3 and no. 4 (October 1967–March 1968): 140; 6, no. 1 (April–June 1965): 72; Government of India, Ministry of Finance, *Economic Survey, 1988–89* (New Delhi: Government of India Press, 1989), p. S-17; and *Agricultural Situation in India* 41, no. 12 (March 1987): 1004.

6. The data for Maharashtra are for the year ending on March 31, 1986, as reported in *Maharashtra Quarterly Bulletin of Economics and Statistics* 28, no. 4 (January–March 1988): 1; the all-India data are for the year ending March 31, 1985, as reported in Government of India, Planning Commission, *Seventh Five Year Plan, 1985–90,* vol. 2 (New Delhi: Government of India Press, 1985), p. 72.

7. Government of Maharashtra, Planning Department, *Annual Plan, 1983–84, Maharashtra* (Bombay: Government of Maharashtra, 1984), p. 95.

8. Sugarcane cultivation is estimated to absorb eight to ten times more water than most foodgrain crops. G. O., "Maharashtra: Fighting Drought," *Economic and Political Weekly* 21, no. 18 (May 3, 1986): 769. Nilakantha Rath and Ashok K. Mitra ("Economics of Utilization of Canal Water in Dry Agricultural Regions," *Indian Journal of Agricultural Economics* 41, no. 2 [1986]: 131–40) suggest that alternative crop rotations reducing the area under sugar cultivation would free up water sufficient to increase the area irrigated by 30 to 100 percent. A commission convened by the Government of Maharashtra estimated that the area under irrigation could be tripled if irrigation were restricted to lightly irrigated crops (see V. M. Dandekar, D. Deshmukh, and V. R. Devskar, *Interim Report of the Committee to Study the Introduction of Eight Monthly Supply of Water on Irrigation Projects in Maharashtra* [Bombay: Government of Maharashtra, 1979]). See also Ashok K. Mitra, "Utilization Revisited: Surface Irrigation in Drought Prone Areas of Western Maharashtra," *Economic and Political Weekly* 21, no. 17 (April 26, 1986): 752–56. Regarding the controversy over sugar cultivators' disproportionate share of irrigation, see Mitra, "Utilization Revisited," 769–70; M. D. Sathe, "Maharashtra: Social Basis of Sharing Irrigation Water, Central Issue in Well-Being of Poor," *Economic and Political Weekly* 21, no. 17 (April 26, 1986): 737–38; G. O.,

"Fighting Famine," *Economic and Political Weekly* 20, no. 43 (November 2, 1985): 885–87.

9. Donald B. Rosenthal, *The Expansive Elite* (Berkeley: University of California Press, 1977); A. R. Kamat, "Political Economic Developments in Maharashtra: A Review of the Post-Independence Era," *Economic and Political Weekly* 15, no. 39 (September 27, 1980): 1627. Rosenthal enunciates the phenomenon for India in general in "Deurbanization, Elite Displacement and Political Changes in India," *Comparative Politics* 2 (January 1970): 1969–2001.

10. B. S. Baviskar, *The Politics of Development: Sugar Co-operatives in Rural Maharashtra* (Delhi: Oxford University Press, 1980), pp. 113–86. See also Rosenthal, *The Expansive Elite,* pp. 13–14, 206–18.

11. Jayant Lele, "One-Party Dominance in Maharashtra: Resilience and Change," in *State Politics in Contemporary India: Crisis or Continuity?* ed. John R. Wood (Boulder, Colo.: Westview Press, 1984), pp. 169–96, especially 180–85. Lele points out that the major cleavage among political elites in the late 1970s and the 1980s has been between pluralists (those who wish to maintain the autonomy of the competitive elite system set up by Y. B. Chavan) and loyalists (those who stress their closeness to Indira Gandhi and rely more on populism to mobilize their support). From his institutional base in the cooperative sector, Patil is a leader of the pluralists.

12. Jayant Lele, *Elite Pluralism and Class Rule: Political Development in Maharashtra* (Bombay: Popular Prakashan, 1981), pp. 45–80; and Anthony T. Carter, *Elite Politics in Rural India* (London: Cambridge University Press, 1974), pp. 101–26.

13. Jayant Lele, "Chavan and the Political Integration of Maharashtra," in *Contemporary India: Socio-economic and Political Processes* (Poona: Continental Prakashan, 1982), pp. 29–54.

14. The phrase is taken from Ronald J. Herring and Rex M. Edwards, "Guaranteeing Employment to the Poor: Social Functions and Class Interests in the Employment Guarantee Scheme in Western India," *World Development* 11, no. 7 (July 1983): 575–92.

15. Since Maharashtra began the EGS on a statewide scale in 1974, Karnataka and Tamilnadu have taken up similar schemes. The EGS served as the inspiration of the central government–sponsored Rural Landless Employment Guarantee Programme initiated in 1983. This program has recently been combined with the National Rural Employment Programme, the Government of India's other major public works program aimed at rural poverty alleviation.

16. Herring and Edwards ("Guaranteeing Employment," p. 585) found that Bombay's annual contribution to total EGS tax revenues ranged from 62 to 70 percent over the years 1975–76 to 1979–80. The minister for social welfare, Pratibha Patil, publicly credited the EGS with reducing the number of workers and beggars coming into Bombay ("EGS Has Helped Reduce Influx," *Times of India* [Bombay], April 7, 1983).

17. Lele, "Chavan and the Political Integration of Maharashtra." See also his "One-Party Dominance in Maharashtra" and his *Elite Pluralism and Class Rule.*

18. Herring and Edwards, "Guaranteeing Employment," pp. 586–87.

19. A government report indicated that 77.6 percent of 2,051 households had an increase in production "to the extent of 25 percent" as a result of using EGS assets. See Government of India, Program Evaluation Organisation, Planning Commission, and Government of Maharashtra, Directorate of Economics and Statistics, *Joint Evaluation of Employment Guarantee Scheme of Maharashtra,* vol. 1 (New Delhi: Controller of Publications, 1980), p. 33.

20. Government of Maharashtra, Planning Department, "Employment Guarantee Scheme," memorandum dated February 8, 1990 (Planning Dept., EMP 9); Madhav Godbole, *Public Expenditures in Maharashtra: A Case for Expenditure Strategy* (Bombay: Himalaya Publishing House, 1989), p. 101; *Census of India, 1981, Series 1, India,* Paper 3: *Provisional Population Totals: Workers and Non-Workers* (New Delhi: Controller of Publications, 1981), p. 210.

21. A sketch of EGS administration can be gleaned from "Employment Guarantee Scheme," directive dated September 1974, "The Maharashtra Employment Guarantee Act, 1977, Maharashtra Act No. XI of 1978"; and "The Maharashtra Employment Guarantee Rules, 1979"; all in Government of Maharashtra, Planning Department, *Employment Guarantee Scheme: A Compendium of Orders* (Bombay: Government of Maharashtra, 1982), pp. 1–9, 906–17, and 933–51.

22. By May 1973, relief works accounted for more than 64,000 projects employing 4.9 million workers. See Sulabha Brahme, *Drought in Maharashtra, 1972* (Pune: Gokhale Institute of Politics and Economics, 1983), p. 87.

23. V. Subramanian, *Parched Earth: The Maharashtra Drought, 1970–73* (New Delhi: Orient Longman, 1975), p. 189.

24. The importance of these early drought relief programs to the evolution of the EGS was highlighted by V. Subramanian, secretary to the Department of Revenue and Forests at the time of the famine relief effort and later secretary to the Planning Department, in an interview in Bombay, January 3, 1984.

25. Technically, planning takes place on the basis of panchayat samiti constituencies. These coincide with tahsils everywhere in Maharashtra except in the eastern Vidharbha region.

26. My survey found that only two of thirty-four technical officers were born in the tahsil where they worked. I was able to inspect the notes of the tahsil-level EGS meetings for Shrirampur and Karjat. The minutes noted that politicians, often the member of the legislative assembly who chairs these meetings, suggested that projects be taken up at four of the seven Shrirampur tahsil meetings that were held from January to July 1983. Politicians made suggestions for projects at all three of the meetings in Karjat from July to December 1983. Officers in charge of planning EGS projects said that local politicians made suggestions for projects and locations in each of the tahsils that I studied.

The superior knowledge of local politicians became obvious to me at meetings in the office of Ahmednagar's collector held to initiate implementation of the Comprehensive Watershed Development Programme (COWDEP) under the EGS (February 6, 1984). The Agriculture Department's subdivisional soil conservation officers (sub discos) for each tahsil were accompanied to this meeting by at least one local politician. The politicians spoke far more knowledgeably about local conditions. Afterward, sub discos told me that they relied on the politicians for suggestions on where the projects should be initiated.

27. Stanley M. Davis and Paul R. Lawrence, *Matrix* (Reading, Mass.: Addison-Wesley, 1977).

28. Samuel S. Lieberman, "An Organizational Reconnaissance of the Employment Guarantee Scheme," *Indian Journal of Public Administration* 30, no. 4 (October 1984): 977–78.

29. Directives dated April 9, 1976; cited in *A Compendium of Orders*, pp. 146–47.

30. Jay R. Galbraith, "Matrix Organization Designs: How to Combine Functional and Project Forms," *Business Horizons* 14, no. 1 (1971): 29–40; Lieberman, "Organizational Reconnaissance," p. 985.

31. In contrast, after four years of NREP implementation, the Government of West Bengal included only forty-five pages on the NREP in its volume on programs implemented by panchayats. See *Compendium for Panchayati Raj in West Bengal* (Calcutta: Government of West Bengal, Director of Panchayats, 1984), pp. 317–62.

32. Interview with deputy commissioner for development, Pune, February 1, 1984.

33. The volatility of labor attendance was a frequent complaint of the field-level officers that I interviewed in Ahmednagar. It was one of the most important concerns discussed at the "Session on EGS Implementation" conducted by the Maharashtra Administrative Staff College in Bombay on December 17–18, 1983. Others who have observed this volatility include Samuel S. Lieberman, "Field-Level Perspectives on Maharashtra's Employment Guarantee Scheme," *Public Administration and Development* 5, no. 2 (1985): 109–27; Kumudini Dandekar, *Employment Guarantee Scheme: An Employment Opportunity for Women* (Pune: Gokhale Institute of Politics and Economics, 1983), p. 32; and Vasant Deshpande, *Employment Guarantee Scheme: Impact on Poverty and Bondage among Tribals* (Pune: Tilak Vidyapeeth, 1982), pp. 74–76.

34. Rozgar Hami Yojana Samiti, 1982–83, Sahaavi Maharashtra Vidhan Sabha, *Saatvaa Ahavaal* (Seventh Session) (Bombay: Maharashtra State Legislative Secretariat, 1983), p. 2.

35. For other fieldwork arriving at a similar conclusion, see Sarthi Acharya and V. G. Panwalkar, "The Maharashtra Employment Guarantee Scheme: Impact on Male and Female Labour," paper prepared under the Population Council, Programme in Asia on Women's Roles and Gender Differences in Development (Bombay: Tata Institute of Social Sciences, 1988), pp. 16–17.

36. The Planning Department's memo entitled "Employment Guarantee Scheme" (note 20 above) provides a good example of the dated information yielded by worker registration. The latest data it was able to provide were registration figures for 1984 (p. 3). See also Rozgar Hami Yojana Samiti, 1983–84, Sahaavi Maharashtra Vidham Sabha, *Navvaa Ahavaal* (Ninth Session) (Bombay: Maharashtra State Legislative Secretariat, 1984), p. 1; and S. Bagchee, "Employment Guarantee Scheme in Maharashtra," *Economic and Political Weekly* 19, no. 37 (September 15, 1984): 1634.

37. Government of India and Government of Maharashtra, *Joint Evaluation* (note 19 above), pp. 42, 59.

38. For a good description of the RDLF, see Government of Maharashtra, Planning Department, Government Resolution No. RoHoYo-2089/72/Rohoyo-6, Mantrayala, Bombay, dated June 22, 1989; and "Employment Guarantee Scheme in a New Form: Rural Development through Labour Power," *Lok Rajya* 45 (August 16, 1989): 56–60. My observation about the limited impact of the RDLF is based on conversations with Martin Ravallion of the World Bank after his return from a May field trip in Maharashtra, Washington, D.C., August 15, 1990.

39. Interview, Bombay, December 8, 1983.

40. My interviews with thirty-four project-level officers were conducted in three tahsils of Ahmednagar district. Situated across the Sahyadri Mountains about 100 miles due west of Bombay, Ahmednagar, with 7,035 square kilometers and 2.3 million people, is Maharashtra's second-largest district in territory and the fifth-largest in population. Climatic conditions are arid, with twelve of the thirteen districts considered drought-prone areas. Irrigation projects in the northern tahsils of Shrirampur, Koparagaon, Rahuri, and Newasa have made possible extensive sugarcane cultivation. The area, proudly claimed to be "the sugar bowl of Maharashtra," accounts for one-fourth of all sugar production in Maharashtra.

In part because of its arid climate, Ahmednagar has received more persondays of EGS employment and more EGS expenditures than any other district. I interviewed field-level officers from three tahsils in the district. Parner and Karjat are backward areas with low ratios of net irrigated area to net sown area (7.3 and 10.2, respectively) and even less of their gross cropped area under surface irrigation (0.2 percent and 0.9 percent). Shrirampur, in contrast, is the most developed tahsil in Ahmednagar. Its 47.6 percent net irrigated area to net sown area is the highest of any tahsil in the district. It also topped the district's tahsils in gross cropped area under reliable surface irrigation (24.2 percent) and gross cropped area under sugarcane (21.6 percent). My interviews included structured and unstructured questions. They lasted for from thirty minutes to two and a half hours. My sample included thirteen project-level officers from Parner, eleven from Karjat, and ten from Shrirampur. With such a small number of interviews, I make no claim to have a representative sample. My selection of tahsils was motivated by the desire to explore the impact of different levels of development on EGS implementation.

41. The state legislature's Employment Guarantee Scheme committee has also observed the existence of large gangs. It recommended that the size of gangs be reduced, and the Planning Department issued a circular asking the implementing agencies to do so. See directive dated October 27, 1976, in *A Compendium of Orders,* p. 201.

42. The Agriculture Department (Soil Conservation) is an exception. It supervises EGS works with its own personnel.

43. Herring and Edwards, "Guaranteeing Employment," p. 590.

44. Michael Lipsky, *Street-Level Bureaucracy* (New York: Russell Sage Foundation, 1980).

45. For instance, one junior engineer recounted an incident that occurred

when he went to pay workers their wages. He found himself short of change—a situation that most Indians should be able to empathize with, given the country's perpetual shortage of coinage. As a result, he was unable to pay each worker his precise earnings. The workers harangued him and then ruined his motor scooter.

46. Letter to Collector from Executive Engineer, Nasik Irrigation Division, dated September 25, 1981; Letter to Collector, Ahmednagar, from Executive Engineer, Upper Pravara Canal Division, Sangamner, dated December 24, 1981; Letter to Collector, Ahmednagar, from Executive Engineer, Ahmednagar Irrigation Circle, dated August 12, 1982; and Letter to Collector from Executive Engineer, MID-I Ahmednagar No. PB/3028/83.

47. Interview, Pune, February 1, 1984.

48. Albert O. Hirschman, *Shifting Involvements: Private Interests and Public Action* (Princeton, N.J.: Princeton University Press, 1982), p. 124.

49. An investigation by the state government's finance minister found 341 cases of corruption at the end of 1983 ("341 EGS Graft Cases Detected," *Indian Express* [Bombay] December 6, 1983, p. 4). An investigation by the EGS committee of the state legislature found graft involving Rs. 11.5 million in a single tahsil from 1978 to 1982 ("12 Engineers Suspended for Fraud," *Indian Express* [Bombay], March 22, 1984; "Rs. 1.15 Crore Graft in Nasik EGS," *Times of India* [Bombay], March 22, 1984).

50. Herring and Edwards, "Guaranteeing Employment," p. 580.

51. In one of the more amusing cases, a member of the state legislature accused EGS administrators of including the names of donkeys on local muster roles. See "Donkey and EGS," *Times of India* (Bombay), March 22, 1983.

52. "341 EGS Graft Cases Detected."

53. B. R. Bawke, leader of a union of EGS workers in Shrirampur tahsil, told me that government officials often "buy off" EGS workers when they threaten to complain about corruption (interview, Shrirampur, March 22, 1984).

54. For a discussion of corruption on the IRDP, see Nilakantha Rath, "Garibi Hatao: Can IRDP Do It?" *Economic and Political Weekly* 26, no. 6 (February 9, 1985): 238–46. For a less critical assessment see Robert V. Pulley, *Making the Poor Creditworthy: A Case Study of the Integrated Rural Development Program in India,* World Bank Discussion Paper 58 (Washington, D.C.: World Bank, 1989).

55. Official reports concerned with the problem of corruption include Sanathanam Commission (Government of India) and National Institute of Public Finance and Policies, *Aspects of Black Money in India* (New Delhi: Government of India Press, 1985). Unofficial accounts of corruption include Robert Wade, "The Market for Public Office: Why the Indian State Is Not Better at Development," *World Development* 13, no. 4 (April 1985): 467–97; Robert Wade, "The System of Administrative and Political Corruption: Land Irrigation in South India," *Journal of Development Studies* 18, no. 3 (April 1982): 287–328; and P. Krishna Gopinath, "Corruption in Political and Public Offices: Causes and Cure," *Indian Journal of Public Administration* 28, no. 4 (December 1982): 897–918.

56. Tevfik F. Nas, Albert C. Price, and Charles T. Weber, "A Policy Ori-

ented Theory of Corruption," *American Political Science Review* 80, no. 1 (March 1986): 107–20; and Barry S. Rundquist, Gerald S. Strom, and John G. Peters, "Corrupt Politicians and Their Electoral Support," *American Political Science Review* 71, no. 3 (September 1977): 955.

57. For a historical overview of these dynamics see B. B. Mishra, *District Administration and Rural Development in India* (Delhi: Oxford University Press, 1983), pp. 133–61.

58. Interviews with tahsildars in Shrirampur and Karjat and with Bombay collector (former collector at Dhule); and minutes of the meeting of Naib tahsildars and *awal karkuns* (EGS administrators), held in the office of the deputy collector (EGS), Ahmednagar, March 3, 1983.

59. Prakash Kardaley, "Dhule Collector Inspired Colleagues," *Indian Express* (Bombay), July 4, 1982.

60. "Gavai Report Reveals Only a Fraction," *Indian Express* (Bombay), September 19, 1982.

61. Prakash Kardaley, "Dhule Crusade against Corruption," *Indian Express* (Bombay), January 16, 1983.

62. Kardaley, "Dhule Collector Inspired Colleagues."

63. Rahul Singh, "EGS Fraud Report Gathering Dust," *Indian Express* (Bombay), January 25, 1984.

64. Interview, Bombay, February 11, 1984.

65. Kardaley, "Dhule Crusade against Corruption."

66. Rahul Singh, "Official Lethargy Shocking," *Indian Express* (Bombay), January 26, 1984.

67. Directives dated December 27, 1977, and August 1, 1979, in *A Compendium of Orders* (note 21 above), pp. 320–21, 526–27.

68. Undated and untitled mimeo given during interview with Sitaram Bajare, representative of the *Rozgar Hami Kaamgaar Sargh* (Employment Guarantee Workers' Union), Pune, February 2, 1984.

69. Interview, Parner, March 5, 1984.

70. Interview with Suryakant Palande, chair of the state legislature's EGS committee, Bombay, March 27, 1984.

71. Interview with Sitaram Bajare, Pune, March 31, 1984; correspondence with Ramkrishna Kalaburge, Pushpa Pandhar Patte, and Bhimrao Zagade, social workers for Surya, Palghar, and Thane, Maharashtra, March 15, 1984.

72. "Pilot Employment Guarantee Scheme in Integrated Area Development Blocks," directive dated July 24, 1969, in *A Compendium of Orders*, pp. 739–44.

73. For an excellent discussion of the relations between the panchayats and local administrators and MLAs, see Rosenthal, *The Expansive Elite* (note 9 above), pp. 48–50, 269–305. The Ashok Mehta Committee, convened by the central government to evaluate the workings of the country's panchayats, mentions tensions between MLAs and panchayat officials as an important reason for the weakening of the panchayats on the national level as well as in Maharashtra. See Government of India, Ministry of Agriculture and Irrigation, Department of Rural Development, *Report of the Committee on Panchayati Raj Institutions* (New Delhi: Government of India Press, 1978), pp. 4–7. The Bon-

girwar Committee, appointed by the Government of Maharashtra in February 1970 to evaluate the state's panchayats, noted the state government's reluctance to transfer programs to the panchayats. See Government of Maharashtra, *Statement of the Recommendations of the Evaluation Committee on Panchayati Raj (Bongirwar Committee) and Government Decisions Thereon* (Bombay: Central Government Press, 1973). For an analysis of the reactions of the state's MLAs to the introduction of the panchayats, see Lawrence L. Shrader and Ram Joshi, "Zilla Parishad Elections in Maharashtra and the District Political Elite," *Asian Survey* 3, no. 3 (March 1963): 143–55.

One manifestation of the weakening of the panchayats in Maharashtra is that zilla parishad elections have not been held since 1979. Chief Minister Sharad Pawar dissolved all of Maharashtra's zilla parishads in June 1990, claiming that these hotbeds of corruption would interfere with the fair elections he had promised within four months. This manipulation of the zilla parishads may be an attempt to replace Pawar's rivals with his supporters. See J. V. Deshpande, "Zilla Parishad Game," *Economic and Political Weekly* 25, no. 27 (July 7, 1990): 1442.

74. Lieberman, "Field-Level Perspectives" (note 33 above), p. 116.

75. Rozgar Hami Yojana Samiti, 1982–83 Sahaavi Maharashtra Vidhan Sabha, *Sahaavaa Ahavaal* (Sixth Session) (Bombay: Maharashtra State Legislative Secretariat, 1983), pp. 3, 17. See also directive dated November 24, 1980, in *A Compendium of Orders*, p. 663.

76. Reported in directives dated February 24, 1981; January 23, 1981; and September 17, 1977. All cited in *A Compendium of Orders*, pp. 282–83, 676–77, and 684–85.

77. Rozgar Hami Yojana Samiti, *Navvaa Ahavaal* (note 36 above), p. 7; *Atthavaa Ahavall* (Eighth Session, 1984), p. 20; *Sahaavaa Ahavaal*, p. 4.

78. Interview, Bombay, January 24, 1985.

79. For reviews of the literature on opportunity structures and collective action, see Sidney Tarrow, "National Politics and Collective Action: Recent Theory and Research in Western Europe and the United States," *Annual Review of Sociology* 14 (1988): 429–33; and Herbert Kitschelt, "Political Opportunity Structures and Political Protest: Anti-Nuclear Movements in Four Democracies," *British Journal of Political Science* 16, no. 1 (January 1986): 57–85.

80. To use the language of Marx, it transforms the conditions that make EGS workers like "homologous potatoes in a sack," living in similar conditions but without entering into manifold relations with one another, thereby incapable of enforcing their class interest in their own name. See Karl Marx, *The Eighteenth Brumaire of Louis Bonaparte* (New York: International Publishers, 1963), pp. 123–24 (originally published in 1852).

81. B. N. Rajhans, president of the Shet Majoor Panchayat, observed that the EGS helps to break down caste barriers because it obliges all workers to drink water from the same source. Interview, Pune, January 28, 1984.

82. Ibid.

83. Interview with B. R. Bawke, president, Ahmednagar Zilla Shet Majoor Union, March 22, 1984.

84. Interview, Parner, March 5, 1984.

85. The analysis on district-level trends is based on Hannan Ezekiel and Johann C. Stuyt, *The Maharashtra Employment Guarantee Scheme: Its Response to Differences in Employment Patterns between Districts* (Washington, D.C.: International Food Policy Research Institute, 1989), pp. 4–5. See also Hannan Ezekiel and Johann C. Stuyt, "Maharashtra Employment Gurantee Scheme: Geographical Distribution of Employment," *Economic and Political Weekly* 25, no. 26 (June 30, 1990): A86–A92.

86. This ranking is based on gross value of output per hectare for Maharashtra's twenty-six districts from 1978–79 to 1980–81. Jalgaon ranked first and Kolhapur ranked sixth in gross value of output per male worker. See Government of Maharashtra, Planning Department, *Report of the Fact Finding Committee on Regional Imbalance,* vol. 2 (Bombay: Government of Maharashtra, 1984), p. 312.

87. Martin Ravallion, "Reaching the Poor through Rural Public Works: Arguments, Evidence and Lessons from South Asia," unpublished paper, World Bank, Washington, D.C., 1990, p. 12.

88. Kumudini Dandekar and Maju Sathe, "Employment Guarantee Scheme and Food for Work Programme," *Economic and Political Weekly* 15, no. 15 (April 12, 1980): 712; Acharya and Panwalkar, "The Maharashtra Employment Guarantee Scheme: Impact on Male and Female Labour" (note 35 above), pp. 43–45; M. J. Bhende et al., "EGS and the Poor: Evidence from Longitudinal Village Studies," *Economic and Political Weekly* 27, no. 13 (March 28, 1992): A19–A22.

89. In addition to the previous incidents that I have cited, see Acharya and Panwalkar, "The Maharashtra Employment Guarantee Scheme," p. 49; Leslie J. Calman, *Protest in Democratic India* (Boulder, Colo.: Westview Press, 1985), pp. 216–17; S. Bagchee, "Employment Guarantee Scheme in Maharashtra" (note 36 above), and "Illegal Activity?" *Economic and Political Weekly* 12, no. 22 (May 28, 1977): 856. Dandekar and Sathe ("Employment Guarantee Scheme," p. 710) estimate that the EGS provides employment to "at best three-fourths of the total reported unemployment among the weaker sections."

90. Acharya and Panwalkar, "The Maharashtra Employment Guarantee Scheme," pp. 17, 50.

91. Government of Maharashtra, Planning Department, *Employment Guarantee Scheme: Statistical Information Book* (Bombay: Government of Maharashtra, 1985), mimeo. Many surveys of EGS sites report a larger proportion of women workers. A study by the Institute of Social Studies (*Impact on Women Workers: Maharashtra Employment Guarantee Scheme,* vol. 1 [New Delhi: Institute of Social Studies, 1979], p. 57) explained the discrepancy by stating that men often register for EGS employment and then send female members of their family to do the work. See also Dandekar, *Employment Guarantee Scheme: An Employment Opportunity for Women* (note 33 above), p. 28; and Government of India and Government of Maharashtra, *Joint Evaluation* (note 19 above), p. 17.

92. Nonetheless, the EGS is not free of gender discrimination. One study (*Impact on Women Workers,* vol. 1, p. 60) found that the headmen of work gangs discriminated against women by underestimating their contribution to

the work accomplished. Many women complained to Acharya and Panwalkar ("The Maharashtra Employment Guarantee Scheme," pp. 51–52) that they were excluded from partaking in some of the more lucrative jobs available on the EGS.

93. Acharya and Panwalkar, "The Maharashtra Employment Guarantee Scheme," p. 48.

94. The average monthly labor attendance from June through August 1979 was 662,820, while the average attendance from June through August in 1978 and 1980 was 423,782. See Government of Maharashtra, Planning Department, *Statistical Information Book*, p. 71.

95. T. S. Walker, R. P. Singh, and M. Asokan, "Risk Benefits, Crop Insurance, and Dryland Agriculture," *Economic and Political Weekly* 21, nos. 25 and 26 (June 21–28, 1986): A-86.

96. Acharya and Panwalkar, "The Maharashtra Employment Guarantee Scheme," p. 44.

97. Ravallion, "Reaching the Poor through Rural Public Works" (note 87 above), pp. 33–35.

98. Acharya and Panwalkar, "The Maharashtra Employment Guarantee Scheme," pp. 30–32.

99. Ezekiel and Stuyt, *The Maharashtra Employment Guarantee Scheme* (note 85 above), pp. 6–7.

100. The study does not include Greater Bombay. By 1985, the number of districts had grown from twenty-five to twenty-nine. The new districts were created by dividing up preexisting ones. My calculations are based on the twenty-five original districts.

101. For instance, see "EGS for Whom?" *Economic and Political Weekly* 19, no. 10 (March 10, 1984): 402–3; Herring and Edwards, "Guaranteeing Employment" (note 14 above); "Who Pays for and Who Gains from EGS?" *Economic and Political Weekly* 17, no. 31 (July 31, 1982): 1226–28; and Amrita Abraham, "Maharashtra's Employment Guarantee Scheme," *Economic and Political Weekly* 15, no. 12 (August 9, 1980): 1339–42.

CHAPTER 4

1. Early advocates of the educational impact of public participation include John Stuart Mill, *Considerations on Representative Government* (Indianapolis: Bobbs-Merrill, 1958, originally published in 1861); and Harold J. Laski, *A Grammar of Politics* (London: Allen and Unwin, 1960), especially p. 61. Paulo Freire has dealt at length with the transformative impact of participation in development. See his *Pedagogy of the Oppressed* (New York: Herder and Herder, 1970) and *Education for Critical Consciousness* (New York: Seabury Press, 1973). See also Carol Pateman, *Participation and Democratic Theory* (Cambridge: Cambridge University Press, 1970), and Benjamin Barber, *Strong Democracy: Participatory Politics for a New Age* (Berkeley: University of California Press, 1984). Denis Goulet wisely stresses the tensions that arise when the transformative impact of participation is taken as an end in itself rather than a means for effective policy. See "Participation in Development: New Avenues,"

World Development 17, no. 2 (February 1989): 165–78. The hypothesis has been supported by an array of experts on development in the Third World. See John D. Montgomery, *Bureaucrats and People: Grassroots Participation in Third World Development* (Baltimore: Johns Hopkins University Press, 1988); Milton J. Esman and Norman T. Uphoff, *Local Organizations: Intermediaries in Rural Development* (Ithaca, N.Y.: Cornell University Press, 1984); Guy Gran, *Development by People: Citizen Construction of a Just World* (New York: Praeger, 1983); David C. Korten, "Social Development: Putting People First," in *Bureaucracy and the Poor,* ed. David C. Korten and Felip B. Alfonso (Singapore: McGraw-Hill International, 1981), pp. 201–21, and "Community Organization and Rural Development: A Learning Process Approach," *Public Administration Review* 40, no. 5 (September–October 1980): 480–501; and Norman Uphoff and Milton Esman, *Local Organizations for Rural Development: Analysis of the Asian Experience* (Ithaca, N.Y.: Cornell University Press, 1974). It has been an explicit justification for the establishment of panchayat institutions in India. See, for instance, Government of India, Planning Commission, *Seventh Five Year Plan, 1985–90,* vol. 2 (New Delhi: Government of India Press, 1985), p. 51; *Report of the Team for the Study of Community Projects and National Service,* vol. 1, sec. 2 (New Delhi: Government of India, 1957), p. 23; and Government of India, Ministry of Agriculture and Irrigation, Department of Rural Development, *Report of the Committee on Panchayati Raj Institutions* (New Delhi: Government of India Press, 1978), p. 8. For a study of panchayat institutions in West Bengal that finds strong support for the hypothesis, see M. Shiviah, K. B. Srivastava, and A. C. Jena, *Panchayati Raj Institutions in West Bengal, 1978: A Study of Institutions Building for Rural Development* (Hyderabad: National Institute for Rural Development, 1980), especially pp. 1–6.

2. The hypothesis has a long history in American political analysis. Classic examples include Grant McConnell, *Private Power and American Democracy* (New York: Knopf, 1966); Theodore J. Lowi, *The End of Liberalism* (New York: Norton, 1969); and Philip Selznick, *TVA and the Grass Roots* (Berkeley: University of California Press, 1980; reprint of 1949 ed.). One of the better-known applications of this hypothesis in analyzing India's political economy during the postindependence period is Francine Frankel, *India's Political Economy, 1947–1977* (Princeton, N.J.: Princeton University Press, 1978). For analyses of panchayats based on this argument, see Indira Hiraway, *Abolition of Poverty in India: With Special Reference to Target Group Approach in Gujarat* (Delhi: Vikas, 1986), and various selections from George Mathews, ed., *Panchayati Raj in Karnataka Today* (New Delhi: Concept, 1985). A sophisticated version of the argument has been applied to an analysis of the Community Development Programme in Birbhum district of West Bengal (see Suraj Bandyopadhyay and Donald Von Eschen, "The Conditions of Rural Progress," report submitted to the Canadian International Development Agency, Ottawa, 1981).

3. This hypothesis originated in Robert Michels's assertion that the institutional interests developed by party organizations shape their pursuit of their stated objectives. See his *Political Parties* (New York: Free Press, 1962). For an updated and more sophisticated treatment, see Angelo Panebianco, *Political*

Parties: Organization and Power (Cambridge: Cambridge University Press, 1988), especially pp. 49–68. The hypothesis has been developed in the literature on political machines in the United States; see, for instance, Martin Shefter, "The Emergence of the Political Machine: An Alternative View," in *Theoretical Perspectives on Urban Politics,* ed. Willis Hawley and Michael Lipsky (Englewood Cliffs, N.J.: Prentice-Hall, 1976), pp. 14–44. A number of scholars have applied the machine model in their analysis of the Congress Party in India. See, for example, Myron Weiner, *Party Building in a New Nation: The Indian National Congress* (Chicago: University of Chicago Press, 1967); Paul R. Brass, *Factional Politics in an Indian State: The Congress Party in Uttar Pradesh* (Berkeley: University of California Press, 1965); and James C. Scott, *Comparative Political Corruption* (Englewood Cliffs, N.J.: Prentice-Hall, 1972), pp. 132–43.

4. Sidney Tarrow, *Struggle, Politics, and Reform: Collective Action, Social Movements, and Cycles of Protest,* 2nd ed. (Ithaca, N.Y.: Center for International Studies, Cornell University, 1991), pp. 32–39.

5. The all-India rural average is 172 persons per square kilometer. The overall average for the United States is 17.9. See *Census of India, 1981, Series 1, India,* Part II-A(i): *General Population Tables* (New Delhi: Controller of Publications, 1985), pp. 72–78; and World Bank, *World Development Report, 1989* (New York: Oxford University Press, 1989), p. 165.

6. For 1971–72, 30.9 percent of rural households were landless, according to the Government of India, *National Sample Survey, Twenty-sixth Round, West Bengal,* Report 215 (New Delhi: Controller of Publications, 1978). A 1981–82 survey based on a sample of sixty villages throughout West Bengal found 35.5 percent of all households to be landless. See Nripen Bandyopadhyay and Associates, "Evaluation of Land Reform Measures in West Bengal: A Report," *Asian Employment Programme Working Papers, ARTEP* (Geneva: International Labour Organisation, 1985), p. 13.

7. These averages were computed for the year 1980–81, as reported in Government of India, Director of Economics and Statistics, Department of Agriculture and Cooperation, Ministry of Agriculture, "Agricultural Census: All India," *Agricultural Situation in India* 40, no. 5 (August 1985): 412.

8. *Census of India, 1981, Series 23, West Bengal,* Paper 1 of 1981: *Supplement: Provisional Population Totals* (Calcutta: Director of the Census, 1981), pp. 74–78. As cited in James K. Boyce, *Agrarian Impasse in Bengal: Institutional Constraints to Technological Change* (Oxford: Oxford University Press, 1987), p. 225.

9. N. Kakawani and K. Subbarao, "Rural Poverty and Its Alleviation in India," *Economic and Political Weekly* 25, no. 13 (March 31, 1990): A-6. West Bengal had the highest ranking of any state according to the "poverty gap" measure created by these authors.

10. Atul Kohli, *The State and Poverty in India: The Politics of Reform* (Cambridge: Cambridge University Press, 1987), p. 107.

11. Ibid., pp. 95–143.

12. Government of India, Ministry of Finance, *Economic Survey of India* (New Delhi: Government of India Press, 1990), p. 31.

13. Ibid.

14. Government of India, Ministry of Finance, *Expenditure Budget, 1990–91*, vol. 2 (New Delhi: Government of India, 1990), p. 12.

15. *West Bengal Panchayat Act, 1973*, as modified up to 11–1–80 (Calcutta: Government of West Bengal, 1980), p. 22.

16. District Planning Officer, Midnapore, *An Approach to the Seventh Five Year Plan for the Midnapore District, West Bengal* (Midnapore: Office of the District Planning Officer, 1985), mimeo.

17. Data in this paragraph were computed from Government of West Bengal, Development and Planning Department, *Report on the NREP,* Statements I, II, and IV (Calcutta: Government of West Bengal, 1985).

18. This last datum includes the transitional subdivisions of Midnapore Sadar and thereby overstates the percentage for Jhargram subdivision. Data in this paragraph were computed from *Annual Plan on Agriculture, 1984–85, Midnapore East* (Tamluk, West Bengal: Office of Principal Agricultural Officer, Midnapore East, 1984), pp. 19, 45, 46, 73; and *Annual Plan on Agriculture, 1984–85, Midnapore West* (Midnapore: Office of Principal Agricultural Officer, Midnapore West, 1984), pp. 2, 31, 32, 45.

19. The scale of agricultural development combined three variables: productivity of *aman* paddy, productivity of *boro* paddy, and fertilizer consumption per hectare. The value of these variables was computed for each block. The blocks were then ranked for each variable, and the rankings were averaged for each block. For the final scale, each block was ranked according to this average.

Ideally, the scale would also have included an indicator of cropping intensity or percentage of net cropped land under irrigation. Since I was unable to acquire a complete set of these data for each block, I had to exclude this variable from my scale. I am confident, however, that had I been able to include either of these variables, it would have had little impact on my selection of blocks. The three relatively developed blocks that I selected ranked first, second, and sixth in cropping intensity among the blocks of eastern Midnapore. After making an extensive tour of the less developed blocks during the *boro* season, I am certain that if I had included cropping intensity or extent of irrigation in the index, the index would have shown the blocks to be even less developed. The rankings were computed from data provided in the *Annual Plans* cited in note 18.

20. The CPI(M) controlled forty-eight of Midnapore's fifty-four panchayati samitis at the time of my research. The research design also included Gopiballavpur II development block. It ranks last among Midnapore's blocks on the index of agricultural development and is under CPI(M) control. Unfortunately, time constraints compelled me to exclude it from my study.

21. Interview with Dileep Bhattacharya, secretary, Department of Panchayats, Government of West Bengal, Calcutta, March 3, 1985.

22. The classic statement is Richard P. Taub, *Bureaucrats under Stress* (Berkeley: University of California Press, 1969).

23. Interview with S. K. Guha, district magistrate, Midnapore, February 22, 1985.

24. Tarun Ganguly, "The Role of the Panchayats," *The Telegraph* (Calcutta), May 22, 1983, p. 5.

25. Interview with S. Bhowmick, district panchayat officer, Midnapore, February 29, 1985.

26. Interview with R. S. Bandhopadhyay, director, Department of Panchayats, Government of West Bengal, Calcutta, February 8, 1985.

27. Interview with Guha.

28. Interview with Bandhopadhyay.

29. For instance, the state government has used the panchayats to collect unpaid irrigation taxes. See "Drive to Collect Dues from Farmers," *The Statesman* (Calcutta), February 2, 1985, p. 9. It has also called upon panchayats to help detect power theft in rural areas. See "West Bengal Drive to Check Power Thefts," *The Telegraph* (Calcutta), March 5, 1985, p. 3.

30. These comments are cited in Suraj Bandyopadhyay and Donald Von Eschen, "The Impact of Politics on Rural Production and Distribution: A Comparative Study of Rural Policies and Their Implementation under Congress and Left Front Governments in West Bengal India," paper presented at the annual meeting of the Association for Asian Studies, San Francisco, March 26, 1988, p. P28.

31. In an interesting comparison of the implementation of the IRDP in two localities, Madhura Swaminathan ("Village Level Implementation of IRDP: Comparison of West Bengal and Tamil Nadu," *Economic and Political Weekly* 25, no. 13 [March 31, 1990]: A17–A27) found that decentralization of authority to gram panchayats improved beneficiary selection and significantly lowered the rural poor's costs of participating in the program.

32. For one of the best analyses of the initiative to decentralize planning, see Arun Ghosh, "Decentralized Planning: West Bengal Experience," *Economic and Political Weekly* 23, no. 13 (March 26, 1988): 655–63.

33. Ghosh ("Decentralized Planning") is relatively enthusiastic about the implementation of decentralized planning in Midnapore and Burdwan. But implementation of the program has been uneven. Bandyopadhyay and Von Eschen ("The Impact of Politics," p. P33) found that "virtually no planning" had been done in the block they studied in Birbhum.

34. Interview with S. Sarkar, district planning officer, Midnapore, February 22, 1985. Mr. Sarkar told me, however, that the district was beginning a new grass-roots planning scheme that would include the participation of panchayati raj institutions. He said that the inclusion of these institutions would improve coordination between the NREP and the other programs.

35. Interview with Benoy Chowdhury, Calcutta, April 11, 1985.

36. Ghosh, "Decentralized Planning," p. 659.

37. Interview with block development officer, Jamboni, Gidhni, March 11, 1985.

38. Memorandum from P. C. Banerji, Secretary, Government of West Bengal, dated January 7, 1983, as cited in *Compendium for Panchayati Raj in West Bengal* (Calcutta: Government of West Bengal, Director of Panchayats, 1984), p. 353.

39. A similar tendency in the planning of the NREP's predecessor program, the Food for Work Programme. See *Evaluation of Food for Work Programme* (New Delhi: Government of India, 1981), p. 11.

40. In her survey of gram panchayats throughout the state, Kirsten Westergaard also found the lack of expertise to be a problem. See *People's Participation, Local Government and Rural Development: The Case of West Bengal India* (Copenhagen: Centre for Development Research, 1986), p. 41. Additional subassistant engineers were to be provided at the block level, but their deployment has been delayed by the resistance of departmental interests in the capital (Ghosh, "Decentralized Planning," p. 662).

41. Kirsten Westergaard (*People's Participation,* p. 41) also notes this problem.

42. *Gram Panchayats in West Bengal and Their Activities: Survey and Evaluation* (Calcutta: Government of West Bengal, Town and Country Planning Department, n.d., c. 1980), p. 36; Narayan Chandra Adak, "Panchayats and Rural Development: Midnapore District—A Case Study," M.Phil. thesis, Jadavpur University, Calcutta, 1983, p. 127.

43. Interview with extension officer, Moyna, March 27, 1985.

44. Interviews with block development officer, Jamboni, Gidhni, March 11, 1985; block development officer, Binpur I, Lalgarh, March 15, 1985; and panchayat clerk, Tamluk II, Mecheda, April 1, 1985.

45. Interview with block development officer, Dashpur II, Sonakhali, April 3, 1985.

46. Ibid. My findings are corroborated by a 1987 newspaper article and another survey in Midnapore, cited in Bandyopadhyay and Von Eschen, "Impact of Politics," p. P36.

47. The data on employment generated by the NREP were provided by the Department of Rural Development, Ministry of Agriculture and Rural Development, Government of India. West Bengal has a total of 3,891,531 main workers classified as agricultural laborers, according to the *Census of India, 1981, Series 23, West Bengal,* Part III-A & B(i): *General Economic Tables* (New Delhi: Controller of Publications, 1987), p. 181. The number of NREP workdays per laborer generated by the NREP varies considerably from village to village. The figure of twenty-five days per worker was selected on the basis of surveys by Kohli (*The State and Poverty in India* [note 10 above], p. 137), who found that the NREP provided twenty-eight days of supplementary employment per worker in his area, and by Westergaard (*People's Participation,* pp. 82–83), who found that the households of landless families secured between fifteen and seventy-nine extra days of work per year.

48. Bihar had the next-largest disparity. It generated 21.8 percent of all NREP employment while possessing 20.0 percent of the ultra-poor. See Kakawani and Subbarao, "Rural Poverty and Its Alleviation in India" (note 9 above), p. A-12.

49. Interview with Bhattacharya (note 21 above).

50. Interview with *sabhapati,* Moyna panchayat samiti, Moyna, March 29, 1985.

51. Computed from Memo no. 473, April 11, 1985, from District Planning

Officer, Midnapore. In addition, the block development officers in the less developed blocks told me that there is always or often an excess of laborers wanting employment on the NREP, while those in the developed blocks said that they rarely or never experience an excess. The pradhans and secretaries, however, almost always seem to feel that there are more workers than NREP jobs available: 88 percent of those in less developed blocks and 92 percent in more developed ones said that they always or frequently had an excess of workers for NREP projects.

52. Information in this paragraph is derived from the following interviews: block development officer, Tamluk II, Mecheda, April 2, 1985; block development officer, Binpur I, Lalgarh, March 19, 1985; subassistant engineer, Binpur I, Lalgarh, March 19, 1985.

53. Allegations are widespread. Adak's survey of one hundred residents of Midnapore ("Panchayats and Rural Development," note 42 above) found that 84 percent believed that rumors of corruption by panchayat members were at least partly true. The sums involved can be considerable. In Binpur I, the block development officer had submitted formal charges alleging that pradhans of Sijua gram panchayat had embezzled Rs. 47,942 (Memo no. 3-E, dated February 2, 1985, from Block Development Officer, Binpur I, to Officer in Charge, Binpur Police Station).

54. For similar observations see Westergaard, *People's Participation*, pp. 41–42; and Krishna Lal Basu, "A Study on the Role That the Panchayats Are Playing in Generating Forces of Development in the Rural Areas of Birbhum," unpublished manuscript, Department of Social Work, Vidya Bhavana, Visva-Bharati, 1982, p. 36.

55. Amrita Basu, "State Autonomy and Agrarian Transformation in India," *Comparative Politics* 22, no. 4 (July 1990): 496.

56. Interview with S. Bhowmick, president, Land Development Bank, Tamluk, April 6, 1985.

57. The trend is toward decline in the number of independent representatives. Twenty-five percent were independents following the 1978 elections. The elections in 1983 reduced the independents to 8 percent. (Data provided by the office of the district panchayat officer, Midnapore, 1985.)

58. These events occurred in gram panchayat no. 3, Srikantha, in Moyna block. (Interviews with Bhushan Dolai, general secretary, Congress (I) block committee, Moyna, April 6, 1985; and CPI(M) MLA, Moyna constituency, Moyna, April 6, 1985.)

59. The information in this paragraph is derived from my interview with S. Bhowmick, district panchayat officer, Midnapore, February 27, 1985.

60. Interviews with Buddhadev Bhakat, CPI(M) local committee secretary, Jamboni, Gidhni, March 13, 1985; Sudhir Pandey, former local committee secretary and *sabhapati*, Binpur I panchayat samiti, Lalgarh, March 19, 1985; *sabhapati*, Tamluk II panchayat samiti, April 2, 1985; and *sabhapati*, Dashpur II panchayat samiti, April 4, 1985. This account is also supported by Westergaard, *People's Participation*, pp. 71, 88, 91.

61. Interview with Paritosh Maiti, CPI(M) local committee member and secretary Krishak samiti, Tamluk II, Mecheda, April 1, 1985.

62. Interview with Sukumar Sen Gupta, secretary, CPI(M) district committee, Midnapore, April 8, 1985; and interview with Dr. S. K. Mishra, *sabhadhipati*, Midnapore, April 9, 1985.

63. Interview with Dr. S. K. Mishra. Sukumar Sen Gupta stated to Amrita Basu that his party expelled 167 elected panchayat members on grounds of corruption in 1983. See Basu, "State Autonomy and Agrarian Transformation in India" (note 55 above), p. 496. In his study of Mahammad Bazar block in Birbhum district, G. K. Lieten ("Panchayat Leaders in a West Bengal District," *Economic and Political Weekly* 23, no. 40 [October 1, 1988]: 270) also observed a relatively high turnover in gram panchayat representatives, due in part to the CPI(M)'s expelling of those considered to be corrupt.

64. Interview with Dashpur I Congress (I) panchayat samiti member, Jotegobardhan, April 4, 1985. Benoy Chowdhury, in a postmortem to the 1984 Lok Sabha elections, observed, "Sectarianism and partisanship while providing relief jobs or recording the names of sharecroppers also led to the alienation of natural allies of the Left" (*The Statesman*, January 9, 1985; cited in T. J. Nossiter, *Marxist State Governments in India: Politics, Economics and Society* [London: Pinter, 1988], p. 141). Westergaard encountered similar charges; see *People's Participation*, pp. 45, 60, 63, 74, 76. Also see Partha S. Banerjee, "The God That Failed," *Illustrated Weekly of India*, February 3, 1985, p. 29.

65. Interview with subassistant engineer, Binpur I, Lalgarh, March 22, 1985; interview with block development officer, Binpur I, Lalgarh, March 22, 1985.

66. Survey response of gram panchayat secretary, Dashpur II, Sonakhali, April 3, 1985. For a similar observation concerning Birbhum district, see Bandyopadhyay and Von Eschen, "The Impact of Politics," pp. P24, P31.

67. Interview with Sukumar Das, former general secretary, West Bengal Pradesh Congress Committee, Tamluk, April 3, 1985.

68. This explanation was provided to me in an interview with Bhushan Dolai, general secretary, Congress (I) Moyna Block Committee, Moyna, April 6, 1985. CPI(M) party leaders attributed their defeat to the fact that one Congress leader had been responsible for an influx of relief funds after the floods in 1978. I found their contention unconvincing, because it fails to explain why the funds should have an impact on the panchayat elections in 1983 and not on the elections that preceded or followed it. (Interview with CPI(M) member of the state legislative assembly, Moyna constituency, Moyna, April 6, 1985.)

69. The fourth gram panchayat in the east was won by the Communist Party of India—a partner with the CPI(M) in the Left Front, though often an electoral rival (interview with block development officer, Binpur I, Lalgarh, March 14, 1985; interview with *sabhapati*, Jarkhand Party, Binpur I panchayat samiti, Lalgarh, March 19, 1985). CPI(M) leaders attributed their losses to the fact that they failed to make the public aware that they were not given sufficient resources to meet everyone's needs (interview with Amiya Sen Gupta, secretary, CPI(M) local committee for Binpur I [West], Dahijuri, March 18, 1985). Sudhir Pandey, the former *sabhapati* and secretary of the CPI(M) local committee for Binpur I (East), denied being involved in any corruption; he attributed the CPI(M)'s defeat to a loss of "the spirit of sacrifice" among party cadre (interview, Lalgarh, March 19, 1983).

70. Interview with Buddhadev Bhakat, secretary, CPI(M) local committee, Jamboni, Gidhni, March 13, 1985.

71. *Report of the Team for the Study of Community Projects* (note 1 above) and *Report of the Committee on Panchayati Raj Institutions* (note 1 above).

72. The CPI(M)'s efforts to fulfill commitments previously made by the Congress Party extend beyond the panchayats. The Left Front's initiatives in land redistribution and enforcing tenant rights were also attempts to fulfill commitments previously legislated by the Congress Party. Explanations for the absence of radical departures from Congress (I) policy include the constraints created by the electoral and legal contexts, the need to maintain a healthy economy, and the state government's dependence on central government resources. See Kohli, *The State and Poverty in India,* pp. 100–102; and Bandyopadhyay and Von Eschen, "The Impact of Politics" (note 30 above), p. P3.

73. Interview with Benoy Chowdhury, Calcutta, April 11, 1985. Biplab Das Gupta, a leading CPI(M) intellectual, also elaborates the political rationale for NREP through panchayats.

74. Prasanta Sengupta, "The Congress Party in West Bengal: Politics, Patronage and Power, 1947–1983," in *Politics in West Bengal,* ed. Rakhahari Chatterji (Calcutta: World Press, 1985), pp. 31–60; and Marcus Franda, *Political Development and Political Decay* (Calcutta: Firma K. L. Mukhopadhyay, 1971).

75. The Asoka Mehta Committee report (*Report of the Committee on Panchayati Raj Institutions,* p. 6) observed, "The lukewarm attitude of the political elite at higher levels towards strengthening the democratic process at the grass roots was generally the crux of the matter. Of particular significance in this is the relative cooling off of enthusiasm of MP's and MLA's in some states towards Panchayati Raj because they would perceive a threat in emerging Panchayati Raj leadership to their position in their respective communities."

76. For an interesting debate on the impact of economic structure on India's rural development programs, see the debate between C. T. Kurien and M. L. Dantwala in *Asian Seminar on Rural Development: The Indian Experience,* ed. M. L. Dantwala, Ranjit Gupta, and Keith C. D'Souza (Delhi: Oxford University Press, 1986), pp. 373–96, 397–406.

77. In Myron Weiner, ed., *State Politics in India* (Princeton, N.J.: Princeton University Press, 1968), p. 268.

78. Ibid. See also Anjali Ghosh, *Peaceful Transition to Power* (Calcutta: Firma K. L. Mukhopadhyay, 1981), pp. 17–18; and Mohit Bhattacharya, "West Bengal," in *Patterns of Panchayati Raj in India,* ed. G. Ram Reddy (Delhi: Macmillan of India, 1977), pp. 295–96.

79. Asok K. Mukhopadhyay, *The Panchayat Administration in West Bengal* (Calcutta: World Press, 1980), p. 75.

80. Marvin Davis, *Rank and Rivalry: The Politics of Inequality in Rural West Bengal* (London: Cambridge University Press, 1983), pp. 185–91.

81. Ibid., p. 184.

82. Tarun Ganguly, "An Atmosphere of Violence," *The Telegraph* (Calcutta), May 29, 1985, p. 9.

83. During the 1988 panchayat election, campaign police reports indicate that there were 67 violent clashes, in which 148 were seriously injured and 7

killed. This is a decline in the level of violence since the 1983 campaign, when 173 violent incidents were reported in which 372 were seriously injured and nine were killed (see "2.63 [Crore] Voters to Elect 6,200 Candidates in 3-Tier Poll," *The Telegraph* (Calcutta), February 28, 1988; and Ganguly, "An Atmosphere of Violence."

84. For instance, see Indranil Banerjie, "Panchayats Are for Making Money," *The Telegraph* (Calcutta), May 25, 1983, p. 9; Apurba Sengupta, "Bitter Fight Likely for Burdwan Panchayat Seats," *Amrita Bazar Patrika* (Calcutta), May 12, 1983, p. 4.

85. Ganguly, "Role of the Panchayats" (note 24 above).

86. Cited in Atul Kohli, "Parliamentary Communism and Agrarian Reform: The Evidence from India's Bengal," *Asian Survey* 23 (July 1983): 792.

87. Twenty-four of the twenty-nine pradhans who were schoolteachers were affiliated with the CPI(M). These accounted for 33 percent of the seventy-three pradhans affiliated with the CPI(M) in the sample. Schoolteachers accounted for only three of the twenty-one pradhans (14 percent) who were affiliated with opposition parties or were independents. Two were members of the Revolutionary Socialist Party, another partner of the Left Front. See *The Gram Panchayats in West Bengal* (note 42 above), p. 29.

88. Studies documenting the backgrounds of panchayat officials consistently corroborate these findings. See Kohli, *The State and Poverty in India,* p. 111; and Westergaard, *People's Participation,* pp. 40–47, 53–54, 62–65, and 69–72. Bandyopadhyay and Von Eschen ("The Impact of Politics," pp. P9–P10, P27) cogently make the argument that the CPI(M) has relied on middle social strata for political leadership at the grass roots in rural West Bengal. The only study that plausibly could be interpreted as contradicting this argument is G. K. Lieten's survey in Mahammad Bazar block in Birbhum district ("Panchayat Leaders in a West Bengal District" [note 63 above], pp. 2069–73). Lieten found that only 10 of the 127 CPI(M) candidates for seats in the block's gram panchayats were schoolteachers, while 74 were either small peasants, sharecroppers, or agricultural laborers. A large number of these CPI(M) candidates (51 percent) were members of scheduled castes and scheduled tribes. The inconsistency with other findings is at least partly explainable by the disparities between the backgrounds of candidates for gram panchayats and those who are selected to be pradhans.

89. "West Bengal State Conference Organisational Report," as cited in *Political Organisational Report of the Twelfth Congress of the Communist Party of India (Marxist)* (New Delhi: Hari Singh Kang, 1986), p. 159.

90. Cited in Amrita Basu, "Democratic Centralism in the Home and the World: Bengali Women and the Communist Movement," in *Promissory Notes: Women in the Transition to Socialism,* ed. Sonia Kruks, Rayna Rapp, and Marilyn B. Young (New York: Monthly Review Press, 1989), p. 220.

91. Kohli, *The State and Poverty in India,* p. 105; Bandyopadhyay and Von Eschen, "The Impact of Politics," p. P2.

92. In 1989, the Public Accounts Committee (PAC) of the West Bengal legislative assembly compiled a highly critical report on the functioning of the Government of West Bengal's Department of Education. Among the irregular-

ities it criticized was the appointment of 1,313 teachers without requisite sanction from the government. For a discussion of the PAC report, see A. N. M. Abdi, "Dubious Deals," *Illustrated Weekly of India*, March 5, 1989, pp. 32–33. See also Kamaljeet Rattan, "West Bengal: Sham Schools," *India Today*, November 30, 1987, p. 47; Bandyopadhyay and Von Eschen, "The Impact of Politics," p. P20.

93. For similar observations, see Bandyopadhyay and Von Eschen, "The Impact of Politics," pp. P10, P22; and Amrita Basu, *Two Faces of Protest: Contrasting Modes of Women's Activism in India* (Berkeley: University of California Press, 1992), pp. 7, 42.

94. For an excellent comparison of the manner in which backward classes have been incorporated into state political systems, see Francine R. Frankel and M. S. A. Rao, eds., *Dominance and State Power in Modern India*, 2 vols. (Delhi: Oxford University Press, 1989 and 1990). Raymond Lee Owens and Ashis Nandy (*The New Vaisyas: Entrepreneurial Opportunity and Response in an Indian City* [Durham, N.C.: Carolina Academic Press, 1978]) provide a fascinating account of the social ascendance of the Mahisyas in Howrah. Of course, in rural areas with fewer industrial opportunities, the Mahisyas rose to power less rapidly than they did in the Calcutta metropolitan area.

95. Atul Kohli, "From Elite Activism to Democratic Consolidation: The Rise of Reform Communism in West Bengal," in Frankel and Rao, *Dominance and State Power*, vol. 2, pp. 367–415; Donald W. Attwood and B. R. Baviskar, "The Barren Grounds in West Bengal?" in *The Political Economy of Cooperation in Rural India*, vol. 2 (unpublished manuscript, McGill University, 1991), pp. 6–7.

96. I tried to check for the extent that the pradhans biased their answers by overstating their contact with the public. First, I asked them about a category that they were unlikely to find advantageous to admit contact with: political workers. The pradhans nevertheless reported very high rates of contact with them. Second, I asked the secretaries of the gram panchayats about their contacts with the public. These government officials have less incentive to present themselves as being in close contact with the public. Their rates of contact with various categories of the public are still high, though slightly lower than those of pradhans. As several secretaries brought to my attention, they have a less direct role in NREP planning and implementation than the pradhans and therefore would have fewer contacts with the public. Westergaard (*People's Participation*, pp. 45, 71) found much less activism among the poor and low-caste groups, though she observes that the gram panchayats have increased their political activism.

97. Max Weber, *The Protestant Ethic and the Spirit of Capitalism*, trans. Talcott Parsons (New York: Scribner's, 1958; originally published in 1920). See also Theodore W. Schultz, *Investing in People: The Economics of Population Quality* (Berkeley: University of California Press, 1981), and *Investment in Human Capital: The Role of Education and of Research* (New York: Free Press, 1971).

98. Interview with panchayat clerk, Binpur I block office, Lalgarh, March 22, 1985.

99. Interview with Paritosh Maiti, secretary of the Krishak samiti and member of the CPI(M) local committee, Tamluk II, Mecheda, April 1, 1985.

100. This point was made to me during an interview with P. C. Banerji, secretary, Department of Planning and Development, Government of West Bengal, Calcutta, June 16, 1984. See also interview with Keshab Chakraborti, chief demographer, Town and Planning Department, Government of West Bengal, Calcutta, June 21, 1984; and interview with S. Sarkar, district planning officer, Midnapore, February 22, 1985.

101. For instance, in Dashpur II, a proposal to build a road to Kelegoda village has been stifled by the resistance of landowners residing outside the village. They refuse to allow soil to be taken from their fields to rebuild the road, which was washed out by floods. The village is populated predominantly by landless laborers from scheduled castes. Interview with block development officer, Dashpur II, Sonakhali, April 3, 1985.

102. Atul Kohli, *The State and Poverty in India* (note 10 above), pp. 140, 143.

103. Communist Party of India (Marxist), *Report on Organisation and Tasks* (adopted by the Fourteenth Party, Congress held at Madras, January 3–9, 1992) (New Delhi: Hari Singh Kang, 1992): 48.

104. In a party letter "for members only," the state committee stated that support for the Congress (I) Party was growing because the CPI(M) was losing contact with the public; mainly, lower-level units were not keeping track of the problems of people in their locality. Cited by Prasanta Sarkar, "Janata Victory in Karnataka Boosts Left Front Morale," *Amrita Bazar Patrika* (Calcutta), March 12, 1985, p. 6. Published party documents also note these problems. See *Political Organisational Report of the Eleventh Congress of the Communist Party of India (Marxist)* (Calcutta: Desraj Chadha, 1982), p. 96; and *Political Organisational Report of the Twelfth Congress*, p. 163.

105. For instance, Westergaard (*People's Participation,* p. 64) found that CPI(M)-affiliated pradhans faced serious charges of corruption in two of the four gram panchayats that she studied in depth. Because of their electoral clout, they retained the CPI(M)'s support and were reelected in the 1983 panchayat elections.

106. Tarun Ganguly, "CPM Reviewing Renewal of Membership," *The Telegraph* (Calcutta), March 3, 1985, p. 1.

107. Prasanta Sarkar, "CPI(M) Is Giving a Second Look at Election Results," *Amrita Bazar Patrika* (Calcutta), February 9, 1985, p. 6; "Change in the CPI(M) Hierarchy Unlikely," *Amrita Bazar Patrika* (Calcutta), February 27, 1985, p. 1; Sattam Ghosh, "What Ails the CPI(M)?" *The Telegraph* (Calcutta), March 17, 1985, p. 7.

108. See the following articles by S. N. M. Abdi, in the *Illustrated Weekly of India:* "Preparing for Battle," December 4, 1988, pp. 30–33; "Jackie O!" November 20, 1988, pp. 21–24; "Derailed," November 13, 1988, pp. 26–29; "The Fall Guy," October 23, 1988, pp. 39–41. See also Payal Singh, "Tough Guy," *Illustrated Weekly of India,* October 9, 1988, pp. 26–27.

109. S. N. M. Abdi, "Sabotaged?" *Illustrated Weekly of India,* December 11, 1988, p. 23.

110. Sujit K. Das, "Left Front's Health Circus," *Economic and Political Weekly* 23, no. 21 (May 21, 1988): 1057.

111. S. N. M. Abdi, "Growing Criminalisation," *Illustrated Weekly of India,* September 9, 1990, pp. 22–23.

112. See, for instance, Sumanta Banerjee, "West Bengal Today: An Anticipatory Post-Mortem," *Economic and Political Weekly* 25, no. 33 (August 1990): 1812–16; Ajit Roy, "West Bengal: Pyrrhic Victory," *Economic and Political Weekly* 25, nos. 24 and 25 (June 16 and 23, 1990): 1293; S. N. M. Abdi, "Day of the Long Knives," *Illustrated Weekly of India,* July 1, 1990, pp. 24–25; and S. N. M. Abdi, "The Politics of Crime," *Illustrated Weekly of India,* November 5, 1989, pp. 34–39.

113. *Census of India, 1981* (note 47 above), p. 367.

114. Kohli, "From Elite Activism to Democratic Consolidation" (note 95 above), especially pp. 372–73, and *The State and Poverty in India,* pp. 127–28.

115. Bandyopadhyay and Von Eschen, "The Impact of Politics," pp. P22–23; and Basu, "State Autonomy and Agrarian Transformation" (note 55 above), pp. 495–96.

116. Kohli, *The State and Poverty in India,* p. 115. However, the employment of elected officials as full-time office workers would help curtail many of the administrative inefficiencies, such as the delays in submitting utilization certificates, that plague NREP implementation in West Bengal.

117. See, for instance, Sanjib Baruah, "The End of the Road in Land Reform? Limits to Redistribution in West Bengal," *Development and Change* 21 (1990): 119–46. Bandyopadhyay and Von Eschen ("The Impact of Politics," pp. P28–P38, S1–S8) argue that the CPI(M) has emphasized redistribution and neglected increasing production in virtually all its rural development programs.

118. Ross Mallick, "West Bengal Development Reform Impass," unpublished paper, Canadian Institute for International Peace and Security, Ottawa, 1991; and "Limits to Radical Intervention: Agricultural Taxation in West Bengal," *Development and Change* 21, no. 1 (January 1990): 157.

119. Atul Kohli, *The State and Poverty in India;* Nossiter, *Marxist State Governments in India* (note 64 above), pp. 137–43.

120. For an argument along these lines, see Bandyopadhyay and Von Eschen, "The Impact of Politics," pp. P32, S3–S4, S8.

121. Atul Kohli, *The State and Poverty in India.*

122. Ibid., p. 95.

123. For an interesting study documenting the declining responsiveness of the CPI(M), see Basu, *Two Faces of Protest* (note 93 above), especially pp. 39–53.

124. This finding is stressed by Basu, pp. 61–78, 159–91. This argument was also made to me by Deepankar Das Gupta, a social activist in Midnapore, during an interview on February 22, 1985.

125. "Panchayat Elections 1988," *The Telegraph* (Calcutta), February 21, 1988.

126. T. J. Pempel, "Introduction," in *Uncommon Democracies: The One-*

Party Dominant Regimes, ed. T. J. Pempel (Ithaca, N.Y.: Cornell University Press, 1990), p. 16.

127. Nora Hamilton, *The Limits of State Autonomy: Post-Revolutionary Mexico* (Princeton, N.J.: Princeton University Press, 1982), pp. 104–41; Wayne A. Cornelius, "Nation Building, Participation, and Distribution: The Politics of Social Reform under Cárdenas," in *Crisis, Choice, and Change: Historical Studies of Political Development,* ed. Gabriel Almond, Scott C. Flanagan, and Robert J. Mundt (Boston: Little, Brown, 1973), pp. 392–498.

128. For an argument that the domination of the Japanese political system by the Liberal Democratic Party is best described as "patterned pluralism," in which political competition has helped maintain the LDP's responsiveness to social needs, see Michio Muramatsu and Ellis S. Krauss, "The Dominant Party and Social Coalitions in Japan," in Pempel, *Uncommon Democracies,* pp. 282–305; and "The Conservative Policy Line and the Development of Patterned Pluralism," in *The Political Economy of Japan,* vol. 1, ed. Kozo Yamamura and Yasukichi Yasuba (Stanford, Calif.: Stanford University Press, 1987), pp. 516–54. Kent E. Calder notes that, despite the longstanding rule of the LDP, LDP politicians still are insecure and therefore continue to be responsive to social needs. See *Crisis and Compensation: Public Policy and Political Stability in Japan, 1949–1986* (Princeton, N.J.: Princeton University Press, 1988), especially pp. 20–26. The Swedish experience is a bit more complicated. From 1932 to 1976, the Social Democratic Party's share of the vote hovered around 46 percent. It garnered a majority of Swedish votes only twice (in 1940 and 1968), each time under exceptional conditions. The defeat of the Social Democrats in 1976 after the party failed to respond to new issues concerning environmental protection and nuclear power, as well as its clumsy handling of collective wage earner funds, illustrates the palpable threat of political competition confronting the party (see Gøsta Esping-Andersen, "Single-Party Dominance in Sweden: the Saga of Social Democracy," in Pempel, *Uncommon Democracies,* pp. 33–57). The Social Democrats' strategy for defusing this threat was first to ally with the Agrarian Party and later to formulate policies that appealed to the country's middle and professional classes. The broad coverage of trade union membership and the Social Democrats' receptiveness to their political initiatives, along with the corporatist system of bargaining between centralized organizations of business and labor, functioned to maintain the social Democrats' responsiveness to a broad array of social needs. See also Gøsta Esping-Andersen, *Politics against Markets: The Social Democratic Road to Power* (Princeton, N.J.: Princeton University Press, 1985); and Jonas Pontusson, "Conditions of Labor Dominance: Sweden and Britain Compared," in Pempel, *Uncommon Democracies,* pp. 58–82.

129. Samuel P. Huntington, *Political Order in Changing Societies* (New Haven, Conn.: Yale University Press, 1968), especially pp. 397–432.

130. Robert Dahl, *Polyarchy* (New Haven, Conn.: Yale University Press, 1971), pp. 1–2.

131. Rajni Kothari, "The Congress 'System' in India," *Asian Survey* 4, no. 12 (December 1964): 1161–73; and W. H. Morris-Jones, *Politics Mainly Indian* (Madras: Orient Longman, 1978).

132. In his most recent work, *Democracy and Discontent: India's Growing Crisis of Governability* (Cambridge: Cambridge University Press, 1990), Atul Kohli has attributed India's crisis of governability to the decline of the Congress Party organization and the failure of any other political party to fill the organizational vacuum that it has left.

133. Barbara Geddes, "A Game Theoretic Model of Reform in Latin American Democracies," *American Political Science Review* 85, no. 2 (June 1991): 371–92.

134. Rajni Kothari, "Decline of Parties and the Rise of Grassroots Movements," in *State against Democracy,* ed. Rajni Kothari (Delhi: Ajanta, 1988), pp. 37–54; and Alberto Melucci, *Nomads of the Present* (Philadelphia: Temple University Press, 1989), pp. 165–79.

135. Sheldon Annis, "Can Small-Scale Development Be a Large-Scale Policy? The Case of Latin America," *World Development* 15, supp. (Autumn 1987): 129.

136. John Keane, *Democracy and Civil Society* (London: Verso, 1988), pp. 101–51. Amrita Basu, in her study of different modes of political activism, also suggests the complementarity of parties and NGOs. See *Two Faces of Protest,* p. 232.

CHAPTER 5

1. The term *logic of appropriateness* is taken from James G. March and Johan P. Olsen, *Rediscovering Institutions: The Organizational Basis of Politics* (New York: Free Press, 1989).

2. Terry M. Moe, "The Politics of Structural Choice: Toward a Theory of Public Bureaucracy," in *Organization Theory: From Chester Barnard to the Present and Beyond,* ed. Oliver E. Williamson (New York: Oxford University Press, 1990), pp. 116–53, and "The Politics of Bureaucratic Structure," in *Can the Government Govern?* ed. John E. Chubb and Paul E. Peterson (Washington, D.C.: Brookings Institution, 1989), pp. 267–329. See also Martin Shefter, "Party, Bureaucracy, and Political Change in the United States," in *Political Parties: Development and Decay,* ed. Louis Maisel and Joseph Cooper (Beverly Hills, Calif.: Sage, 1978), pp. 211–65.

3. I follow March and Olsen (*Rediscovering Institutions*) in stressing that the selection of institutionalized rules does not necessarily conform to a single logic of appropriateness. In instances where inconsistent and contradictory rules initially appear "appropriate" to a particular situation, politics may play an important role in determining which rule is most "appropriate."

4. John D. Steinbruner, *The Cybernetic Theory of Decision* (Princeton, N.J.: Princeton University Press, 1974), p. 66.

5. This observation is also supported by Sarthi Acharya and V. G. Panwalkar, "The Maharashtra Employment Guarantee Scheme: Impact on Male and Female Labour," paper prepared under the Population Council, Programme in Asia on Women's Roles and Gender Differences in Development (Bombay: Tata Institute of Social Sciences, 1988), pp. 16–17. Apparently, information about available workers is also not collected for the Jawahar Rozgar Yojana. See Gov-

ernment of India, Programme Evaluation Organisation, Planning Commission, *Jawahar Rozgar Yojana* (New Delhi: Government of India, Planning Commission, 1992), pp. 10–11, mimeo.

6. See, for instance, the Planning Department memorandum entitled "Employment Guarantee Scheme" and dated February 8, 1990; Rozgar Hami Yojana Samiti, 1983–84, Sahaavi Maharashtra Vidhan Sabha, *Navvaa Ahavaal* (Ninth Session) (Bombay: Maharashtra State Legislative Secretariat, 1984), p. 1; and S. Bagchee, "Employment Guarantee Scheme in Maharashtra," *Economic and Political Weekly* 19, no. 37 (September 15, 1984): 1634.

7. Asim Das Gupta, *Rural Development Planning under the Left Front Government in West Bengal* (Calcutta: Government of West Bengal, Information and Cultural Affairs Department, 1981), pp. 7–8.

8. Interviews with block development officer, Jamboni, Gidhni, March 11, 1985; block development officer, Binpur I, Lalgarh, March 15, 1985; panchayat clerk, Tamluk II, Mecheda, April 1, 1985.

9. *Gram Panchayats in West Bengal and Their Activities: Survey and Evaluation* (Calcutta: Government of West Bengal, Town and Country Planning Department, n.d., c. 1980), p. 36. Inadequate record-keeping is also a problem with the current employment program, the Jawahar Rozgar Yojana. See Programme Evaluation Organisation, *Jawahar Rozgar Yojana*, pp. 43–44.

10. This finding is based on my fieldwork in Midnapore, Spring 1985.

11. For a similar argument made from observations of the U.S. Department of Housing and Urban Development during the 1970s, see Robert Bell, *The Culture of Policy Deliberations* (New Brunswick, N.J.: Rutgers University Press, 1985), pp. 179–96.

12. One of the best examples of the technical department officers' reluctance to get involved with the EGS occurred in the early 1980s, when the district collector of Ahmednagar district asked district-level officers to serve as monitors of EGS implementation in one of the district's thirteen tahsils. District records show that at least four officers refused to do so—because, according to the collector, they wished to avoid the political pressures that accompanied such work. For more details, see chapter 3.

13. This is the basic premise of agency theory. For an excellent review, see Kathleen M. Eisenhardt, "Agency Theory: An Assessment and Review," *Academy of Management Review* 14, no. 1 (1989): 57–74. Also see Daniel Levinthal, "A Survey of Agency Models of Organizations," *Journal of Economic Behavior and Organization* 9 (1988): 153–85; Terry M. Moe, "The New Economics of Organization," *American Journal of Political Science* 28, no. 4 (November 1984): 739–77; and Kenneth Arrow, "The Economics of Agency," in *Principals and Agents,* ed. John Pratt and Richard Zeckhauser (Cambridge, Mass.: Harvard University Press, 1985), pp. 37–51.

14. For a study of the NREP in Madhya Pradesh that reaches similar conclusions, see R. K. Tiwari, *Rural Employment Programmes in India: The Implementation Process* (New Delhi: Indian Institute of Public Administration, 1990).

15. For instance, Barbara Geddes, "Building 'State' Autonomy in Brazil, 1930–1964," *Comparative Politics* 22, no. 2 (January 1990): 217–35.

16. Ronald J. Herring, *Land to the Tiller: The Political Economy of Agrarian Reform in South Asia* (New Haven, Conn.: Yale University Press, 1983), pp. 38–42, 286.

17. Patronage appointments occur much more frequently in Latin American countries such as Mexico and Brazil than in South Asia, which has relatively strong civil service traditions. See, for instance, Merilee Serrill Grindle, *Bureaucrats, Politicians, and Peasants in Mexico* (Berkeley: University of California Press, 1977); and Geddes, "Building 'State' Autonomy."

18. Joel S. Migdal, *Strong Societies and Weak States: State-Society Relations and State Capabilities in the Third World* (Princeton, N.J.: Princeton University Press, 1988), especially chap. 7, pp. 238–58.

19. For India see Robert Wade, "The Market for Public Office: Why the Indian State Is Not Better at Development," *World Development* 13, no. 4 (1985): 467–97. For observations concerning the predatory nature of the Indian state, see Pranab Bardhan, *The Political Economy of Development in India* (Oxford: Blackwell, 1984); and Lloyd I. Rudolph and Susanne Hoeber Rudolph, *In Pursuit of Lakshmi: The Political Economy of the Indian State* (Chicago: University of Chicago Press, 1987). Perhaps the strongest testimony to the Indian state's predatory character was provided by Rajiv Gandhi. During the 1989 general election campaign, the then prime minister admitted that only 15 percent of the funds allocated to poverty alleviation ever reaches the poor. See Inderjit Badhwar, "Frantic Pace," *India Today,* November 30, 1989, p. 16. For more general observations see Dietrich Rueschemeyer and Peter B. Evans, "The State and Economic Transformation: Toward an Analysis of the Conditions underlying Effective Intervention," in *Bringing the State Back In,* ed. Peter B. Evans, Dietrich Rueschemeyer, and Theda Skocpol (Cambridge: Cambridge University Press, 1985), p. 61; Edward Banfield, "Corruption as a Feature of Governmental Organization," *Journal of Law and Economics* 18 (1975): 587–605; Anne Krueger, "The Political Economy of the Rent Seeking Society," *American Economic Review* 64, no. 3 (June 1974): 291–303; and the discussion of "market" corruption in James C. Scott, *Comparative Political Corruption* (Englewood Cliffs, N.J.: Prentice-Hall, 1972), p. 88.

20. Theda Skocpol, "Bringing the State Back In: Strategies of Analysis in Current Research," in Evans, Rueschemeyer, and Skocpol, *Bringing the State Back In,* p. 9. For a similar definition see Eric A. Nordlinger, "Taking the State Seriously," in *Understanding Political Development,* ed. Myron Weiner and Samuel P. Huntington (Boston: Little, Brown, 1987), p. 361.

21. Geddes ("Building 'State' Autonomy in Brazil," pp. 226–27) provides a graphic example. She approvingly quotes officials of Brazil's National Development Bank, who depict their work as "global rationality" rather than "political rationality." Theda Skocpol is more cautious. See her "Bringing the State Back In," pp. 14–15.

22. Eric Nordlinger ("Taking the State Seriously," p. 368) is an exception to the general tendency to view relations between states and social groups in adversarial terms; nevertheless, his analysis also neglects the need for ensuring the social responsiveness of state agencies.

23. Skocpol, "Bringing the State Back In," pp. 15–17.

24. This view is pervasive in the work of scholars such as Migdal (*Strong States and Weak States,* pp. 10–41), although he does incorporate a Durkheimian concept of "social control," which suggests that a state's strength can be enhanced through its ability to secure compliance, legitimation, and participation.

25. Richard J. Samuels, *The Business of the Japanese State* (Ithaca, N.Y.: Cornell University Press, 1987), especially pp. 8–9.

26. Ibid., p. 9.

27. See Peter B. Evans, "Predatory, Developmental and Other Apparatuses: A Comparative Political Economy Perspective on the Third World State," *Sociological Forum* 4, no. 4 (1989): 561–87.

28. C. T. Kurien, "Reconciling Growth and Social Justice: Strategies versus Structure?" in *Asian Seminar on Rural Development: The Indian Experience,* ed. M. L. Dantwala, Ranjit Gupta, and Keith C. D'Souza (Delhi: Oxford University Press, 1986), pp. 373–96; and Herring, *Land to the Tiller,* especially pp. 268–88.

29. See, for instance, Sanjib Baruah, "The End of the Road in Land Reform? Limits to Redistribution in West Bengal," *Development and Change* 21 (1990): 119–46; and B. S. Minhas, "Rural Poverty, Land Redistribution and Economic Development," *Indian Economic Review* 5, no. 1 (April 1970): 97–128.

30. Herring, *Land to the Tiller,* pp. 210–16, 279–88.

31. M. L. Dantwala, "Reconciling Growth and Social Justice: Agrarian Structure and Poverty," in Dantwala, Gupta, and D'Souza, *Asian Seminar on Rural Development,* pp. 397–406.

32. This formulation is taken from Milton J. Esman and Norman T. Uphoff, *Local Organizations: Intermediaries in Rural Development* (Ithaca, N.Y.: Cornell University Press, 1984), p. 254. For a useful discussion of government initiatives and the development of NGOs, see pp. 253–88.

33. Mahatma Gandhi's emphasis on "constructive work," or social work to uplift the poor, has been an important factor in this regard.

34. Government of India, Planning Commission, *Seventh Five Year Plan, 1985–90,* vol. 2 (New Delhi: Government of India Press, 1985), p. 68.

35. Jai Mangal Deo, "Voluntary Agencies vis-à-vis Government," *Yojana* 31, no. 4 (March 1, 1987): 12–13.

36. Lawrence Gomes, "Role of Voluntary and Other Organisations in Development," *Yojana,* December 1, 1989, p. 30.

37. Those who document the Indian state's efforts to control the NGO sector include Rajesh Tandon, "The State and Voluntary Agencies in Asia," in *Doing Development: Government, NGOs and the Rural Poor in Asia,* ed. Richard Holloway (London: Earthscan Publications, 1989), pp. 12–29; Aloysius P. Fernandez, "NGOs in South Asia: People's Participation and Partnership," *World Development* 15, supp. (1987): 39–49; Rajni Kothari, "NGO's, the State and World Capitalism," *Economic and Political Weekly* 21, no. 50 (December 13, 1986): 2177–82; Walter Fernandes, "The National NGO Convention: Voluntarism, the State and the Struggle for Change," *Social Action* 36 (October 1986): 431–41; L. C. Jain, "Debates in the Voluntary Sector: Some Reflections," *Social Action* 36 (October 1986): 404–16; and the es-

says by Harsh Sethi and Smitu Kothari, Jai Sen, Rajesh Tandon, Samkhya, and Sharad Kulkarni in *Lokayan Bulletin* 4, no. 3/4 (1986). For a different perspective see the writings of Bunker Roy in *Mainstream* (June 14, 1986; November 28, 1987; July 23, 1988).

38. The provision did allow an exemption for donations to a rural development fund, to be set up by the prime minister. But to my knowledge such a fund was never established.

39. Atul Kohli, *The State and Poverty in India: The Politics of Reform* (Cambridge: Cambridge University Press, 1987).

40. Ibid., p. 43. See also Atul Kohli, "Democracy, Economic Growth, and Inequality in India's Development," *World Politics* 32, no. 4 (July 1980): 623–38. Kohli's historical study of the rise of Communists in West Bengal emphasizes the conjunctural variables that create "Bengali exceptionalism." See "From Elite Activism to Democratic Consolidation: The Rise of Reform Communism in West Bengal," in *Dominance and State Power in Modern India: Decline of a Social Order*, vol. 2, ed. Francine R. Frankel and M. S. A. Rao (Delhi: Oxford University Press, 1990), pp. 367–415.

41. For a review of the literature that illustrates this approach, see Joan M. Nelson, "Political Participation," in *Understanding Political Development*, ed. Myron Weiner and Samuel P. Huntington (Boston: Little, Brown, 1987), pp. 103–15. For the classic statement concerning the development of parties and modernization, see Joseph LaPalombara and Myron Weiner, "The Origin and Development of Political Parties," in *Political Parties and Political Development*, ed. Joseph LaPalombara and Myron Weiner (Princeton, N.J.: Princeton University Press, 1966), pp. 3–42.

42. Two of the first works to emphasize crises and instability in this process were Samuel P. Huntington, *Political Order in Changing Societies* (New Haven, Conn.: Yale University Press, 1968); and Leonard Binder et al., *Crises and Sequences in Political Development* (Princeton, N.J.: Princeton University Press, 1971). For a review of the literature that elaborates this point, see Samuel P. Huntington, "The Goals of Development," in Weiner and Huntington, *Understanding Political Development*, pp. 3–32.

Sidney Verba's stress on sequences and development was especially important in laying the basis for a greater concern for history. See "Sequences and Development," in Binder et al., *Crises and Sequences*, pp. 283–316. Later work along these lines includes Charles Tilly, ed., *The Formation of National States in Western Europe* (Princeton, N.J.: Princeton University Press, 1975); and Raymond Grew, ed., *Crises of Political Development in Europe and the United States* (Princeton, N.J.: Princeton University Press, 1978).

The works on state formation include Tilly, *Formation of National States;* Perry Anderson, *Lineages of the Absolutist State* (London: New Left Books, 1974); Reinhard Bendix, *Kings or People: Power and the Mandate to Rule* (Berkeley: University of California Press, 1978); and Gianfranco Poggi, *The Development of the Modern State: A Sociological Introduction* (Palo Alto, Calif.: Stanford University Press, 1978).

43. Richard A. Higgott, *Political Development Theory* (London: Croon Helm, 1983).

44. Some analysts have argued that essential to the success of South Korea

and Taiwan was their market-driven export-oriented industrial policy. See, for instance, Bela Balassa, "Exports and Economic Growth: Further Evidence," *Journal of Development Economics* 5 (1978): 181–89; Gustav Ranis, "Industrial Development," and Ian Little, "An Economic Renaissance," both in *Economic Growth and Structural Change in Taiwan,* ed. Walter Galenson (Ithaca, N.Y.: Cornell University Press, 1979), pp. 206–62, 448–507. More recent interpretations have argued for the importance of state-led industrialization. See, for instance, Alice Amsden, *Asia's Next Giant: South Korea and Late Industrialization* (New York: Oxford University Press, 1989); Robert H. Wade, *Governing the Market: Economic Theory and the Role of Government in East Asian Industrialization* (Princeton, N.J.: Princeton University Press, 1990); Stephan Haggard, *Pathways from the Periphery: The Politics of Growth in Newly Industrializing Countries* (Ithaca, N.Y.: Cornell University Press, 1990); and the essays by Gereffi, Bradford, Ranis, Wade, and Schive in *Manufacturing Miracles,* ed. Gary Gereffi and Donald L. Wyman (Princeton, N.J.: Princeton University Press, 1990).

45. For a useful exception that explores the impact of public policy on the development of NGOs, see Sheldon Annis, "Can Small-Scale Development be a Large-Scale Policy? The Case of Latin America," *World Development* 15, supp. (Autumn 1987): 129–34.

46. Gøsta Esping-Andersen, *The Three Worlds of Welfare Capitalism* (Princeton, N.J.: Princeton University Press, 1990); Bo Rothstein, "Marxism, Institutional Analysis, and Working-Class Power: The Swedish Case," *Politics and Society* 18, no. 3 (1990): 317–45; Theda Skocpol, "Comparing National Systems of Social Provision: A Polity Centered Approach," paper presented at the meeting of the International Political Science Association, August 28–31, 1988, Washington, D.C.; Margaret Weir, Ann Shola Orloff, and Theda Skocpol, eds., *The Politics of Social Policy in the United States* (Princeton, N.J.: Princeton University Press, 1988); Theda Skocpol and Edwin Amenta, "States and Social Policies," *Annual Review of Sociology* 12 (1986): 131–57; and Gøsta Esping-Andersen, *Politics against Markets: The Social Democratic Road to Power* (Princeton, N.J.: Princeton University Press, 1985).

47. For instance, John W. Thomas and Merilee S. Grindle, "After the Decision: Implementing Policy Reforms in Developing Countries," *World Development* 18, no. 8 (August 1990): 1163–81; Robert H. Bates, *Beyond the Miracle of the Market: The Political Economy of Agrarian Change in Kenya* (Cambridge: Cambridge University Press, 1989); and John Echeverri-Gent, "Guaranteed Employment in an Indian State," *Asian Survey* 28, no. 12 (December 1988): 1294–1310.

48. See, for instance, Myron Weiner, "Capitalist Agriculture and Rural Well-Being," in Myron Weiner, *The Indian Paradox: Essays in Indian Politics,* ed. Ashutosh Varshney (New Delhi: Sage, 1989), pp. 99–132; Gail Omvedt, "New Movements," *Seminar* 352 (December 1988): 39–44; and Rudolph and Rudolph, *In Pursuit of Lakshmi* (note 19 above), pp. 312–32.

49. For Latin America see Merilee S. Grindle, *State and Countryside: Development Policy and Agrarian Politics in Latin America* (Baltimore: Johns Hopkins University Press, 1986); for Egypt see Richard H. Adams, Jr., *Devel-*

opment and Social Change in Rural Egypt (Syracuse, N.Y.: Syracuse University Press, 1986); and Leonard Binder, *In a Moment of Enthusiasm: Political Power and the Second Stratum in Egypt* (Chicago: University of Chicago Press, 1978).

50. Charles Tilly's *From Mobilization to Revolution* (Reading, Mass.: Addison-Wesley, 1978) remains his most systematic treatment. For applications of this basic model, see *The Contentious French: Four Centuries of Popular Struggle* (Cambridge, Mass.: Harvard University Press, 1986); "Social Movements and National Politics," in *State Building and Social Movements*, ed. W. Bright and S. Harding (Ann Arbor: University of Michigan Press, 1984), pp. 297–317; and "Introduction" and "The Web of Contention in Eighteenth-Century Cities," both in *Class Conflict and Collective Action*, ed. Louise A. Tilly and Charles Tilly (Beverly Hills, Calif.: Sage, 1981), pp. 13–25, 27–51. For surveys of other sociological literature on collective action, see Sidney Tarrow, *Struggle, Politics and Reform: Collective Action, Social Movements and Cycles of Protest* (Ithaca, N.Y.: Center for International Studies, Cornell University, 1991); Susan Olzak, "Analysis of Events in the Study of Collective Action," *Annual Review of Sociology* 15 (1989): 119–41; Sidney Tarrow, "National Politics and Collective Action: Recent Theory and Research in Western Europe and the United States," *Annual Review of Sociology* 14 (1988): 421–40; and Craig Jenkins, "Resource Mobilization Theory and the Study of Social Movements," *Annual Review of Sociology* 9 (1983): 527–53.

51. Tilly, *From Mobilization to Revolution*, pp. 59–62.

52. Ibid., p. 70.

53. John D. McCarthy and Mayer N. Zald, *The Trend of Social Movements in America: Professionalization and Resource Mobilization* (Morristown, N.J.: General Learning Corporation, 1973), especially p. 13; and Robert H. Salisbury, "An Exchange Theory of Collective Action," in *Interest Group Politics in America*, ed. Robert H. Salisbury (New York: Harper and Row, 1970), pp. 32–47.

54. M. L. Dantwala, "Growth and Equity in Agriculture," *Indian Journal of Agricultural Economics* 42, no. 2 (April–June 1987): 154; and A. Vaidyanathan, "Agricultural Development and Rural Poverty," in *The Indian Economy: Recent Developments and Future Prospects*, ed. Robert E. G. Lucas and Gustav F. Papanek (Boulder, Colo.: Westview Press, 1988), p. 81.

55. For the classic treatment of this issue, see Jan Breman, *Patronage and Exploitation: Changing Agrarian Relations in South Gujarat, India* (Berkeley: University of California Press, 1974). See also Ronald Herring, "Contesting the 'Great Transformation': Land and Labor in South India" unpublished manuscript, Northwestern University, 1991.

56. My comments below are indebted to James C. Scott, *Weapons of the Weak: Everyday Forms of Peasant Resistance* (New Haven, Conn.: Yale University Press, 1985); and Herring, "Contesting the 'Great Transformation.'"

57. For an excellent study of the major parties' appeals to the poor during India's 1989 general elections, see Francine R. Frankel, "India's Democracy in Transition," *World Policy Journal* 7, no. 3 (Summer 1990): 521–55.

58. The most developed elaboration of Sen's capacity-enhancing strategy can be found in Jean Dreze and Amartya Sen, *Hunger and Public Action* (Ox-

ford: Clarendon Press, 1989). See also the following works by Sen: *On Ethics and Economics* (Oxford: Blackwell, 1987); *Commodities and Capabilities* (Amsterdam: Elsevier, 1985); "Development: Which Way Now?" in *Resources, Values and Development* (Cambridge, Mass.: Harvard University Press, 1984), pp. 485–508; and *Poverty and Famines* (Oxford: Clarendon Press, 1981). For a selection of Schultz's work on human capital, see *Restoring Economic Equilibrium: Human Capital in the Modernizing Economy* (Cambridge, Mass.: Blackwell, 1990); *Investing in People: The Economics of Population Quality* (Berkeley: University of California Press, 1981); *Investment in Human Capital: The Role of Education and of Research* (New York: Free Press, 1971); and *Transforming Traditional Agriculture* (New Haven, Conn.: Yale University Press, 1964).

59. The quotes are from Marx. They are quoted by Sen to describe the objective of his strategy. See "Development: Which Way Now?" p. 497.

60. James A. Hanson and Samuel S. Lieberman, *India: Poverty, Employment, and Social Services* (Washington, D.C.: World Bank, 1989); Jandhyala B. G. Tilak, *The Economics of Inequality in Education* (New Delhi: Sage, 1987); Government of India, Ministry of Education, *Challenge of Education: A Policy Perspective* (New Delhi: Government of India Press, 1985); and Stephen P. Heyneman, "Investment in Indian Education: Uneconomic?" *World Development* 8, no. 2 (February 1980): 145–63.

61. Arun Ghosh, "Education for All," *Economic and Political Weekly* 27, no. 14 (April 4, 1992): 679.

62. S. R. Osmani, "Social Security in Asia," in *Social Security in Developing Countries*, ed. Etisham Ahmad et al. (Oxford: Clarendon Press, 1991), p. 342; and B. M. Bhatia, *A Study of India's Food Policy* (Kuala Lumpur: Asian Pacific Development Centre, 1983), p. 69.

63. Hanson and Lieberman, *India: Poverty, Employment and Social Services*, p. 132.

64. D. Bandyopadhyay, "Direct Intervention Programmes for Poverty Alleviation: An Appraisal," *Economic and Political Weekly* 23, no. 26 (June 25, 1988): A77–A88; Moni Nag, "Political Awareness as a Factor in Accessibility of Health Services: A Case Study of Rural Kerala and West Bengal," *Economic and Political Weekly* 24, no. 8 (February 25, 1989): 417–26; John C. Caldwell, "Routes to Low Mortality in Poor Countries," *Population and Development Review* 12, no. 2 (June 1986): 171–220; Joan P. Mencher, "The Lessons and Non-Lessons of Kerala: Agricultural Labourers and Poverty," *Economic and Political Weekly* 15, special no. (October 1980): 1781–1802.

65. For theories of collective action see note 50 above.

66. For instance, Hanson and Lieberman, *India: Poverty, Employment and Social Services;* World Bank, *The World Bank's Support for the Alleviation of Poverty* (Washington, D.C.: World Bank, 1988), and *Poverty and Hunger: Issues and Options for Food Security in Developing Countries* (Washington, D.C.: World Bank, 1986). For a concise and balanced discussion of targeting, see Robin Burgess and Nicholas Stern, "Social Security in Developing Countries: What, Why, Who and How?" in Ahmad et al., *Social Security in Developing Countries*, pp. 62–65.

67. For comparative analyses demonstrating the greater political viability of universalistic social policy, see Peter Baldwin, *The Politics of Social Solidarity: Class Bases of the European Welfare State, 1875–1975* (Cambridge: Cambridge University Press, 1990); Esping-Andersen, *The Three Worlds of Welfare Capitalism* and *Politics against Markets* (note 48 above); Sara A. Rosenberry, "Social Insurance: Distributive Criteria and the Welfare Backlash: A Comparative Analysis," *British Journal of Political Science* 12 (1982): 421–47; and Walter Korpi, "Social Policy and Distributional Conflict in the Capitalist Democracies: A Preliminary Comparative Framework," *West European Politics* 3 (October 1980): 296–315.

68. Martin Ravallion, Gaurav Datt, and Shubham Chaudhuri, *Higher Wage Rates for Relief Work Can Make Many of the Poor Worse Off: Recent Evidence from Maharashtra's "Employment Guarantee Scheme"* (Washington, D.C.: World Bank, 1990).

69. While the financial constraints confronting countries like India are very serious, it is important to remember that universalistic social welfare programs are not only associated with advanced capitalist countries with well-organized working classes. In fact, the first universalistic social welfare policies in Scandinavia were pension programs enacted in the 1890s (Denmark) and 1913 (Sweden), largely at the behest of the countries' farmers. See Baldwin, *The Politics of Social Solidarity*, especially pp. 55–94.

70. My discussion here is indebted to Theda Skocpol's concept of "targeting within universalism." See "Targeting within Universalism: Politically Viable Policies to Combat Poverty in the United States," paper presented at the annual meeting of the American Political Science Association, San Francisco, August 31, 1990. For a study that acknowledges the importance of building support for poverty alleviation programs by including the "nearly poor" as well as the poor, see World Bank, *Targeted Programs for the Poor during Structural Adjustment* (Washington, D.C.: World Bank, 1988), especially pp. 2–4, 32–33.

71. In 1978–79, 20 percent of India's villages did not have schools, and a large share of schools lacked proper facilities. More than half of India's primary schools were without proper buildings; 70 percent had no library books; 40 percent had no blackboards; and 85 percent did not have lavatories. In more than one-third of India's primary schools, a single teacher is employed to handle three or four classes. Poor quality as well as poor coverage is a consequence of the paucity of funding and lack of facilities. The dropout rate for primary school was 60 percent. Only twenty-three of every one hundred children enrolled in primary school make it to the eighth grade. According to India's National Sample Survey, less than a quarter of poor rural girls and only 43 percent of poor rural boys ages six to fourteen went to school in 1983. On the whole, it is estimated that only half of the eligible children attend school. As a consequence of this poor performance, the number of illiterates has grown from 300 million in 1951 to 437 million in 1988. For these data and more, see Ghosh, "Education for All," p. 679; Myron Weiner, *The Child and the State in India: Child Labor and Education Policy in Comparative Perspective* (Princeton, N.J.: Princeton University Press, 1991), especially pp. 90–96; Government of India, Ministry of Education, *Challenge of Education* (note 60 above); Hanson and

Lieberman, *India: Poverty, Employment and Social Services,* pp. 55, 122–23; and Jandhyala B. G. Tilak, "The Political Economy of Education in India," paper presented at the Seventh World Congress of Comparative Education, Montreal, July 1989, pp. 15–18.

72. For a theoretical model and a historical case that illuminates this insight, see Doug McAdam, *Political Process and the Development of Black Insurgency, 1930–1970* (Chicago: University of Chicago Press, 1982). See also Richard A. Couto, *Ain't Gonna Let Nobody Turn Me Around: The Pursuit of Racial Justice in the Rural South* (Philadelphia: Temple University Press, 1991).

73. For an excellent summary of the relation between education and agricultural productivity, see Jandhyala B. G. Tilak, "Education and Its Relation to Economic Growth, Poverty and Income Distribution: Past Evidence and Further Analysis," Discussion Paper no. 46, World Bank, Washington, D.C., 1989, pp. 23–28. For more general observations, see World Bank, *World Development Report, 1990* (Oxford: Oxford University Press, 1990), p. 80.

74. This is an especially remarkable finding, since the study it is based on (Tilak, *Economics of Inequality in Education,* pp. 114–22) does not take into account the quality of education received (backward castes generally receive an inferior education) or wage discrimination against the backward castes.

75. Tilak, "Education and Its Relation to Economic Growth," especially pp. 63–84; Irma Adelman and A. Levy, "The Equalizing Role of Human Resource Intensive Growth Strategies: A Theoretical Model," *Journal of Policy Modelling* 6, no. 2 (July 1984): 271–87; Gary S. Fields, *Poverty, Inequality and Development* (Cambridge: Cambridge University Press, 1980); Jan Tinbergen, *Income Distribution: Analysis and Policies* (Amsterdam: North Holland, 1975); Montek S. Ahluwalia, "Income Inequality: Some Dimensions of the Problem," in *Redistribution with Growth,* ed. Hollis Chenery et al. (Oxford: Oxford University Press, 1974) p. 337; and Irma Adelman and Cynthia T. Morris, *Economic Growth and Social Equity in Developing Countries* (Palo Alto, Calif.: Stanford University Press, 1973).

76. Hanson and Lieberman, *India: Poverty, Employment and Social Services,* pp. 54, 62–71; and Rati Ram and Theodore W. Schultz, "Life Span, Health, Savings, and Productivity," *Economic Development and Cultural Change* 27, no. 3 (April 1979): 399–421.

77. I am indebted to Martin Ravallion for drawing my attention to the possibilities of coordinating the implementation of public works with the Integrated Rural Development Programme.

78. Ghosh, "Education for All," pp. 681–82.

79. My comment here draws from Amartya Sen, "Indian Development: Lessons and Non-Lessons," *Daedalus* 118, no. 4 (Fall 1989): 369–92.

80. Peter Gourevitch, *Politics in Hard Times: Comparative Responses to International Economic Crisis* (Ithaca, N.Y.: Cornell University Press, 1986).

81. For a discussion of "silences" in public policy, see Ira Katznelson, "Rethinking the Silences of Social and Economic Policy," *Political Science Quarterly* 101, no. 2 (1986): 307–25.

82. For an excellent study of the development of the "farm lobby," see John Mark Hansen, *Gaining Access: Congress and the Farm Lobby, 1919–1981* (Chicago: University of Chicago Press, 1991).

83. James T. Bonnen, "Why is There No Coherent U.S. Rural Policy?" *Policy Studies Journal* (forthcoming).

84. U.S. Bureau of the Census, *Statistical Abstract of the United States, 1991* (Washington, D.C.: U.S. Government Printing Office, 1991), pp. 395–97, and *State and Metropolitan Area Data Bank, 1991* (Washington, D.C.: U.S. Government Printing Office, 1991), p. 77.

85. Michael Lipton, *Why Poor People Stay Poor: Urban Bias in World Development* (Cambridge, Mass.: Harvard University Press, 1977).

86. Ann R. Tickamyer and Cynthia M. Duncan, "Poverty and Opportunity Structure in Rural America," *Annual Review of Sociology* 16 (1990): 70.

87. U.S. Bureau of the Census, *Current Population Reports,* Series P-60, no. 175: *Poverty in the United States, 1990* (Washington, D.C.: U.S. Government Printing Office, 1991), pp. 6, 68.

88. William P. O'Hare, *The Rise of Poverty in Rural America* (Washington, D.C.: Population Reference Bureau, 1988), p. 5.

89. Mark Henry, Mark Drabenstott, and Lynn Gibson, "A Changing Rural America," *Economic Review* 72, no. 1 (July 1985): 23–41.

90. Ann R. Tickamyer and Cynthia M. Duncan, "Work and Poverty in Rural America," in *Rural Policies for the 1990s,* ed. Cornelia B. Flora and James A. Christenson (Boulder, Colo.: Westview Press, 1991), p. 102.

91. Kenneth L. Deavers and Robert A. Hoppe, "The Rural Poor: The Past as Prologue," in Flora and Christenson, *Rural Policies for the 1990s,* p. 91.

92. D. Bellamy, "Economic and Socio-Demographic Change in Persistent Low-Income Counties: An Update," paper presented at the meeting of the Southern Rural Sociological Association, New Orleans, 1988; U.S. Department of Agriculture, *The Diverse Social and Economic Structure of Nonmetropolitan America,* Rural Development Research Report no. 49 (Washington, D.C.: U.S. Government Printing Office, 1985).

93. William P. O'Hare and Brenda Curry-White, *The Rural Underclass: Examination of Multiple-Problem Populations in Urban and Rural Settings* (Washington, D.C.: Population Reference Bureau, 1992); and William P. O'Hare, *Can the Underclass Concept Be Applied to Rural Areas?* (Washington, D.C.: Population Reference Bureau, 1992).

94. John Ferejohn, "Logrolling in an Institutional Context: A Case Study of Food Stamp Legislation," in *Congress and Policy Change,* ed. Gerald C. Write, Jr., Leroy N. Rieselbach, and Lawrence C. Dodd (New York: Agathon Press, 1986), pp. 223–53; and Norwood Allen Kerr, "Drafted into the War on Poverty: USDA Food and Nutrition Programs, 1961–1969," *Agricultural History* 64, no. 2 (Spring 1990): 154–68.

STATISTICAL APPENDIX TO CHAPTER 3

1. The average yield per hectare of *rabi jowar, bajra,* and pulses in Maharashtra over the period 1979–80 through 1981–82 was 486 kgs., 439 kgs., and 354 kgs., respectively. The average yield of more productive crops, such as rice, wheat, *kharif jowar,* and sugarcane, was 1,395 kgs., 868 kgs., 1,017 kgs., and 10,084 kgs. respectively. See Government of Maharashtra, Department of Agriculture, *Districtwise Statistical Information of Agricultural Depart-*

ment (Pune: Government of Maharashtra, n.d.), pp. 112–16, 122, 124, 164 (mimeo).

2. Government of Maharashtra, Planning Department, *Report of the Fact Finding Committee on Regional Imbalance* (note 86 above), pp. 312, 317, 321; *Census of India, 1981* (note 20 above), pp. 150–53.

3. Government of Maharashtra, Directorate of Economics and Statistics, *Statistical Abstract of Maharashtra State for the Year 1978–79* (Nagpur: Government Press, 1983), pp. 109, 136–37; Government of Maharashtra, Department of Agriculture, *Districtwise Statistical Information*, pp. 17, 19, 21, 45.

4. *Census of India, 1981* (note 20 above), pp. 210–13; *Census of India, 1981, Series 12, Maharashtra,* Paper 2 of 1982: *Scheduled Castes and Tribes* (Bombay: Central Government Press, 1982), pp. 8–11, 84–87); Government of Maharashtra, Department of Agriculture, *Report on Agricultural Census, 1970–71: Maharashtra State* (Bombay: Central Government Press, 1976), pp. 107–229; and Directorate of Economics and Statistics, *Statistical Abstract*, pp. 64–69.

5. Alwyn R. Rouyer, "Political Capacity and the Decline of Fertility in India," *American Political Science Review* 81, no. 2 (June 1987): 453–70.

6. Government of Maharashtra, *Statistical Abstract*, pp. 96–97; *Census of India, 1981* (note 20 above), pp. 210–12.

7. For an excellent historical account of these disparities, see Jayant Lele, "Caste, Class and Dominance: Political Mobilization in Maharashtra," in *Dominance and State Power in Modern India: Decline of a Social Order*, ed. Francine R. Frankel and M. S. A. Rao (Delhi: Oxford University Press, 1990), pp. 115–211. See also Lele, "Chavan and the Political Integration of Maharashtra" (note 13 above).

8. Dandekar and Sathe, "Employment Guarantee Scheme and Food for Work" (note 88 above), p. 711; Government of India and Government of Maharashtra, *Joint Evaluation*, p. 64.

9. The poverty data are from the 1982–83 National Sample Survey, as cited in Godbole, *Public Expenditures in Maharashtra* (note 20 above), p. 57. For a village-level study that supports observations about higher rates of unemployment in dryland areas than in the Vidharbha region, where there is a higher share of agricultural laborers, see Bhende et al., "EGS and the Poor" (note 88 above).

10. For thorough documentation of the regional bias in Government of Maharashtra's expenditures, see Government of Maharashtra, Planning Department, *Report of the Fact Finding Committee on Regional Imbalance* (note 86 above).

Works Cited

GOVERNMENT DOCUMENTS

India

Annual Plan on Agriculture, 1984–85, Midnapore East. Tamluk, West Bengal: Office of the Principal Agricultural Officer, Midnapore East, 1984.

Annual Plan on Agriculture, 1984–85, Midnapore West. Midnapore: Office of the Principal Agricultural Officer, Midnapore West, 1984.

Census of India, 1981. Series 1, India. Paper 3: *Provisional Population Tables: Workers and Non-Workers.* New Delhi: Controller of Publications, 1981.

Census of India, 1981. Series 1, India. Part II-A(i): *General Population Tables.* New Delhi: Controller of Publications, 1985.

Census of India, 1981. Series 12, Maharashtra. Paper 2 of 1982: *Scheduled Castes and Tribes.* Bombay: Central Government Press, 1982.

Census of India, 1981. Series 23, West Bengal. Paper 1 of 1981: *Supplement: Provisional Population Totals.* Calcutta: Director of the Census, 1981.

Census of India, 1981. Series 23, West Bengal. Part III-A & B(i): *General Economic Tables.* New Delhi: Controller of Publications, 1987.

Compendium for Panchayati Raj in West Bengal. Calcutta: Government of West Bengal, Director of Panchayats, 1984.

Dandekar, V. M., D. Deshmukh, and V. R. Devskar. *Interim Report of the Committee to Study the Introduction of Eight Monthly Supply of Water on Irrigation Projects in Maharashtra.* Bombay: Government of Maharashtra, 1979.

Election Commissioner of India. *Report on the General Elections to the Legislative Assemblies.* New Delhi: Controller of Publications, 1984.

Election Commissioner of India. *Report on the General Elections to the Legislative Assemblies.* New Delhi: Controller of Publications, 1979.

District Planning Officer, Midnapore. *An Approach to the Seventh Five Year Plan for the Midnapore District, West Bengal.* Midnapore: Office of the District Planning Officer, 1985. Mimeo.

Government of India. *National Sample Survey, 26th Round, West Bengal,* Report 215. New Delhi: Controller of Publications, 1978.

Government of India, Director of Economics and Statistics, Department of Agriculture and Cooperation, Ministry of Agriculture. "Index Numbers of Net Area Sown, Cropping Intensity, Cropping Pattern and Productivity Per Hectare of Net Area Sown—India." *Agricultural Situation in India* 41, no. 12 (March 1987): 1000–1018.

Government of India, Director of Economics and Statistics, Department of Agriculture and Cooperation, Ministry of Agriculture. "Agricultural Census: All India." *Agricultural Situation in India* 40, no. 5 (August 1985): 401–12.

Government of India, Ministry of Agriculture and Irrigation, Department of Rural Development. *Report of the Committee on Panchayati Raj Institutions.* New Delhi: Government of India Press, 1978.

Government of India, Ministry of Agriculture and Rural Development, *Report on the National Rural Employment Programme.* New Delhi: Government of India Press, 1985.

Government of India, Ministry of Agriculture and Rural Development, Department of Rural Development. *Annual Report, 1989.* New Delhi: Government of India Press, 1989.

Government of India, Ministry of Education. *Challenge of Education: A Policy Perspective.* New Delhi: Government of India Press, 1985.

Government of India, Ministry of Finance. *Economic Survey, 1988–89.* New Delhi: Government of India Press, 1989.

Government of India, Ministry of Finance. *Economic Survey of India.* New Delhi: Government of India Press, 1990.

Government of India, Ministry of Finance. *Expenditure Budget, 1990–91.* 2 vols. New Delhi: Government of India, 1990.

Government of India, Ministry of Planning, Department of Statistics. *Estimates of State Domestic Product, 1970–71 to 1987–88.* New Delhi: Controller of Publications, 1988.

Government of India, Planning Commission. *Seventh Five Year Plan, 1985–90.* 2 vols. New Delhi: Government of India Press, 1985.

Government of India, Programme Evaluation Organisation, Planning Commission. *Jawahar Rozgar Yojana.* New Delhi: Government of India, Planning Commission, 1992. Mimeo.

Government of India, Programme Evaluation Organisation, Planning Commission. *Evaluation of Food for Work Programme.* New Delhi: Government of India, 1981.

Government of India, Programme Evaluation Organisation, Planning Commission, and Government of Maharashtra, Directorate of Economics and Statistics. *Joint Evaluation of Employment Guarantee Scheme of Maharashtra.* 2 vols. New Delhi: Controller of Publications, 1980.

Government of Maharashtra. *Statement of the Recommendations of the Evaluation Committee on Panchayati Raj (Bongirwar Committee) and Government Decisions Thereon.* Bombay: Central Government Press, 1973.

Government of Maharashtra, Bureau of Economics and Statistics. *Quarterly Bulletin of Economics and Statistics,* various issues, vols. 6–28 (1965–1988).

Government of Maharashtra, Department of Agriculture. *Districtwise Statistical Information of Agricultural Department.* Pune: Government of Maharashtra, n.d. Mimeo.

Government of Maharashtra, Department of Agriculture. *Report on Agricultural Census, 1970–71: Maharashtra State.* Bombay: Central Government Press, 1976.

Government of Maharashtra, Directorate of Economics and Statistics. *Statistical Abstract of Maharashtra State for the Year 1978–79.* Nagpur: Government Press, 1983.

Government of Maharashtra, Planning Department. *Annual Plan, 1983–84, Maharashtra.* Bombay: Government of Maharashtra, 1984.

Government of Maharashtra, Planning Department. *Employment Guarantee Scheme: A Compendium of Orders.* Bombay: Government of Maharashtra, 1982.

Government of Maharashtra, Planning Department. *Employment Guarantee Scheme: Statistical Information Book.* Bombay: Government of Maharashtra, 1985. Mimeo.

Government of Maharashtra, Planning Department. *Report of the Fact Finding Committee on Regional Imbalance.* 2 vols. Bombay: Government of Maharashtra, 1984.

Government of West Bengal, Development and Planning Department. *Report on the NREP.* Calcutta: Government of West Bengal, 1985. Mimeo.

Gram Panchayats in West Bengal and Their Activities: Survey and Evaluation. Calcutta: Government of West Bengal, Town and Country Planning Department, n.d., c. 1980.

Gupta, Asim Das. *Rural Development Planning under the Left Front Government in West Bengal.* Calcutta: Government of West Bengal, Information and Cultural Affairs Department, 1981.

Report of the Team for the Study of Community Projects and National Service. Vol. 1, sec. 2. New Delhi: Government of India, 1957.

Rozgar Hami Yojana Samiti, 1982–83, Sahaavi Maharashtra Vidhan Sabha. *Sahaavaa Ahavaal* (Sixth Session). Bombay: Maharashtra State Legislative Secretariat, 1983.

Rozgar Hami Yojana Samiti, 1982–83, Sahaavi Maharashtra Vidhan Sabha. *Satvaa Ahavaal* (Seventh Session). Bombay: Maharashtra State Legislative Secretariat, 1983.

Rozgar Hami Yojana Samiti, 1983–84, Sahaavi Maharashtra Vidhan Sabha. *Athavaa Ahavaal* (Eighth Session). Bombay: Maharashtra State Legislative Secretariat, 1984.

Rozgar Hami Yojana Samiti, 1983–84, Sahaavi Maharashtra Vidhan Sabha. *Navvaa Ahavaal* (Ninth Session). Bombay: Maharashtra State Legislative Secretariat, 1984.

Sanathanam Commission (Government of India) and National Institute of Public Finance and Policies. *Aspects of Black Money in India.* New Delhi: Government of India Press, 1985.

West Bengal Panchayat Act, 1973. As modified up to 11-1-80. Calcutta: Government of West Bengal, 1980.

United States

Bankhead-Jones Farm Tenant Act. *United States Statutes at Large.* Vol. 50, pt. 1, pp. 522–33. Washington, D.C.: U.S. Government Printing Office, 1937.

Department of Agriculture Appropriation Act, fiscal year 1941. *U.S. Statutes at Large.* Vol. 54, pt. 1, pp. 532–70. Washington, D.C.: U.S. Government Printing Office, 1941.

Department of Agriculture Appropriation Act, fiscal year 1942. *U.S. Statutes at Large.* Vol. 55, pt. 1, pp. 408–46. Washington, D.C.: Government Printing Office, 1942.

Department of Agricultural Appropriation Act, fiscal year 1943. *U.S. Statues at Large.* Vol. 56, pt. 1, pp. 664–702. Washington, D.C.: U.S. Government Printing Office, 1943.

Emergency Relief Appropriation Act, fiscal year 1937. *U.S. Statutes at Large.* Vol. 50, pt. 1, pp. 353–58. Washington, D.C.: U.S. Government Printing Office, 1937.

Emergency Relief Appropriation Act, fiscal year 1938. *U.S. Statutes at Large.* Vol. 52, pt. 1, pp. 809–20. Washington, D.C.: U.S. Government Printing Office, 1938.

Emergency Relief Appropriation Act, fiscal year 1939. *U.S. Statutes at Large.* Vol. 53, pt. 2, pp. 927–39. Washington, D.C.: U.S. Government Printing Office, 1939.

Emergency Relief Appropriation Act, fiscal year 1941. *U.S. Statutes at Large.* Vol. 54, pt. 1, pp. 611–28. Washington, D.C.: U.S. Government Printing Office, 1941.

Hoffsommer, Harold. "Landlord-Tenant Relations and Relief in Alabama." *Monthly Report of the Federal Emergency Relief Administration,* October 1935, pp. 1–4.

Larson, Olaf F., ed. *Ten Years of Rural Rehabilitation in the United States.* Washington, D.C.: Bureau of Agricultural Economics, 1949. Mimeo.

Records of the Commodity Stabilization Service, Record Group 145. National Archives, Washington, D.C.

Records of the Office of the Secretary of Agriculture, Record Group 16. National Archives, Washington, D.C.

Records of the Resettlement Administration and Farm Security Administration, Record Group 96. National Archives, Washington, D.C.

Records of the Works Projects Administration, Record Group 69. National Archives, Washington, D.C.

Report of the Administrator of the Farm Security Administration, 1939. Washington, D.C.: U.S. Government Printing Office, 1939.

Report of the Administrator of the Resettlement Administration, 1937. Washington, D.C.: U.S. Government Printing Office, 1936.

Resettlement Administration. *First Annual Report.* Washington, D.C.: U.S. Government Printing Office, 1937.

U.S. Bureau of the Census. *Current Population Reports.* Series P-60, no. 175. *Poverty in the United States: 1990.* Washington, D.C.: U.S. Government Printing Office, 1991.

U.S. Bureau of the Census. *Fifteenth Census of the United States: 1930.* Vol. 4: *Agriculture.* Washington, D.C.: U.S. Department of Commerce, 1932.

U.S. Bureau of the Census. *State and Metropolitan Area Data Bank, 1991.* Washington, D.C.: U.S. Government Printing Office, 1991.

U.S. Bureau of the Census. *Statistical Abstract of the United States, 1991.* Washington, D.C.: U.S. Government Printing Office, 1991.

U.S. Congress, Select Committee of the House Committee on Agriculture. *Investigating the Activities of the Farm Security Administration.* House of Representatives, 78th Cong., 2d sess., Report no. 1430. Washington, D.C.: U.S. Government Printing Office, 1944.

U.S. Congress, Subcommittee on Low-Income Families of the Joint Committee on the Economic Report. *Low-Income Families and Economic Stability.* Senate Document 146. Washington, D.C.: U.S. Government Printing Office, 1950.

U.S. Department of Agriculture. *The Diverse Social and Economic Structure of Nonmetropolitan America.* Rural Development Research Report no. 49. Washington, D.C.: U.S. Government Printing Office, 1985.

U.S. National Emergency Council. *Report on Economic Conditions of the South.* Washington, D.C.: U.S. Government Printing Office, 1938.

UNPUBLISHED WORKS

India

Acharya, Sarthi, and V. G. Panwalkar. "The Maharashtra Employment Guarantee Scheme: Impact on Male and Female Labour." Paper prepared under the Population Council, Programme in Asia on Women's Roles and Gender Differences in Development. Bombay: Tata Institute of Social Sciences, 1988.

Adak, Narayan Chandra. "Panchayats and Rural Development: Midnapore District—A Case Study." M. Phil. Thesis, Jadavpur University, Calcutta, 1983.

Attwood, Donald W., and B. R. Baviskar, "The Barren Grounds in West Bengal?" In *The Political Economy of Cooperation in Rural India,* vol. 2, chap. 4. Unpublished manuscript, McGill University, 1991.

Bandyopadhyay, Nripen, and Associates. "Evaluation of Land Reform Measures in West Bengal: A Report." *Asian Employment Programme Working Papers, ARTEP.* Geneva: International Labour Organisation, 1985.

Bandyopadhyay, Suraj, and Donald Von Eschen. "The Conditions of Rural Progress." Report submitted to the Canadian International Development Agency, Ottawa, 1981.

———. "The Impact of Politics on Rural Production and Distribution: A Comparative Study of Rural Policies and Their Implementation under Congress and Left Front Governments in West Bengal India." Paper presented at the annual meeting of the Association for Asian Studies, San Francisco, March 26, 1988.

Basu, Krishna Lal. "A Study on the Role That the Panchayats Are Playing in Generating Forces of Development in the Rural Areas of Birbhum." Unpublished manuscript, Department of Social Work, Vidya Bhavana, Visva-Bharati, 1982.

Herring, Ronald. "Contesting the 'Great Transformation': Land and Labor in South India." Unpublished manuscript, Northwestern University, 1991.

Institute of Social Studies. *Impact on Women Workers: Maharashtra Employment Guarantee Scheme: A Study.* 2 vols. New Delhi: Institute of Social Studies, 1979.

Mallick, Ross. "West Bengal Development Reform Impasse." Unpublished paper, Canadian Institute for International Peace and Security, Ottawa, 1991.

Ravallion, Martin. "Reaching the Poor through Rural Public Works: Arguments, Evidence and Lessons from South Asia." Unpublished paper, World Bank, Washington, D.C., 1990.

———, Gaurav Datt, and Shubham Chaudhuri. *Higher Wage Rates for Relief Work Can Make Many of the Poor Worse Off: Recent Evidence from Maharashtra's "Employment Guarantee Scheme."* Washington, D.C.: World Bank, 1990.

Tilak, Jandhyala B. G. "The Political Economy of Education in India," paper presented at the Seventh World Congress of Comparative Education, Montreal, July, 1989.

Varshney, Ashutosh. "Organizing the Countryside: Peasant Mobilization in the 1980s." Unpublished paper, Massachusetts Institute of Technology, 1989.

United States

Bellamy, D. "Economic and Socio-Demographic Change in Persistent Low-Income Counties: An Update." Paper presented at the meeting of the Southern Rural Sociological Association, New Orleans, 1988.

Finegold, Kenneth, and Theda Skocpol. "Capitalists, Farmers and Workers in the New Deal—The Ironies of Government Intervention." Paper presented at the annual meeting of the American Political Science Association, Washington, D.C., August 31, 1980.

Maddox, James G. "The Farm Security Administration." Ph.D. diss., Harvard University, 1950.

Panor, Marie. "The Resettlement Administration: A Study in the Evolution of Major Purpose." M.A. thesis, University of Chicago, 1951.

Skocpol, Theda. "Comparing National Systems of Social Provision: A Polity Centered Approach." Paper presented at the meeting of the International Political Science Association, Washington, D.C., August 28–31, 1988.

———. "Targeting within Universalism: Politically Viable Policies to Combat Poverty in the United States." Paper presented at the annual meeting of the American Political Science Association, San Francisco, August 31, 1990.

Wilson, G. K. "The Political Behavior of Large Corporations." Paper presented at the annual meeting of the American Political Science Association, Chicago, September 3–6, 1987.

JOURNAL ARTICLES AND BOOKS

India

Abraham, Amrita. "Maharashtra's Employment Guarantee Scheme." *Economic and Political Weekly* 15, no. 12 (August 9, 1980): 1339–42.

Bagchee, S. "Employment Guarantee Scheme in Maharashtra." *Economic and Political Weekly* 19, no. 37 (September 15, 1984): 1633–38.

———. "Illegal Activity?" *Economic and Political Weekly* 12, no. 22 (May 28, 1977): 856–57.

Bandyopadhyay, D. "Direct Intervention Programmes for Poverty Alleviation: An Appraisal." *Economic and Political Weekly* 23, no. 26 (June 25, 1988): A77–A88.

Banerjee, Sumanta. "West Bengal Today: An Anticipatory Post-Mortem." *Economic and Political Weekly* 25, no. 33 (August 18, 1990): 1812–16.

Bardhan, Pranab. *The Political Economy of Development in India.* Oxford: Blackwell, 1984.

Baruah, Sanjib. "The End of the Road in Land Reform? Limits to Redistribution in West Bengal." *Development and Change* 21 (1990): 119–46.

Basu, Amrita. "Democratic Centralism in the Home and the World: Bengali Women and the Communist Movement." In *Promissory Notes: Women in the Transition to Socialism,* ed. Sonia Kruks, Rayna Rapp, and Marilyn B. Young. New York: Monthly Review Press, 1989.

———. "State Autonomy and Agrarian Transformation." *Comparative Politics* 22, no. 4 (July 1990): 483–500.

———. *Two Faces of Protest: Contrasting Modes of Women's Activism in India.* Berkeley: University of California Press, 1992.

Baviskar, B. S. *The Politics of Development: Sugar Co-operatives in Rural Maharashtra.* Delhi: Oxford University Press, 1980.

Bhatia, B. M. *A Study of India's Food Policy.* Kuala Lumpur: Asian Pacific Development Centre, 1983.

Bhattacharya, Mohit. "West Bengal." In *Patterns of Panchayati Raj in India,* ed. G. Ram Reddy, pp. 285–98. Delhi: Macmillan of India, 1977.

Bhende, M. J., et al. "EGS and the Poor: Evidence from Longitudinal Village Studies." *Economic and Political Weekly* 27, no. 13 (March 28, 1992): A19–A22.

Boyce, James K. *Agrarian Impasse in Bengal: Institutional Constraints to Technological Change.* Oxford: Oxford University Press, 1987.

Brahme, Sulabha. *Drought in Maharashtra, 1972.* Pune: Gokhale Institute of Politics and Economics, 1983.

Brass, Paul R. *Factional Politics in an Indian State: The Congress Party in Uttar Pradesh.* Berkeley: University of California Press, 1965.

———. *The Politics of India since Independence.* Cambridge: Cambridge University Press, 1990.

Breman, Jan. *Patronage and Exploitation: Changing Agrarian Relations in South Gujarat, India.* Berkeley: University of California Press, 1974.

Calman, Leslie J. *Protest in Democratic India.* Boulder, Colo.: Westview Press, 1985.

Carter, Anthony T. *Elite Politics in Rural India.* London: Cambridge University Press, 1974.

Communist Party of India (Marxist). *Report on Organisation and Tasks* (adopted by the Fourteenth Party Congress held at Madras, January 3–9, 1992). New Delhi: Hari Singh Kang, 1992.

Dandekar, Kumudini. *Employment Guarantee Scheme: An Employment Opportunity for Women.* Pune: Gokhale Institute for Politics and Economics, 1983.

———, and Maju Sathe. "Employment Guarantee Scheme and Food for Work Programme." *Economic and Political Weekly* 15, no. 15 (April 12, 1990): 707–13.

Dantwala, M. L. "Growth and Equity in Agriculture." *Indian Journal of Agricultural Economics* 42, no. 2 (April–June 1987): 149–54.

———. "Reconciling Growth and Social Justice: Agrarian Structure and Poverty." In *Asian Seminar on Rural Development,* ed. M. L. Dantwala, Ranjit Gupta, and Keith C. D'Souza, pp. 397–406. Delhi: Oxford University Press, 1986.

Das, Sujit K. "Left Front's Health Circus." *Economic and Political Weekly* 23, no. 21 (May 21, 1988): 1057–58.

Davis, Marvin. *Rank and Rivalry: The Politics of Inequality in Rural West Bengal.* London: Cambridge University Press, 1983.

Deo, Jai Mangal. "Voluntary Agencies vis-à-vis Government." *Yojana* 31, no. 4 (March 1, 1987): 10–13.

Deshpande, J. V. "Zilla Parishad Game." *Economic and Political Weekly* 25, no. 27 (July 7, 1990): 1442.

Deshpande, Vasant. *Employment Guarantee Scheme: Impact on Poverty and Bondage among Tribals.* Pune: Tilak Vidyapeeth, 1982.

Documents of the Eleventh Congress of the CPI(M). New Delhi: Desraj Chadha, 1982.

Echeverri-Gent, John. "Guaranteed Employment in an Indian State." *Asian Survey* 28, no. 12 (December 1988): 1294–1310.

"EGS for Whom?" *Economic and Political Weekly* 19, no. 10 (March 10, 1984): 402–3.

"Employment Guarantee Scheme in a New Form: Rural Development through Labor Power." *Lok Rajya* 45 (16 August 1989): 56–60.

Ezekiel, Hannan, and Johann C. Stuyt. "Maharashtra Employment Guarantee Scheme: Geographical Distribution of Employment." *Economic and Political Weekly* 25, no. 26 (June 30, 1990): A86–A92.

———. *The Maharashtra Employment Guarantee Scheme: Its Responses to Differences in Employment Patterns between Districts.* Washington, D.C.: International Food Policy Research Institute, 1989.

Fernandes, Walter. "The National NGO Convention: Voluntarism, the State and the Struggle for Change." *Social Action* 36 (October 1986): 431–41.

Fernandez, Aloysius P. "NGOs in South Asia: People's Participation and Partnership." *World Development* 15, supp. (1987): 39–49.

Frankel, Francine R. "India's Democracy in Transition." *World Policy Journal* 7, no. 3 (Summer 1990): 521–55.

————. *India's Political Economy, 1947–1977.* Princeton, N.J.: Princeton University Press, 1978.

Frankel, Francine R., and M. S. A. Rao, eds. *Dominance and State Power in Modern India.* 2 vols. Delhi: Oxford University Press, 1989 and 1990.

Ghosh, Anjali. *Peaceful Transition to Power: A Study of Marxist Political Strategies in West Bengal, 1967–1977.* Calcutta: Firma K. L. Mukhopadhyay, 1981.

Ghosh, Arun. "Decentralized Planning: West Bengal Experience." *Economic and Political Weekly* 23, no. 13 (March 26, 1988): 655–63.

————. "Education for All." *Economic and Political Weekly* 27, no. 14 (April 4, 1992): 679–83.

G. O. "Fighting Famine." *Economic and Political Weekly* 20, no. 43 (November 2, 1985): 885–87.

————. "Maharashtra: Fighting Drought." *Economic and Political Weekly* 21, no. 18 (May 3, 1986): 769–70.

Godbole, Madhav. *Public Expenditures in Maharashtra: A Case for Expenditure Strategy.* Bombay: Himalaya Publishing House, 1989.

Gomes, Lawrence. "Role of Voluntary and Other Organisations in Development." *Yojana* 33, no. 22 (December 1, 1989): 28–31.

Gopinath, P. Krishna. "Corruption in Political and Public Offices: Causes and Cure." *Indian Journal of Public Administration* 28, no. 4 (December 1982): 897–918.

Hanson, James A., and Samuel S. Lieberman. *India: Poverty, Employment, and Social Services.* Washington, D.C.: World Bank, 1989.

Heginbotham, Stanley. *Cultures in Conflict: Four Faces of Indian Bureaucracy.* New York: Columbia University Press, 1975.

Herring, Ronald J. *Land to the Tiller: The Political Economy of Agrarian Reform in South Asia.* New Haven, Conn.: Yale University Press, 1983.

Herring, Ronald J., and Rex M. Edwards. "Guaranteeing Employment to the Poor: Social Functions and Class Interests in the Employment Guarantee Scheme in Western India." *World Development* 11, no. 7 (July 1983): 575–92.

Heyneman, Stephen P. "Investment in Indian Education: Uneconomic?" *World Development* 8, no. 2 (February 1980): 145–63.

Hiraway, Indira. *Abolition of Poverty in India: With Special Reference to Target Group Approach in Gujarat.* Delhi: Vikas, 1986.

Jain, L. C. "Debates in the Voluntary Sector: Some Reflections." *Social Action* 36 (October 1986): 404–16.

Kakawani, N., and K. Subbarao. "Rural Poverty and Its Alleviation in India." *Economic and Political Weekly* 25, no. 13 (March 31, 1990): A2–A16.

Kamat, A. R. "Political Economic Developments in Maharashtra: A Review of the Post-Independence Era." *Economic and Political Weekly* 15, nos. 39 and 40 (September 27, 1980, and October 4, 1980): 1627–40, 1669–78. (Article was published under the same title in two consecutive issues of *EPW.*)

Kohli, Atul. *Democracy and Discontent: India's Growing Crisis of Governability.* Cambridge: Cambridge University Press, 1990.

———. "Democracy, Economic Growth, and Inequality in India's Development." *World Politics* 32, no. 4 (July 1980): 623–38.

———. "From Elite Activism to Democratic Consolidation: The Rise of Reform Communism in West Bengal." In *Dominance and State Power in Modern India: Decline of a Social Order,* ed. Francine R. Frankel and M. S. A. Rao, vol. 2, pp. 367–415. Delhi: Oxford University Press, 1990.

———. "Parliamentary Communism and Agrarian Reform: The Evidence from India's Bengal." *Asian Survey* 23 (July 1983): 783–809.

———. *The State and Poverty in India: The Politics of Reform.* Cambridge: Cambridge University Press, 1987.

Kothari, Rajni. "The Congress 'System' in India." *Asian Survey* 4, no. 12 (December 1964): 1161–73.

———. "Decline of Parties and the Rise of Grassroots Movements." In *State against Democracy,* ed. Rajni Kothari, p. 37–54. Delhi: Ajanta, 1988.

Kurien, C. T. "Reconciling Growth and Social Justice: Strategies versus Structure?" In *Asian Seminar on Rural Development: The Indian Experience,* ed. M. L. Dantwala, Ranjit Gupta, and Keith C. D'Souza, pp. 373–96. Delhi: Oxford University Press, 1986.

Lele, Jayant. "Caste, Class and Dominance: Political Mobilization in Maharashtra." In *Dominance and State Power in Modern India: Decline of a Social Order,* ed. Francine R. Frankel and M. S. A. Rao, pp. 115–211. Delhi: Oxford University Press, 1990.

———. "Chavan and the Political Integration of Maharashtra." In *Contemporary India: Socio-economic and Political Processes,* pp. 29–54. Poona: Continental Prakashan, 1982.

———. *Elite Pluralism and Class Rule: Political Development in Maharashtra.* Bombay: Popular Prakashan, 1981.

———. "One-Party Dominance in Maharashtra: Resilience and Change." In *State Politics in Contemporary India: Crisis or Continuity?* ed. John R. Wood, pp. 169–96. Boulder, Colo.: Westview Press, 1984.

Lieberman, Samuel S. "Field-Level Perspectives on Maharashtra's Employment Guarantee Scheme." *Public Administration and Development* 5, no. 2 (1985): 109–27.

———. "An Organisational Reconnaissance of the Employment Guarantee Scheme." *Indian Journal of Public Administration* 30, no. 4 (October 1984): 976–90.

Lieten, G. K. "Panchayat Leaders in a West Bengal District." *Economic and Political Weekly* 23, no. 40 (October 1, 1988): 2069–73.

Mallick, Ross. "Limits to Radical Intervention: Agricultural Taxation in West Bengal." *Development and Change* 21, no. 1 (January 1990): 147–64.

Mathews, George, ed. *Panchayati Raj in Karnataka Today.* New Delhi: Concept, 1985.

Mencher, Joan P. "The Lessons and Non-lessons of Kerala: Agricultural Labourers and Poverty." *Economic and Political Weekly* 15, special number (October 1980): 1781–1802.

Minhas, B. S. "Rural Poverty, Land Redistribution and Economic Development." *Indian Economic Review* 5, no. 1 (April 1970): 97–128.

Mishra, B. B. *District Administration and Rural Development in India.* Delhi: Oxford University Press, 1983.

Mitra, Ashok K. "Utilization Revisited: Surface Irrigation in Drought Prone Areas of Western Maharashtra." *Economic and Political Weekly* 21, no. 17 (April 26, 1986): 752–56.

Morris-Jones, W. H. *Politics Mainly Indian.* Madras: Orient Longman, 1978.

Mukhopadhyay, Asok K. *The Panchayat Administration in West Bengal.* Calcutta: World Press, 1980.

Myrdal, Gunnar. *Asian Drama.* 3 vols. New York: Twentieth Century Fund, 1968.

Nag, Moni. "Political Awareness as a Factor in Accessibility of Health Services: A Case Study of Rural Kerala and West Bengal." *Economic and Political Weekly* 24, no. 8 (February 25, 1989): 417–26.

Nossiter, T. J. *Marxist State Governments in India: Politics, Economics and Society.* London: Pinter, 1988.

Omvedt, Gail. "New Movements." *Seminar* 352 (December 1988): 39–44.

Owens, Raymond Lee, and Ashis Nandy. *The New Vaisyas: Entrepreneurial Opportunity and Response in an Indian City.* Durham, N.C.: Carolina Academic Press, 1978.

Political Organisational Report of the Eleventh Congress of the Communist Party of India (Marxist). Calcutta: Desraj Chadha, 1982.

Political Organisational Report of the Twelfth Congress of the Communist Party of India (Marxist). New Delhi: Hari Singh Kang, 1986.

Pulley, Robert V. *Making the Poor Creditworthy: A Case Study of the Integrated Rural Development Programs in India.* World Bank Discussion Paper 58. Washington, D.C.: World Bank, 1989.

Rath, Nilakantha. "Garibi Hatao: Can IRDP Do It?" *Economic and Political Weekly* 26, no. 6 (February 9, 1985): 238–46.

Rath, Nilakantha, and Ashok K. Mitra. "Economics of Utilization of Canal Water in Dry Agricultural Regions." *Indian Journal of Agricultural Economics* 41, no. 2 (April 1986): 131–40.

Rosenthal, Donald B. "Deurbanization, Elite Displacement and Political Changes in India." *Comparative Politics* 2 (January 1970): 1969–2001.

———. *The Expansive Elite.* Berkeley: University of California Press, 1977.

Rouyer, Alwyn R. "Political Capacity and the Decline of Fertility in India." *American Political Science Review* 81, no. 2 (June 1987): 453–70.

Roy, Ajit. "West Bengal: Pyrrhic Victory." *Economic and Political Weekly* 25 nos. 24 and 25 (June 16 and 23, 1990): 1293.

Rudolph, Lloyd I., and Susanne Hoeber Rudolph. *In Pursuit of Lakshmi: The Political Economy of the Indian State.* Chicago: University of Chicago Press, 1987.

Sathe, M. D. "Maharashtra: Social Basis of Sharing Irrigation Water, Central Issue in Well-Being of Poor." *Economic and Political Weekly* 21, no. 17 (April 26, 1986): 737–38.

Scott, James C. *Weapons of the Weak: Everyday Forms of Peasant Resistance.* New Haven, Conn.: Yale University Press, 1985.

Sen, Amartya. "Indian Development: Lessons and Non-Lessons." *Daedalus* 118, no. 4 (Fall 1989): 369–92.

Sengupta, Prasanta. "The Congress Party in West Bengal: Politics, Patronage and Power, 1947–1983." In *Politics in West Bengal,* ed. Rakhahari Chatterji, pp. 31–60. Calcutta: World Press, 1985.

Shiviah, M., K. B. Srivastava, and A. C. Jena. *Panchayati Raj Institutions in West Bengal, 1978: A Study of Institutions Building for Rural Development.* Hyderabad: National Institute for Rural Development, 1980.

Shrader, Lawrence L., and Ram Joshi. "Zilla Parishad Elections in Maharashtra and the District Political Elite." *Asian Survey* 3, no. 3 (March 1963): 143–55.

Subramanian, V. *Parched Earth: The Maharashtra Drought, 1970–73.* New Delhi: Orient Longman, 1975.

Swaminathan, Madhura. "Village Level Implementation of IRDP: Comparison of West Bengal and Tamil Nadu." *Economic and Political Weekly* 25, no. 13 (March 31, 1990): A17–A27.

Tandon, Rajesh. "The State and Voluntary Agencies in Asia." In *Doing Development: Government, NGOs and the Rural Poor in Asia,* ed. Richard Holloway, pp. 12–29. London: Earthscan Publications, 1989.

Taub, Richard P. *Bureaucrats under Stress.* Berkeley: University of California Press, 1969.

Tilak, Jandhyala B. G. *The Economics of Inequality in Education.* New Delhi: Sage, 1987.

Tiwari, R. K. *Rural Employment Programmes in India: The Implementation Process.* New Delhi: Indian Institute of Public Administration, 1990.

Vaidyanathan, A. "Agricultural Development and Rural Poverty." In *The Indian Economy: Recent Developments and Future Prospects,* ed. Robert E. G. Lucas and Gustav F. Papanek, pp. 77–90. Boulder, Colo.: Westview Press, 1988.

Wade, Robert. "The Market for Public Office: Why the Indian State Is Not Better at Development." *World Development* 13, no. 4 (1985): 467–97.

———. "The System of Administrative and Political Corruption: Land Irrigation in South India." *Journal of Development Studies* 18, no. 3 (April 1982): 287–328.

Walker, T. S., R. P. Singh, and M. Asokan. "Risk Benefits, Crop Insurance, and Dryland Agriculture." *Economic and Political Weekly* 21, nos. 25 and 26 (June 21–28, 1986): A81–A87.

Weiner, Myron. "Capitalist Agriculture and Rural Well-Being." In *The Indian Paradox: Essays in Indian Politics,* ed. Ashutosh Varshney, pp. 99–132. New Delhi: Sage, 1989.

———. *The Child and the State in India: Child Labor and Education Policy in Comparative Perspective.* Princeton, N.J.: Princeton University Press, 1991.

———. *Party Building in a New Nation: The Indian National Congress.* Chicago: University of Chicago Press, 1967.

———, ed. *State Politics in India.* Princeton, N.J.: Princeton University Press, 1968.

Westergaard, Kirsten. *People's Participation, Local Government and Rural De-*

velopment: The Case of West Bengal India. Copenhagen: Centre for Development Research, 1986.

"Who Pays for and Who Gains from EGS?" *Economic and Political Weekly* 17, no. 31 (July 31, 1982): 1226–28.

United States

Albertson, Dean. *Roosevelt's Farmer: Claude R. Wickard in the New Deal.* New York: Columbia University Press, 1961.

Alston, Lee J., and Joseph P. Ferrie. "Labor Costs, Paternalism, and Loyalty in Southern Agriculture: A Constraint on the Growth of the Welfare State." *Journal of Economic History* 45, no. 1 (March 1985): 95–118.

———. "Resisting the Welfare State: Southern Opposition to the Farm Security Administration." In *Emergence of the Modern Political Economy,* ed. Robert Higgs, pp. 83–120. Greenwich, Conn.: JAI Press, 1985.

Auerback, Jerold. "Southern Tenant Farmers: Socialist Critiques of the New Deal." *Labor History* 7 (Winter 1966): 3–18.

Baldwin, Sidney. *Poverty and Politics: The Rise and Decline of the Farm Security Administration.* Chapel Hill: University of North Carolina Press, 1968.

Banfield, Edward C. "Ten Years of the Farm Tenant Purchase Program." *Journal of Farm Economics* 31, no. 3 (August 1949): 469–86.

Benedict, Murray R. *Farm Policies of the United States, 1790–1950.* New York: Octagon Books, 1966.

Bensel, Richard Franklin. *Sectionalism and American Political Development.* Madison: University of Wisconsin Press, 1984.

Bonnen, James T. "Why Is There No Coherent U.S. Rural Policy?" *Policy Studies Journal* (forthcoming).

Brody, David. "The New Deal and World War II." In *The New Deal: The National Level,* ed. John Braeman, Robert H. Bremner, and David Brody, pp. 277–78. Columbus: Ohio State University Press, 1975.

Campbell, Christiana McFadyen. *The Farm Bureau and the New Deal.* Urbana: University of Illinois Press, 1962.

Conkin, Paul K. *Tomorrow a New World: The New Deal Community Program.* Ithaca, N.Y.: Cornell University Press, 1959.

Conrad, David Eugene. *The Forgotten Farmers: The Story of the Sharecroppers in the New Deal.* Urbana: University of Illinois Press, 1965.

Couto, Richard A. *Ain't Gonna Let Nobody Turn Me Around: The Pursuit of Racial Justice in the Rural South.* Philadelphia: Temple University Press, 1991.

Daniel, Pete. "The Transformation of the Rural South, 1930 to the Present." *Agricultural History* 55, no. 3 (July 1981): 321–49.

Dollard, John. *Caste and Class in a Southern Town.* New York: Doubleday, 1957.

Ferejohn, John. "Logrolling in an Institutional Context: A Case Study of Food Stamp Legislation." In *Congress and Policy Change,* ed. Gerald C. Write, Jr, Leroy N. Rieselbach, and Lawrence C. Dodd, pp. 223–53. New York: Agathon Press, 1986.

Finegold, Kenneth. "From Agrarianism to Adjustment: The Political Origins of New Deal Agricultural Policy." *Politics and Society* 11, no. 1 (1982): 1–27.

Fite, Gilbert C. "The Agricultural Trap in the South." *Agricultural History* 60, no. 4 (Fall 1986): 38–50.

———. *Cotton Fields No More: Southern Agriculture, 1865–1980.* Lexington: University of Kentucky Press, 1984.

Flynn, Charles L., Jr. *White Land, Black Labor: Caste and Class in Late Nineteenth-Century Georgia.* Baton Rouge: Louisiana State University Press, 1983.

Gilbert, Jess, and Carolyn Howe. "Beyond 'State vs. Society': Theories of the State and New Deal Agricultural Policies." *American Sociological Review* 56, no. 3 (April 1991): 204–20.

Grubbs, Donald H. *Cry from the Cotton: The Southern Tenant Farmers' Union and the New Deal.* Chapel Hill: University of North Carolina Press, 1971.

Hansen, John Mark. *Gaining Access: Congress and the Farm Lobby, 1919–1981.* Chicago: University of Chicago Press, 1991.

Henry, Mark, Mark Drabenstott, and Lynn Gibson. "A Changing Rural America." *Economic Review* 72, no. 1 (July 1985): 23–41.

Hoffsommer, Harold. "The AAA and the Cropper." *Social Forces* 13, no. 3 (March 1935): 494–500.

Holley, Donald. "The Negro in the New Deal Resettlement Programs." *Agricultural History* 45, no. 3 (July 1971): 179–93.

Hooks, Gregory. "From an Autonomous to a Captured State Agency: The Decline of the New Deal in Agriculture." *American Sociological Review* 55 (February 1990): 33–34.

Johnson, Charles S., Edwin Embree, and W. W. Alexander. *The Collapse of Cotton Tenancy.* Chapel Hill: University of North Carolina Press, 1935.

Johnson, Hugh. "The Cabinet: "Flop, Mess, Tangle." *Time,* November 11, 1935, p. 11.

Kerr, Norwood Allen. "Drafted into the War on Poverty: USDA Food and Nutrition Programs, 1961–1969." *Agricultural History* 64, no. 2 (Spring 1990): 154–68.

Key, V. O. *Southern Politics in State and Nation.* New York: Knopf, 1949.

Kile, Orville. *The Farm Bureau through Decades.* Baltimore: Waverly Press, 1948.

Kirby, Jack Temple. "The Transformation of Southern Plantations, c. 1920–1960." *Agricultural History* 57, no. 3 (July 1983): 257–76.

Kirkendall, Richard S. "The New Deal and Agriculture." In *The New Deal: The National Level,* ed. John Braeman, Robert H. Bremner, and David Brody, pp. 83–109. Columbus: Ohio State University Press, 1975.

———. *Social Scientists and Farm Politics in the Age of Roosevelt.* Columbia: University of Missouri Press, 1966.

Kousser, J. Morgan. *The Shaping of Southern Politics: Suffrage Restriction and the Establishment of the One-Party South, 1880–1910.* New Haven, Conn.: Yale University Press, 1974.

Lash, Joseph P. *Eleanor and Franklin.* New York: Norton, 1971.

Lord, Russell. *The Wallaces of Iowa.* Boston: Houghton Mifflin, 1947.

McConnell, Grant. *The Decline of Agrarian Democracy.* Berkeley: University of California Press, 1953.

————. *Private Power and American Democracy.* New York: Knopf, 1966.

MacMahon, Arthur W., John D. Millett, and Gladys Ogden. *The Administration of Federal Work Relief.* Chicago: Public Administration Service, 1941.

Maris, Paul V. "Policy Interpretation." *Rural Rehabilitation,* February 15, 1935, pp. 12–15.

Mertz, Paul E. *New Deal Policy and Southern Rural Poverty.* Baton Rouge: Louisiana State University Press, 1978.

Mowry, George E. *Ar. other Look at the Twentieth Century South.* Baton Rouge: Louisiana State University Press, 1973.

Myrdal, Gunnar. *An American Dilemma: The Negro Problem and Modern Democracy.* 2 vols. New York: Harper and Brothers, 1944.

Odum, Howard. *Southern Regions of the United States.* Chapel Hill: University of North Carolina Press, 1936.

O'Hare, William P. *Can the Underclass Concept Be Applied to Rural Areas?* Washington, D.C.: Population Reference Bureau, 1992.

————. *The Rise of Poverty In Rural America.* Washington, D.C.: Population Reference Bureau, 1988.

O'Hare, William P., and Brenda Curry-White. *The Rural Underclass: Examination of Multiple-Problem Populations in Urban and Rural Settings.* Washington, D.C.: Population Reference Bureau, 1992.

Patterson, James T. *Congressional Conservatism and the New Deal: The Growth of the Conservative Coalition in Congress, 1933–1939.* Lexington: University of Kentucky Press, 1967.

Peck, P. G., and James C. Jensen. "Contributions of Farm Security Borrowers to Agricultural Production Goals." *Journal of Farm Economics* 25 (February 1943): 101–10.

Polenberg, Richard. "The Decline of the New Deal, 1937–40." In *The New Deal: The National Level,* ed. John Braeman, Robert H. Bremner, and David Brody, pp. 246–66. Columbus: Ohio State University Press, 1974.

Roosevelt, Franklin D. *Public Papers and Addresses.* Vol. 1. New York: Random House, 1938.

Salamon, Lester M. "The Time Dimension in Policy Evaluation: The Case of the New Deal Land-Reform Experiments." *Public Policy* 27, no. 2 (Spring 1979): 129–83.

Schapsmeier, Edward L., and Frederick H. Schapsmeier. "Farm Policy from FDR to Eisenhower: Southern Democrats and the Politics of Agriculture." *Agricultural History* 53, no. 1 (January 1979): 352–71.

Schlesinger, Arthur M., Jr. *The Coming of the New Deal.* Vol. 3 of *The Age of Roosevelt.* Boston: Houghton Mifflin, 1959.

Skocpol, Theda, and Kenneth Finegold. "State Capacity and Economic Intervention in the Early New Deal." *Political Science Quarterly* 97, no. 2 (Summer 1982): 255–78.

Sterner, Richard. *The Negroes Share: A Study of Income Consumption, Housing and Public Assistance.* New York: Harper and Brothers, 1943.

Sternsher, Bernard. *Rexford Tugwell and the New Deal.* New Brunswick, N.J.: Rutgers University Press, 1964.

Taylor, Carl C., Helen W. Wheeler, and E. L. Kirkpatrick. *Disadvantaged Classes in American Agriculture.* Washington, D.C.: U.S. Government Printing Office, 1938.

Thomas, Norman, ed. *Plight of the Sharecropper.* New York: League for Industrial Democracy, 1933.

Tickamyer, Ann R., and Cynthia M. Duncan. "Poverty and Opportunity Structure in Rural America." *Annual Review of Sociology* 16 (1990): 67–86.

———. "Work and Poverty in Rural America." In *Rural Policies for the 1990s,* ed. Cornelia B. Flora and James A. Christenson, pp. 102–13. Boulder, Colo.: Westview Press, 1991.

Tindall, George Brown. "The 'Colonial Economy' and the Growth Psychology: The South in the 1930's." *South Atlantic Quarterly* 44 (Autumn 1965): 465–77.

———. *The Emergence of the New South, 1913–1945.* Baton Rouge: Louisiana State University Press, 1967.

Tontz, Robert L. "Memberships of General Farmers' Organizations, United States, 1874–1960." *Agricultural History* 38, no. 3 (July 1964): 143–56.

Tugwell, Rexford G. "Changing Acres." *Current History* 44, no. 6 (September 1936): 57–64.

———. "Cooperation and Resettlement." *Current History* 45 no. 5 (February 1937): 71–76.

———. "Down to Earth." *Current History* 44, no. 4 (July 1936): 33–38.

———, and E. C. Banfield. "Grass Roots Democracy—Myth or Reality?" *Public Administration Review* 10, no. 1 (1950): 47–55.

Vance, Rupert. *Human Geography of the South.* Chapel Hill: University of North Carolina Press, 1932.

Venkataramani, M. S. "Norman Thomas, Arkansas Sharecroppers, and the Roosevelt Agricultural Policies, 1933–1937." *Mississippi Valley Historical Review* 47, no. 2 (September 1960): 225–45.

Webb, Walter Prescott. *Divided We Stand: The Crisis of Frontierless Democracy.* New York: Farrar and Rinehart, 1937.

Westbrook, Lawrence. "The Program of Rural Rehabilitation of the FERA." *Journal of Farm Economics* 17, no. 1 (February 1935): 89–101.

Wilson, M. L. "How New Deal Agencies Are Affecting Family Life." *Journal of Home Economics* 27, no. 5 (1935): 274–80.

———. "Place of Subsistence Homesteads in Our National Economy." *Journal of Farm Economics* 16, no. 1 (January 1934): 73–84.

———. "Report on Land of the National Resources Board." *Journal of Farm Economics* 17, no. 1 (February 1935): 39–54.

Wolters, Raymond. *The Negroes and the Great Depression: The Problem of Economic Recovery.* Westport, Conn.: Greenwood Press, 1970.

———. "The New Deal and the Negro." In *The New Deal: The National Level,* ed. John Braeman, Robert H. Bremner, and David Brody, pp. 170–217. Columbus: Ohio State University Press, 1975.

Woodman, Harold D. "Post–Civil War Southern Agriculture and the Law." *Agricultural History* 53, no. 1 (January 1979): 319–37.

Woodward, C. Vann. *The Origins of the New South*. Baton Rouge: Louisiana State University Press, 1951.

Wright, Gavin. *Old South, New South: Revolutions in the Southern Economy since the Civil War*. New York: Basic Books, 1986.

NEWSPAPERS AND MAGAZINES

Amrita Bazar Patrika (Calcutta).
India Today.
Indian Express (Bombay).
The Illustrated Weekly of India
The Statesman (Calcutta).
The Telegraph (Calcutta).
Time (U.S.A.)
Times of India (Bombay).

THEORETICAL

Ackerloff, G. A. "The Market for 'Lemons': Qualitative Uncertainty and the Market Mechanism." *Quarterly Journal of Economics* 84, no. 3 (August 1970): 488–500.

Adams, Richard H., Jr. *Development and Social Change in Rural Egypt*. Syracuse, N.Y.: Syracuse University Press, 1986.

Adelman, Irma, and A. Levy. "The Equalizing Role of Human Resource Intensive Growth Strategies: A Theoretical Model." *Journal of Policy Modelling* 6, no. 2 (July 1984): 271–87.

Adelman, Irma, and Cynthia T. Morris. *Economic Growth and Social Equity in Developing Countries*. Palo Alto, Calif.: Stanford University Press, 1973.

Ahluwalia, Montek S. "Income Inequality: Some Dimensions of the Problem." In *Redistribution with Growth*, ed. Hollis Chenery et al. Oxford: Oxford University Press, 1974.

Amsden, Alice. *Asia's Next Giant: South Korea and Late Industrialization*. New York: Oxford University Press, 1989.

Anderson, Perry. *Lineages of the Absolutist State*. London: New Left Books, 1974.

Annis, Sheldon. "Can Small-Scale Development Be a Large-Scale Policy? The Case of Latin America." *World Development* 15, supp. (Autumn 1987): 129–34.

Appleby, Paul. *Big Democracy*. New York: Knopf, 1945.

Arrow, Kenneth. "The Economics of Agency." In *Principals and Agents*, ed. John Pratt and Richard Zeckhauser, pp. 37–51. Cambridge, Mass.: Harvard University Press, 1985.

Bacharach, Samuel B., and E. J. Lawler. *Power and Politics in Organizations*. San Francisco: Jossey-Bass, 1980.

Balassa, Bela. "Exports and Economic Growth: Further Evidence." *Journal of Development Economics* 5 (1978): 181–89.

Baldwin, Peter. *The Politics of Social Solidarity: Class Bases of the European Welfare State, 1875–1975.* Cambridge: Cambridge University Press, 1990.

Banfield, Edward. "Corruption as a Feature of Governmental Organization." *Journal of Law and Economics* 18 (1975): 587–605.

Barber, Benjamin. *Strong Democracy: Participatory Politics for a New Age.* Berkeley: University of California Press, 1984.

Bardach, Eugene. *The Implementation Game: What Happens after a Bill Becomes a Law.* Cambridge, Mass.: MIT Press, 1977.

Bardhan, Pranab. "Alternative Approaches to the Theories of Institutions in Economic Development." In *The Economic Theory of Agrarian Institutions,* ed. Pranab Bardhan, pp. 3–17. Oxford: Clarendon Press, 1989.

Bates, Robert H. *Beyond the Miracle of the Market: The Political Economy of Agrarian Change in Kenya.* Cambridge: Cambridge University Press, 1989.

Bates, Robert H., and Da-Hsiang Donald Lien. "A Note on Taxation, Development and Representative Government." *Politics and Society* 14, no. 1 (1985): 53–70.

Bell, Robert. *The Culture of Policy Deliberations.* New Brunswick, N.J.: Rutgers University Press, 1985.

Bendix, Reinhard. *Kings or People: Power and the Mandate to Rule.* Berkeley: University of California Press, 1978.

Bendor, Jonathan, Serge Taylor, and Roland Van Gaalen. "Stacking the Deck: Bureaucratic Missions and Policy Design." *American Political Science Review* 81, no. 3 (September 1987): 873–96.

Benson, J. Kenneth. "The Interorganizational Network as a Political Economy." *Administrative Science Quarterly* 20, no. 2 (June 1975): 229–49.

Berreman, Gerald D. "Caste in India and the United States." *American Journal of Sociology* 66, no. 2 (September 1966): 120–27.

Binder, Leonard. *In a Moment of Enthusiasm: Political Power and the Second Stratum in Egypt.* Chicago: University of Chicago Press, 1978.

Binder, Leonard, et al., eds. *Crises and Sequences in Political Development.* Princeton, N.J.: Princeton University Press, 1971.

Boje, David M., and David A. Whetten. "Effects of Organizational Strategies and Contextual Constraints on Centrality and Attributions of Influence in Interorganizational Networks." *Administrative Science Quarterly* 26, no. 3 (September 1981): 378–95.

Bowman, John R. "Transaction Costs and Politics." *Archives Européennes de Sociologie* 30 (1989): 150–68.

Bozeman, Barry. *All Organizations Are Public.* San Francisco: Jossey-Bass, 1987.

Bozeman, Barry, and Jeffrey D. Straussman. "'Publicness' and Resource Management Strategies." In *Organizational Theory and Public Policy,* ed. Richard H. Hall and Robert E. Quinn, pp. 75–91. Beverly Hills, Calif.: Sage, 1983.

Burgess, Robin, and Nicholas Stern. "Social Security in Developing Countries:

What, Why, Who and How?" In *Social Security in Developing Countries,* ed. Etisham Ahmad et al., pp. 41–80. Oxford: Clarendon Press, 1991.

Burstein, Paul. "Policy Domains: Organization, Culture and Policy Outcomes." *Annual Review of Sociology* 16 (1991): 327–50.

Burt, Ronald S. "Autonomy in a Social Typology." *American Journal of Sociology* 85, no. 4 (January 1980): 892–923.

———. *Toward a Structural Theory of Social Action.* New York: Academic Press, 1982.

Calder, Kent E. *Crisis and Compensation: Public Policy and Political Stability in Japan, 1949–1986.* Princeton, N.J.: Princeton University Press, 1988.

Caldwell, John C. "Routes to Low Mortality in Poor Countries." *Population and Development Review* 12, no. 2 (June 1986): 171–220.

Child, John. "Organizational Structure, Environment and Performance: The Role of Strategic Choice." *Sociology* 6, no. 1 (January 1972): 1–22.

Chubb, John E. *Interest Groups and the Bureaucracy: The Politics of Energy.* Stanford, Calif.: Stanford University Press, 1983.

Cook, Karen S., and Richard M. Emerson. "Exchange Networks and the Analysis of Complex Organizations." In *Research in the Sociology of Organizations,* vol. 3, pp. 1–30. Greenwich, Conn.: JAI Press, 1984.

Cook, Karen S., and Margaret Levi, eds. *The Limits of Rationality.* Chicago: University of Chicago Press, 1990.

Cornelius, Wayne A. "Nation Building, Participation, and Distribution: The Politics of Social Reform under Cárdenas." In *Crisis, Choice, and Change: Historical Studies of Political Development,* ed. Gabriel Almond, Scott C. Flanagan, and Robert J. Mundt, pp. 392–498. Boston: Little, Brown, 1973.

Cox, Oliver Cromwell. *Caste, Class, and Race: A Study in Social Dynamics.* Garden City, N.Y.: Doubleday, 1948.

Crozier, Michel. *The Bureaucratic Phenomenon.* Chicago: University of Chicago Press, 1964.

Crozier, Michel, and Erhard Friedberg. *Actors and Systems,* trans. Arthur Goldhammer. Chicago: University of Chicago Press, 1980.

Dahl, Robert. *Polyarchy.* New Haven, Conn.: Yale University Press, 1971.

Davis, Stanley M. and Paul R. Lawrence. *Matrix.* Reading, MA: Addison Wesley, 1977.

Deavers, Kenneth L., and Robert A. Hoppe. "The Rural Poor: The Past as Prologue." In *Rural Policies for the 1990s,* ed. Cornelia B. Flora and James A. Christenson, pp. 85–101. Boulder, Colo.: Westview Press, 1991.

Demski, J. *Information Analysis.* Reading, Mass.: Addison-Wesley, 1980.

DiMaggio, Paul J. "Interest and Agency in Institutional Theory." In *Institutional Patterns and Organizations: Culture and Environment,* ed. Lynne G. Zucker, pp. 3–21. Cambridge, Mass.: Ballinger, 1988.

DiMaggio, Paul J., and Walter W. Powell. "The Iron Cage Revisited: Institutional Isomorphism and Collective Rationality in Organizational Fields." *American Sociological Review* 48, no. 1 (April 1983): 147–60.

Dreze, Jean, and Amartya Sen. *Hunger and Public Action.* Oxford: Clarendon Press, 1989.

Dumont, Louis. *Homo Hierarchus,* trans. Mark Sainsbury, Louis Dumont, and Basia Gulati. Chicago: University of Chicago Press, 1980.

Eisenhardt, Kathleen M. "Agency Theory: An Assessment and Review." *Academy of Management Review* 14, no. 1 (1989): 57–74.

Elster, Jon. *The Cement of Society: A Study of Social Order.* Cambridge: Cambridge University Press, 1989.

Esman, Milton J., and Norman T. Uphoff. *Local Organizations: Intermediaries in Rural Development.* Ithaca, N.Y.: Cornell University Press, 1984.

Esping-Andersen, Gøsta. *Politics against Markets: The Social Democratic Road to Power.* Princeton, N.J.: Princeton University Press, 1985.

———. "Single-Party Dominance in Sweden: The Saga of Social Democracy." In *Uncommon Democracies: The One-Party Dominant Regimes,* ed. T. J. Pempel, pp. 33–57. Ithaca, N.Y.: Cornell University Press, 1990.

———. *The Three Worlds of Welfare Capitalism.* Princeton, N.J.: Princeton University Press, 1990.

Evans, Peter B. "Predatory, Developmental and Other Apparatuses: A Comparative Political Economy Perspective on the Third World State." *Sociological Forum* 4, no. 4 (1989): 561–87.

———. "The State as Problem and Solution: Predation, Embedded Autonomy, and Structural Change." In *The Politics of Economic Adjustment: International Constraints, Distributive Conflicts, and the State,* ed. Stephan Haggard and Robert Kaufman, pp. 139–81. Princeton, N.J.: Princeton University Press, 1992.

Evans, Peter B., Dietrich Rueschemeyer, and Theda Skocpol, eds. *Bringing the State Back In.* Cambridge: Cambridge University Press, 1985.

Feldman, Martha S., and James G. March. "Information in Organizations as Signal and Symbol." *Administrative Science Quarterly* 26, no. 2 (June 1981): 171–86.

Ferejohn, John. "Rationality and Interpretation: Parliamentary Elections in Early Stuart England." In *The Economic Approach to Politics,* ed. Kirsten R. Monroe, pp. 279–305. New York: HarperCollins, 1991.

Fields, Gary S. *Poverty, Inequality and Development.* Cambridge: Cambridge University Press, 1980.

Foucault, Michel. "The Subject and Power." In *Michel Foucault: Beyond Structuralism and Hermeneutics,* ed. Hubert L. Dreyfus and Paul Rabinow, pp. 208–26. Chicago: University of Chicago Press, 1983.

Franda, Marcus. *Political Development and Political Decay.* Calcutta: Firma K. L. Mukhopadhyay, 1971.

Freire, Paulo. *Education for Critical Consciousness.* New York: Seabury Press, 1973.

———. *Pedagogy of the Oppressed.* New York: Herder and Herder, 1970.

Friedland, Roger, and Robert R. Alford. "Bringing Society Back in: Symbol, Practices, and Institutional Contradictions." In *The New Institutionalism in Organizational Analysis,* ed. Walter W. Powell and Paul J. DiMaggio, pp. 232–63. Chicago: University of Chicago Press, 1991.

Galbraith, Jay R. "Matrix Organization Designs: How to Combine Functional and Project Forms." *Business Horizons* 14, no. 1 (1971): 29–40.

————. *Organizational Design*. Reading, Mass.: Addison-Wesley, 1977.

Geddes, Barbara. "Building 'State' Autonomy in Brazil, 1930–1964," *Comparative Politics* 22, no. 2 (January 1990): 217–35.

————. "A Game Theoretic Model of Reform in Latin American Democracies." *American Political Science Review* 85, no. 2 (June 1991): 371–92.

Gereffi, Gary, and Donald L. Wyman, eds. *Manufacturing Miracles*. Princeton, N.J.: Princeton University Press, 1990.

Goggin, Malcolm, et al. *Implementation Theory and Practice: Toward a Third Generation*. Glenview, Ill.: Scott, Foresman, 1990.

Goulet, Denis. "Participation in Development: New Avenues." *World Development* 17, no. 2 (February 1989): 165–78.

Gourevitch, Peter. "Keynesian Politics: The Political Sources of Economic Policy Choices." In *The Political Power of Keynesian Ideas: Keynesianism across Nations*, ed. Peter A. Hall, pp. 87–106. Princeton, N.J.: Princeton University Press, 1989.

————. *Politics in Hard Times: Comparative Responses to International Economic Crisis*. Ithaca, N.Y.: Cornell University Press, 1986.

Grafstein, Robert. *Institutional Realism: Social and Political Constraints on Rational Actors*. New Haven, Conn.: Yale University Press, 1992.

————. "The Problem of Institutional Constraint." *Journal of Politics* 50, no. 3 (August 1988): 577–99.

Gran, Guy. *Development by People: Citizen Construction of a Just World*. New York: Praeger, 1983.

Grew, Raymond, ed. *Crises of Political Development in Europe and the United States*. Princeton, N.J.: Princeton University, 1978.

Grindle, Merilee S. *Bureaucrats, Politicians, and Peasants in Mexico*. Berkeley: University of California Press, 1977.

————. *State and Countryside: Development Policy and Agrarian Politics in Latin America*. Baltimore: Johns Hopkins University Press, 1986.

Haggard, Stephan. *Pathways from the Periphery: The Politics of Growth in Newly Industrializing Countries*. Ithaca, N.Y.: Cornell University Press, 1990.

Hall, Peter A. "Conclusion: The Politics of Keynesian Ideas." In *The Political Power of Keynesian Ideas: Keynesianism across Nations*, ed. Peter A. Hall, pp. 361–91. Princeton, N.J.: Princeton University Press, 1989.

————. *Governing the Economy: The Politics of State Intervention in Britain and France*. New York: Oxford University Press, 1986.

Hamilton, Nora. *The Limits of State Autonomy: Post-Revolutionary Mexico*. Princeton, N.J.: Princeton University Press, 1982.

Hardin, Russell. "Groups in the Regulation of Collective Bads." In *Public Choice*, ed. Gordon Tullock, pp. 91–102. New Orleans: Public Choice Society, 1980.

Heclo, Hugh. "Issue Networks and the Executive Establishment." In *The New American Political System*, ed. Anthony King, pp. 87–124. Washington, D.C.: American Enterprise Institute, 1978.

————. *Modern Social Politics in Britain and Sweden*. New Haven, Conn.: Yale University Press, 1974.

Herriott, S. R., D. Levinthal, and J. G. March. "Learning from Experience in Organizations." *American Economic Review* 75, no. 2 (1985): 298–302.

Hickson, D. J., et al. "A Strategic Contingencies Theory of Intraorganizational Power." *Administrative Science Quarterly* 19, no. 1 (March 1974): 45–59.

Higgot, Richard A. *Political Development Theory.* London: Croom Helm, 1983.

Hinings, Bob, and Royston Greenwood. "The Normative Prescription of Organizations." In *Institutional Patterns and Organizations: Culture and Environment,* ed. Lynne G. Zucker, pp. 53–70. Cambridge, Mass.: Ballinger, 1988.

Hirschman, Albert O. "Policy Making and Policy Analysis in Latin America: A Return Journey." *Policy Science* 6, no. 4 (1975): 385–402.

———. *Shifting Involvements: Private Interests and Public Action.* Princeton, N.J.: Princeton University Press, 1982.

Huntington, Samuel P. "The Goals of Development." In *Understanding Political Development,* ed. Myron Weiner and Samuel P. Huntington, pp. 3–32. Boston: Little, Brown, Company, 1987.

———. *Political Order in Changing Societies.* New Haven, Conn.: Yale University Press, 1968.

Jacobs, David. "Corporate Economic Power and the State: A Longitudinal Assessment of Two Explanations." *American Journal of Sociology* 93, no. 4 (January 1988): 852–81.

Jenkins, Craig. "Resource Mobilization Theory and the Study of Social Movements." *Annual Review of Sociology* 9 (1983): 527–53.

Jervis, Robert. *Perception and Misperception in International Politics.* Princeton, N.J.: Princeton University Press, 1976.

Jessop, Bob. *State Theory: Putting Capitalist States in Their Place.* University Park: Pennsylvania State University Press, 1990.

Katznelson, Ira. "Rethinking the Silences of Social and Economic Policy." *Political Science Quarterly* 101, no. 2 (1986): 307–25.

Keane, John. *Democracy and Civil Society.* London: Verso, 1988.

Kingdon, John W. *Agendas, Alternatives, and Public Policies.* Boston: Little, Brown, 1984.

Kitschelt, Herbert. "Political Opportunity Structures and Political Protest: Anti-Nuclear Movements in Four Democracies." *British Journal of Political Science* 16, no. 1 (January 1986): 57–85.

Korpi, Walter. "Social Policy and Distributional Conflict in the Capitalist Democracies: A Preliminary Comparative Framework." *West European Politics* 3 (October 1980): 296–315.

Korten, David C. "Community Organization and Rural Development: A Learning Process Approach." *Public Administration Review* 40, no. 5 (September–October 1980): 480–501.

———. "Social Development: Putting People First." In *Bureaucracy and the Poor,* ed. David C. Korten and Felip B. Alfonso, pp. 201–21. Singapore: McGraw-Hill International, 1981.

Kothari, Rajni. "NGO's, the State and World Capitalism." *Economic and Political Weekly* 21, no. 50 (December 13, 1986): 2177–82.

Krasner, Stephen D. "Approaches to the State: Alternative Conceptions and Historical Dynamics." *Comparative Politics* 16, no. 2 (January 1984): 223–46.

———. "Sovereignty: An Institutional Perspective." *Comparative Political Studies* 21, no. 1 (April 1988): 66–94.

Krueger, Anne. "The Political Economy of the Rent Seeking Society." *American Economic Review* 64, no. 3 (June 1974): 291–303.

LaPalombara, Joseph, and Myron Weiner. "The Origin and Development of Political Parties." In *Political Parties and Political Development,* ed. Joseph LaPalombara and Myron Weiner, pp. 3–42. Princeton, N.J.: Princeton University Press, 1966: 3–42.

Laski, Harold J. *A Grammar of Politics.* London: Allen and Unwin, 1960.

Laumann, Edward O., and David Knoke. *The Organizational State.* Madison: University of Wisconsin Press, 1987.

Lawler, Edward J., and Samuel B. Bacharach. "Political Action and Alignments in Organizations." *Research in the Sociologiy of Organizations,* vol. 2, pp. 83–107. Greenwich, Conn.: JAI Press, 1983.

Lawrence, Paul R., and Jay W. Lorsch. *Organizations and Environment: Managing Differentiation and Integration.* Boston: Graduate School of Business Administration, Harvard University, 1967.

Lebow, Richard Ned. *Between Peace and War: The Nature of International Crisis.* Baltimore: Johns Hopkins University Press, 1981.

Levi, Margaret. *Of Rule and Revenue.* Berkeley: University of California Press, 1988.

Levinthal, Daniel. "A Survey of Agency Models of Organizations." *Journal of Economic Behavior and Organization* 9 (1988): 153–85.

Levitt, Barbara, and James G. March. "Organizational Learning." *Annual Review of Sociology* 14 (1988): 319–40.

Lindblom, Charles E. *Politics and Markets.* New York: Basic Books, 1977.

Lipsky, Michael. *Street-Level Bureaucracy.* New York: Russell Sage Foundation, 1980.

Lipton, Michael. *Why Poor People Stay Poor: Urban Bias in World Development.* Cambridge, Mass.: Harvard University Press, 1977.

Little, Ian. "An Economic Reconnaissance." In *Economic Growth and Structural Change in Taiwan,* ed. Walter Galenson, pp. 448–507. Ithaca, N.Y.: Cornell University Press, 1979.

Loomis, Burdett A. "Coalitions of Interests: Building Bridges in a Balkanized State." In *Interest Group Politics,* 2nd ed., ed. Allan J. Cigler and Burdett A. Loomis, pp. 258–74. Washington, D.C.: Congressional Studies Quarterly, 1986.

Lowi, Theodore J. *The End of Liberalism.* New York: Norton, 1969.

Lynn, L. E. *Managing the Public's Business.* New York: Basic Books, 1981.

McAdam, Doug. *Political Process and the Development of Black Insurgency, 1930–1970.* Chicago: University of Chicago Press, 1982.

McCarthy, John D., and Mayer N. Zald. *The Trend of Social Movements in America: Professionalization and Resource Mobilization.* Morristown, N.J.: General Learning Corporation, 1973.

MacRae, Douglas. *Policy Indicators.* Chapel Hill: University of North Carolina Press, 1985.

Majone, Giodominco, and Aaron Wildavsky. "Implementation as Evolution." In *Policy Studies Review Annual,* ed. Howard E. Freeman, pp. 103–17. Beverly Hills, Calif.: Sage, 1978.

Mann, Michael. "The Autonomous Power of the State: Its Origins, Mechanisms and Results." *Archives Européenes de Sociologie* 25, no. 2 (1984): 185–213.

March, James G. "Bounded Rationality, Ambiguity and the Engineering of Choice." *Bell Journal of Economics* 9 (Autumn 1978): 587–608.

March, James G., and Johan P. Olsen. "The New Institutionalism: Organizational Factors in Political Life." *American Political Science Review* 78, no. 3 (September 1984): 734–49.

———. *Rediscovering Institutions: The Organizational Basis of Politics.* New York: Free Press, 1989.

Maris, Paul V. "Policy Interpretation." *Rural Rehabilitation* (February 15, 1935): 12–15.

Marx, Karl. *The Eighteenth Brumaire of Louis Bonaparte.* New York: International Publishers, 1963. (Originally published in 1852.)

———. "On the Jewish Question." In *Karl Marx: Early Writings,* trans. Rodney Livingstone and Gregor Benton, pp. 212–41. New York: Vintage, 1975. (Originally published in 1843.)

Melucci, Alberto. *Nomads of the Present.* Philadelphia: Temple University Press, 1988.

Meyer, John W. "Centralization of Funding and Control in Educational Governance." In *Organizational Environments,* ed. John W. Meyer and W. Richard Scott, pp. 179–98. Beverly Hills, Calif.: Sage, 1983.

———. "The World Polity and the Authority of the Nation-State." In *Institutional Structure: Constituting State, Society and the Individual,* ed. George M. Thomas et al., pp. 41–70. Newbury Park, Calif.: Sage, 1987.

Meyer, John, John Boli, and George M. Thomas. "Ontology and Rationalization in the Western Cultural Account." In *Institutional Structure: Constituting State, Society and the Individual,* ed. George M. Thomas et al., pp. 12–37. Newbury Park, Calif.: Sage, 1987.

Meyer, John W., and Brian Rowan. "Institutionalized Organizations: Formal Structure as Myth and Ceremony." *American Journal of Sociology* 83, no. 2 (September 1977): 340–63.

Meyer, John W., and W. Richard Scott, eds. *Organizational Environments: Ritual and Rationality.* Beverly Hills, Calif.: Sage, 1983.

Michels, Robert. *Political Parties.* New York: Free Press, 1962.

Migdal, Joel. *Strong Societies and Weak States: State-Society Relations and State Capabilities in the Third World.* Princeton, N.J.: Princeton University Press, 1988.

Mill, John Stuart. *Considerations on Representative Government.* Indianapolis: Bobbs-Merrill, 1961. (Originally published in 1861.)

Moe, Terry. "The New Economics of Organization." *American Journal of Political Science* 28, no. 4 (November 1984): 739–77.

———. "The Politics of Bureaucratic Structure." In *Can the Government Govern?* ed. John E. Chubb and Paul E. Peterson, pp. 267–329. Washington, D.C.: Brookings Institution, 1989.

———. "The Politics of Structural Choice: Toward a Theory of Public Bureaucracy." In *Organization Theory: From Chester Barnard to the Present and Beyond,* ed. Oliver E. Williamson, pp. 116–53. New York: Oxford University Press, 1990.

Moley, Raymond. *Twenty-Seven Masters of Politics.* New York: Funk and Wagnalls, 1949.

Montgomery, John D. *Bureaucrats and People: Grassroots Participation in Third World Development.* Baltimore: Johns Hopkins University Press, 1988.

Montjoy, Robert S., and Laurence J. O'Toole, Jr. "Toward a Theory of Policy Implementation: An Organizational Perspective." *Public Administration Review* 39, no. 5 (September 1979): 455–76.

Muramatsu, Michio, and Ellis S. Krauss. "The Conservative Policy Line and the Development of Patterned Pluralism." In *The Political Economy of Japan,* ed. Kozo Yamamura and Yasukichi Yasuba, vol. 1, pp. 516–54. Stanford, Calif.: Stanford University Press, 1987.

———. "The Dominant Party and Social Coalitions in Japan." In *Uncommon Democracies: The One-Party Dominant Regimes,* ed. T. J. Pempel, pp. 282–305. Ithaca, N.Y.: Cornell University Press, 1990.

Nas, Tevfik F., Albert C. Price, and Charles T. Weber. "A Policy Oriented Theory of Corruption." *American Political Science Review* 80, no. 1 (March 1986): 107–20.

Nelson, Joan M. "Political Participation." In *Understanding Political Development,* ed. Myron Weiner and Samuel P. Huntington, pp. 103–59. Boston: Little, Brown, 1987.

Nordlinger, Eric A. "Taking the State Seriously." In *Understanding Political Development,* ed. Myron Weiner and Samuel P. Huntington, pp. 353–90. Boston: Little, Brown, 1987.

North, Douglass C. *Institutions, Institutional Change and Economic Performance.* Cambridge: Cambridge University Press, 1990.

Offe, Claus. "The Divergent Rationalities of Administrative Action." In *Disorganized Capitalism,* ed. John Keane, pp. 300–316. Cambridge, Mass.: MIT Press, 1985.

———. "The Theory of the Capitalist State and the Problem of Policy Formation." In *Stress and Contradiction in Modern Capitalism,* ed. Leon N. Lindberg et al., pp. 125–43. Lexington, Mass.: Heath, 1975.

Olzak, Susan. "Analysis of Events in the Study of Collective Action." *Annual Review of Sociology* 15 (1989): 119–41.

Osmani, S. R. "Social Security in Asia." In *Social Security in Developing Countries,* ed. Etisham Ahmad et al., pp. 305–55. Oxford: Clarendon Press, 1991.

O'Toole, Laurence J., Jr., and Robert S. Montjoy. "Interorganizational Policy Implementation: A Theoretical Perspective." *Public Administration Review* 44, no. 6 (November 1984): 491–503.

298 Works Cited

Ouchi, William G. "Markets, Bureaucracies and Clans." *Administrative Science Quarterly* 25, no. 1 (March 1980): 129–41.

Panebianco, Angelo. *Political Parties: Organization and Power.* Cambridge: Cambridge University Press, 1988.

Pateman, Carol. *Participation and Democratic Theory.* Cambridge: Cambridge University Press, 1970.

Pempel, T. J. "Introduction." In *Uncommon Democracies: The One-Party Dominant Regimes,* ed. T. J. Pempel, pp. 1–32. Ithaca, N.Y.: Cornell University Press, 1990.

Perrow, Charles. "Economic Theories of Organization." *Theory and Society* 15, nos. 1–2 (1986): 11–45.

———. "Markets, Hierarchies and Hegemony: A Critique of Chandler and Williamson." In *Perspectives on Organization Design and Behavior,* ed. Andrew Van De Ven and William Joyce, pp. 371–90. New York: Wiley Interscience, 1981.

Peters, B. Guy. "Bureaucracy, Politics, and Public Policy." *Comparative Politics* 11, no. 3 (April 1979): 339–58.

Pettigrew, Andrew M. "Information Control as a Power Resource." *Sociology* 6, no. 2 (May 1972): 187–204.

Pfeffer, Jeffrey. *Power in Organizations.* Marshfield, Mass.: Pitman, 1981.

Pfeffer, Jeffrey, and Gerald R. Salancik. *The External Control of Organizations: A Resource Dependence Perspective.* New York: Harper and Row, 1978.

Poggi, Gianfranco. *The Development of the Modern State: A Sociological Introduction.* Palo Alto, Calif.: Stanford University Press, 1978.

Pontusson, Jonas. "Conditions of Labor Dominance: Sweden and Britain Compared." In *Uncommon Democracies: The One-Party Dominant Regimes,* ed. T. J. Pempel, pp. 58–82. Ithaca, N.Y.: Cornell University Press, 1990.

Powell, Walter W., and Paul J. DiMaggio, eds. *The New Institutionalism in Organizational Analysis.* Chicago: University of Chicago Press, 1991.

Pratt, John, and Richard Zeckhauser, eds. *Principals and Agents.* Cambridge, Mass.: Harvard University Press, 1985.

Pressman, Jeffrey L., and Aaron B. Wildavsky. *Implementation.* Berkeley: University of California Press, 1973.

Ram, Rati, and Theodore W. Schultz, "Life Span, Health, Savings, and Productivity." *Economic Development and Cultural Change* 27, no. 3 (April 1979): 399–421.

Ramirez, Francisco O. "Institutional Analysis." In *Institutional Structure: Constituting State, Society and the Individual,* ed. George M. Thomas et al., pp. 316–28. Newbury Park, Calif.: Sage, 1987.

Ranis, Gustav. "Industrial Development." In *Economic Growth and Structural Change in Taiwan,* ed. Walter Galenson, pp. 206–62. Ithaca, N.Y.: Cornell University Press, 1979.

Ritti, Richard, and Jonathan H. Silver. "Early Processes of Institutionalization: The Dramaturgy of Exchange in Interorganizational Relations." *Administrative Science Quarterly* 31, no. 1 (March 1986): 25–42.

Rosenberry, Sara A. "Social Insurance: Distributive Criteria and the Welfare

Backlash: A Comparative Analysis." *British Journal of Political Science* 12 (1982): 421–47.

Rosenthal, Donald B. *The Expansive Elite.* Berkeley: University of California Press, 1977.

Rothstein, Bo. "Marxism, Institutional Analysis, and Working-Class Power: The Swedish Case." *Politics and Society* 18, no. 3 (1990): 317–45.

Rowan, Brian. "Organizational Structure and Institutional Environment: The Case of Public Schools." *Administrative Science Quarterly* 27 (1982): 259–87.

Rundquist, Barry S., Gerald S. Strom, and John G. Peters. "Corrupt Politicians and Their Electoral Support." *American Political Science Review* 71, no. 3 (September 1977): 954–63.

Rueschemeyer, Dietrich, and Peter B. Evans, "The State and Economic Transformation: Toward an Analysis of the Conditions underlying Effective Intervention." In *Bringing the State Back In,* ed. Peter B. Evans, Dietrich Rueschemeyer, and Theda Skocpol, pp. 44–77. Cambridge: Cambridge University Press, 1985.

Sabatier, Paul. "An Advocacy Coalition Framework of Policy Change and the Role of Policy-Oriented Learning Therein." *Policy Sciences* 21 (Fall 1988): 129–68.

———. "Social Movements and Regulatory Agencies." *Policy Sciences* 6, no. 3 (1975): 301–42.

———. "Towards Better Theories of Policy Process." *PS: Political Science and Politics* 24, no. 2 (1991): 147–56.

Salancik, Gerald R. "An Index of Subgroups' Influence in Dependency Networks." *Administrative Science Quarterly* 31, no. 2 (June 1986): 194–211.

Salisbury, Robert H. "An Exchange Theory of Collective Action." In *Interest Group Politics in America,* ed. Robert H. Salisbury, pp. 332–67. New York: Harper and Row, 1970.

———. "The Paradox of Interest Groups in Washington—More Groups, Less Clout." In *The New American Political System,* 2nd ed., ed. Anthony King, pp. 203–30. Washington, D.C.: AEI Press, 1990.

Samuels, Richard J. *The Business of the Japanese State.* Ithaca, N.Y.: Cornell University Press, 1987.

Schultz, Theodore W. *Investing in People: The Economics of Population Quality.* Berkeley: University of California Press, 1981.

———. *Investment in Human Capital: The Role of Education and of Research.* New York: Free Press, 1971.

———. "Reflections on Poverty within Agriculture." *Journal of Political Economy* 58 (February 1950): 1–15.

———. *Restoring Economic Equilibrium: Human Capital in the Modernizing Economy.* Cambridge, Mass.: Blackwell, 1990.

———. *Transforming Traditional Agriculture.* New Haven, Conn.: Yale University Press, 1964.

Scott, James C. *Comparative Political Corruption.* Englewood Cliffs, N.J.: Prentice-Hall, 1972.

Scott, W. Richard. "The Adolescence of Institutional Theory." *Administrative Science Quarterly* 32 (1987): 493–511.

———. "Introduction: From Technology to Environment." In *Organizational Environments: Ritual and Rationality*, ed. John W. Meyer and W. Richard Scott, pp. 13–17. Beverly Hills, Calif.: Sage, 1983.

———. "The Organization of Environments: Network, Cultural and Historical Elements." In *Organizational Environments: Ritual and Rationality*, ed. John W. Meyer and W. Richard Scott, pp. 165–75, Beverly Hills, Calif.: Sage, 1983.

Selznick, Philip. *Leadership and Administration*. Evanston, Ill.: Row, Peterson, 1957.

———. *TVA and the Grass Roots*. Berkeley: University of California Press, 1980; reprint of 1949 ed.

Sen, Amartya. *Commodities and Capabilities*. Amsterdam: Elsevier, 1985.

———. "Development: Which Way Now?" In *Resources, Values and Development*, ed. Amartya Sen, pp. 485–508. Cambridge, Mass.: Harvard University Press, 1984.

———. *On Ethics and Economics*. Oxford: Blackwell, 1987.

———. *Poverty and Famines*. Oxford: Clarendon Press, 1981.

———. *Resources, Values and Development*. Cambridge, Mass.: Harvard University Press, 1984.

Shefter, Martin, "The Emergence of the Political Machine: An Alternative View," in *Theoretical Perspectives on Urban Politics*, ed. Willis Hawley and Michael Lipsky, 14–44, Englewood Cliffs, N.J.: Prentice-Hall, 1976.

———. "Party, Bureaucracy, and Political Change in the United States." In *Political Parties: Development and Decay*, ed. Louis Maisel and Joseph Cooper, pp. 211–65. Beverly Hills, Calif.: Sage, 1978.

Shepsle, Kenneth, and Barry Weingast. "Why Are Congressional Committees Powerful?" *American Political Science Review* 81, no. 3 (September 1977): 935–45.

Shweder, Richard A. *Thinking through Cultures: Expeditions in Cultural Psychology*. Cambridge, Mass.: Harvard University Press, 1991.

Simon, Herbert. *Administrative Behavior*. 2nd ed. New York: Macmillan, 1961.

———. "Human Nature in Politics: The Dialogue of Psychology with Political Science." *American Political Science Review* 79, no. 2 (June 1985): 293–304.

———. *Models of Man*. New York: Wiley, 1957.

Skocpol, Theda. "Bringing the State Back In." In *Bringing the State Back In*, ed. Peter B. Evans, Dietrich Rueschemeyer, and Theda Skocpol, pp. 3–37. Cambridge: Cambridge University Press, 1985.

———. *States and Social Revolutions* (Cambridge: Cambridge University Press, 1978).

Skocpol, Theda, and Edwin Amenta. "States and Social Policies." *Annual Review of Sociology* 12 (1986): 131–57.

Sorensen, Georg. *Democracy, Dictatorship and Development*. New York: St. Martin's Press, 1990.

Steinbruner, James D. *The Cybernetic Theory of Decision.* Princeton, N.J.: Princeton University Press, 1974.

Steinmo, Sven, Kathleen Thelen, and Frank Longstreth, eds. *Structuring Politics: Historical Institutionalism in Comparative Analysis.* New York: Cambridge University Press, 1992.

Stigler, George J. "The Theory of Regulation." *Bell Journal of Economics and Management Science* 2, no. 1 (Spring 1971): 3–21.

Stinchcombe, Arthur L. *Creating Efficient Industrial Administrations.* New York: Academic Press, 1974.

———. *Information and Organizations.* Berkeley: University of California Press, 1990.

Swidler, Ann. "Culture in Action: Symbols and Strategies." *American Sociological Review* 51, no. 2 (April 1986): 273–86.

Tarrow, Sidney. "National Politics and Collective Action: Recent Theory and Research in Western Europe and the United States." *Annual Review of Sociology* 14 (1988): 421–40.

———. *Struggle, Politics, and Reform: Collective Action, Social Movements, and Cycles of Protest.* 2nd ed. Ithaca, N.Y.: Center for International Studies, Cornell University, 1991.

Thelen, Kathleen, and Sven Steinmo. "Historical Institutionalism in Comparative Politics." In *Structuring Politics,* ed. Sven Steinmo, Kathleen Thelen, and Frank Longstreth, pp. 1–32. New York: Cambridge University Press, 1992.

Thomas, John W., and Merilee S. Grindle. "After the Decision: Implementing Policy Reforms in Developing Countries." *World Development* 18, no. 8 (August 1990): 1163–81.

Thompson, James D. *Organizations in Action.* New York: McGraw-Hill, 1967.

Tilak, Jandhyala B. G. "Education and Its Relation to Economic Growth, Poverty and Income Distribution: Past Evidence and Further Analysis." Discussion Paper no. 46, World Bank, Washington, D.C., 1987.

Tilly, Charles. *The Contentious French: Four Centuries of Popular Struggle.* Cambridge, Mass.: Harvard University Press, 1986.

———. *From Mobilization to Revolution.* Reading, Mass.: Addison-Wesley, 1978.

———. "Introduction." In *Class Conflict and Collective Action,* ed. Louise A. Tilly and Charles Tilly, pp. 13–25. Beverly Hills, Calif.: Sage, 1981.

———. "Social Movements and National Politics." In *State Building and Social Movements,* ed. W. Bright and S. Harding, pp. 297–317. Ann Arbor: University of Michigan Press, 1984.

———. "The Web of Contention in Eighteenth Century Cities." In *Class Conflict and Collective Action,* ed. Louise A. Tilly and Charles Tilly, pp. 27–51. Beverly Hills, Calif.: Sage, 1981.

———, ed. *The Formation of National States in Western Europe.* Princeton, N.J.: Princeton University Press, 1975.

Tinbergen, Jan. *Income Distribution: Analysis and Policies.* Amsterdam: North Holland, 1975.

Tolbert, Pamela S. "Institutional Environments and Resource Dependence:

Sources of Administrative Structure in Institutions of Higher Education." *Administrative Science Quarterly* 30, no. 1 (March 1985): 1–13.

Tolbert, Pamela, and Lynne Zucker. "Institutional Sources of Change in Organizational Structure: The Diffusion of Civil Service Reform, 1880–1930." *Administrative Science Quarterly* 28, no. 1 (1983): 22–39.

Tullock, Gordon. *The Politics of Bureaucracy.* Washington, D.C.: Public Affairs Press, 1965.

Uphoff, Norman, and Milton Esman. *Local Organizations for Rural Development: Analysis of the Asian Experience.* Ithaca, N.Y.: Cornell University Press, 1974.

Van Horn, Carl E., and Donald S. Van Meter. "The Implementation of Intergovernmental Policy." In *Public Policy Making in a Federal System,* ed. Charles O. Jones and Robert D. Thomas, pp. 39–62. Beverly Hills, Calif.: Sage, 1976.

Verba, Sidney. "Sequences and Development." In *Crises and Sequences in Political Development,* ed. Leonard Binder et al., pp. 283–316. Princeton, N.J.: Princeton University Press, 1971.

Verba, Sidney, Bashiruddin Ahmed, and Anil Bhatt. *Caste, Race and Politics: A Comparative Study of India and the United States.* Beverly Hills, Calif.: Sage, 1971.

Wade, Robert H. *Governing the Market: Economic Theory and the Role of Government in East Asian Industrialization.* Princeton, N.J.: Princeton University Press, 1990.

Weber, Max. *The Protestant Ethic and the Spirit of Capitalism,* trans. Talcott Parsons. New York: Scribner's, 1958. (Originally published in 1920.)

Weir, Margaret. "Ideas and Politics: The Acceptance of Keynesianism in Britain and the United States." In *The Political Power of Keynesian Ideas: Keynesianism across Nations,* ed. Peter A. Hall, pp. 53–86. Princeton, N.J.: Princeton University Press, 1989.

———. *Politics and Jobs: The Boundaries of Employment Policy in the United States.* Princeton, N.J.: Princeton University Press, 1992.

Weir, Margaret, Ann Shola Orloff, and Theda Skocpol, eds. *The Politics of Social Policy in the United States.* Princeton, N.J.: Princeton University Press, 1988.

Weir, Margaret, and Theda Skocpol. "State Structures and the Possibilities for 'Keynesian' Responses to the Great Depression in Sweden, Britain and the United States." In *Bringing the State Back In,* ed. Peter B. Evans, Dietrich Rueschemeyer, and Theda Skocpol, pp. 107–63. Cambridge: Cambridge University Press, 1985.

Wildavsky, Aaron. *Speaking Truth to Power: The Art and Craft of Policy Analysis.* Boston: Little, Brown, 1979.

Williamson, Oliver E. *The Economic Institutions of Capitalism.* New York: Free Press, 1985.

———. *Markets and Hierarchies.* New York: Free Press, 1975.

Wilson, James Q. *Bureaucracy: What Government Agencies Do and Why They Do It.* New York: Basic Books, 1989.

Wood, B. Dan. "Principals, Bureaucrats, and Responsiveness in Clean Air Enforcement." *American Political Science Review* 82, no. 1 (March 1988): 213–34.

World Bank. *Poverty and Hunger: Issues and Options for Food Security in Developing Countries.* Washington, D.C.: World Bank, 1986.

World Bank. *Targeted Programs for the Poor during Structural Adjustment.* Washington, D.C.: World Bank, 1988.

World Bank. *The World Bank's Support for the Alleviation of Poverty.* Washington, D.C.: World Bank, 1988.

World Bank. *World Development Report, 1989.* New York: Oxford University Press, 1989.

World Bank. *World Development Report, 1990.* Oxford: Oxford University Press, 1990.

Wuthnow, Robert. *Meaning and Moral Order: Explorations in Cultural Analysis.* Berkeley: University of California Press, 1987.

Zald, Meyer N., and John D. McCarthy, eds. *Social Movements in an Organizational Society.* New Brunswick, N.J.: Transaction Books, 1987.

Zucker, Lynne G. "Institutional Theories of Organization." *Annual Review of Sociology* 13 (1988): 443–64.

———. "The Role of Institutionalization in Cultural Persistence." *American Sociological Review* 42, no. 3 (October 1977): 725–43.

———, ed. *Institutional Patterns and Organizations: Culture and Environment.* Cambridge, Mass.: Ballinger, 1988.

Index

AAA. *See* Agricultural Adjustment Administration
Acharya, Sarthi, 122, 123, 124
Administrative network, 20
Aerospace industry, and resource dependence, 25–26
AFBF. *See* American Farm Bureau Federation
African-Americans: disfranchisement of, 76, 84; and FSA, 66–67, 86–87; in rural U.S., 203; in Southern agriculture, 75, 76
Agency theory, 1, 2, 17; and EGS, 103, 179
Agrarian structure, in Midnapore, 156–57
Agricultural Adjustment Act of 1933, 40
Agricultural Adjustment Administration (AAA): and AFBF, 39, 78, 86; Committee on Violations of Rental and Benefit Contracts, 43; controversy over legal status of tenants, 42–43; Cotton Division, 43–44; and dependence on commercial farmers, 41; and extension service, 41, 68; and FSA, 70; Land Policy Section, 49; Legal Advisory Committee, 43; Legal Division, 44; production control, 41–42; purge of liberals, 42; and rural poverty, 39, 41–44; and transformation of Southern agriculture, 74
Agricultural fundamentalism, 201
Agricultural laborers: and EGS, 208, 212, 213; and NREP, 162, 166; and West Bengal politics, 157–58

Agricultural policy: constitutive impact in U.S., 78
Agricultural sector: depression in U.S., 40, 74; in Maharashtra, 238–39n.8; state intervention in U.S., 38
Ahmednagar, 240n.40
Ahmednagar Zilla Shet Majoor Union, 112
Alexander, Will, 72, 92
Amberson, William, 43
American Farm Bureau Federation (AFBF): and AAA, 41, 78, 86; and Congress, 71–72, 85; and FSA, 11, 78–81, 177; and grass-roots democracy, 71; membership in South, 80; opposition to New Deal poverty programs, 39; and U.S. Department of Agriculture, 80, 201–2
American South: agriculture in, 74–76; as colonial economy, 6; Democratic Party in, 9; disfranchisement in, 8, 9; elite domination in, 8; and FSA, 74; industrial development of, 6; nature of agricultural production, 6; one-party system in, 77; parallels with developing economies, 6; political disorganization of rural poor, 84; political institutions of, 8; politics in, 76–78; populism in, 8, 77–78; poverty in, 7, 76; racism in, 8; Republicans in, 77; tenancy and sharecropping in, 7
American state, 38
Analytical framework, 5
Appalachia, 202, 203
Appleby, Paul, 61, 70

Information networks: and government
agencies, 27
Information resources, 26–27
Institutionalization, 3
Institutionalized rules, 5, 16, 22, 28–32,
37, 177; and EGS, 176; and FSA, 81–
84; and NREP, 155
Institutional rationality, 2
Institutions, 2, 4
Integrated Area Development Scheme, 96
Integrated Rural Development Pro-
gramme, 107, 199–200 ; and NREP
in West Bengal, 142; and panchayats,
251n.31
Interorganizational conflict, 20

Jackson, Gardner, 42
Jamboni, 137, 153–54
Janata Dal, 195
Jawahar Rozgar Yojana, 134
Jefferson, Thomas, 81
Jesnes, O. B., 69
Jharkhand Party, in Binpur I, 138
Johnson, D. Gale, 7, 64
Joint Committee on Reduction of Non-
essential Federal Expenditures, 72

Karnataka: primary education in, 200
Knoke, David, 28
Kohli, Atul, 133, 164, 166, 167, 169,
171, 188, 189
Kudal Commission, 188

Land acquisition: and EGS, 117–18; and
NREP, 163
Landlords, in Southern agriculture, 75
Landowners, social power of, 7
Land reform, 186–87
Land use planning, in early New Deal,
48–50
Lasswell, Harold, 60
Laumann, Edward O., 28
Legal regime: constitutive impact of,
32–33
Lipsky, Michael, 3
Literacy tests: in American South, 76
Logics of appropriateness, 3

Macrocomparative analysis, 1, 2, 4
Maddox, James, 58, 63
Maharashtra: agricultural sector, 91–92,
238–39n.8, 271n.1; Congress Party
dominance, 93; economy, 89; geography, 89; panchayat institutions, 94;
political competition, 239n.11; political power in, 92–93; State Employment Guarantee Council, 98, 103;
state legislature, 93

Mahishyas, 159
Marathas: and politics, 92–93, 162
March, James G., 31
Maris, Paul V., 45
Members of Legislative Assembly: and
EGS, 113; and panchayats in West
Bengal, 156, 163
Methodology: for Indian cases, 10; for
American case, 11
Mexico: one-party dominant system in,
154
Meyer, John W., 34
Midnapore: agrarian structure in, 156–
57; agricultural development,
250n.19; ecology and development,
136–37
Migdal, Joel, 181
Mississippi delta, 202, 203
Monitoring: and EGS, 179; and imple-
mentation, 17; and politics, 178–80;
and tacked-on programs, 179
Moyna, 137, 153
Myrdal, Gunnar, 79

National Farmers Union, 11, 71, 79
National Industrial Recovery Act, Section
208, 46
National Land Use Planning Committee,
48–49
National Resources Board, 49, 52
National Rural Employment Programme
(NREP), 5, 133: administrative accountability, 144; administrative
structure, 10, 173; and agricultural
laborers, 162, 166; and corruption,
148, 150–51, 180, 253n.53; and cultivators, 162; and decentralized authority, 200; and elite domination hypothesis, 127–28, 129; employment
generated in West Bengal, 147; and
greater responsiveness hypothesis
127, 128–29; and institutionalized
rules, 155; and Integrated Rural Development Programme, 142; and land
acquisition, 163; and level of agricultural development, 147–48; low rate
of fund utilization, 144–47, 167; and
mobilization of the poor, 12, 191–93;
monitoring, 148; national impact,
133–34; and panchayats, 135–36,
139, 140–41, 143–47, 148–49, 151,
178–79, 180; planning, 140–41,
143–44; and political parties, 148,
151–54; and political patronage hypothesis, 128, 129; and popular participation, 139, 148–49; record-keeping, 144; and scheduled castes,

Compositor:	Graphic Composition, Inc.
Text:	10/13 Sabon
Display:	Sabon
Printer and Binder:	Braun-Brumfield, Inc.